THE GOSPEL AND THE CHURCHES

Books by WILHELM NIESEL

Published by The Westminster Press:

THE GOSPEL AND THE CHURCHES

A Comparison of Catholicism, Orthodoxy, and Protestantism

THE THEOLOGY OF CALVIN

THE GOSPEL AND THE CHURCHES

A COMPARISON OF CATHOLICISM, ORTHODOXY, AND PROTESTANTISM

by

WILHELM NIESEL

Translated by

DAVID LEWIS

THE WESTMINSTER PRESS
PHILADELPHIA

A translation of *Das Evangelium und die Kirchen, Ein Lehrbuch der Symbolik*, by Dr Wilhelm Niesel, first published by Verlag der Buchhandlung des Erziehungsverein, Neukirchen Kreis Moers, second edition 1960. This edition is also published in Great Britain by Oliver and Boyd Ltd., Edinburgh, under the title *Reformed Symbolics*.

Library of Congress Catalog Card No. 62-17753

Printed in Great Britain
by Robert Cunningham and Sons Ltd., Alva

TRANSLATOR'S PREFACE

Dr Wilhelm Niesel is already known in the English-speaking world as an outstanding Calvin scholar. He has contributed much to the better understanding of Calvin's work which is so encouraging a feature of theological life today, not least in Britain and America. In the present work he appears as a true follower of *Calvinus oecumenicus*. Writing from a long and close engagement in ecumenical discussions on faith and order, he says what he has to say with clarity, vigour and frankness, as becomes a true friend. The positions he states and, above all, the questions he asks should be carefully considered, especially where they touch and probe the tender spots, and where the temptation to evade is correspondingly strong. 'Faithful are the wounds of a friend: profuse are the kisses of an enemy' (Prov. 27.6)!

In its order and proportions, as well as in what is left out, the book inevitably reflects an ecclesiastical landscape more familiar to continental churchmen than to us, their English-speaking neighbours. Yet we still find ourselves here on strangely familiar ground, amid essentially the same conflicts, though viewed from a refreshingly helpful, if unfamiliar, angle. And in the section on the Anglo-Saxon Churches, Dr Niesel even ventures into territory which is more familiar to us than to him. The great economic, political, and cultural realignment taking shape in Europe today, midway between East and West, only underlines the need for a 'common market' in theology, a free and responsible exchange in both directions. Dr Niesel's book points the way to a better understanding both of ourselves and of our fellow Christians on the continent.

He writes from within the experience of the German Reformed Church of which he has been Moderator for some years. He was himself, from the very beginning, actively involved in the critical events leading to the Barmen Declaration in 1934 and the emergence of the Confessing Church. He spent some time in prison during the Church conflict, time which he wisely employed in teaching himself to read and speak English with the aid of an English grammar from the prison library. The renewal of the German Church in those fateful years and the significance of its experience for the whole Church has not yet been anything like sufficiently understood in the English-speaking world. Here too Dr Niesel's book will help to redress the balance.

The work of translation presented special problems only in the matter of footnotes and the bibliography. For the sake of readers with no knowledge of German I have, with the author's approval, expanded the footnotes where it seemed desirable to do so, adding further details and references to works in English. Also with Dr Niesel's approval, I have replaced his own suggestions for further reading by a selected and amplified list of comparable English works, though retaining all the English works cited by him. I have also added as appendixes a translation of the Düsseldorf Theses and the Barmen Declaration, together with an index of names.

I acknowledge gratefully the assistance given me in compiling the bibliography by Canon H. E. W. Turner and the Rev. Dr W. A. Whitehouse of Durham, the Rev. A. Raymond George of Headingley, the Rev. Dr E. A. Payne of London, and Father H. Swanston of The Oratory, Birmingham. At all stages I have been greatly helped by the author himself who patiently and promptly answered all my many enquiries, both in correspondence and at the meeting I was privileged to have with him when attending the Assembly of the German Reformed Church at Barmen in October 1960. For a country minister with a limited library the editorial work would have been quite impossible without the ready help afforded by various libraries, and particularly that of New College Edinburgh, and the Chapter and University Libraries at Durham. To my friend C. E. B. Cranfield of Durham I owe the initial encouragement to study German theology and I hope he may regard this translation as a small token of thanks for that and for many other things beside. My thanks are also due to Mrs J. Foggin of Tosson Tower, who typed the whole of a very difficult manuscript, and, not least, to the editorial staff of

Oliver and Boyd, who have supervised this work and saved me from many pitfalls by their wise and helpful counsel.

D.A.L.

THROPTON
June 1961

FOREWORD
to the Second German Edition

This book originated in lectures which I gave at the Wuppertal Theological College, founded by the Confessing Church during the German Church struggle. Though primarily intended as a textbook for theological students it can be read by interested Church members, since all quotations in foreign languages have been translated. This at once indicates both the scope and the limits of the book. I have intentionally not attempted to provide in each chapter a complete and detailed account, which would have meant expanding the work to several volumes and so hindered the purpose I had in mind. I have tried to give a brief, and, I hope, clear outline of the problems involved, and, so far as possible, allowed the sources to speak for themselves. Quotations from Roman Catholic sources have in almost every case been reproduced in the original as well, to enable the reader to compare what I have said with the official wording. I have made it clear in the preliminary section that my aim in this book is not to provide a descriptive handbook to the denominations, but simply to ask the central question: how do the various churches communicate the Gospel? There is a bibliography of books for further study.

For this edition, which is also appearing in an English translation, I have revised the book and almost completely rewritten the final chapters. My sincere thanks are due to the translator, whose labours will make my work available to a wider circle of the *oikoumene*. Since the Second World War I have had the privilege of sharing in the work of the Faith and Order Commission and of serving on the Central Committee of the World Council of Churches. I hope that my friends in the various churches will feel they have been rightly understood in what follows, and will note that my concern has not been to canvass for a particular confession of faith. Both in its positive assertions and in its criticisms the following work is intended solely as a summons to the One Lord of the One Church.

WILHELM NIESEL
Schöller, Wuppertal
Advent 1958

CONTENTS

II

THE GOSPEL AND THE ORTHODOX CHURCH

III

THE GOSPEL AND THE CHURCHES OF THE REFORMATION

PRELIMINARY REMARKS

1. Introduction

In what follows, we shall be dealing with the branch of theology which used to be called *Symbolics*,[1] a term still used in technical theological discussion. It acquired this name on Lutheran soil. Although the term may since have been used occasionally in Roman Catholic and Reformed circles, it has never become firmly established there. There are good reasons for this.

Embedded in the title Symbolics is the word *symbolum*.[2] In the language of the early Church the symbol meant, in effect, the recognisable sign of the Christians. The confession of faith in which Christians were instructed before their baptism and which they then had to profess, was regarded as this 'password'. Thus the symbol was the confession of faith affirmed by Christians before the Church.

The oldest symbol known to us is the Roman Baptismal Creed, which took shape in the second or third century, and later emerged in southern Gaul in the fifth century, in the form best known to us as the Apostles' Creed (*Apostolicum*). This symbol was not recognised at all in the Eastern Church, where another symbol gained acceptance and in time came to be acknowledged by the Western Church as well, though here it was regularly used only in the Mass. This was the Nicene Creed (*Nicaeno-Constantinopolitanum*). It is well known that this had no connexion with the actual creed drawn up at Nicea (325), nor

[1] See C. A. Briggs, *Theological Symbolics*, Edinburgh 1914, pp. 3-33; F. Kattenbusch, 'Symbolics', in the *New Schaff-Herzog Encyclopaedia of Religious Knowledge*, ed. S. M. Jackson, henceforth cited as *New-Schaff-Herzog*, New York and London 1908-12, VOL. XI, pp. 199ff; Karl Barth, *Church Dogmatics*, VOL. I, 2, trans. G. T. Thomson, Edinburgh 1935, pp. 827f.

[2] For the various possible meanings of this word see F. Loofs, *Symbolik oder christliche Konfessionskunde* ('Symbolics or the study of Christian denominations'), Tübingen 1902, henceforth cited as *Symbolik*, VOL. I, p. 1. Also J. N. D. Kelly, *Early Christian Creeds*, London 1950, pp. 52ff.

was it composed by the Council of Constantinople (381), but it somehow found its way into the official acts of this Council and was universally recognised at the Council of Chalcedon (451). To this was added later, in the West, the so-called Athanasian Creed (*Athanasianum*), which was not in fact the work of Athanasius, but already presupposes the theology of Ambrose and Augustine.

The Lutheran Formula of Concord (1580)[3] distinguishes between these three 'ecumenical creeds'[4] or the 'ancient and accepted symbols',[5] and the '*symbol of the present time*',[6] i.e. the Augsburg Confession (1530), and also includes under this description the other Lutheran confessions.[7] By symbol it meant a 'comprehensive, unanimously agreed summary and form, wherein is brought together from God's Word the common doctrine . . . which the Churches that are of the true Christian religion confess'. 'The ancient Church always had for this use its fixed symbols.'[8] 'In the Formula of Concord a symbol means simply a *compendiaria doctrinae forma* derived from scripture, a *typus doctrinae* having public and legal authority, an ecclesiastical norm for doctrinal teaching.'[9]

This interpretation was further strengthened by the fact that most of the Reformed Churches also accepted these three ancient symbols as authoritative and themselves produced a whole series of confessional documents. The *Formula consensus*

[3] The Lutheran confessions are quoted by the author from *Die Bekennenisschriften der evangelischlutheranischen Kirche*, 2nd edn. Göttingen 1952 (and 3rd edn. 1956), henceforth cited as *Bekenntnisschriften* (*Luth.*). See *Concordia Triglotta*, edd. F. Bente and W. H. T. Dau, 1917 (reprinted 1921 and 1955), which contains the original German text, the official 1584 Latin version, and an English translation. This translation is reprinted in *Concordia or Book of Concord, The Symbols of the Evangelical Lutheran Church*, Concordia Publishing House, St Louis 1957, henceforth cited as *Concordia*. P. Schaff, *The Creeds of the Evangelical Protestant Churches*, London 1877, 6th edn. New York 1931, VOL. II of *The Creeds of Christendom*, henceforth cited as Schaff, contains the Augsburg Confession, Luther's Small Catechism, and the Formula of Concord (Epitome), with English versions. *Luther's Primary Works*, edd. H. Wace and C. A. Buchheim, London 1896, includes translations of the Small and Large Catechisms. See also *Reformation Writings of Martin Luther*, trans. B. L. Woolf, 2 vols. 1952, 1956.

[4] Thorough Declaration. Comprehensive Summary 2 (*Bekenntnisschriften* (*Luth.*), p. 834; *Concordia*, p. 234).

[5] Preface to the Christian Book of Concord (*Bekenntnisschriften* (*Luth.*), p. 742; *Concordia*, p. 3). [6] *Ibid.*

[7] Thorough Declaration 3ff (*Bekenntnisschriften* (*Luth.*), p. 834; *Concordia*, p. 234).

[8] Thorough Declaration, introd. (*Bekenntnisschriften* (*Luth.*), p. 833; *Concordia*, p. 234). [9] Loofs, *Symbolik*, p. 63.

Helvetica (1675) actually used the term 'symbolic' in referring to the *Confessio Helvetica posterior* (1562).[10]

Once a standard for Church doctrine as comprehensive as that which the Lutherans possessed in the Formula of Concord was available, the occasion arose for commentaries on this standard. A scholarly interest in the symbol emerged. It also became necessary to come to terms with the declared teaching of other ecclesiastical bodies, until finally, in the period of the Enlightenment, men began to take for granted the existence of the various Confessional Churches and to examine and compare their doctrinal positions as expressed above all in the symbols. Thus in 1796 the Church historian, Gottlieb Jakob Planck of Göttingen wrote 'An historical and comparative sketch of the dogmatic systems of our main Christian denominations, according to their basic ideas, the differences in doctrine derived from them, and their practical consequences'.[11] A few years later, Professor Phillip Konrad Marheineke of Berlin, for the reasons just mentioned, expressly gave the title 'Christian Symbolics' to a similarly ambitious work, only the first part of which was ever published.[12]

Unlike his nineteenth-century successors, Marheineke did not limit himself to a description of the doctrinal positions of the Churches, but also enquired into their organisation, worship, and day-to-day life. He aimed, that is to say, at giving a comprehensive picture of the various denominations. It can indeed be asked whether theologians were well advised to describe and compare the doctrinal positions of the different Churches solely on the basis of their symbols. For, in the first place, the concept 'symbol' itself raises many questions. It is quite fictitious to speak of three ecumenical symbols of the Ancient Church. We have already seen that the Eastern Church recognised only one, the *Nicaeno-Constantinopolitanum*. It is true that all three symbols are in force in the Roman Church, but

[10] E. F. K. Müller, *Die Bekenntnisschriften der reformierten Kirche*, Leipzig 1903, p. 869, 40.

[11] *Abriss einer historischen und vergleichenden Darstellung der dogmatischen Systeme unserer verschiedenen christlichen Hauptpartheyen nach ihren Grundbegriffen, ihren daraus abgeleiteten Unterscheidungslehren und ihren praktischen Folgen.* Planck (1751-1833) was a Lutheran. See *New Schaff-Herzog*, VOL. IX, pp. 86f.

[12] *Das System des Katholizismus*, Heidelberg 1810-14. For Marheineke see *New Schaff-Herzog*, VOL. VII, pp. 179f.

here they are not regarded as doctrinal norms in the same sense as in Lutheran theology. The Roman Church recognises other norms too, which cannot simply be summarised in a collection of credal documents. Reformed theology speaks of 'Confessions' and, with one late exception, never applies to these the term 'symbol'. This is no accident. Clearly the emphasis placed on these confessions is not the same as in Lutheranism. As soon as the attempt was made in a 'Symbolics' to describe and compare the doctrinal positions of the different Churches essentially on the basis of the symbols, violence was already done to other Churches by the very nature of this approach to them. In the second place, the question arises: what did the writers of Symbolics mean by the doctrine they wished to extract from the symbolic documents? Had not the concept of *doctrina* as used by them, long since become something fixed and hardened, whereas in the Reformation period it had meant something very much alive, and almost equivalent to a doctrine or gospel of salvation? There is, of course, doctrine in the Church, just as there is a theology. But does the word 'doctrine' accurately describe what is affirmed in the Confessions of Faith, or attested in the ancient Church by the symbols of baptism or the Mass? Is the really decisive factor in the different Churches the particular doctrinal system which each of them recognises? Symbolics, especially as this branch of theology has been pursued in Lutheranism, has to face these critical questions.

It is doubtful whether this damage is repaired by extending Symbolics to cover the study of Christian denominations, as Marheineke intended to do, and as Ferdinand Kattenbusch,[13] E. F. K. Müller,[14] F. Loofs[15] and, more recently, Hermann Mulert[16] have done. No objection can possibly be raised when historians try to construct the most comprehensive picture possible of the various denominations. The Churches do, in fact, present such a picture; why then should it not be described? But we must at least ask whether this represents any advance

[13] F. Kattenbusch, *Lehrbuch der vergleichende Konfessionskunde*, VOL. 1, *Die orthodox-anatolische Kirche*, Freiburg 1892.

[14] E. F. K. Müller, *Symbolik, vergleichende Darstellung der christlichen Hauptkirchen nach ihren Grundzüge und ihren wesentlichen Lebensäusserungen*, henceforth cited as *Symbolik*, Erlangen 1896.

[15] *Symbolik.*

[16] Hermann Mulert, *Konfessionskunde*, 3rd edn. Berlin 1957.

on the older type of Symbolics, which, though it dealt in a questionable way with doctrine only, nevertheless to some extent still remained aware of a norm standing above the Church's speech and action. This is certainly not Mulert's position, for he says that the purpose of the study of Christian denominations is 'critically to trace governing ideas and ultimate truths'.[17] On the other hand a theologian like E. F. K. Müller, who does not approach the subject as an historian, shows insight here when he says that the aim of his work is 'to reach a comprehensive understanding, directed to ultimate principles, of the differences between the various Christian Confessional bodies, with a view to confirming or correcting one's own standpoint'.[18] But even here, what does he mean by 'principles' and 'standpoint'?

Is not Werner Elert right when, by contrast, in his *Form and Structure of Lutheranism*,[19] he seeks to bring out the particular point 'which suffices to account for the whole structure of subsequent Lutheranism in history' and finds it in what he calls '*dynamis*' (i.e. inherent power)? Is there not, in fact, something about the Church which can be called '*dynamis*'? But even Elert appears not to take this quite seriously, for he speaks of a *dynamis* operating as a 'denominational constant' and regards the denominations as 'supra-individual forces with a morphology of their own'.[20] For him even Lutheranism is one such form, born of Luther's experience, arising out of his encounter with the Gospel, and from then on continually unfolding itself with a 'supra-individual vitality'[21] After his efforts to clarify to his own satisfaction the driving force behind this development, Elert goes on to describe it in all its forms. But is this organic interpretation of the denominations any more satisfactory than the static one found, for example, in E. F. K. Muller?

2. Foundations

(*a*) *Theological Reconsideration*

The theological reconsideration which began with the publication of Karl Barth's *Commentary on Romans* at the end of the

[17] *Op. cit.*, p. 20. [18] Müller, *Symbolik*, p. 11.

[19] Werner Elert, *Morphologie des Luthertums*, 2 vols., Munich 1931-3. New edn. 1958, p. 8. [20] *Op. cit.*, p 6. [21] *Op. cit.*, p. 9.

First World War, the great interest shown at that time in the teaching of the Reformers, in Kierkegaard's criticism of modern Church life, and in the work and witness of the two Blumhardts,[22] led to the rediscovery of insights which had long been dormant within Protestantism. A few preachers of God's free grace, men hardly noticed by the great theological faculties, but listened to by 'the quiet in the land', alone had maintained the insights of the Reformation during the nineteenth century. None of the young theological students attending the lectures of Karl Barth and other leaders of the new theological movement in the 1920's suspected how soon the words to which they then listened so attentively and with such emotion, were to acquire the most immediate relevance to their situation. What had been learned in the lecture rooms and seminars had soon, in Germany and neighbouring countries, to be tested and proved in open conflict.

In 1933, a year of great trial and much spiritual confusion, the newly recovered insights of the Reformation proved a powerful aid. In the spring, a group of ministers and elders from the Rhineland met together in Düsseldorf, to consider what an Evangelical Church is. Some words spoken 400 years earlier by our spiritual forefathers helped to disperse the clouds and had a really liberating effect. 'The Holy Christian Church, whose Sole Head is Christ, is born of the Word of God, abides in the same, and hears not the voice of a stranger.'[23]

Against the prevailing spirit of those days, which thought it found divinity in race, nation, blood, and soil, witness was borne to the Churches, with strict Reformed exclusiveness, that the Word of God, on which the Church rests, comes to us only from the Holy Scriptures. Above all, the Word was not identified with any philosophical, ethical, or religious content of the Bible. On the contrary, in opposition to every orthodox or

[22] Johann Christoph Blumhardt (1805-80) a German Lutheran, and his son Christoph (1842-1919). See *New Schaff-Herzog, sub. nom.*

[23] First Bern Thesis 1528. Latin text in B. J. Kidd, *Documents illustrative of the Continental Reformation* (henceforth cited as Kidd, *Documents*), Oxford 1911, p. 460. English translation in Schaff, *Creeds of Christendom*, VOL. I, *A History of the Creeds of Christendom*, p. 365. The Düsseldorf Theses are given in *Bekenntnisschriften und Kirchenordnungen der nach Gottes Wort reformierten Kirche*, ed. W. Niesel, 3rd edn. Zollikon 1948, henceforth cited as *Bekenntnisschriften und Kirchenordnungen*, pp. 327f. An English translation is given in Appendix I to the present volume, pp. 355f.

liberal misunderstanding of Scripture, and adopting what had once come with new force to the Reformers, it was affirmed: '*The Word of God spoken to us*' (through Holy Scripture) '*is our Lord Jesus Christ*.'[24] Thus at a moment when a philosophy of life was claiming to be master in the life of the German State and Church, the Helper Himself was in the field, 'the Saviour of the world, and the only Lord of the elect Church'.[25] Christians in the Evangelical Church in Germany realised afresh that the Church does not live of itself, and that, in the last resort, all doctrinal and legal safeguards are of no avail. One thing alone upholds the Church and enables it to overcome all things—namely the Gospel, God's own Word. This was declared in the fifth of the Düsseldorf Theses: 'The Church lives solely because day by day it is newly called and upheld, comforted and governed by its Lord.' The Church does not simply have the Gospel at its disposal, nor can it be taken for granted that it is imbued with it. On the contrary, the Gospel comes to the Church where and when God wills, and places it under His promise and His healing judgment. Because the Church found itself really confronted by the Gospel, it had no cause to fear the proximity of the champions of the creed that had so suddenly gained the upper hand, nor even to be anxious because of its own weakness. Its strength was superior to all this and from then on it showed itself able to prevail.

(*b*) *The Barmen Theological Declaration*[26]

The Düsseldorf Theses had been drawn up by an unofficial group of ministers and elders. Soon afterwards, in May 1934, representatives of the Churches and congregations which rejected the heresy, met together in the Reformed Church at Barmen-Gemarke in the Rhineland as the Confessional Synod of the entire German Evangelical Church, declared itself to be a lawfully constituted synodical organ of the Church in Germany, and in this capacity issued the Barmen Theological

[24] Düsseldorf Thesis No. 3. [25] Düsseldorf Thesis No. 4.

[26] See *The Significance of the Barmen Declaration for the Oecumenical Church, Theology* Occasional Paper, New Series No. 5, London 1943. This contains a translation of the acts of the Barmen Confessional Synod, including the Barmen Theological Declaration (pp. 9-14). For the German text see *Bekenntnisschriften und Kirchenordnungen*, ed. W. Niesel p. 334ff. An English translation is given in Appendix II to the present volume, pp. 357f.

Declaration. The substance of both sets of theses is the same, but whereas the Düsseldorf Theses amplified a confessional statement made during the Reformation and related it to the needs of the present hour, the Barmen Declaration placed in the immediate forefront the testimony of Scripture itself, and regarded statements made on the basis of a word of Scripture, simply as an exegesis of this word of Scripture.

The *substance of the Church* is, according to the Barmen Declaration, *a person*, Jesus Christ. In support of this the Synod referred to the saying of Jesus: 'I am the way, and the truth, and the life; no one comes to the Father but by me' (John 14.6). Jesus Christ is 'God's revelation' for us. The foundation which upholds the Church is this person who lived in the past, almost 2,000 years ago. In this person, God Himself has made Himself known to mankind. This is what the Church has always taught. It already stood in the ancient symbols of the Church, and was explicitly reaffirmed by the confessional statements of the Reformation. But the Barmen Declaration did not simply adopt the Christology and Trinitarian doctrine of the ancient Church. It declared that Jesus Christ is the *one* Word of God to us today. The man who was crucified under Pontius Pilate is not just an important figure of past history. Because it was God's Son Himself who then adopted human form, He became the person with power to present Himself. Death could not end his existence or his influence. He who was is also He who is, and He who is to come. He is not only the one in whom God made Himself known to mankind then, but, in Him, God also encounters us today. The Barmen Synod was not therefore seeking to proclaim doctrine in the form of a theory; it was concerned rather to testify that in that treacherous time it had heard out of Holy Scripture the voice of the Good Shepherd.

Later, at the Amsterdam Conference in 1948, there was much discussion about whether the Church is something that exists or an event which happens. It is unnecessary for us to take up a position on this whole question here, but we must be clear about one thing, namely, that for the Church the essential thing is this event in which Jesus Christ deals with us as the Living One, this event in which He comes to us, in which, in Him today, God emerges from His hiddenness, Himself speaks

His word to us. In the true understanding of the Church it is not a question of 'being' or 'event' in the abstract, it is a question of this event in which the Word of God comes to us, that same Word who became flesh and dwelt among us men in the years A.D. 1-30. Anyone wishing to speak here exclusively of an 'act' as the factor which upholds the Church, would be speaking just as philosophically as one who wished to regard the Church exclusively in terms of 'being'. What is involved here is an enormously significant act, one that is quite without parallel. Only here can we properly learn what an event is, when we realise that God Himself is speaking to us today. To understand this event, we have to think of the burning bush out of which God's voice once spoke to Moses (Exod. 3). 'God reveals His presence', that was what was apprehended anew at the synods, in the meetings of congregations, in the prisons and concentration camps, when the Scriptures came alive there.

We do not mean that people at that time had strange experiences. This particular Word of God came to the members of synods, to Christians at worship, or to those behind prison bars, when the Bible was opened. Moreover this happened just because Jesus Christ is attested to us in Holy Scripture. We hear of Him only through His messengers, His forerunners and His eye- and ear-witnesses. This is so because Jesus Christ lived at a definite place and time in history. The Church lives, not by any Christ-idea, but by the Son of God who came to us in our world. The Barmen Synod confesses this quite plainly by directing us to the Scriptures. What happens is that this event comes to us from that past time as an event which concerns us today. The Barmen Synod does not bind us to the Bible as to a paper-Pope. The Word of God was not incarnated again in the Scriptures. The Bible simply bears witness to Jesus Christ the One Word of God. It proclaims Him as the Saviour who comes, came once, and is coming again. It is called *Holy* Scripture because the testimonies it contains were chosen by God with this end in view and therefore they and no others perform this service for us. But Scripture is not holy in the sense that in it we encounter the Holy One Himself. Rather is it like the burning bush from which God's Word spoke to Moses. But we too may expect this to happen. That was how the

Reformers read and heard the Bible afresh. Such a reading and hearing is also granted to us.

When, in what follows, we consider the various Christian denominations, the most important question to all of them will therefore be: 'What do you think of Christ?' (Matt. 22.42) and this question will assume concrete form when we ask the Churches about the status of Holy Scripture, the witness to Christ, in their midst. These two questions are inseparable. We cannot speak of Christ and, at the same time, ignore Holy Scripture, nor can we keep close to Scripture without constantly seeking for Christ in it.

A further point must be added. The Barmen Declaration rejected 'the false doctrine that the Church can and must acknowledge as sources of her proclamation, except and beside this one Word of God, other events and powers, forms and truths, as God's revelation'. When God came down to us, when He became man, when in this way He revealed Himself in Jesus Christ, we were given access to Him, and we are warned against seeking access to salvation anywhere else. The Barmen Thesis quotes Jesus' claim: 'I am the door' (John 10.9). By doing so it shows that it is not attributing to revelation a theoretical exclusiveness nor one based on some principle or other, but simply pointing to the event of God's self-revelation in the flesh, to the uniqueness of the God who comes to be known in this miraculous act of His. It is the First Commandment which is set clearly before us in the miracle of the Incarnation and Redemption. God's self-revelation brands as unusable all the other approaches to God which are pressed upon us. To seek other approaches or even to assert that they exist, is to call in question God's revelation in Christ, indeed means ultimately a denial that it is God's self-revelation. It is to turn God's self-revelation into information about God, a disclosure of a part of God, behind which God himself remains hidden. Thus it will be important for our evaluation of the various Churches to ask whether they cleave to Christ alone, and therefore to the Scriptures alone, or on the contrary recognise and use other sources for their message.

The Synod at Barmen offered no proof that Jesus Christ is the One Word of God, it simply declared this to be so. If this could be proved, Jesus Christ would not be Who He is. For it would mean that there was still some court of appeal superior to Him which had to and could pass judgment on Him. The Synod kept strictly to the biblical witness to Christ. It knew that this witness liberated it from the powers and bound it to Jesus Christ. We today are all of us asked if we are willing to let the same decision hold good for us too. The Synod was concerned with the truth which proves its power in life and in death, and which can be and wills to be this because it is in fact God Himself, and indeed the God who is with us, Immanuel. The members of the Synod knew that they stood in the presence of this God, they listened to Him and were therefore His people. So in Barmen, and always whenever Christ comes on the scene, it was a question of *faith* and *obedience*. At Barmen then there was no negotiating with opponents in order to reach a theological compromise. The faith was simply confessed to them.

In the second Barmen Thesis, the *liberating and binding authority of Jesus Christ* over us is defined more precisely: 'As Jesus Christ is God's declaration of the forgiveness of all our sins . . . so, with the same seriousness . . . He is God's mighty claim on the whole of our life.' It becomes quite clear at this point that the Synod had no wish to defend a dogma against novel doctrines. It was not a 'parsons' squabble', as people too readily and wrongly asserted at the time. Of course each of the Barmen Theses contains a doctrine. They are not just pious vapourings. But these doctrines serve as flying buttresses. The hearer has still to be convinced and brought under the dominion of Christ. The second Barmen thesis asserts the gracious rule of Jesus Christ over us, and speaks of it even more clearly than does the first thesis. It brings out the fact that we have access to God in Jesus Christ because in Him we receive the forgiveness of sins. The all-important thing which we receive from God we obtain not just anyhow, but solely and exclusively in Christ. But just because we receive everything from God in Christ, our whole life belongs to Him.

So we have to ask the different denominations: *Do they acknowledge this gracious rule of Christ over them?* We shall let them tell us whether they seek salvation solely and exclusively in

Christ, and whether they know that they are therefore under a total obligation to serve Him. We shall have to be sure that when they extol Christ as the Great Prophet they also glorify Him as our sole High Priest and Eternal King. The second Barmen thesis explicitly rejected the false doctrine 'that there are areas of our life in which we belong not to Jesus Christ but to other masters, realms where we do not need to be justified and sanctified by Him'. Otherwise Christ's reconciling work would be called in question. If a good and ethically neutral area of life and conduct existed apart from Christ, it would mean that for this area His sacrifice for us was unnecessary. Anyone who thought that, would not be taking God's presence in Christ seriously, but would really be refusing to let himself be delivered by Him 'from the godless bondage of this world' and would not come to a 'free grateful service of His creatures'. We need the forgiveness and guidance of God's Word, of Christ the Lord, in everything we do in every sphere.

But in the Church it is not simply that Jesus Christ is always meeting us afresh. God's gift and claim not only come to us again and again, we are also actually claimed and enlisted in Christ's service by them. Through Christ's call there comes into being a serving community. His word bears fruit. Otherwise it would not be His creative Word. According to the third Barmen thesis, this fruit is *the Church*. This community is not a human contrivance. It is neither an association of like-minded people for the cultivation of the religious life (the misunderstanding which threatens all Free Churches) nor a form of society embracing, ordering and controlling the religious side of human life (the misunderstanding which threatens national and established Churches). Least of all is it a divine institution in this world created once and for all in order to superintend and distribute supernatural blessings (as Roman Catholicism imagines). On the contrary, the Church is the congregation of those who hear and accept God's Word. Luther laid great stress on this truth and held that the word 'Kirche' should be discarded since it only served to obscure the reality in view here. He wished to see it replaced by the word 'Gemeinde' (community, congregation). This conception of the Church was reaffirmed afresh in the Barmen Declaration. The surprise which greeted Karl Barth's contribution to the Amsterdam Conference in 1948: 'The Church—the living congregation of the living Lord Jesus Christ',[27] was therefore quite unnecessary. What Barth then called attention to had already been confessed at Barmen. The Church is the mutual association of those who have been called and claimed by Jesus Christ. As their Saviour, Jesus Christ is also their Lord, or (as Eph. 4 says), their Head. In relation to Him all those who have been called out stand together on a different level, just because they are so closely bound to Him. Therefore whatever their status may be in other respects, they are all placed on the same level. Not that their personal individuality is destroyed; on the contrary, it is summoned to new life. It is their self-seeking which has been broken and forgiven. They have therefore been made free for one another. Instead of standing against each other, they stand by each other under their common Lord. Through him they have become brothers.

What has just been said about the word 'Church' must, of course, be rightly understood. We have not replaced an institutional concept of the Church by one drawn from modern sociology. The Church is certainly a society, an association, but congregationalism can be just as perverse as any institutionalism. We are not to substitute a principle centred on the congregation for one centred on the ministry. The only principle, in the quite unphilosophical sense expressed in the words: 'I am the Alpha and the Omega, the beginning and the end' (Rev. 21.6), is Jesus Christ. An assembly of Christians is the community of the Lord Jesus Christ only when He demonstrates His presence in it as its living Lord, when, as the third Barmen thesis says, He 'acts presently' in it. To arrive at a true picture of the Church, of course, one must not consider it only from the standpoint of its Head; but it ceases to be the Church and becomes a religious society like any other when the living relationship between the Head and the members is broken off, when the Church's life is no longer nourished and supplied from its Head. What is not included in the German word 'Gemeinde'

[27] See World Council of Churches, Amsterdam Assembly Series, *Man's Disorder and God's Design*, VOL. I, *The Universal Church in God's Design*, henceforth cited as *Universal Church*, London 1948, pp. 67-76.

(community), and not necessarily implied even in the word 'Versammlung' (congregation), is clearly expressed in the Greek word for 'Church', ἐκκλησία. This word makes it clear that the constitutive factor in the Church is an action. The Church is the summoned flock. The summons comes by an act of Jesus Christ Himself. Barmen says: 'Jesus Christ acts presently [in the Church] . . . by the Holy Spirit' in Word and Sacrament. The Church's Lord is present by the agency of His Spirit. He is never there as a thing, an object which we can control. On the contrary, He comes to us with sovereign freedom where and when He wills. Through the Holy Spirit He comes into our midst from the world of God. For this purpose of course He employs His instruments, preaching and the sacraments which accompany it. We saw earlier that although Jesus Christ Himself is the one Word of God, this Word is attested by the word of Holy Scripture, and that this word in turn is proclaimed here and now. The living Lord uses this proclamation, which adopts the testimony of Scripture, in order to reach men today with His gift and claim. The seal is set to this proclamation by the actions which Christ commanded, namely, by Baptism and the Lord's Supper.

With splendid clarity, the third Barmen thesis affirms the solidarity of the Church, this summoned flock, with the world. The world is the world of sin and estrangement from God. Its character is therefore the very negation of that communion with God which constitutes the Church. But this communion does not rest on the Church's superiority to the world. In themselves, the members of this society are just as self-seeking and so just as godless as the rest of mankind. The Church must acknowledge the truth that there is no distinction. But it knows of forgiveness. It is not by its own piety or goodness that it hears this Divine declaration. It owes this solely and exclusively to its Lord, who enables it to hear and accept His gift. It is 'the Church of pardoned sinners', living wholly and utterly *in* the world, but not of the world.

As the society of sinners summoned by the Lord, the Church has to serve in the world. Its business is not to be like the world, in a false solidarity with it, but to declare to the world the basis of the Church's own life. Recalling what was said in the first thesis, the third declares that this witness is given 'by its faith and obedience'. Not therefore simply by the inner attention of its members to their Lord, but by the whole conduct of their life. To emphasise this it adds that the Church must perform its service of witness by 'its message and its order'. The practical ordering of the Church's life must make it clear whether or not the Church itself is subject to its Lord, here on the way, whether its message is only theory, or whether it really summons men in obedience to Christ the Lord. The order of the congregation of Christ the Lord can never be like a temple of stone, but only like the tabernacle of the children of Israel in the wilderness. It is a witness that here is a company on the move, comforted and guided by its coming Lord and longing for Him.

The Barmen Declaration thereby provided a very necessary clarification. The distinction between the visible Church and the invisible Church, which stems from Augustine and was adopted by the Reformers, left Protestantism an easy prey to a dangerous error. Everything we have said about the Church on the basis of the third Barmen thesis applies, it was said then, to the Church of faith, to the true Church which is invisible. The Church in which we live is not to be confused with this Church of faith. Of course it shares the life of that true Church, but in itself it is a sociological phenomenon in an imperfect world. The Barmen Declaration affirms however, that it is the Church as the Church of forgiven sinners which is the society in which Jesus Christ 'acts presently'. Precisely in this questionable existence is it the Church of Jesus Christ. In itself it is nothing. It is what it is, in Christ. But it has to confess Him in and with its entire existence.

The third Barmen thesis underlines all that when it goes on to reject the doctrine 'that the Church is permitted to form its message or its order according to its own desire or according to prevailing philosophical or political convictions'. If, that is to say, the content and form of the Church's message are distinguished so as to suggest that while the content remains unalterable the form can, if necessary, be altered to fit in with the needs of the hour, that means the substance of the message has been secretly changed into a philosophy and the message is no longer the Christian Gospel at all. The Church is certainly called by Christ into liberty, but that means wholly and completely into His service. The Church must never forget that everything it says and does in every respect, it says and does as His servant. Because it is a free community it knows no licence. Neither will it submit to the yoke of the philosophical and political opinions prevailing at any particular time. It cannot serve two masters. When we deal with the different denominations we shall have to ask if they *know that they are summoned to bear witness in this comprehensive way in utter solidarity with the world*, to ask if they know they have been made wholly dependent on the Lord and could not live even for a moment without His presence?

The fourth Barmen thesis develops the statements made in the third in a direction which is very important for our enquiry into the various Church structures. It points out that by the service to which the Church is summoned, what is meant is usually called 'Ministry' ('Amt'). In the various 'ministries' in the Church, what is involved is '*the service* (*Dienst*) . . . *entrusted to and required of the whole congregation*'. That accords with the facts. The New Testament does not contain the term 'Amt' (office). The New Testament word which Luther translates by 'Amt' is διακονία, 'Dienst', service, ministry (Latin: *ministerium*, not *munus*). The Reformation Confessions correctly rendered this New Testament word by *ministerium*. Unfortunately the German versions used the questionable term 'Amt' (office), which suggests something fixed and institutional. It certainly no longer reminds us of the revolutionary change which took place when Jesus described His work, indeed His entire mission, as 'service' and regarded his disciples' task therefore as something which could be summed up as a 'serving' (διακονεῖν), as for example in the passage quoted in the fourth thesis (Matt. 20 25f), and in the explanation which follows: 'even as the Son of Man came not to be served but to serve, and to give his life as a ransom for many' (Matt. 20.28). We should compare, too, the account of the feet-washing in John 13. Jesus extols as the highest thing what was regarded as the lowest, namely, διακονεῖν, waiting at table, carrying out the menial duties of a slave According to Jesus, the greater is not the one who sits at table but the one who waits. Jesus Himself is such a διακονῶν. He is so in the absolute sense, because He served us to the point of laying down His life for us. Hence, all who are His are summoned to serve to the utmost (John 12.25f). It is therefore constitutive of the very essence of the Church that it should be in service, in solidarity with Christ its Head.[28]

When the fourth Barmen thesis speaks of 'various ministries' in the Church it does not explain how this variety arises or how it is to be understood. This was clearly not of first importance to the members of the Synod. One thing had to be made clear, however. If in the Lord's Church it is a matter of service and only of service, then it is not permissible for one ministry in the Church to exercise lordship over another. If it is by her Lord's presence that the Church lives and is distinct from all other societies, then here it applies: 'You have one teacher and you are all brethren' (Matt. 23.8). A statutory subordination of some ministers to others, such as was being demanded at that time in Germany, is never permissible in the Church. If such a subordination and superordination is nevertheless introduced, it is not just a secondary disorder that is caused but the sole sovereignty of Jesus Christ is assailed. What is then denied is that He, the Head, gives to each member of His body the spiritual gifts needed to perform his ministry and that, in this way, the servant members of His servant body are utterly subordinate to Him.

In our examination of the various denominations we shall need therefore to see whether *they acknowledge this rule of the Church by Jesus Christ*, or, on the contrary, establish within themselves a rule by man; whether they wish only to be the Church of Jesus Christ, or to leave room for man and man's will to rule. It becomes clear at this point whether a Church wishes to be governed by her Lord or by sin, for sin is essentially man's desire to be himself the master, and the rejection of the gracious rule of Jesus Christ.

The fifth Barmen thesis declares that *the State too stands under God's rule* and therefore has no independent authority of its own. If it wishes to perform a helpful service in the still unredeemed

[28] Cf. also *Sao Paulo Story*, The Eighteenth General Council of the World Alliance of Reformed and Presbyterian Churches, 1959, ed. Marcel Pradervand, Geneva 1960.

world and not to pervert its mission by making itself the sole and total order of human life, then it is directed to God's commandment and righteousness and thus to the message of the Church. The sixth thesis again defines the Church's task, this time from one special viewpoint. The two biblical passages placed at the beginning of this thesis speak of the living and present Lord and of the royal freedom of His word. It is the freedom of the Lord who means to abide with His Church, and therefore is the exact opposite of despotic licence. It is the freedom of His love. The Church's task is to proclaim the Word of His free loving-kindness. It is significant that the Barmen Declaration ends as it began by pointing *to the Gospel of God's free grace*. Quite clearly, the first thesis is being expounded once more. If what is said here in conclusion is not heeded, everything which the Barmen Declaration has said about the Church's task in the earlier theses will be misunderstood. This passage will test whether or not the Church knows the cause entrusted to it. The sixth thesis is therefore of special importance in our enquiry.

In the fourth thesis we were told of a service entrusted to and required of the Church. Now we are told that it has a mission. It stands here on earth in Christ's stead. Not that the Church itself has to accomplish, extend, or complete His work. It has all been done already by Christ Himself. It is finished. What the Church has to do is to proclaim this news 'to all men'. It is not the will of Jesus Christ to leave us as orphans after His resurrection and ascension. He, the Heavenly King, who lived in our midst and spoke to us as a man like ourselves, condescends to us still further with such humility that now He employs human lips to invite all men to come to Him. This is the service He has committed to the Church as His representative. The Church is allowed to be an instrument of this Lord, His spokesman. It is the herald of Jesus Christ. Not in such a way that this task is superimposed on its real self. The Church is not the body of Christ in which particular members are subsequently given the special task of proclaiming Christ. On the contrary, the proclamation and glorification of Christ constitute this body. The Church is not a worshipping or educational society which now and again also has to make forays into the world alienated from God. On the contrary, the Church is a mission or it is nothing at all.[29]

According to the sixth thesis, the Church's task is 'to deliver the message of the free grace of God'. It has to proclaim the God whose name is 'I am who I am' or 'I will be who I will be'. The Church testifies to the Lord of Lords and King of Kings, who needs no one and who does what He purposes. But the Church can announce that this same God has made it known to us that He is our Immanuel, God with us. In inconceivable mercy, He created man to be His partner, reconciled to Himself this creature who spurns His love, by claiming us for Himself as His own, in His Son, and now He wills to be glorified in us. The Church is permitted to glorify the name of this God in the sight of the nations.

Its task is not just to impart doctrine. The free grace of God will not let itself be imprisoned in a textbook, not even in one approved by all the Christian councils. Any Church content to do no more than hand on a doctrine set down in some creed or other would be mistaking its mission. A Church making this its aim would have become a synagogue and its ministers rabbis. The Church is concerned not with doctrine but with the Doctor, with the Word, with Jesus Christ the Risen Lord.

Nor is it the Church's task to proclaim a morality. The view that the Church's main business is to teach people the Ten Commandments is questionable. The Church will have to guard against turning God's law into a collection of rules, a sort of Jewish version of the old Saxon law. If it were to do that, it would become like the sect of the Pharisees which Jesus opposed. A Church that thought its main task was to improve morals and manners would be like the opponents of Jesus who 'tithed mint and dill and cummin and neglected the weightier matters of the law, justice and mercy and faith' (Matt. 23.23). The Church's real message concerns Him who fulfilled the Law for us, and has translated us into the liberty of the children of God.

The Gospel of Jesus Christ does not presuppose any particular disposition or readiness in the hearts of the hearer. It

[29] Cf. *The Calling of the Church to Mission and to Unity*, a statement adopted by the Executive Committee of the World Council of Churches at Rolle (Switzerland) in 1951. (Minutes of the Fourth Meeting, pp. 63ff.)

does not rely on men being made receptive to it by distress, nor on satisfactory social conditions providing a good soil for the seed of the Word. The Spirit blows where He wills. Once again we are reminded that the Lord through His Spirit 'acts presently', opening men's hearts to Him where and when He wills.

This Gospel of God's free grace is entrusted to the Church, not handed over to it and therefore placed at its disposal. The Gospel is not affected by the circumstances in which the Church finds itself at any given time. It is not true that the Church only has to order its life aright for it to be able to deliver this message. Even a perfect liturgy is not a prerequisite. On the contrary, all this could even be a hindrance to the free course of this message. Certainly this message is in no way guaranteed by any Church order or liturgy. It is nevertheless true that outside the Church there is no salvation (*extra ecclesia nulla salus*). This is true, however, only so far as the Church is the handmaid of the Lord. It is true in virtue of the Gospel which is the vital nerve of the Church. It has pleased God again and again to allow the message of His free grace to shine forth even in the deepest confusions of the Church. That must never be forgotten.

The message entrusted to the Church is the announcement of God's free *grace*. It is the news that the last shall be first. It is the message for the woman who was a great sinner, for Zacchaeus the collaborator and quisling, for the thief on the Cross, but not for the strong who have no need of a physician. It is good news to the poor in the land, but not to the Scribes and Pharisees. It is good news for all who hunger and thirst for righteousness, but not for the satisfied and complacent.

This Gospel of free grace is addressed to all people. God is no respecter of persons (Acts 10.34). It is addressed to atheists and to religious people, to communists and to capitalists, to the good and the evil, the just and the unjust.

In proclaiming this message the Church demonstrates its own freedom. It is free as the society commissioned by Christ. In serving the Gospel it is free from all philosophies. As it obeys and serves Christ it is free from all other Lords, all other powers, and from the Devil. But it is not so in its own strength. Its obligation ennobles it. Its Lord is its freedom. It will therefore always have to pray again and again for this freedom, for true submission to Christ.

Enjoying this freedom the Church knows that all licence is excluded. It will not use the Word entrusted to it to pursue a strategy of self-glorification. As the postscript to the sixth thesis says, the Church will not use it 'to serve any self-chosen desires, purposes and plans.' It was unable to lend itself to the building of spiritual foundations to uphold the Third Reich, as it was then expected to do. It did not exist to provide the German people with inner resources for their selfish enterprises. No more is it its task today either to support the Christian West or to prepare the way for a Communist order of society. The Church's sole concern is the free grace of its free Lord. *Soli Deo gloria.* Everything else which is right in God's sight will then be added unto us (Matt. 6.33).

Is this what the denominations are concerned for—this free grace, this free Lord? That is the decisive question to be put to them. It may be objected that this whole enquiry is superfluous because we are approaching our task with dogmatic prejudice; that we have taken our stand on the Barmen Theological Declaration and are going to look one-sidedly at the different denominations from that standpoint. We cannot forestall this objection, of course, but anyone raising it should realise that he himself is 'in the same condemnation'. There is no such thing as an impartial study of denominations. Even the attempts made by historians cannot completely conceal the dogmatic or philosophical assumptions on which their work rests. It is, moreover, relatively unimportant for the interpretation of other denominations whether the standpoint of an author of a Symbolics is that of orthodoxy or of liberal Protestantism. Why should the concerns of the different denominations be better understood from the latter standpoint in particular?

We have deliberately set the Düsseldorf Theses and the Barmen Theological Declaration at the beginning of this enquiry. In the time of great testing which overtook the Church in Germany at that time, we ourselves were obliged to confess in these words what the Church stands for. Indeed we were then faced with the question and had to confess openly what the basis of our life was. For what is attested in these theses on the basis of Holy Scripture, many Church members had to stake their very existence. In return they incurred the shame of being despised by the many. For these statements they suffered persecution at the hands of the Gestapo. They went to prison and to concentration camps. For these statements they had to give up their work, their families, some even life itself. To us these theses are no mere scrap of paper, merely a sentimental memory, one confession of faith among so many others on our library shelves. In them we confessed our faith in the Word which called us and never forsook us, which upheld and comforted us. These theses are the response of Christians in Germany to the One Word of God heard speaking afresh in Holy Scripture.

Anyone who imagines that we have thereby established a judicial court from which to pass judgment on the denominations has not understood the Barmen Declaration, which in fact bears witness to the Lord who has reserved final judgment to Himself. But this same Lord summons us to watchfulness. That is why the Barmen Declaration warns us against the ways which lead away from Him. We shall confront the denominations with this testimony. We shall question them from this standpoint. We shall also have to issue warning signals. How could it possibly be otherwise when we recognise the message of free grace? Ecumenical thinking, far from making everything relative, requires each of us to take seriously the truth which has found him and to speak frankly about it to the others. Such a conversation assumes that the others are ready for it. If not, the necessary conversation can become instead simply a protest. Any ecumenical conversation also presupposes that we ourselves are ready to be asked questions by the others and, when necessary, to be instructed by them. The Barmen Theological Declaration is not itself the Truth. All we did by our words then was to bear witness to that Truth. We must be ready to listen to others if a better testimony to Jesus Christ has been given them.

3. The Task

From the above it will be clear that it is not my intention to write a Symbolics in the old sense of the word. For in the different denominations we are dealing not simply with theological doctrines but, behind all doctrines and all expressions of the Church's life, with the question of *Christ's presence in His Church.* It would not serve our purpose, therefore, to give a purely descriptive account of the denominations, for the important thing is not the form of an ecclesiastical society but what has shaped and moulded this form. As I have already stressed, our task is essentially a critical one. We must ask the denominations how they respect the Gospel entrusted to them, how they relate themselves to it and how they communicate it.

This means we shall keep to the contemporary form and witness of the denominations. Not that we shall not also have to glance at their past, for the denominations regard their understanding of the Gospel as to a great extent formulated in documents of the past. But it is not our concern to describe the origins of the denominations or the development of their doctrinal positions. Such matters will only be mentioned occasionally as need arises.

We renounce any idea of starting our survey of the different Churches from some highest common factor. Loofs says soberly: 'There are no formulae, confessions, or liturgies common to all Christians. Even the so-called "ecumenical" creeds are not common property.'[30] He quotes the words of the Roman Catholic theologian Bellarmine: 'The faith is not in the words but in their meaning; we do not have the same creed, therefore, if we disagree about its interpretation.'[31]

The question with which denomination it is best to begin can be answered in different ways. If we choose to deal first with the Roman Church and then with the Orthodox, this is not because (like E. F. K. Müller) we find life and movement in the Roman Church but in the Orthodox only static tradition.[32] The reason is rather that the Roman Church stands furthest away from us, whereas with the Orthodox Church we are engaged in a continuing conversation within the World Council of Churches.[33] In its isolation from all other Christian socie-

[30] Loofs, *Symbolik*, p. 76.

[31] *Op. cit.*, p. 65. 'Non in verbis, sed in sensu est fides; non ergo habemus idem symbolum, si in explicatione dissidemus.'

[32] Müller, *Symbolik*, p. 198.

[33] World Council of Churches, Amsterdam Assembly Series, VOL. V, official report, *The First Assembly of the World Council of Churches in Amsterdam*, ed. W. A. Visser't Hooft, London 1948.

ties,[34] the Roman Church today presents such special features that we must deal with it at the outset and only then turn to those denominations which are in vital communication with one another as Churches.

[34] It should be thankfully acknowledged that individual Roman Catholic theologians are often astonishingly eager for discussions, especially with the ecumenical movement. We are speaking here, however, of the official Roman Church. Will the 'ecumenical council' announced by Pope John XXIII on 25 January 1959 lead to a fundamental change in the Curia and end its isolation from the Churches united in the World Council?

I

THE GOSPEL AND ROMAN CATHOLICISM

CHAPTER I

THE SOURCES[1]

1. THE OBJECT OF FAITH

THE last ecumenical council of the Roman Church, the Vatican Council (1869-70), defined exactly what Roman Catholics must believe: 'Further, all those things must be believed with divine and Catholic faith, which are contained in the Word of God, whether written or handed down by tradition, and which the Church, either by a solemn judgment or by her ordinary and universal *magisterium*, proposes for belief as having been divinely revealed.'[2] The teaching and message of the Roman Church is not a truth accessible to all men but one given to the Church by divine revelation. Yet the Vatican Council makes the rather strange assertion that it is not because of the present condition of mankind that 'revelation must be regarded as absolutely necessary',[3] and, as we shall see later, the distinction between natural and supernatural revelation[4] plays a very important part in Roman theology and practice. Bartmann is nevertheless right when he says: 'Since, strictly speaking, dogma requires supernatural revelation, those doctrines which the Church in its preaching does not derive from this source are not essential dogmas.'[5]

[1] Cf. Karl Barth, *Kirchliche Dogmatik*, VOL. I, 2, Zollikon 1938, pp. 607-37; Eng. trans. *Church Dogmatics*, VOL. I, 2, Edinburgh 1956, pp. 545-72.

[2] 'Porro fide divina et catholica ea omnia credenda sunt, quae in verbo Dei scripto vel tradito continentur et ab Ecclesia sive solemni iudicio sive ordinario et universali magisterio tanquam divinitus revelata credenda proponuntur.' Sess. 3, ch. 3 (H. Denzinger, *Enchiridion symbolorum definitionum de rebus fidei et morum*, henceforth cited as D., 31st edn., ed. K. Rahner, Freiburg im Breisgau 1960, 1792; K. Mirbt, *Quellen zur Geschichte des Papsttums und des römischen Katholizismus*, henceforth cited as M., 4th edn. Tübingen 1924, 458.16; Schaff, II.244f).

[3] 'Non hac tamen de causa revelatio absolute necessaria dicenda est.' Sess. 3, ch. 2 (D., 1786; M., 457.13; Schaff, II.240f).

[4] D., 1785; M., 457.4; Schaff, II.240.

[5] B. Bartmann, *Lehrbuch der Dogmatik*, 8th edn., Freiburg im Breisgau 1932, VOL. I, p. 5.

2. Holy Scripture and Tradition

The Roman Church derives its doctrine from Holy Scripture, the 'Word of God written', as the Vatican Council calls it. The Council supported this by referring to the explanation given at the Council of Trent (1546). This spoke of the Gospel 'which, before promised through the prophets in the Holy Scriptures, our Lord Jesus Christ, the Son of God, first promulgated with His own mouth, and then commanded to be preached by His Apostles to every creature, as the fountain of all, both saving truth and moral discipline', and added 'that this truth and discipline are contained in the written books and the unwritten traditions'.[6]

As the Vatican fathers recalled, the Council of Trent gave a complete list of all the books of the Old and New Testaments, in which the divine truth is to be found. This list has two significant features: (i) The Old Testament Apocrypha, i.e. the books not found in the Hebrew canon but only in the Greek, are recognised as equally Holy Scripture. These apocryphal books are of great importance as a Scriptural warrant for Roman Catholic teaching. (ii) The listed writings are stated to be 'sacred and canonical' *only* in the form they have assumed in the old Latin Vulgate edition.[7] To its parallel statement, Trent added the warning 'that no one is to dare or presume to reject this edition under any pretext whatever'.[8] The Roman Church thus restricts the hearing of the testimony of the Apostles and Prophets to a translation made by itself and therefore, since all translation inevitably involves interpretation, to its own word. Here already the Church interposes itself between the biblical message and its hearers.

The prophetic and apostolic writings, closely defined even to their linguistic form and including the Old Testament Apocrypha, are regarded by the Roman Church as canonical,

[6] 'Hanc veritatem et disciplinam contineri in libris scriptis et sine scripto traditionibus' (D., 783; M., 291.34; Schaff, II.80). Vatican Sess. 3, ch. 2 (D., 1787; M., 457.18; Schaff, II.241).

[7] Vatican Council, *loc. cit.* Even the recent papal encouragement of textual criticism in no way diminishes the 'juridical authenticity' of the Vulgate for the Latin Church. See the Encyclical *Divino afflante Spiritu* of Pius XII, 1943 (D., 2292; English trans. *Biblical Studies,* trans. G. D. Smith, London 1959, pp. 15f).

[8] 'Quod nemo illam [sc. vulgatam editionem] reicere quovis praetextu audeat vel praesumat' (D., 785; M., 292.20; Schaff, II.82.)

however, not because of the Church's recognition, nor even simply because of their contents, but also and primarily because of their origin. The Vatican Council states: 'The Church holds these to be sacred and canonical not merely . . . because they contain revelation with no admixture of error but because, having been written by the inspiration of the Holy Ghost, they have God for their Author and have been delivered as such to the Church herself.'[9] What determines the authority of Holy Scripture, therefore, is, in addition to its contents, its *inspiration* by the Holy Spirit. The Bible is a divine production.

Offsetting this tremendous assertion about Scripture is the fact that the Church has already shared in the production of this divinely created book, by making the authorised Latin version. God and the Church have co-operated in this work. It is no surprise then, when the Roman Church assigns equal authority alongside the written Word to the *unwritten traditions*. Trent is quite explicit about this: 'This truth and discipline are contained in the written books and the unwritten traditions which, received from the mouth of Christ Himself, or from the Apostles themselves, the Holy Ghost dictating, have come down to us, transmitted as it were from hand to hand.'[10] This oral tradition, dictated to the Apostles by Christ Himself, or by the Holy Spirit, and preserved by the Church continually since then, is accepted and respected by the Church 'with an equal affection of piety and reverence'[11] alongside Holy Scripture. Before long this concept of tradition was enlarged by the *Professio fidei tridentinae* (1564), which put even *ecclesiastical tradition* on a par with Apostolic tradition. Every Roman priest since then has had to accept and subscribe to both: 'I most steadfastly admit and embrace apostolic and ecclesiastical traditions, and all other observances and constitutions of the same

[9] 'Eos vero Ecclesia pro sacris et canonicis habet non ideo . . . dumtaxat, quod revelationem sine errore contineant; sed propterea, quod Spiritu Sancto inspirante conscripti Deum habent auctorem, atque ut tales ipsi Ecclesia traditi sunt' (Schaff, II.241f).

[10] 'Hanc veritatem et disciplinam contineri in libris scriptis et sine scripto traditionibus, quae ab ipsius Christi ore ab Apostolis acceptae, aut ab ipsis Apostolis Spiritu Sancto dictante quasi per manus traditae ad nos usque pervenerunt' (D., 783; M., 291.37; Schaff, II.80).

[11] 'Pari pietatis affectu ac reverentia.'

Church.'[12] Before considering what is meant by tradition, we must first look at a further point which has an important bearing on the authority of Scripture and tradition.

3. The Church's Teaching Office

The source of Roman Catholic doctrine is not the Bible as such nor tradition as such, but both these only as—in the words of the Vatican Council quoted in the opening paragraph—'proposed for belief as having been divinely revealed', 'either by the solemn judgment of the Church or by her ordinary and universal *magisterium* (teaching office)'.[13] The present teaching office of the Church alone decides what must be accepted by members of the Roman Church from these two sources, Scripture and tradition. As regards Scripture, Trent had already stated 'that no one relying on his own skill, shall, . . . wresting the Sacred Scripture to his own senses, presume to interpret the said Sacred Scripture contrary to that sense which Holy Mother Church, whose it is to judge of the true sense and interpretation of the Holy Scriptures, has held and does hold: or even contrary to the unanimous consent of the Fathers'.[14] When, therefore, in answer to the question what must the Church teach as the basis of belief, Rome replies: Scripture *and* tradition, we are bound to say that Scripture does not, according to the Tridentine statements, keep its place alongside tradition, but is in practice subordinated to it, since it can only be interpreted in accord with the unanimous consent of the Fathers. In the last instance, it is the Church itself which alone determines the true meaning and interpretation of Scripture. In keeping with this dogmatic definition, Karl Adam praises

[12] 'Apostolicas et ecclesiasticas traditiones reliquasque eiusdem Ecclesiae observationes et constitutiones firmissime admitto et amplector' (D., 995; M. 339.33; Schaff, II.207).

[13] 'Ab Ecclesia sive solemni iudicio sive ordinario et universali magisterio tanquam divinitus revelata credenda proponuntur' (D., 1792; M., 458.16; Schaff, II.244f). Nevertheless the doctrine of *fides implicita* developed by medieval scholasticism, according to which the ordinary Christian need believe personally only the most important doctrines and can trust the Church for all other matters of faith, has never become a dogma.

[14] 'Ut nemo . . . sacram Scripturam ad suos sensus contorquens, contra eum sensum, quem tenuit et tenet sancta mater Ecclesia cuius est iudicare de vero sensu et interpretatione Scripturarum, aut, etiam contra unanimum consensum Patrum ipsam Scripturam sacram interpretari audeat' (D., 786; M., 292.21; Schaff, II.83).

the 'vitality' of ecclesiastical tradition in contrast to the 'dead word' of the Bible.[15]

What was already suggested at Trent was made explicit by the Vatican Council: above the tradition stands the *Church's teaching office*. It is the Church that settles what the orally transmitted, unwritten Word of God says to men.[16] Moreover, only the Church is in a position to know the unanimous patristic interpretation of Holy Scripture, so that when interpreting Scripture no one may appeal to this or that Father in isolation. The type of biblical exegesis which appealed to Augustine, for example, and which, when used by the Reformers, caused the Roman theologians such embarrassment, was henceforth ruled out of order.

The dogmatic theologians therefore teach that 'Scripture and tradition are the distant rule of faith (*regula fidei remota*), the Church is the immediate rule of faith (*regula fidei proxima*)'.[17] The Roman Catholic who wants to know what he has to believe must abide by the latter rule. The 'distant rule of faith' operates for him only through the Church as intermediary. 'The Catholic Christian must believe all that God has revealed and that the Church proposes for his belief, whether it stands in Holy Scripture or not.'[18] F. Kattenbusch is surely right when he concludes that the Roman Church 'really wants to listen only to itself'.[19] The fundamental objection to Rome's position here has been stated by Karl Barth: 'If then, apart from the Church's undeniable and distinctive vitality, there exists over against the Church a concrete authority with a distinctive vitality of its own, an authority whose utterance means, not that the Church is speaking to itself but is being spoken *to*, an authority which can occupy the position of an autonomous power and so of a criterion, then clearly this authority must be distinguished from and superior to the merely intangible and oral vigour of Church tradition, precisely by its written character as "Bible".'[20]

[15] *Das Wesen des Katholizismus*, 4th edn. 1927, p. 162, English trans. *The Spirit of Catholicism*, London 1932, pp. 55f; cited in Barth, *Church Dogmatics*, VOL. I, 1, p. 118.

[16] Vatican Council, *ad loc.*

[17] Bartmann, *Dogmatik*, VOL. II, pp. 33f.

[18] J. Deharbe, *Katholischer Katechismus*, Regensburg 1847, Q.36. Similarly in other catechisms.

[19] J. J. Herzog, *Realenzyklopädie für protestantische Theologie und Kirche*, henceforth cited as *R.E.*, 3rd edn. ed. A. Hauck, Leipzig 1896-1913, VOL. XVII, p. 104.

[20] *Church Dogmatics*, VOL. II, pp. 118f (Eng. trans. altered slightly).

We shall better understand the Roman view giving the Church the last word in all matters of faith and morals, if we consider the distinction made in the words: 'either by a solemn judgment or by her ordinary and universal *magisterium*'.[21] The former refers to the decisions of Ecumenical Councils and *ex cathedra* Papal announcements. Serious difficulties arise, however, when we ask which texts fall within this description. First, there is the problem which Councils are to be reckoned as ecumenical. The general view is that there have been twenty.[22] Secondly, we have to remember that not all the decisions of these Councils are binding. Last but not least, we must bear in mind that, since the Vatican Council, conciliar decisions are authoritative only in conjunction with the teaching office of the Pope. This latest Ecumenical Council asserted 'that the Roman Pontiffs have, according as the needs of the times suggested, either summoned a General Council, or explored the mind of the Church throughout its length and breadth, or again used local synods or other means which Providence might offer, and so have come to define as obligatory what, with God's help, they came to recognise as being in harmony with Sacred Scripture and Apostolic Tradition'.[23] It is not the status of a synod which determines the importance of its decisions. The teaching of a local synod can be just as significant as that of an ecumenical one, if it agrees in substance with Scripture and tradition. Only the Pope, however, can say whether such agreement exists.

As regards the authority of the Pope as the occupant of the Church's teaching office, the Vatican Council proclaimed as divinely revealed dogma: 'that the Roman Pontiff, when he speaks *ex cathedra*, that is, when in discharge of the office of pastor and doctor of all Christians, he defines a doctrine regarding faith or morals to be held by the universal Church, by the divine assistance promised to him in blessed Peter, is possessed of that infallibility with which the divine Redeemer willed that

[21] 'Sive solemni iudicio sive ordinario et universali magisterio.' [22] M., 593.

[23] 'Romani autem Pontifices, prout temporum et rerum conditio suadebat, nunc convocatis oecumenicis Conciliis aut explorata Ecclesiae per orbem dispersae sententia, nunc per Synodos particulares, nunc, aliis, quae divina suppeditabat providentia, adhibitis auxiliis, ea tenenda definiverunt, quae sacris Scripturis et apostolicis traditionibus consentanea, Deo adiutore, cognoverant.' Sess. 4 (D., 1836; M., 464.42; Schaff, II.268f).

His Church should be endowed for defining doctrine regarding faith or morals, and that such definitions of the Roman Pontiffs are irreformable, of themselves and not by the consent of the Church'.[24] It is clear from this that the Church's teaching office, to which every Catholic is directed if he wishes to be certain what he must believe, culminates in the Pope. Of course the Pope only makes a 'solemn judgment' when he comes forward explicitly as the teacher of all Christendom, speaks on matters of faith and morals, and states his intention to announce a doctrinal definition. Papal pronouncements which are intended simply to exhort or instruct do not fall within this category. But which papal decisions have been spoken *ex cathedra*? It used to be said by some theologians that no Pope had ever used this authority, and that there were therefore no *ex cathedra* pronouncements. This opinion became untenable, however, after the solemn definition of the dogma of the bodily assumption of Mary. We must notice too, that in announcing the dogma of papal infallibility, the Vatican Council gave it retrospective force. Yet it is still very difficult to say just which papal decisions have this character. They certainly include the Bull *Unam sanctam* of Boniface VIII (1302), which affirmed the primacy of the spiritual authority over that of the state; the Bull *Exsurge Domine* (1502) in which Leo X condemned forty-one errors of Luther; the Constitution *Unigenitus Dei filius* of Clement XI (1713) against the Augustinian views of the Jansenist, Paschasius Quesnel; the Bull *Ineffabilis Deus* (1854) of Pius IX, which defined as dogma the immaculate conception of Mary; and the Encyclical *Quanta Cura*, issued by Pius IX with the 'Syllabus errorum' (1864), containing eighty propositions rejecting Modernism. It is significant that under these circumstances the Pope of the Vatican Council, Pius IX, could coin the phrase: 'I am the tradition.'[25] We must not, however,

[24] 'Romanum Pontificem, cum ex cathedra loquitur, id est, cum omnium Christianorum pastoris et doctoris munere fungens pro suprema sua Apostolica auctoritate doctrinam de fide vel moribus ab universa Ecclesia tenendam definit, per assistentiam divinam ipsi in beato PETRO promissam, ea infallibilitate pollere, qua divinus Redemptor Ecclesiam suam in definienda doctrina de fide vel moribus instructam esse voluit, ideoque eiusmodi Romani Pontificis definitiones ex sese, non autem ex consensu Ecclesiae, irreformabiles esse.' Sess. 4, ch. 4 (D., 1839; M., 465.24; Schaff, II.270f).

[25] See J. B. Bury, *History of the Papacy in the Nineteenth Century*, London 1930, p. 124.

overlook the following statement made by that Council: 'The Holy Spirit was promised to the successors of Peter not as if He were going to reveal some new doctrine for them to publish, but in order that His assistance might enable them to preserve with all reverence the revelation or deposit of faith, transmitted through the Apostles, and to expound it faithfully.'[26] The Pope, in whom all doctrinal authority is concentrated, has no power to proclaim new doctrine, but may only expound the revelation transmitted by the Apostles. In his teaching office, the Pope is not free but controlled. Since, however, he has no real counterpart, this is not a genuine control and the door is wide open to every kind of arbitrariness.

Papal pronouncements and conciliar decrees form only a part of the deposit of faith which the Church proposes for acceptance by believers. The other part is proclaimed by the Church '*ordinario et universali magisterio*'.

This 'ordinary and universal *magisterium*' is the function of the bishops, which they exercise by means of pastoral letters, by the approval of catechisms and religious books, and so on. They are not infallible in their teaching office, but simply transmit the Christian truth which believers must hold.

The 'ordinary and universal *magisterium*' also operates in the life and practice of the Church, above all in the liturgy. The liturgical books used by the priesthood should therefore be mentioned: the *Missale Romanum* (1570), containing the Order of Mass; the *Rituale Romanum* (1614), giving the formularies for the sacraments and other ecclesiastical rites and ceremonies performed by the priests; the *Pontificale Romanum* (1596), regulating the ceremonies performed by the bishops; and the *Breviarium Romanum* (1074 and 1568), compiled from various sources and giving the daily offices for the secular clergy.

From all that has been said, it follows that there is no official body of documents setting forth the faith of the Roman Church. Even Denzinger's collection of conciliar decrees and papal decisions is of quite uncertain status and certainly not infallible in the Roman sense. Unlike the Lutheran Church, with its

[26] 'Neque enim PETRI successoribus Spiritus Sanctus promissus est, ut eo revelante novam doctrinam patefacerent, sed ut, eo assistente, traditam per Apostolos revelationem seu fidei depositum sancte custodirent et fideliter exponerent' (D., 1836; M., 465.4; Schaff, II.269).

Book of Concord, the Roman Church does not regard any single book as a testament of its faith. That would not be in accord with its view of the Church's teaching office.

4. Where is the Tradition Located?

Various sources of tradition are used by the Church's teaching office. They include, in addition to those already mentioned, 'the unanimous consent of the Fathers' (*consensus patrum*), referred to above but very difficult to define; the Acts of the Martyrs; and, according to Bartmann,[27] even pictures, sculptures, monuments, and Christian inscriptions.

The Roman Church does not, in fact, maintain a mere *dogma formale* (*dogma quoad nos*), which it has already formulated, but at the deepest level, the *dogma materiale* (*dogma quoad se*), the divine legacy (*divinum depositum*) entrusted to the Church which she must faithfully guard and unfailingly teach.[28] The Church keeps and administers the hidden treasure of the *dogma materiale*. From it she can bring out whatever she thinks fit. This happens when she defines a dogma.

We must also listen to the Church when we wish to know what has already been defined as dogma (*dogma formale declaratum*). In the last analysis, only the Pope can give reliable information on this point. In a negative and defensive sense this is done by means of the *Index librorum prohibitorum* which has been continuously published at Rome since 1562.

In general the criteria of authentic tradition are the three mentioned by Vincent of Lerins in his *Commonitorium* (434): 'In the Catholic Church the greatest care is to be taken to hold that which has been believed everywhere, always, and by all; for that is Catholic in the true and strict sense.'[29]

[27] *Dogmatik*, VOL. I, p. 29.

[28] Vatican Sess. 3, ch. 4 (D., 1800; M., 460.2; Schaff, II.250).

[29] 'In ipsa item catholica ecclesia magnopere curandum est, ut id teneamus, quod ubique, quod semper, quod ab omnibus creditum est; hoc est enim vere proprieque catholicum' (M., 73.27; English trans, in *Documents of the Christian Church*, ed. H. Bettenson, henceforth cited as Bettenson, *Documents*, London 1943, p. 119). Vincent's *Commonitorium* is found in Migne, P.L., VOL. L, pp. 637ff. A translation is given in VOL. IX of the Library of Christian Classics, *Early Mediaeval Theology*, ed. George E. McCracken. London 1957.

CHAPTER 2

THE ROMAN VIEW OF THE CHURCH[1]

In Chapter 1 we learned the sources from which Roman Catholicism derives its doctrine and how it assesses them. As we saw, it is impossible to confine ourselves to these sources for, along with them, we have to consider the Church, or, more precisely, the Church's teaching office. There is no access to the sources except through this teaching office. The Church is the 'immediate rule of faith', to which the believer must adhere. It is, therefore, appropriate to ask now what Rome means by the Church.

Roman theologians have said, with some truth, that Rome has no doctrine of the Church. The doctrine of the Church is of course, dealt with in all textbooks on dogmatics, but whereas in other matters Roman Catholic dogmatics is essentially the exposition of dogma, the section devoted to the Church refers to very few propositions representing defined dogma. Councils and Papal documents have developed no explicit doctrine of the Church. That in itself is very significant. It was obviously enough for the Church to exist and to carry on its work. Any reflexion about itself was regarded as unnecessary. The Church was in fact infallible. It was aware of no position superior to itself from which it could be challenged. It was only 'the special conditions of our time' during the Second World War which constrained Pius XII to issue his Encyclical *Mystici corporis Christi*.[2] In the preface to the German edition of this document, the translator says: 'This is the first dogmatic presentation of the doctrine of the Church as the mystical body of Christ.'[3] Whether that is the case, or whether this encyclical was simply

[1] Cf. R. Newton Flew, 'The Church of Rome', in *The Nature of the Church*, ed. R. N. Flew, London 1952, pp. 17-40.

[2] D., 2287ff; Eng. trans. G. D. Smith, *The Mystical Body of Jesus Christ*, London 1943, p. 6.

[3] *Unsere Kirche*, Rundschr. *Mystici corporis*, Heidelberg 1946, p. 5.

meant as instruction, cannot be determined with certainty. Either way, it is very important. Yet even without it we would not be groping in the dark. There is a whole series of important statements about the Church setting forth defined dogma.

1. The Divine Foundation of the Church

The opening words of the *Decretum pro Iacobitis*, from the Bull *Cantate Domino* issued by Eugenius IV in 1441, 'The Holy Roman Church founded on the Word of our Lord and Redeemer,'[4] remind us of the first Berne thesis, reaffirmed at Düsseldorf in 1933. The statements of the modern Papacy, however, show that it is not the living, and therefore present, Word of the Lord which is here in view, but the Word which He once spoke during his lifetime on earth. In the Anti-Modernist oath (1910), it is asserted that the Church was 'founded immediately and personally by the true and historic Christ during His earthly life',[5] and the immediately following words, about the foundation of the Church on Peter and his successors, show that this appeal to the 'historic Christ' is not intended merely as a safeguard against a modern, unbiblical view of the Church. The intention is rather to present the Church as a society which began to exist from that point of time onwards and continues to exist in this time of ours. Without this background, the important concept of 'tradition', which we met in Chapter 1, would be meaningless. Most papal pronouncements speak of the foundation of the Church in this temporal sense. 'The Divine Redeemer began to build the mystical Temple of His Church when He was preaching and giving His Commandments; He completed it when He hung in glory on the Cross; He manifested and promulgated it by the visible mission of the Paraclete, the Holy Spirit, upon His disciples.'[6]

According to the Vatican Council the Church was founded 'in order to continue for all time the life-giving work of redemption',[7] so that in the Church 'as the house of the living God, all

[4] 'Sacrosancta Romana Ecclesia, domini et salvatoris nostri voce fundata' (D., 703).

[5] 'Per ipsum verum atque historicum Christum, cum apud nos degeret, proxime ac directo institutam' (D., 2145; M., 516.20).

[6] Pius XII, *Mystici corporis*, Eng. trans. pp. 17f.

[7] 'Ut salutiferum redemptionis opus perenne redderet.'

who believe might be united in the bond of one faith and one charity'.[8] The Church 'is a mystical body whose Head is Christ'.[9] The most recent papal statement about the Church also refers repeatedly to the Church as Christ's mystical body. This does not mean that an attempt was made here to speak of the Church in genuinely biblical terms. On the contrary, in this description of the Church as a body, a particular sociological concept is being employed which is alien to Scripture. In the Encyclical *Mystici corporis* (1943), Pius XII says: 'We therefore deplore and condemn also the calamitous error which invents an imaginary Church, a society nurtured and shaped by charity, with which it disparagingly contrasts another society which it calls juridical. Those who make this totally erroneous distinction fail to understand that it was . . . the purpose . . . of perpetuating on this earth the salutary work of the Redemption . . . which caused the Divine Redeemer . . . to give the community of human beings founded by Him the constitution of a *society perfect in its own order, provided with all its juridical and social elements*.'[10] An earlier Pope had rejected the view that the Church comes into being when individuals accept Christ and thus constitute a society. Individuals are called by Christ as 'united and joined together in truth and conviction, so that instead of a crowd there emerges a people united by law.'[11] What this 'perfect society' (*societas perfecta*), this 'people united by law' (*populus iure sociatus*) looks like we shall learn in what follows.

2. The Church as a Priestly, Sacramental Institution for Salvation

The Church fulfils its mission of giving permanence to the work of redemption and of incorporating men into the body of Christ, by handing on what it has itself received from Christ.[12] Pius XII says that 'Christ Jesus on the Cross opened up to His

[8] Sess. 4 (D., 1821; M., 461.25; Schaff, II.256).

[9] Bull *Unam Sanctam*, 1302 (D., 468; M., 210.22).

[10] Pius XII, *Mystici corporis*, Eng. trans. p. 39.

[11] 'Consociati atque invicem re animisque iuncti, ut ex multitudine populus existeret iure sociatus.' Encyclical *Satis cognitum*, 1896 (D., 1959).

[12] 'Partam per Iesum Christum salutem simulque beneficia omnia, quae inde proficiscuntur, late fundere in omnes homines atque ad omnes propagare aetates debet Ecclesia.' *Satis cognitum*, 1896 (D., 1955).

Church the well-spring of Divine gifts'. It was thus equipped 'to bathe men with a rain of Heavenly graces'.[13]

This stream of gifts, of which the Church is the channel and which makes and maintains those taken into it as members of the Church, flows from the Cross of Christ. Just as the Church, the fruit of Christ's redeeming work, is continually increased and preserved by this stream, so too it owes its existence to it. As we saw earlier, though Christ began to found the Church by His preaching, He completed it on the Cross. 'After the [Incarnate] Word of God had yielded up His spirit, and His side had been pierced with the lance, He caused the immaculate virgin, Holy Mother Church, to be formed from the water and the blood which flowed from His side, just as from the side of the sleeping Adam, Eve was formed to be his wife.'[14] In view of the Church's origin and mission, Möhler even goes so far as to say (in his *Symbolik*) that the Church is 'the Son of God continuing to manifest Himself in human form, constantly renewing and ever rejuvenating Himself, *the permanent incarnation of the same*' Son of God.[15] 'The Church is the Lord's body, His visible form in its totality, His abiding, *eternally rejuvenated* humanity, His *eternal manifestation*.'[16] That is not defined dogma, of course, but it surely makes plain Rome's doctrine of the Church and its mission. It is not only Möhler who has said that the Church is the 'eternally self-rejuvenating Son of God', and to this extent, 'His eternal manifestation'. Even Pope Pius XII calls on the faithful to regard the Church as 'Christ Himself'.[17] While the physical body of Christ is 'now seated at the right hand of the Father', His 'mystical body' derives from and is continually nourished by the sacrifice on the Cross.[18]

How does this happen? The Church founded by Christ and perfected on the Cross can conduct the stream of grace to men because it is authorised to repeat again and again the sacrifice

[13] Pius XII, *Mystici corporis*, Eng. trans. p. 21.

[14] 'Dei Verbum . . . emisso iam spiritu perforari lancea sustinuit latus suum, ut exinde profluentibus undis aquae et sanguinis formaretur unica et immaculata ac virgo sancta mater Ecclesia, coniunx Christi, sicut de latere primi hominis soporati Eva sibi in coniugium est formata.' Constitution *De Summa Trinitate et fide catholica* (D., 480).

[15] J. A. Möhler, *Symbolik oder Darstellung der dogmatischen Gegensätze der Katholiken und Protestanten*, Mainz 1832, p. 333.

[16] *Op. cit.*, p. 356.

[17] *Mystici corporis*, Eng. trans. p. 56.

[18] *Op. cit.*, p. 36.

offered by Christ once for all on the Cross, and in this way to cause the spring of all graces to flow again. The Council of Trent stated that 'Sacrifice and priesthood are, by God's ordinance, in such wise conjoined as that both have existed in every law. Whereas, therefore, in the New Testament, the Catholic Church has received, from the institution of Christ, the holy visible sacrifice of the Eucharist, it must needs also be confessed that there is in that Church a new, visible, and external priesthood, into which the old has been translated. And the Sacred Scriptures show, and the tradition of the Catholic Church has always taught, that this priesthood was instituted by the same Lord our Saviour, and that to the Apostles, and their successors in the priesthood, was the power delivered of consecrating, offering, and administering His body and blood, as also of forgiving and retaining sins.'[19] The Church's continuing power to cause the spring of grace to flow again is located in the priesthood into which the Apostles and their successors, the Bishops, have been called. The latter ensure the continuation of the priesthood, in virtue of an uninterrupted succession which, it is claimed, links them to the Apostles (*successio apostolica*). By the sacrament of ordination they are able to make priests and to transmit to these the same power to offer up Christ's sacrifice.[20]

According to Roman doctrine, therefore, there is in the Church a priesthood instituted by Christ Himself, a special order (*ordo*) of priests, having an indestructible character (*character indelibilis*).[21] This priesthood does not exist in virtue of the sacrifice of the Mass, for both the Mass and the priestly office are held to derive directly from Christ. The priesthood causes the spring of grace to flow. Without this priestly order (*ordo*) the Roman Church would be unthinkable. She is a priestly, sacramental institution for salvation.

[19] 'Sacrificium et sacerdotium ita Dei ordinatione coniuncta sunt, ut utrumque in omni lege exstiterit. Cum igitur in Novo Testamento sanctum Eucharistiae sacrificium visibile ex Domini institutione catholica Ecclesia acceperit: fateri etiam oportet, in ea novum esse visibile et externum sacerdotium (can. 1), in quod vetus translatum est (Heb. 7.12ff). Hoc autem ab eodem Domino Salvatore nostro institutum esse (can. 3), atque Apostolis eorumque successoribus in sacerdotio potestatem traditam consecrandi, offerendi et ministrandi corpus et sanguinem eius, nec non et peccata dimittendi et retinendi, sacrae Litterae ostendunt, et catholicae Ecclesiae traditio semper docuit (can. 1).' Sess. 23, ch. 1 (D., 957; M., 326.29; Schaff, II.186f).

[20] Sess. 23, ch. 4 (D., 960; M., 327.14; Schaff, II.188ff). [21] *Ibid.*

3. The Church as a Legally Constituted Monarchy

The priesthood is at the same time called to govern the Church. 'The Church is a hierarchy headed by a monarch. It is indeed based on this hierarchy, on Peter, the Prince of the Apostles, and all his successors.'[22] This hierarchy is as 'an army set in array'.[23] It consists of bishops, presbyters, and deacons.[24]

The Bishops are regarded as the successors of the Apostles. The promise given to the Apostles has been transferred to them. They are therefore the mainstay of the Church's hierarchical structure. The Council of Trent states 'that . . . bishops, who have succeeded to the place of the Apostles, principally belong to this hierarchical order . . . they are placed by the Holy Ghost to rule the Church of God, they are superior to priests'.[25] Similarly, the most recent Papal pronouncement about the Church says: 'Therefore the bishops are not only to be regarded as more eminent members of the Universal Church, by reason of the truly unique bond which unites them with the divine Head of the whole Body and so makes them indeed "the primary parts of the members of the Lord"; but each of them is also, as far as his own diocese is concerned, a true Pastor who tends and rules in the name of Christ the flock committed to his care.'[26] As the successors of the Apostles, bishops have 'juridical authority' (*potestas jurisdictionis*) over their dioceses including the priests. This authority consists in 'governing and restraining the Christian community and guiding it to the eternal Heavenly bliss'.[27] Within this authority a distinction is made between legislative, judicial, and coercive power (*potestas legifera, iudicalis, coactiva*). This organisation of the Roman Church is in sharp contrast to the 'community of brethren', confessed by the Barmen Declaration, in which 'the various

[22] 'Super PETRUM, apostolicae hierarchiae principem, eiusque in aevum successores aedificatam.' Anti-modernist oath, 1910 (D., 2145; M., 516.21).

[23] 'Ut castrorum acies ordinata' (cf. Song of Sol. 6.3). Trent Sess. 23, ch. 4 (D., 960; M., 327.21; Schaff, II.189).

[24] Sess. 23, can. 6 (D., 966; M., 328.12; Schaff, II.192).

[25] 'Episcopos, qui in Apostolorum locum successerunt, ad hunc hierarchicum ordinem praecipue pertinere, et 'positos (sicut idem Apostolus ait) a Spiritu Sancto regere Ecclesiam Dei' [Acts 20.28], eosque presbyteris superiores esse.' *Loc. cit.* (D., 960; M., 327.24; Schaff, II.189).

[26] Pius XII, *Mystici corporis*, Eng. trans. pp. 25ff.

[27] 'Christianum populum gubernare et moderari et ad aeternam coelestemque beatitudinem dirigere.' Roman Catechism, 1566, PT. II, ch. 7, Q. 6 (M., 347.12).

ministries . . . do not establish any lordship of some over others'.

The monarchical head. This contrast becomes quite unmistakable when we learn that the episcopate has a monarchical head, the Pope at Rome. The Vatican Council simply completed the structure of the Roman Church, which all along required a head with absolute authority to govern. It teaches that '*it is by the institution of Christ the Lord*, or by *divine right*, that blessed Peter should have a perpetual line of successors in the primacy over the universal Church'.[28] This was of course an ancient view. The Vatican Fathers could appeal to the Council of Florence (1438-45) to support their statement that 'the Roman Pontiff himself is the successor of blessed Peter, Prince of the Apostles, and is *true Vicar of Christ* and head of the whole Church, and father and teacher of all Christians, and that in blessed Peter full power was given to him by Jesus Christ our Lord to rule, feed, and govern the universal Church'.[29] The government of the Church by Christ its invisible Head is an 'extraordinary' one, that by the Pope, His vicar on earth, is the 'ordinary' one.[30] Since the Vatican Council, however, this papal function is not a primacy of honour, nor of mere leadership or oversight, but a primacy of jurisdiction, i.e. the Pope now has supreme legislative, judicial and coercive authority. This primacy over the whole Church was 'immediately and directly [*immediate et directe*] promised and given' to the Apostle Peter 'by Christ the Lord'.[31] And what was given to Peter belongs to all his successors in the Papacy. 'This power of jurisdiction of the Roman Pontiff which is truly episcopal, is immediate: to which all, of whatever rite and dignity, both pastors and faithful, both individually and collectively, are bound, by their duty of hierarchical subordination and true obedience, to submit.'[32] The

[28] 'Esse ex ipsius Christi Domini institutione seu iure divino, ut beatus PETRUS in primatu super universam ecclesiam habeat perpetuos successores.' Sess. 4, ch. 2, canon (D., 1825; M., 462.41; Schaff, II. 261f).

[29] 'Ipsum Pontificem Romanum successorem esse beati PETRI, principis Apostolorum, et verum Christi vicarium totiusque Ecclesiae caput et omnium Christianorum patrem ac doctorem existere; et ipsi in beato PETRO pascendi, regendi ac gubernandi universalem Ecclesiam a Domino nostro Iesu Christo plenam potestatem traditam esse.' Sess. 4, ch. 3 (D., 1826; M., 463.6; Schaff, II.262).

[30] Pius XII, *Mystici corporis*, Eng. trans, p. 24.

[31] Vatican Sess. 4, ch. 1 (D., 1822; M., 462.3; Schaff, II.260).

[32] 'Hanc Romani Pontificis iurisdictionis potestatem, quae vere episcopalis est, immediatam esse: erga quam cuiuscunque ritus et dignitatis pastores atque fideles,

function exercised by the Pope, therefore, is not one originally committed to the whole Church and only now transferred to the Pope.[33] He is what he is directly from Christ. He is not just the pinnacle of the hierarchical structure of the Roman Church, but in fact, 'the abiding principle and visible foundation' of the unity both of the episcopate and of the whole company of the faithful.[34] Anyone who challenges his position attacks the very essence of the Church. 'For with this visible head eliminated and the visible bonds of unity broken, the mystical Body of the Redeemer is so obscured and disfigured that it becomes impossible for those who are seeking the harbour of eternal salvation to see or discover it.'[35]

The Bishops' position under the Pope. Once it has defined as dogma the overriding authority of the Pope, the Vatican Council does not hesitate to give the bishops their due. 'So far is this power of the Supreme Pontiff from being any prejudice to the ordinary and immediate power of episcopal jurisdiction, by which bishops, who have been set by the Holy Ghost to succeed and hold the place of the Apostles, feed and govern each his own flock, as true pastors, that this their episcopal authority is really asserted, strengthened and protected by the Supreme and universal Pastor.'[36] Bishops are therefore regarded as having an immediate juridical authority, since they are instituted in their office by the Holy Ghost. The most recent papal pronouncement on the Church appears to restrict still further the authority allowed to bishops by the Vatican Council. 'In discharging this function however they are not completely independent but are subject to the proper authority of the Roman Pontiff, although they enjoy ordinary power of jurisdiction received immediately from the Sovereign Pontiff himself.'[37] A

tam seorsum singuli quam simul omnes, officio hierarchicae subordinationis veraeque obroedientiae obstringuntur.' Vatican Sess. 4, ch. 3 (D., 1827; M., 463.14; Schaff, II.263).

[33] Vatican Sess. 4, ch. 1 (D., 1822; M., 462.18; Schaff, II.259).

[34] *Loc. cit.* (D., 1821; M., 461.34; Schaff, II.257).

[35] Pius XII, *Mystici corporis*, Eng. trans. p. 25.

[36] 'Tantum autem abest, ut haec Summi Pontificis potestas officiant ordinariae ac immediatae illi episcopalis iurisdictionis potestati, qua episcopi, qui positi a Spiritu Sancto [cf. Acts 20.28] in Apostolorum locum successerunt, tanquam veri pastores assignatos sibi greges singuli singulos pascunt et regunt, ut eadem a supremo et universali pastore asseratur, roboretur ac vindicetur.' Sess. 4, ch. 3 (D., 1828; M., 463.22; Schaff, II.263f).

[37] 'Id tamen dum faciunt, non plane sui iuris sunt, sed sub debita Romani

remarkable way of putting it! The Vatican Council could still speak of an 'immediate power' possessed by bishops. The adjective has now become an adverb, and the ordinary power of jurisdiction possessed by bishops is said to be received by them immediately from the Pope.[38] But apart from this new restriction of episcopal authority, we must also notice that in any case this authority is attached only to their office and not to their person. It leaves them if they leave this office.

The Vatican Council had already restricted episcopal authority in the Pope's favour in three respects:

(1) The Pope has 'the right of free communication with the pastors of the whole Church and with their flocks'.[39]

(2) The Pope is 'the supreme judge of the faithful and . . . recourse may be had to his tribunal'.[40]

(3) It is unlawful 'to appeal from the judgments of the Roman Pontiff to an Ecumenical Council, as to an authority higher than that of the Roman Pontiff'.[41] There is no right of appeal against the Pope. He really is the supreme court of the Roman Church, he really claims the place of Christ here on earth. In contrast to this, the Barmen Declaration is expressing the basic New Testament view (and not just 'existential difficulties') when it says that in the Church it can only be a matter of service and that 'special "leaders" equipped with power to rule' have no place in her.

Under the bishop, the priest exercises jurisdiction only in the confessional (*forum poenitentiale*), in the sacrament of penance. This jurisdiction belongs to his office for his work in the cure of souls. This qualification does not diminish the tremendous importance of this jurisdiction for the individual Church mem-

Pontificis auctoritate positi, quamvis ordinaria iurisdictionis potestate fruantur, immediate sibi ab eodem Pontifice Summo impertita.' Pius XII, *Mystici corporis* (D., 2287; Eng. trans. p. 26).

[38] Bartmann (*Dogmatik*, VOL. II, p. 177) could still write: 'Acts 20.28, the passage referred to by the Council, states that the Holy Spirit established the bishops to rule the Church. That means that they too have also received from God their whole authority by consecration. . . . The Pope simply appoints the bishop to his diocese, the episcopal power of jurisdiction comes from God.'

[39] 'Libere communicandi cum pastoribus et gregibus totius ecclesiae.' Vatican Sess. 4, ch. 3 (D., 1829; M., 463.31; Schaff, II.264).

[40] 'Iudicem supremum fidelium et . . . ad ipsius posse iudicium recurri.' *Loc. cit.* (D., 1830; M., 463.39; Schaff, II.265).

[41] 'Ab iudiciis Romanorum Pontificum ad oecumenicum Concilium tanquam ad auctoritatem Romano Pontifice superiorem appellare.' *Ibid.*

bers, for in virtue of it the priest decides matters of life and death to the individual.[42] But even the bishop's judicial power can sometimes be delegated to a priest, e.g. to the episcopal Vicar-General.

4. The Church as a Visible Institution

It follows from all this that the Roman Church is something so clearly and firmly ordered that it can be seen and identified by all. 'God has bestowed on it manifest notes of that institution, that it can be recognised *by all men* as the guardian and teacher of the revealed Word.'[43] As we saw earlier, the Pope is the 'visible foundation' of the Church's unity, and anyone questioning his authority obscures and destroys the warning lights of the harbour of salvation. The Pope is therefore regarded as the earthly head of the Church. Pius XII quotes some words of Leo XIII: 'By the very fact of being a body, the Church is visible.'[44] The Jesuit Bellarmine does not go beyond accepted Church doctrine when he writes: 'The Church is a human society as visible and palpable as the Roman Empire or the Kingdom of France or the State of Venice.'[45] It is significant that he should compare the Church with various national States, for it is precisely the juridical order of the Church, culminating in the Pope as monarch, which is its most distinctive feature.

The Roman Church affirms that there are several recognisable marks (*notae*) of the Church. The Nicene Creed names four: unity, holiness, catholicity, and apostolicity. Roman doctrine stresses the indissoluble unity of these marks, and interprets the last of them in the sense of apostolic succession. As we said earlier, the Church's unity rests in the Papacy. 'The Catholic Church is therefore *one*, with a visible and perfect unity throughout the world and embracing all nations, a unity with its basis, root and unfailing source in the authority of

[42] See below, Chapter 7, pp. 80ff.

[43] 'Deus . . . manifestis notis instruxit, ut ea tanquam custos et magistra verbi revelati ab omnibus posset agnosci.' Vatican Sess, 3, ch. 3 (D., 1793; M., 458.23; Schaff, II.245).

[44] Encyclical *Satis cognitum*, 1896, as quoted in *Mystici corporis* (Eng. trans. p. 12).

[45] 'Ecclesia enim est coetus hominum ita visibilis et palpabilis, ut est coetus populi Romani vel regnum Galliae aut res publica Venetorum.' *Disputationes de controversiis Christianae fidei*, 1586-93, BK III, c. 2 (M., 361.28).

St Peter, Prince of the Apostles, and his successors in the See of Rome.'[46] The Papacy is the centre of ecclesiastical unity.[47]

Since, in Roman doctrine, the Church is essentially a hierarchical institution, membership of it is also defined in a special way. All who have been baptised are members of the Church.[48] Pius IX wrote to Kaiser Wilhelm I: 'Everyone who has received baptism is in some degree and in some sense related to the Pope.'[49] Benedict XIV had said the same in 1749: 'Anyone who receives baptism in proper form even from a heretic, thereby becomes a member of the Catholic Church. . . . Heretics are therefore subject to the Church and its laws.'[50] It can be said that all believers belong to the Church 'even though their faith is not alive'.[51] They are then 'dead members' but still members. All who have been baptised belong *ipso facto* to the mystical body of the Church of which Christ is the Heavenly Head.

The following propositions have been rejected: 'that only believers who worship perfectly in the Spirit and in the truth, belong to the Church'[52]; the assertions of Paschasius Quesnel that the Church includes 'all the angels in heaven, with all the elect and just, on earth and in all ages'[53]; and that 'the Church is . . . solely the one Christ, who unites the many Saints, whom He Himself sanctifies'.[54]

According to Bellarmine, there are three recognisable marks of full Church membership: 'The confession of the true faith,

[46] 'Ecclesia igitur catholica una est unitate conspicua perfectaque orbis terrae et omnium gentium ea profecto unitate, cuius principium, radix et origo indefectibilis est beati PETRI Apostolorum principis, eiusque in Cathedra Romana successorum suprema auctoritas.' Pius IX, 1864 (D., 1686).

[47] *Satis cognitum*, 1896 (D., 1960).

[48] Trent Sess. 7, can. 13f (D., 869f; M., 304.42; Schaff, II.122).

[49] M., 470.3.

[50] 'Eum, qui baptisma ab haeretico rite suscepit, illius vi ecclesiae catholicae membrum effici . . . sic haeretici ecclesiae subditi sunt et legibus ecclesiasticis tenentur' (M., 470.45).

[51] 'Licet fides non sit viva.' Trent Sess. 6, can. 28 (D., 838; M., 302.29; Schaff, II.116).

[52] 'Ut ad corpus Ecclesiae non pertineant nisi fideles, qui sunt perfecti adoratores in spiritu et veritate.' Pius VI in *Auctorem fidei*, 1794, condemning the Reform Synod of Pistoia of 1786 (D., 1515).

[53] 'Omnes angelos coeli et omnes electos et iustos terrae et omnium saeculorum.' Clement XI in the Constitution *Unigenitus Dei Filius*, 1713 (D., 1422; M., 398.11);

[54] 'Ecclesia est unus solus Christus compositus ex pluribus sanctis, quorum est sanctificator.' *Op. cit.* (D., 1425; M., 398.17).

participation in the sacraments, and submission to the lawful Shepherd, the Roman Pontiff.'[55] But, in certain circumstances, as we have seen, Popes could reduce these conditions to the single one of baptism. As Rome sees it, baptism, in claiming a man for Christ, at the same time automatically requisitions him for Christ's vicar.

Outside the visible, hierarchical institution of the Roman Church, there is no salvation. This exclusive character follows logically from the power of the priestly office (*potestas ordinis*) and from the power of jurisdiction (*potestas iurisdictionis*) which are found only in this Church. Pius IX announced: 'It is of faith that outside the Apostolic Roman Church no one can be saved, that she is the one Ark of Salvation, and that whoever fails to enter it will be lost in the deluge.'[56] Later, in the *Syllabus* of 1864, he condemned the proposition that we may at least entertain good hope of the salvation of those 'who are not members of the true Church of Christ'.[57] Pius XII expressed himself more guardedly. He states that 'those who do not belong to the visible structure of the Catholic Church are in a position in which they cannot be certain of their own eternal salvation: for though they may be related to the mystical body of the Redeemer by some unconscious yearning and desire, yet they are deprived of those many great heavenly gifts and aids which can be enjoyed only in the Catholic Church'.[58]

Salvation is found, not where the One Word of God is proclaimed and heard, but in the institution of the Roman Church, because this priestly sacramental organisation as such is the sole means of salvation. The individual's salvation does not depend on the Word, on Christ, but on the Church. This is not surprising since, as we saw earlier, the Church alone controls the Word. The Church is not the servant of the Word, obliged always to submit to His renewed questioning but, on

[55] 'Professio verae fidei, sacramentorum communio et subiectio ad legitimum pastorem, Romanum Pontificem.' *Op. cit.* (M., 361.12).

[56] 'Tenendum quippe ex fide est, extra apostolicam Romanam Ecclesiam salvum fieri neminem posse, hanc esse unicam salutis arcam, hanc qui non fuerit ingressus, diluvio periturum.' Allocution *Singulari quadam*, 1854 (D., 1647. M., 447.23).

[57] 'Qui in vera Christi Ecclesia nequaquam versantur.' (D., 1717; M., 451.36).

[58] *Mystici corporis*, Eng. trans. p. 61.

the contrary, the master of the Word, 'His eternal manifestation'', the Word given shape and form, and not the community 'in which Jesus Christ acts presently as Lord in Word and Sacrament, through the Holy Spirit'.[59]

[59] Barmen Thesis No. 3.

CHAPTER 3

THE DOCTRINE OF MAN[1]

HAVING seen how the Roman Church regards itself as the bearer of salvation, we now ask about its doctrine of man, the intended beneficiary of this salvation.

1. MAN'S ORIGINAL STATE

The Vatican Fathers appealed to the words of the Fourth Lateran Council (1215) when they affirmed that 'God . . . created out of nothing . . . both the spiritual and the corporeal creature . . . and afterwards the human creature as . . . consisting of spirit and body'.[2] The mortality of the human soul had been explicitly rejected.[3]

The original state of grace. The first man possessed a holiness and righteousness 'wherein he had been constituted'.[4] As was later affirmed in opposition to the view of Michael Baius, man was therefore 'elevated above his natural state by a supernatural and gracious gift, so that he worshipped God supernaturally in faith, hope, and love'.[5] To human nature, consisting of body and soul, another gift had been added, in the person of the first man, a gift completely transcending the capacity and title of all created nature and resting on a divine act. In respect of human nature, it is also called an 'additional gift' (*donum superadditum*) and, in respect of the divine act, an 'undeserved gift' (*donum indebitum*), since God was not obliged to confer it on man. Roman theology regards this divine gift added

[1] For further study see Hans Emil Weber, *Der Mensch in katholischer und evangelischer Auffassung*, Beiträge zur Ev. Theologie. VOL. IV, Munich 1941, pp. 84ff.

[2] 'Deus . . . "utramque de nihilo condidit naturam spiritualem et corporalem . . . ac deinde humanam quasi communem ex spiritu et corpore constitutam".' Vatican Sess. 3, ch. 1 (D., 1783; M., 456.45; Schaff, II.239).

[3] 5th Lateran Council, 1512-17 (D., 738).

[4] 'In qua constitutus fuerat.' Trent Sess. 5 (D., 788; M., 293.26; Schaff, II. 84).

[5] 'Dono quodam supernaturali et gratuito supra conditionem naturae suae fuisse exaltatum, ut fide, spe et caritate Deum supernaturaliter coleret.' Pius V, Bull *Ex omnibus afflictionibus*, 1567 (D., 1023).

to human nature, as the *image of God* in the first man.

This absolutely supernatural gift (*donum supernaturale per se*) imparted to the first man must be distinguished from the relatively supernatural gifts (*dona praeternaturalia*) also given to him. The latter surpass human nature, but not all created nature, that of the angels for example. They include: (1) freedom from desire (*concupiscentia*)[6]; (2) exemption from physical death[7]; and (3) from pain.[8]

Man in possession of all these gifts, both the *dona supernaturalia* and the *dona praeternaturalia*, is in the state of elevated nature (*status naturae elevatae*), in his proper original state. By state (*status*) is meant not a condition but the goal God sets for man, and man's equipment with the necessary means to reach it. In this state of elevated nature man was destined and equipped for communion with God.

Roman theology distinguishes between this state and the state of pure nature (*status naturae purae*). No theologian teaches the actuality of this state, in which man would have to be regarded as a spiritual being endowed with freedom and capable of a natural knowledge and love of God. The official teaching is that this pure natural human state was once a possibility. It is significant that in speaking of man's original state the Council of Trent did not say, as we might have expected, 'in which he had been created' (*in qua creatus fuerat*), but more ambiguously, 'in which he had been constituted' (*in qua constitutus fuerat*). Pius V condemned the proposition of Michael Baius: 'God could not have created man in the beginning as he is now born.'[9] This abstract distinction between man's supernatural endowment (*donum supernaturale*) and his pure nature (*natura pura*) is not unimportant. It shows clearly that Roman theology is in a position to construct a complete idea of man without taking account of his relationship to God. Man is a being composed of body and soul. That is the essential concept of man.

Between the purely natural state and the state of elevated nature lies the state of unimpaired nature (*status naturae integrae*).

[6] Trent Sess. 5 (D., 792; M., 294; Schaff, II.88). Cf. Bartmann, *Dogmatik*, VOL. II, p. 303.

[7] Trent Sess. 5 (D., 788f; M., 293; Schaff, II.84f).

[8] *Loc. cit.* (D., 789; M., 293; Schaff, II.85).

[9] 'Deus non potuisset ab initio talem creare hominem, qualis nunc nascitur.' Bull *Ex omnibus afflictionibus* (D., 1055).

We have already indicated its special gifts: in this state, the conflict between body and soul is overcome. The sensual impulse (*concupiscentia*) is subordinated to reason, because of a divine gift of grace which, as we saw, does not exceed the order of all created nature. The possibility of this state is accepted Roman teaching. The school of Duns Scotus affirmed its reality. In this state a man will have prepared himself to receive supernatural grace and made himself worthy of it. The Thomists teach that man's endowment with the *dona praeternaturalia* and *supernaturalia* is simultaneous. The formula of the Council of Trent (*in qua constitutus fuerat*) did not decide in favour of Thomas against Duns. Its ambiguity leaves room for both views. This difference between the theological schools is unimportant, however, compared with the conceptual distinction already mentioned, between man's proper original state and his nature without the grace of this original state.

2. The Fall of Man

Only in the doctrine of sin does the full significance of what we have just heard about man become clear.

According to Trent, Adam by disobedience *lost the supernatural gifts* of holiness and righteousness.[10] The *praeternatural gifts*, freedom from physical pain and death, have also been lost.[11] This means further that man has lost his freedom from concupiscence, since 'concupiscence', it is said, 'stems from sin and inclines to sin'.[12] It is actually stated 'that the entire Adam was changed in body and soul for the worse'.[13] Is this tantamount to the Scholastic view that, by Adam's sin, man was deprived of the gift of grace and his natural capacities injured?[14] The Council of Trent inclines towards the teaching of Thomas, who said that, formally, original sin is a lack of original righteousness and that 'all the parts of the soul are disordered'.[15] It

[10] Trent Sess. 5, 2 (D., 789; M., 293; Schaff, II.85). [11] *Ibid.*

[12] 'Concupiscentia ex peccato est et ad peccatum inclinat.' Sess. 5, 5 (D., 792; M., 294; Schaff, II.88).

[13] 'Totumque Adam . . . secundum corpus et animam in deterius commutatum fuisse.' Sess. 5 (D., 788; M., 293; Schaff, II.85).

[14] 'Privatio in gratuitis, vulneratio in naturalibus.' Petrus Lombardus, I.ii d., 25ff.

[15] 'Inordinatio in omnibus aliis animae viribus.' *Summa Theologica*, I.ii, Q. 82, Art. 3, Ob. 3 (English Dominicans' translation, London 1947, VOL. I, p. 957).

is still true, however, that to the Tridentine statement that the 'entire Adam was changed for the worse' the words 'because no part of the soul remained unimpaired'[16] would have to be added. That was not done. Trent did therefore not side unambiguously with Thomas. It was still possible for the Scotists to put their interpretation on the phrase 'for the worse'. They do not apply it to man's whole nature. They take it to mean that man has lost not only the grace proper to his original nature but also the grace of integrity, and now exists in the state of pure nature. Man's essential being has therefore remained untouched. Whereas for Thomas concupiscence is 'an inordinate disposition of nature'[17] and is indeed 'contrary to nature',[18] in the Scotist view it is a neutral capacity of human nature. The Jesuit Bellarmine gave classical expression to this permissible interpretation of the Tridentine statement, when he wrote: 'After Adam's fall, man's state differs from his purely natural state no more than *one who has been robbed* differs *from one who is naked*; and, if you leave original guilt out of account, human nature is no worse *than it was*, and suffers no more weakness and ignorance *than it suffered in the state of pure nature*. The corruption of nature stems therefore not from the lack of any natural gifts nor from the acquisition of any evil capacity, but solely from the loss of the supernatural gift because of Adam's sin.'[19]

Since the Vatican Council, Rome has inclined more to the Scotist and Jesuit doctrine of sin. The proclamation of Papal Infallibility by this Council gives new importance in our enquiry to the Bull *Ex omnibus afflictionibus* and the Constitution *Unigenitus*, which condemned respectively the doctrines of Michael Baius (*d.* 1589) and Paschasius Quesnel (*d.* 1719). The words 'changed for the worse' can no longer be taken to mean that body and soul have been affected by the Fall, or that con-

[16] 'Nulla etiam animae parte illaesa durante.'

[17] *Summa Theol.*, I.ii, Q. 82, Art. 1, Reply Ob. 2 (Eng. trans. VOL. I, p. 956).

[18] *Op. cit.*, Art. 3, Ob. 1 (VOL. I, p. 957).

[19] 'Non magis differt status hominis post lapsum Adae a statu eiusdem in puribus naturalibus quam differt spoliatus a nudo; neque deterior est humana natura, si culpam originalem detrahes, neque magis infirmitate et ignorantia laborat, quam esset et laboraret in puris naturalibus condita. Proinde corruptio naturae non ex alicuius doni naturalis carentia neque ex alicuius malae qualitatis accessu, sed ex sola doni supernaturalis ob Adae peccatum omissione profluxit'. Bellarmine, *op. cit.*, III.i.5.

cupiscence rules man 'contrary to nature' and corrupts all his acts. For the following propositions have been condemned: 'Without the aid of God's grace free will can only sin'[20]; and 'When God's love no longer rules in the sinner's heart, fleshly desire must dominate him and corrupt all his actions.'[21] Always the possibility remains that man may, of himself, do something good, within the limits of his natural state.

This departure from the Thomist, Augustinian interpretation of the Tridentine statement is not the only thing to emerge. The Vatican Council made a positive statement about fallen man's *capacity to know God*. 'God, the beginning and end of all things may be certainly known by the natural light of human reason, by means of created things.'[22] According to Rome this is a possibility which is continually being actualised among men, and not something which, as Paul shows in Rom. 1.19-23, never happens at all, because man blinded by sin cleaves to the creature rather than to the Creator. In this view, philosophy and theology are directly related. Within its own limits, philosophy can make true statements even about God. The beliefs which flourish in the non-Christian world do not necessarily conflict with Roman dogma. On the contrary a place can be found for them in the theology of the Roman Church.

On *the freedom of man's will*, the Council of Trent says that it is 'by no means extinguished, although attenuated in its powers and bent down'.[23] This is a vague ambiguous formula. What exactly is left of the freedom of the will? We gathered from the

[20] 'Liberum arbitrium, sine gratiae Dei adiutorio, nonnisi ad peccandum valet' (d., 1027; M., 347.32). Cf. 'Omnia opera infidelium sunt peccata et philosophorum virtutes sunt vitia' (All the works of unbelievers are sinful and the 'virtues' of the philosophers are vices. D., 1925; M., 347.30).

[21] 'Amore Dei in corde peccatorum non amplius regnante necesse est, ut in eo carnalis regnet cupiditas omnesque actiones eius corrumpat' (D., 1395; M., 397.21). Cf. 'Cupiditas aut caritas usum sensuum bonum vel malum faciunt' (D., 1396; M., 397.22). 'Omnis cognitio Dei, etiam naturalis, etiam in philosophicis ethnicis, non potest venire nisi a Deo; et sine gratia non producit nisi praesumptionem, vanitatem et oppositionem ad ipsum Deum loco affectuum adorationis, gratitudinis et amoris' (All knowledge of God, whether natural or that of the pagan philosophers, can only lead away from God. Without grace, it only results in pride, vanity and rebellion against God instead of in feelings of worship, gratitude and love. D., 1391; M., 397.11).

[22] 'Deum, rerum omnium principium et finem, naturali humanae rationis lumine e rebus creatis certo cognosci posse.' Vatican Sess. 3, ch. 2 (D., 1785; M., 457.4; Schaff, II. 240).

[23] 'Minime exstinctum, viribus licet attenuatum et inclinatum.' Trent Sess. 6, ch. 1 (D., 793; M., 295.19; Schaff, II.89).

Bull *Ex omnibus afflictionibus* that the freedom of the will does not of itself necessarily incline to sin. This Bull also defends the view 'that a good or non-evil use of free will' is possible.[24] By his own decision and strength, fallen man can choose and do good, within the limits of his state.

Yet we have to realise that in the last analysis this does not help man at all. For, in the first place, he can only attain a right relation to God with the help of actual grace, which has to be given him. All the same, as we shall see more fully later,[25] Rome does reckon with a sufficiency of grace in the non-Christian world so that the question can even be asked whether by its aid man cannot acquire a merit not his own (*meritum de congruo*), and, in this way, prepare himself for justification. In the second place, we must notice that anyone dying in original sin incurs Hell, since, according to the Council of Trent, original sin means 'the death of the soul'.[26] It is stated, however, that these are punished only negatively, by being deprived of the vision of God.[27] To mitigate the severity of this view, a special ante-Hell is envisaged for children dying unbaptised.[28]

3. SUMMARY

Rome does not regard man as being always before the judgment seat of the living, revealed God. Man is not therefore measured and judged by the living Word of this God. The result is an almost mechanical and impersonal view of man which regards him as essentially 'pure nature'. At his creation God added two different kinds of grace but man lost these when he fell, just as one can lose something one is carrying. Since then he has existed in the state of 'pure nature'. Man's nature has become worse not in itself but only in comparison with his erstwhile original state of supernature. The negative aspect is the loss he has suffered. He lacks a richness he once had. The positive aspect is his concupiscence This is a dangerous 'material for sin' (*fomes peccati*) but not sinful in itself.[29] Rome does not deny

[24] 'Usus aliquis liberi arbitrii bonus, sive non malus' (D., 1065; M., 397.7.44; cf. D., 1388, 1414). [25] See below, p. 58.

[26] Trent Sess. 5, can. 2 (D., 789; M., 293.35; Schaff, II.85).

[27] 'Poena damni citra poenam ignis.' Pius VI, 1794, against the Synod of Pistoia (D., 1526). [28] 'Limbus puerorum', maintained by Pius VI, *loc. cit.*

[29] Bartmann, *Dogmatik*, VOL. I, p. 303. 'The post-Tridentine theologians also declare that concupiscence comes *from* sin but explain this as follows: concupiscence

original sin but regards it simply as an absence of gifts man once possessed. It is *original guilt*. The life of man, fallen from communion with God, is therefore assessed in an altogether positive and tolerant way. This is possible because it is as if he lived his life sheltered from God's claim. The serious question for Rome is whether there is in fact any such shelter from God. Evangelical theology can regard man only in the light of revelation. Just because it does so it knows him to be, in and for himself, in utter darkness and utterly lost (John 1.9-11). Roman theology, on the other hand, thinks that in his reason and freedom of will, man possesses an important 'point of contact with the Sublime'.[30]

is an ordinary natural force deriving from the act of creation. In Paradise, its evil effects were kept in check by a *donum integritatis*, but the latter was lost in the Fall, and so these natural forces, which in themselves are capable of the worst excesses now pour like waters through the broken dykes which hitherto had restrained them. *To that extent* concupiscence derives *from sin*.' (Trent Sess. 5, can. 5; D., 792; Schaff, II.88. Bartmann's italics.)

[30] J. H. Oswald, *Rel. Urgeschichte der Menschheit*, Paderborn 1887, p. 151.

CHAPTER 4

THE DOCTRINE OF JUSTIFICATION[1]

1. Preparation for Justification

EVEN Roman doctrine agrees that fallen man cannot by his own strength recover communion with God. His nature is not strong enough to do this, even though it has remained unimpaired. Yet, because it has not been impaired by sin, it cannot surprise us that the Council of Trent rejects the proposition that 'it is not in any way necessary that the [impious] man be *prepared and disposed* by the movement of his own will'[2] for justification. What is meant by this disposition? It is only required, of course, in the case of adults. Children are not yet capable of it and receive justification simply by the administration of baptism. 'In adults, the beginning of the said justification is to be derived from the prevenient grace of God,[3] through Jesus Christ, that is to say, *from His vocation*, whereby, without any merits existing on their part, they are called; so that they, who by sins were alienated from God, may *be disposed* through His quickening and assisting grace, to convert themselves to their own justification, by *freely assenting to and co-operating with that said grace*: in such sort that, while God touches the heart of man by the illumination of the Holy Ghost, neither is man himself utterly inactive while he receives that inspiration,

[1] See Hans Rückert, *Die Rechtfertigungslehre auf dem Tridentinischen Konzil*, Berlin 1925; Hans Küng, *Rechtfertigung. Die Lehre Karl Barths und eine katholische Besinnung*, Einsiedeln 1957 [Barth's own words about this book may be quoted: 'A young man from Lucerne, for seven years thoroughly trained in Rome and having become a doctor of theology in Paris, has presented razor-sharp arguments for the thesis that between the Reformation teaching as now interpreted and presented by myself, and the rightly understood doctrine of the Roman Catholic Church, there is, precisely on the central point of justification by grace, no essential difference! So far this book has not been repudiated by Catholic officialdom, but, on the contrary, has been openly lauded by various representatives of that Church.' *Christian Century*, 25 January 1960, p. 75. Tr.].

[2] 'Nulla ex parte necesse esse, eum (impium) suae voluntatis motu praeparari atque disponi.' Trent Sess. 6, can. 9 (D., 819; M., 301.28; Schaff, II.112).

[3] This is also known as *gratia actualis*; cf. p. 61.

forasmuch as he is also able to reject it; yet he is not able, by his own free will, without the grace of God, to move himself unto justice in His sight.'[4]

That means: (1) that *prevenient grace is unconditionally necessary*, if man is to take even one step towards salvation. To that extent it can be said on the Roman side that everything depends on the grace of God. The Second Council of Orange had affirmed this in 529: 'Anyone who says that the beginning of faith is in us by nature and not by a gift of grace, i.e. by the inspiration of the Holy Spirit, who raises our wills from unbelief to faith, from ungodliness to religion, shows himself an enemy of apostolic doctrine.'[5] Man neither has access to salvation nor can he earn by his works the grace which gives him access to it. That is strongly emphasised. The Second Council of Orange said that 'the reward is owed to good works when they are done, but the grace which is not owed precedes in order that good works may be done'.[6]

But: (2) *man's will is active in the reception of grace*, by his free consent and co-operation. Man's acceptance of the divine call is not simply an act of the Holy Spirit, for, in fact, man could also reject it. Of course the Holy Spirit co-operates in man's acceptance, but man is equally engaged in it. The Reformers' denial of all human co-operation was expressly condemned at Trent: 'If anyone saith that man's free will, moved and excited by God, by assenting to God exciting and calling, nowise co-operates towards disposing and preparing itself for obtaining the grace of justification; that it cannot refuse its consent, if it would, but that, as something inanimate, it does nothing what-

[4] 'Ipsius iustificationis exordium in adultis a Dei per Christum Iesum praeveniente gratia sumendum esse, hoc est, ab eius vocatione, qua nullis eorum exsistentibus meritis vocantur, ut qui per peccata a Deo aversi erant, per eius excitantem atque adiuvantem gratiam ad convertendum se ad suam ipsorum iustificationem eidem gratiae libere assentiendo et cooperando, disponantur, ita ut, tangente Deo cor hominis per Spiritus Sancti illuminationem, neque homo ipse nihil omnino agat, inspirationem illam recipiens, quippe qui illam et abicere potest, neque tamen sine gratia Dei movere se ad iustitiam coram illo libera sua voluntate posse.' Trent Sess. 6, ch. 5 (D., 797; M., 292.5; Schaff, II.92).

[5] 'Si quis . . . initium fidei . . . non per gratiae donum, id est, per inspirationem Spiritus Sancti corrigentem voluntatem nostram ab infidelitate ad fidem, ab impietate ad pietatem, sed naturaliter nobis inesse dicit, Apostolicis dogmatibus adversarius approbatur.' Conc. Arausicanum II (529), can. 5 (D., 178).

[6] 'Debetur merces bonis operibus, si fiant, sed gratia, quae non debetur, praecedit, ut fiant.' Can. 18 (D., 191).

ever and is merely passive; let him be anathema.'[7] By the Holy Spirit, God does not work as the Creator creating something new, as once He called the world into being out of nothing, solely by His deed. '*Veni Creator Spiritus*' can in fact be sung by Rome today only in a qualified sense.

(3) We ask: Is this actual, prevenient grace really as seriously intended as it seemed? This question is inevitable in view of Rome's rejection of the Jansenist[8] proposition: 'Pagans, Jews, heretics and the like are in no way influenced by Jesus Christ; it is right therefore to assume that they have an empty unprepared will, lacking all sufficient grace.'[9] Rome does not mean that actual grace is at every man's disposal, but simply that sufficient grace is there in the non-Christian world and that it rests with men how they use it.

How, exactly, does man *prepare* himself for justification? 'With the prevenient inspiration of the Holy Spirit and with His help, man can believe, love, hope or be penitent as he ought, so that the grace of justification may be bestowed on him.'[10] Notice that, helped by the influence of divine grace, man can to some extent do all this even before his relation to God has been put right. The restoration of his relation to God is prepared for in this way. Not that man can actually earn this restoration. He needs for that not only *gratia actualis* but also *gratia habitualis*, sanctifying grace.[11] Only the latter makes true merit possible. But God justifies a man in consideration of the fact that, to some extent, he believes, hopes, loves and therefore repents. It is worth noticing the meaning attached to these distinct preparatory acts. So far as faith is concerned, the Council of Trent condemned the view 'that justifying faith is

[7] 'Si quis dixerit, liberum hominis arbitrium a Deo motum et excitatum nihil cooperari assentiendo Dei excitanti atque vocanti, quo ad obtinendam iustificationis gratiam se disponat ac praeparet, neque posse dissentire, si velit, sed velut inanime quoddam nihil omnino agere mereque passive se habere, A.S.' Trent Sess. 6, can. 4 (D., 814; M., 301.13; Schaff, II.111).

[8] Cornelius Jansen, *d.* 1638.

[9] 'Pagani, Iudaei, haeretici aliique huius generis nullum omnino accipiunt a Iesu Christo influxum; adeoque hinc recte inferes, in illis esse voluntatem nudam et inermem sine omni gratia sufficienti.' Jansenist errors condemned in 1690 (D., 1295).

[10] 'Praeveniente Spiritus Sancti inspiratione atque eius adiutorio hominem credere, sperare et diligere aut poenitere posse, sicut oportet, ut ei iustificationis gratia conferatur.' Trent Sess. 6, can. 3 (D., 813; M., 301.11; Schaff, II.111).

[11] See p. 61.

simply confidence in the divine mercy which remits sins for Christ's sake, or that this confidence alone is that whereby we are justified'.[12] In the act of faith, those impelled by grace believe 'those things to be true which God has revealed and promised'.[13] The Vatican Fathers defined faith as a 'supernatural virtue whereby, inspired and assisted by God's grace, we believe that the things which He has revealed are true'.[14] The faith that prepares the way for justification is, therefore, 'a dogmatic, credal faith'.[15] It is called *fides informis*, to distinguish it from the 'faith which is formed by love' (*fides caritata formata*). This acceptance of revealed truth does not justify. A man must further be given the virtue of love, to mould his faith,[16] which in itself is neutral. This bare assent to truth, this *fides informis*, is nevertheless, in the Roman view, faith in the full sense of the word. Rome does not regard faith as a personal relationship and union between the whole man and Jesus Christ, God's declaration of the forgiveness of all our sins and His claim to the whole of our life.[17] Roman theology does not reckon with a gracious presence of God that wakens the response of faith in the sinner. We must also bear in mind that not only is this 'dogmatic credal faith' not what the Reformers meant by faith, but that even its source conflicts with their understanding of the matter. It is of course 'a gift of God', yet by it 'man yields voluntary obedience to God Himself, by assenting to and co-operating with His grace, which he is able to resist'.[18] This dogmatic credal faith, necessary for justification, is the product of joint divine and human action.

As we saw, hope and love are necessary as further steps on the ways to justification. By these men are 'moved by a certain hatred and detestation against sins, i.e. by that penitence which

[12] 'Fidem iustificantem nihil aliud esse quam fiduciam divinae misericordiae peccata remittentis propter Christum, vel eam fiduciam solam esse, qua iustificamur.' Trent Sess. 6, can. 12 (D., 822; M., 301.34; Schaff, II.113).

[13] 'Disponuntur . . . dum . . . libere moventur in Deum, credentes, vera esse quae divinitus revelata et promissa sunt.' Trent Sess. 6, ch. 6 (D., 798; M., 296.16; Schaff, II.93).

[14] 'Virtutem esse supernaturalem, qua, Dei aspirante et adiuvante gratia, ab eo revelata vera esse credimus.' Vatican Sess. 3, ch. 3 (D., 1789; M., 457.39; Schaff, II.243).

[15] Bartmann, *Dogmatik*, VOL. II, p. 89.

[16] See p. 61f.

[17] Barmen Thesis No. 2.

[18] 'Fides ipsa in se . . . donum Dei est . . . quo homo liberam praestat ipsi Deo obedientiam gratiae eius, cui resistere posset, consentiendo et cooperando.' Vatican Sess. 3, ch. 3 (D., 1791; M., 458.14; Schaff, II.244).

must be performed before baptism'.[19] Finally, there must be a decision 'to receive baptism, to begin a new life, and to keep the commandments of God'.[20] In other words, *a full and varied activity* is required of man, in his inner attitude at least, if not in his outward action as well. The view 'that the ungodly man is justified by faith alone, in such wise as to mean that nothing else is required to co-operate in order to the obtaining of justification'[21] is therefore condemned.

2. Justification

Justification itself is 'a translation from that state wherein man is born a child of the first Adam, to the state of grace and of the adoption of the sons of God'.[22] It is not, therefore, a process initiated in man by God, but a divine act. That arouses our interest. Only the preparation just described can be regarded as a process.

In this divine act two elements are to be distinguished:

(*a*) Trent is quick to insist, against the Reformers, that justification is '*not merely the forgiveness of sins*'.[23] It includes this of course, though here again Rome has a different view of the forgiveness of sins. 'We are not only reputed but are truly called and are just.'[24] Justification is not simply a divine act by which we are declared just and receive a promise. It is an event whereby a change begins in us, so that we become just. What this means is clear from the rejection of the view which 'denies that, by the grace of our Lord Jesus Christ conferred in baptism, the guilt of original sin is remitted, or even asserts that the whole of that which has the true and proper nature of sin is not

[19] 'Illumque tanquam omnis iustitiae fontem diligere incipiunt ac propterea moventur adversus peccata per odium aliquod et detestationem, hoc est, per eam poenitentiam, quam ante baptismum agi oportet.' Trent Sess. 6, ch. 6 (D., 798; M., 296.16ff; Schaff, II.93).

[20] 'Denique dum proponunt suscipere baptismum inchoare, novam vitam et servare divina mandata.' *Ibid.*

[21] 'Sola fide impium iustificare, ita ut intelligat nihil aliud requiri, quo ad iustificationis gratiam consequendam cooperetur.' Sess. 6, can. 9 (D., 819; M., 301.27; Schaff, II.112).

[22] 'Ut sit translatio ab eo statu, in quo homo nascitur filius primi Adae, in statum gratiae et "adoptionis filiorum" Dei.' Sess. 6, ch. 4 (D., 796; M., 295.40; Schaff, II.91).

[23] 'Iustificatio ipsa . . . quae *non est sola peccatorum remissio*.' Sess. 6, ch. 7 (D., 799; M., 296.35; Schaff, II.94).

[24] 'Non modo reputamur sed vere iusti nominamur et sumus.' (D., 799; M., 297.4; Schaff, II.95).

taken away but only rased or not imputed'.[25] In Rome's view, Luther's worst heresy was his statement that original sin is not destroyed by grace but simply forgiven. Rome's teaching is that, after the act of justification, there remains in man only inordinate desire (*concupiscentia*), an impulse which is not evil in itself, and which serves to test the justified man in his life-long struggle. Original sin, or, as Rome prefers to call it, original guilt, is completely eliminated.

(*b*) The second element in the divine act of justification is '*the sanctification and renewal* of the inward man, through the voluntary reception of the grace and of the gifts whereby man becomes just instead of unjust'.[26] Not only is the state of original guilt set aside by justification, but a renewal also begins to take place in man. What this renewal means is clear from the following anathema: 'If anyone says that men are justified either by the sole imputation of the justice of Christ, or by the sole remission of sins, to the exclusion of *the grace* and *the charity* which is poured forth in their hearts by the Holy Ghost and *is inherent in them*, or even that the grace whereby we are justified is only the favour of God: let him be anathema.'[27] Man is renewed because, along with the grace which sets aside his original guilt, love is poured into him, creating in him a new disposition (*habitus*). This *habitual* grace is distinct from *actual* grace, the enabling initial grace granted only for the moment, of which we heard in the last section. Habitual or sanctifying grace enters into man, though of course not in such a way that it cannot be lost. Bartmann calls it 'an inner supernatural energy which the Holy Spirit produces in us by baptism'.[28] It makes man just in a positive sense. Since this justifying grace is infused into men, there are differences between its individual

[25] 'Si quis per Iesum Christum Domini nostri gratiam quae in baptismate confertur, reatum originalis peccati remitti negat, aut etiam asserit, non tolli totum id, quod veram et propriam peccati rationem habet, sed illud dicit tantum radi aut non imputari: A.S.' Sess. 5, ch. 5 (D., 792; M., 294.16; Schaff, II.87).

[26] 'Sanctificatio et renovatio interioris hominis per voluntariam susceptionem gratiae et donorum, unde homo ex iniusto fit iustus.' Sess. 5, ch. 7 (D., 799; M., 296.36; Schaff, II.94).

[27] 'Si quis dixerit homines iustificare vel sola imputatione iustitiae Christi, vel sola peccatorum remissione, exclusa gratia et caritate quae in cordibus eorum per Spiritum Sanctum diffundatur atque illis inhaereat, aut etiam gratiam, qua iustificamur, esse tantum favorem Dei: A.S.' Sess. 6, can. 11 (D., 821; M., 301.31; Schaff, II.112f).

[28] *Dogmatik*, VOL. II, p. 96.

recipients. Each receives it 'according to his own measure, which the Holy Ghost distributes to everyone as He wills, and according to each one's special disposition and co-operation'.[29] Clearly the act of justification itself is also conditioned by a man's preparatory action and co-operation. Human preparation is not just a prerequisite for receiving justification but affects justification itself.

Infused sanctifying grace has thus a twofold effect. It destroys sin and sanctifies man. It also confers on him the adoption of sonship, and, with this, the hope of his heavenly inheritance. Finally, it makes him a fit dwelling-place for the Holy Spirit.[30] This grace is not to be identified with the Holy Spirit. Though supernatural, it is still a created essence. It is, as we heard, 'a supernatural energy'.

As the fruits of sanctifying grace, man acquires faith, hope, and love.[31] Even before, he was able and under obligation to act in accordance with these *theological virtues*, by the help of actual grace. Now he is infused with sanctifying grace and thus with the *qualities* of faith, hope, and love. He not merely believes; he *is* a believer. He not only does particular acts of love, he is imbued with divine love.[32]

3. The Increase of Justification

Since in Roman theology justification means, not that Jesus Christ encounters, justifies and also sanctifies us in His Word, but that a supernatural energy is infused into us, it comes as no surprise to hear further that there is an 'increase of the justification received'.[33] Just as a process conditions the act of justification and influences the extent of its effects, so the event of justification is followed by a further process. '*They* [the justified] . . . *increase in that justice* which they have received through

[29] 'Secundum mensuram, quam "Spiritus Sanctus partitur singulis prout vult" et secundum propriam cuiusque dispositionem et cooperationem.' Sess. 6, ch. 7 (D., 799; M., 297.5; Schaff, II.95). [30] Bartmann, *Dogmatik*, VOL. II, pp. 103ff.

[31] Trent Sess. 6, ch. 7 (D., 800; M., 297.11; Schaff, II.96).

[32] It appears that Rome now wishes to make justification depend upon our attitude to Mary. Cf. the Encyclical *Le Pèlerinage de Lourdes* of Pius XII, 1957. 'There is no land redeemed by Christ's blood but loves to proclaim Mary as its Mother and Patron' (Eng. trans. *Our Lady of Lourdes*, trans. V. J. Matthews, London 1957, p. 4, § 2).

[33] 'De acceptae iustificationis incremento.' Sess. 6, ch. 10 (D., 903; M., 298.4; Schaff, II.99).

Christ, and are still further justified, faith co-operating with good works'.[34] Because of indwelling grace, real progress in sanctification takes place and so an increase in justifying grace itself. This is not to say that the justified man is not truly justified at the deepest levels of his life. For when those who have been justified 'fall into at least light and daily sins which are also called venial, they do not for that reason cease to be just'.[35] They are not sinners and do not sin in fact, when they do good works. The contrary view was condemned.[36]

The progress made in sanctification does not of itself automatically produce an increase in justification. This increase results from *the meritorious character of the works* done by the justified man. That was stated by the Council of Trent: 'If anyone says that the good works of one that is justified are in such manner the gift of God, that they are not also the good merits of him that is justified: or that the said justified, by the good works he performs through the grace of God and the merits of Jesus Christ, whose living member he is, *does not truly merit increase of grace* . . . let him be anathema.'[37] Therefore the justified man produces an increase in grace by what he does. If he uses the gift he has received, God bestows more supernatural energy on him. The Reformers' view, 'that the justified man sins if he performs good works with a view to an eternal recompense' was condemned.[38] Yet it can still be said: 'God forbid that a Christian should either trust or glory in himself, and not in the Lord, whose bounty towards all men is so great that He will have the things which are His own gifts be their merits.'[39]

[34] 'Sic ergo iustificati . . . in ipsa iustitia per Christi gratiam accepta, cooperante fide bonis operibus, crescunt atque magis iustificantur.' *Ibid.*

[35] 'Licet enim in hac mortali vita quantumvis sancti et iusti in levia saltem et quotidiana, quae etiam "venialia" dicuntur, peccata quandoque cadant, non propterea desinunt esse iusti.' Sess. 6, ch. 11 (D., 804; M., 298.21; Schaff, II.100f).

[36] *Ibid.*

[37] 'Si quis dixerit hominis iustificati bona opera ita esse dona Dei, ut non sint etiam bona ipsius iustificati merita, aut ipsum iustificatum bonis operibus, quae ab eo per Dei gratiam et Iesu Christi meritum (cuius vivum membrum est) fiunt, non vere mereri augmentum gratiae . . . A.S.' Sess. 6, can. 32 (D., 842; M., 302.39; Schaff, II.117f).

[38] 'Iustificatum peccare, dum intuitu aeternae mercedis bene operatur.' Sess. 6, can. 31 (D., 841; M., 302.38; Schaff, II.117).

[39] 'Absit tamen, ut christianus homo in se ipso vel confidat vel "glorietur" et non "in Domino" cuius tanta est erga omnes homines bonitas ut eorum velit esse merita quae sunt ipsius dona.' Sess. 6, can. 16 (D., 810; M., 300.37; Schaff II.109).

Taken in conjunction with Canon 32 quoted above, this can only mean that human merit always originates in infused grace, but is not itself, so to speak, a pure gift of divine grace, which God subsequently allows to be called 'merit'. On the contrary, it depends on human co-operation with infused grace, and is therefore real merit.

A word must be added here on the Roman *concept of merit*. Bartmann writes: 'According to Thomas, merit (reward) is the inner connexion linking action and response in accordance with the requirements of justice.'[40] He allows that the term was introduced into Christian theology from the field of law by Tertullian, though this theologian 'merely substituted the term "merit" for the biblical word "reward" '.[41] Protestant scholars are surely right in thinking that this substitution completely changed the biblical concept. The gracious gift of God, the gracious reward which He bestows as He wills (Matt. 20.15), became instead something man may *claim* because of what he does.

A distinction is drawn between 'deserved merit' (*meritum de condigno*), which is merit in the strict sense, and 'equitable or congruous merit' (*meritum de congruo*) which God allows without any obligation to do so.

To acquire *strict merit*, a man must be in a state of grace, and do the works required by God's Commandments and the Church's commandments. According to the catechisms there are five Church commandments: (1) To keep the holy days of obligation, (2) to attend Mass every Sunday and feast day, (3) to keep the appointed fasts, (4) to go to confession at least once a year, and (5) to receive communion at least once a year. But even an act which in itself is morally indifferent becomes a meritorious work, if in it an act of Christian virtue comes to life as a result of infused grace, i.e. if, in conjunction with this neutral act, there is also an act of faith, hope or love.

Equitable or congruous merit exists when someone, not in a state of grace and thus lacking any divine promise for what he does, nevertheless voluntarily performs a morally good act.[42] Rome indeed holds that even if a man is not in a state of grace and has only his natural resources, he can nevertheless do morally

[40] *Dogmatik*, VOL. II, p. 119. [41] *Op. cit.*, p. 118. [42] *Op. cit.*, p. 122.

good works within the limits of this condition. Even apart from God, even in rebellion against Him, and alienated from Him, man can do something good. In what he does and does not do he is not measured in relation to God.

The Council of Trent describes *the reward of merit* in a sentence whose opening words we have already quoted: the justified man 'merits increase of grace, eternal life, and, if he departs this life in grace, the attainment of eternal life, and also an increase of glory'.[43] Three things, then, are won by the works of justified man: an increase in sanctifying grace, a right to eternal life, and an increase in eternal glory. It is not unfair to say, therefore, that the Roman Catholic has to earn heaven for himself. However, 'because man's capacity for merit depends on God's grace, eternal life also can be called a "grace"'.[44]

If the justified man lapses into sin, he can, by his acts of preparation, earn justification for himself, at least indirectly.[45] If justification is restored to him then merits previously acquired by him are revived.

The measure of grace bestowed on man because of his good works always varies in proportion to his co-operation.

Moreover a Christian in a state of grace can also perform 'non-obligatory works' (*opera supererogatoria*).[46] The obligatory works are defined above all in the commandments, mentioned earlier. In the Roman view, men can really obey these commandments with the help of grace. The works which go beyond what is commanded (*super-erogatoria*) are, in particular, the 'evangelical counsels' of the Sermon on the Mount (*consilia evangelica*), which a man may keep if he wishes to do what is exceptional. These 'evangelical counsels' are the means of attaining Christian perfection. Above all they include (1) voluntary poverty, (2) self-denial or complete obedience to a spiritual superior, and (3) perpetual chastity. Acts in keeping with these 'counsels' are 'works of supererogation', which acquire 'superfluous merit', provided they exceed what the person concerned has to do to make satisfaction for temporal punishments. The

[43] 'Vere mereri augmentum gratiae, vitam aeternam et ipsius vitae aeternae (si tamen in gratia decesserit) consecutionem, atque etiam gloriae augmentum. Sess. 6, can. 32 (D., 842; M., 302.40; Schaff, II.117f).

[44] Bartmann, *Dogmatik*, VOL. II, p. 123. [45] *Op. cit.*, p. 124.

[46] With this phrase cf. Luke 10.35.

way of the 'evangelical counsels' is the way chosen by those in orders. Yet even in a secular calling one can live a perfect life by keeping not only the commandments but the evangelical counsels as well. This does not alter the fact that there are, according to Rome, *two classes of Christians* in God's sight: those who simply live in accordance with the commandments, and acquire merit by doing so, and those who, by following the 'evangelical counsels', accomplish more. This division is only possible because of two errors: firstly, the Ten Commandments whose profound and penetrating significance Jesus made clear in the Sermon on the Mount, are trimmed and scaled down to match the capacity of the average Christian, and secondly the directives issued in the Sermon on the Mount are turned into non-obligatory counsels which we are free to heed or ignore at our will.

4. The Threat to Justification

The justification we have received can be lost. That is not surprising. If it is not an act of God alone, but a capacity imprinted in man, it can of course be destroyed. That is what happens as a result of each *mortal sin*. A mortal sin is committed 'when man voluntarily breaks the divine law in some serious matter'.[47] All other sins are venial since they can be wiped out by simple contrition.[48] Mortal sin is so named because it deprives man of sanctifying grace and makes him liable to eternal death. He loses the *habitus* of love, but not necessarily that of faith and hope. 'If anyone says that grace being lost through sin, faith also is always lost with it, or that the faith which remains, though it be not a lively faith, is not a true faith, or that he who has faith without charity is not a Christian: let him be anathema.'[49] Such language is possible only because faith is regarded, not as a living relationship to Christ, but as a mere assent to the truth. If that is all faith is, it can of course

[47] Trèves Catechism.

[48] 'Peccata mortalia et venialia.' This distinction is defined dogma: cf. Trent Sess. 6, ch. 11; Sess. 14, ch. 6 (D., 804, 902; M., 298.23, 314.23; Schaff, II.100, 151f).

[49] 'Si quis dixerit, amissa per peccatum gratia simul et fidem semper amitti, aut fidem, quae remanet, non esse veram fidem, licet non sit viva, aut eum, qui fidem sine caritate habet, non esse Christianum: A.S.' Sess. 6, can. 28 (D., 838; M., 302.27; Schaff, II.116).

still remain when the relationship to God has been broken.

Moreover according to Roman doctrine, not only can man fall out of grace, but all his life he remains *uncertain about his state of grace*. The view of the Reformers, 'that it is necessary for everyone, for the obtaining the remission of sins, that he believe for certain and without any wavering arising from his own infirmity and indisposition, that his sins are forgiven him',[50] and 'that he is assuredly in the number of the predestinate'[51] was condemned. Bartmann says that the rejection of the assurance of faith by the Council of Trent does not result in 'a religion of trembling anxiety' for 'there is still a middle way between assurance of faith and doubt, namely, a moral certainty which banishes all anxiety and despair'.[52] That is a revealing answer and the only one possible if, as Rome teaches, our justification is not enclosed in Jesus Christ, but is an energy which, though dwelling in us, can in fact be lost.

5. Prayer and Justification

One of the good works by which man acquires merit and a consequent increase in grace, is prayer. Prayer does not have its *raison d'être* simply as man's response to God's Word. It is one human religious exercise among many others. This clearly follows from the rejection of a decision of the reforming Synod of Pistoia (1786) which 'described any effect attributed to a fixed number of prayers and pious salutations as a superstitious invention, as if an effect were superstitious that was certainly not regarded as due to the number itself, but solely to the Church's prescription of a certain number of prayers or outward acts as necessary in order to gain an indulgence . . . and in a general way for the proper and orderly practice of our holy religion'.[53] In the Roman Church, therefore, it is not just the

[50] 'Omni homini ad remissionem peccatorum assequendam necessarium esse, ut credat certo et absque ulla haesitatione propriae infirmitatis et indispositionis peccata sibi esse remissa.' Sess. 6, can. 13 (D., 823; M., 301.36; Schaff, II.113).

[51] 'Hominem renatum et iustificatum teneri ex fide ad credendum, se certo esse in numero praedestinatorum.' Sess. 6, can. 15 (D., 825; M., 301.41; Schaff, II.113).

[52] *Dogmatik*, VOL. II, p. 109. On this view, which was already advanced by the scholastics, cf. Calvin, *Institutio*, BK III, ch. 2, § 38 (trans. McNeill and Battles, VOL. I, pp. 585f).

[53] 'Doctrina, quae velut superstitiosam universe notat quamcunque efficaciam, quae ponatur in determinato numero precum et piarum salutationum; tanquam superstitiosa censenda esset efficacia, quae sumitur non ex numero in se spectato,

content of prayer which matters, but the *number of prayers* as well. The best-known example of this is the Rosary prayer.[54] Moreover, *some forms of prayer are more valuable than others*. This is clear from the system of indulgences in use in the Roman Church, which determines the exact value of the various prayers.[55] One element in every prayer of course, as in every good work, is the *bona intentio*, the 'intention' with which it is prayed, i.e. the realisation of the purpose it is to serve. It is not enough just to recite prayers thoughtlessly, though one is not expected to think of the 'intention' of every single prayer. One can also pray 'in the intention' of some other person, of a bishop or of the Pope for example, and, by doing so, further his intercessions.

All this is not to say there is no genuine prayer in the Roman Church. We need only recall the devotional books in use there, such as the *De imitatione Christi* of Thomas À Kempis (*d.* 1471). The fact remains that every prayer has a meritorious character and is one of the means by which man's justification is increased.

The Saints as Intercessors. Considering the influence which the religious man and his actions have on God according to Roman teaching, the special mediatorial role between men and God assigned by this teaching to exceptionally religious men, to the Saints, comes as no surprise. By their intercessions they plead for men. It is advantageous therefore to invoke them and the

sed ex praescripto Ecclesiae certum numerum precum vel externarum actionum praefinientis pro indulgentiis consequendis, pro adimplendis poenitentiis, et generatim pro sacro et religioso cultu rite et ex ordine peragendo: falsa . . . pietati fidelium iniuriosa, Ecclesiae auctoritati derogans, erronea.' Pius VI, *Auctorem fidei*, 1794 (D., 1564; M., 412.31).

[54] Cf. Müller, *Symbolik*, p. 177n. 'Nothing certain is known about the name and origin of the Rosary, a string of beads used in the counting of prayers. It was the Dominicans who specially fostered its use in honour of the Virgin Mary. The complete Rosary, supposed to have been revealed to St Dominic *circa* 1206, consists of 15 "decades" of smaller beads for the Ave Maria, each of which is separated from the next by a larger bead for the Paternoster. During the recitation of the decades, the principal mysteries of the life of Jesus are recalled and when His name is mentioned in each decade the variant words are added: "whom thou, O virgin, didst conceive by the Holy Ghost," "whom thou, O virgin, didst carry in thy womb to Elisabeth," and so on. In all therefore, 15 Paternosters and 150 Ave Marias, with 15 additional variant clauses. This is known as the "Mary Psalter". According to a ruling of Pope Benedict XIII in 1726, anyone who recites it daily for a whole year receives plenary indulgence. Cf. T. Esser, *Rosenkranz*, 1889.'

[55] Cf. the extracts given by Mirbt (pp. 565ff) from F. Béringar and P.A. Steinen, *Die Ablässe: ihr Wesen und Gebrauch* (Indulgences, their nature and use), 2 vols. Paderborn 1921-2. For example, the prayer 'My God and all' gains 50 days' indulgence, whereas the prayer of faith in the privileges of Mary and in the infallibility of the Pope gains 100 days.

aid of their prayers.[56] This was defined as dogma by the Council of Trent. What the Second Council of Nicea (787) said about the images of the saints, applies also to the saints themselves. We owe them only our reverence, our worship we owe to God.[57] It must further be noted that one Pope declared: 'We so honour the servants [i.e. the saints] that the glory is the Lord's who said: "Whoever receives you, receives me," and so that we, who have no certainty of our own justice, are continually upheld by their prayers to the God of grace and by their merits in His sight.'[58] That is typical Roman teaching; there is no question of worshipping the creature, yet an important influence on justification is assigned to the creature. The Christian labouring by prayer and other good works to increase his justification and to win eternal life can still never have complete assurance. In this plight he is never pointed to Jesus Christ as his 'only comfort in life and in death',[59] but to other Christians. They must lend him their aid, if he is to reach the goal.

One aspect of the reverence paid to the saints is *the honouring of their relics*, i.e. their bodies or parts of them. The Council of Trent expressly defended the cult of relics: 'Also the holy bodies of martyrs and of others now living with Christ—which bodies were the living members of Christ and the temples of the Holy Ghost, and which are by Him to be raised unto eternal life and

[56] 'Sanctos una cum Christo regnantes, orationes suas pro hominibus Deo offerre. bonum atque utile esse, suppliciter eos invocare et ob beneficia impetrando a Deo per Filium eius Iesum Christum Dominum nostrum, qui solus noster Redemptor et Salvator est, ad eorum orationes, opem auxiliumque confugere' (the saints who reign together with Christ, offer up their own prayers to God for men: it is good and useful suppliantly to invoke them, and to have recourse to their prayers, aid (and) help for obtaining benefits from God through His Son, Jesus Christ our Lord, who is our alone Redeemer and Saviour). Trent Sess. 25 (D., 984; M., 333.31; Schaff, II.200).

[57] τιμητικὴ προσκύνησις (honoraria adoratio)—λατρέια (latria) (D., 302; M., 116.33). In the case of the Saints the term προσκύνησις (adoratio) is usually avoided, and it is said that we owe them 'dulia' and Mary 'hyperdulia'.

[58] 'Honoramus servos, ut honor redundet in dominum qui dixit: "Qui vos recipit, me recipit" ac proinde nos qui fiduciam nostrae iustitiae non habemus illorum precibus et meritis apud clementissimum Deum iugiter adiuvemur.' John XV, 993 (D., 342; M., 134.18). But in 1687 Innocent XI rejected the proposition of Michael Molinos that 'no creature, not even the Blessed Virgin, or the saints, should occupy our heart because God alone wills to occupy and possess it'. (Nulla creatura, nec beata Virgo nec Sancti sedere debent in nostro corde: quia solus Deus vult illud occupare et possidere. D., 1256.)

[59] Heidelberg Catechism, Q. 1.

to be glorified, are to be venerated by the faithful through which [bodies] many benefits are bestowed by God on men.'[60]

In a wider sense the relics of saints include everything which has been in contact with them. The Council of Trent rejected the view that the veneration of these objects is useless.[61] Although this cult may have been checked since the Reformation, we can see the importance it still has, e.g. by the fact that the Holy Shroud of Turin was brought out once again as recently as 1951. The purpose of the cult of relics is always the same, to gain the assistance of the saints.[62]

Finally, there is the cult of the images of the saints. Rome's teaching on this matter will be dealt with in the concluding chapter on Mariology.[63]

[60] Sess. 25, *De invocatione . . . Sanctorum* (D., 985; M., 333.42).
[61] *Loc. cit.* (M., 334.1). [62] *Ibid.* [63] See p. 117f.

CHAPTER 5

THE SACRAMENT OF BAPTISM

1. Baptism, the Entrance to the Christian Life

Baptism was described by Pope Eugenius IV as 'the gateway to the spiritual life'.[1] Its institution was necessary because, by Adam's fall, death came upon all men. It is 'the perfect remedy for adults and children alike'.[2] What is this remedy?

By baptism, the candidates, who are in a state of original guilt, are infused with the habitual grace which justifies and renews them: 'By the power of baptism guilt is taken from the children', 'and children and adults are given in baptism formative grace and virtues.'[3] Those regenerated by baptism become so pure 'that there is nothing to retard their entrance into heaven'.[4]

Baptism is the instrumental cause by which men pass from a state of original guilt into a state of grace. Concerning justification, understood as sanctification and renewal, Trent says: 'The causes of this justification are these: . . . the instrumental cause is the sacrament of baptism, which is the "sacrament of faith", without which no man was ever justified.'[5]

Since it is only by baptism that sanctifying grace is infused into man, baptism is absolutely necessary for salvation: 'if anyone says that baptism is free, i.e. is not necessary to salvation, let him be anathema'.[6]

[1] 'Vitae spiritualis ianua.' Eugenius IV, Bull *Exultate Deo*, 1493 (D., 696; M., 235.19).

[2] 'Tam adultis quam parvulis communiter perfectum remedium ad salutem.' Const. *de Summa Trinitate*, 1311-12 (D., 480).

[3] 'Per virtutem baptismi parvulis quidem culpam remitti.' 'Tam parvulis quam adultis conferri in baptismo informantem gratiam et virtutes.' *Loc. cit.* (D., 483).

[4] Trent Sess. 5, can. 5 (D., 792; M., 294.23; Schaff, II.88).

[5] 'Huius iustificationis causae sunt . . . instrumentalis item sacramentum baptismi, quod est "sacramentum fidei" sine qua nulli unquam contigit iustificatio.' Sess. 6, ch. 7 (D., 799; M., 296.38; Schaff, II.95).

[6] 'Si quis dixerit baptismum liberum esse, hoc est, non necessarium ad salutem: A.S.' Trent Sess. 7, can. 5 *de bapt.* (D., 861; N., 304.26; Schaff, II.123).

Water baptism can be replaced by the blood baptism (*baptismus sanguinis*) undergone by those martyrs who were not able to receive baptism in the prescribed way. In certain circumstances, the desire (*votum*) for baptism is a sufficient substitute, provided perfect contrition is also there in the person concerned.[7]

Baptism and its effect do not however suffice for the whole of man's lifetime. Through mortal sin, the baptised can lose the grace of sanctification. To wipe out mortal sin and all other sins, he needs further gifts of grace. The opposite view, held by the Reformers, that the sinner can always take refuge again and again in the promise given by baptism, was explicitly condemned: 'If anyone says that by the sole remembrance and the faith of the baptism which has been received, all sins committed after baptism are either remitted or made venial, let him be anathema.'[8] This is not surprising, for in Roman doctrine what is involved in baptism is not the declaration of the forgiveness of sins and Christ's presence in His Word, but the infusion of grace. This grace leaves a man, once he commits mortal sin. To look up to Christ in faith is of no avail. Grace must first be re-infused by some other agency.

One thing a baptised person cannot lose, even by the deadliest sin; namely the character, the mark which baptism has imprinted on his soul. In baptism, he receives a spiritual seal that is indestructible. He thereby enters 'the state of created faith' (*status fidei genitae*), which distinguishes him from all other men. Hence baptism cannot be repeated.[9] Once he has been baptised a man remains a member of the Church, even if by the loss of sanctifying grace he has become a dead member.[10]

At what point does baptism take effect? According to Roman teaching baptism works '*ex opere operato*', like all sacraments. It works, that is, by the objective performance of the act, and not

[7] Trent Sess. 6, ch. 4 (D., 796; M., 296.1; Schaff, II.91). Neither of these forms of baptism confers any *character indelebilis* (see § c). Those baptised in these ways do not therefore belong to the visible Church.

[8] 'Si quis dixerit, peccata omnia, quae post baptismum fiunt, sola recordatione et fide suscepti baptismi vel dimitti vel venialia fieri: A.S.' Trent Sess. 7, can. 10 *de bapt.* (D., 866; M., 304.36; Schaff, II.124).

[9] Trent Sess. 7, can. 9 *de sacr.* (D., 852; M., 304.1; Schaff, II.121). Cf. *Exultate Deo*, 1439 (D., 695; M., 235.14).

[10] See above, Chapter 2, § 4, p. 46.

'*ex opere operantis*', i.e. not in virtue of the attitude of the person who administers or receives it. Trent rejected the contrary view in respect of the sacrament's recipient: 'If anyone says that by the said sacraments of the New Law, grace is not conferred through the act performed but that faith alone in the divine promise suffices for the obtaining of grace, let him be anathema.'[11] That necessarily follows, if by baptism grace is infused into man and if the decisive thing in baptism is not the Word of promise which demands faith in the recipient.

What has been said is subject to one qualification, of course. As we saw, the Roman Church is the sole dispenser of grace. If a baptism is administered by someone not belonging to this Church, then the sanctifying grace, which is what counts, is not given by that baptism. If, however, the recipient of it subsequently joins the Roman Church, his baptism revives and he receives its real gift.

Baptism is valid, however, whenever it is rightly administered, i.e. when the administrant baptises by sprinkling with water in the name of the Triune God, and has the intention, i.e. the will, to accomplish by baptism what the Roman Church intends by it.[12] If these conditions are fulfilled, baptism can be administered even by a non-Christian, Jew or heretic, without thereby diminishing its validity.[13]

According to the principle stated, such a baptism may not be repeated. In practice, however, this is often done, on the ground that it is uncertain whether baptism has been properly administered. In such cases the following formula is used: 'If thou art baptised I baptise thee not; but if thou art not yet baptised, I baptise thee in the Name, etc.'[14] The Roman Church maintains that this is not a repetition of baptism. It can use the name of the Triune God as if it were a formula which, in certain circumstances, i.e. if it has already once been pronounced over someone, is null and void.

[11] 'Si quis dixerit, per ipsa novae Legis sacramenta ex opere operato non conferri gratiam sed solam fidem divinae promissionis ad gratiam consequendam sufficere: A.S.' Sess. 7, can. 8 *de sacr.* (D., 851; M., 303.44; Schaff, II.121).

[12] Trent Sess. 7, can. 11 *de sacr.* (D., 854; M., 304.5; Schaff, II.121).

[13] Nicholas I, 866 (D., 335; M., 129.18); Eugenius IV, 1439 (D., 696; M., 235.31); Trent Sess. 7, can. 4 *de bapt.* (D., 860; M., 304.24; Schaff, II.123).

[14] 'Si baptizatus es, non te baptizo, sed, si nondum baptizatus es, ego te baptizo in nomine....' Cf. D., 399 and 1848.

For valid baptism, what is required of the recipient is simply that he should offer no impediment, which would prevent the influx of grace. In other words, he must not persist in unbelief and impenitence. 'If anyone says that the Sacraments of the New Law do not contain the grace which they signify, or that they do not confer that grace on those who do not place an obstacle thereunto . . . let him be anathema.'[15] This condition is not surprising if we remember that infused grace requires the recipient's co-operation. Without this willingness and activity, it cannot begin to flow. Only in the case of infant baptism is this condition not required.[16] Even the baptism of a candidate who is unwilling cannot be repeated, for in every case, even when the candidate offers an impediment, it produces that indestructable mark (*character indelebilis*) which distinguishes a Christian from the heathen.

2. What Constitutes Baptism?

For baptism ordinary water is essential. 'The material of this sacrament is true natural water, and it matters not whether it be cold or warm.'[17] The immediate material (*materia proxima*), as it is called, is the washing of the candidate by immersion (*immersio*), pouring (*infusio*), or sprinkling (*aspersio*). Today this last is no longer recognised as proper baptism. As a rule consecrated water is used, i.e. water which has been consecrated by prayers and exorcisms on Easter Day or Whit Sunday.

Various ceremonies are also attached to this use of the material, and, though these are not essential for the sacrament, the use of them is protected by dogma: 'If anyone says that the received and approved rites of the Catholic Church, wont to be used in the solemn administration of the sacraments may be condemned, or without sin be omitted at pleasure by the ministers or be changed by every pastor of the Churches, into other new ones: let him be anathema.'[18] In baptism the priest

[15] 'Si quis dixerit, sacramenta novae Legis non continere gratiam quam significant, aut gratiam ipsam non ponentibus obicem non conferre . . .A.S.' Trent Sess. 7, can. 6 *de sacr.* (D., 849; M., 303.38; Schaff, II.120).

[16] Innocent III, 1201 (D., 410).

[17] 'Materia huius sacramenti est aqua vera et naturalis: nec refert, frigida sit an calida.' Bull *Exultate Deo*, 1439 (D., 696; M., 235.21). Trent Sess. 7, can. 2 *de bapt.* (D., 858; M., 304.19; Schaff, II.122).

[18] 'Si quis dixerit, receptos et approbatos Ecclesiae catholicae ritus in solemni

puts the salt of wisdom (*sal sapientiae*) into the candidate's mouth, and wipes the ears and nose with spittle (*Ephphatha*, Mark 7.34), the breast and shoulders with the oil of salvation (*oleum salutis*), and the head with the chrism of salvation (*chrism salutis*). Finally the baptised person receives a white garment and a lighted taper, as the light of salvation.

It is not the water alone which produces the effect of the sacrament. To the material must be added the words which declare what this action with the water is intended to accomplish. 'Let the Word be added to the element and it will become a sacrament.'[19] The mere naming of the Name of the Triune God in baptism is therefore not sufficient.[20] The material is unformed and must be formed by the words—*the form of the sacrament*. The form is: 'I baptise thee in the Name of the Father and of the Son and of the Holy Ghost.'[21] These words have consecrating power in respect both of the material and the recipient of baptism. The effect of the sacrament, the infusion of habitual grace, is produced by the material and the form together.

To the proper administration of baptism the minister of the sacrament also belongs. What applies to the sacraments generally applies also to baptism. 'All these sacraments are performed in three parts: by the things as material, by the words as form, and by the person of the administrant who performs the sacrament with the intention of doing what the Church does.'[22] The minister of baptism is normally the priest. He alone can administer solemn baptism with all the ceremonies attached to it. 'The administrant of this sacrament is the priest, to whom baptism pertains in virtue of his office. In cases of necessity, however, not only the priest or the deacon, but even a layman or a woman, indeed even a pagan or heretic

sacramentorum administratione adhiberi consuetos aut contemni aut sine peccato, a ministris pro libito omitti, aut in novos alios per quemcunque ecclesiarum pastorem mutari posse: A.S.' Trent Sess. 7, can. 13 *de sacr.* (D., 856; M., 304.9; Schaff, II.122).

[19] 'Accedit verbum ad elementum et fit sacramentum.' Augustine, *In Ioann.*, 80.3.

[20] D., 398.

[21] 'Forma autem est: "Ego te baptizo in nomine Patris et Filii et Spiritus Sancti."' Bull *Exultate Deo* (D., 696; M., 235.23).

[22] 'Haec omnia sacramenta tribus perficiuntur videlicet rebus tanquam materia, verbis tanquam forma, et *persona ministri* conferentis sacramentum cum intentione faciendi, quod facit Ecclesia.' *Exultate Deo* (D., 695; M., 235.15).

can baptise, so long as he keeps to the form used by the Church and intends to do what the Church does.'[23] When a baptism does take place in such an emergency, the ceremonies are afterwards to be performed by the priest.

[23] 'Minister huius sacramenti est sacerdos cui ex officio competit baptizare. In causa autem necessitatis non solum sacerdos vel diaconus, sed etiam laicus vel mulier, immo etiam paganus et haereticus baptizare potest, dummodo formam servet Ecclesiae et facere intendat, quod facit Ecclesia.' *Loc. cit.* (D., 696; M., 235.29).

CHAPTER 6

THE SACRAMENT OF CONFIRMATION

1. The Effect of this Sacrament

The sacrament of confirmation completes the sacrament of baptism. 'Those who have become Christians by baptism still have a certain tenderness and frailty just like new-born babes, but by the sacrament of chrism, they are strengthened against all the temptations of the world, the flesh and the devil, and are confirmed inwardly in faith to confess and glorify the name of our Lord Jesus Christ, whence also doubtless the term "confirmation" is derived.'[1] 'The result of this sacrament is that in it the Holy Ghost is given for strengthening, just as it was given to the Apostles at Pentecost, in order that the Christian should boldly confess the name of Christ.'[2] Since, in the Roman view, baptism is not the declaration of forgiveness, but the infusion of habitual grace, we are not surprised to hear that by a further sacrament, something more can still be added to baptism, namely, an increase of grace, consisting of the spirit of strength. When grace is thought of as a heavenly substance, it can be a case of more or less. Like baptism, confirmation imprints an indelible mark on man (*character indelebilis*).[3] It means that the confirmed person is spiritually strengthened to confess and defend the faith publicly.

Confirmation is *not absolutely necessary* for salvation.[4] Thomas says: 'All the sacraments are in some way necessary for salvation: but some so that there is no salvation without them; some as conducing to the perfection of salvation: and thus it is that confirmation is necessary for salvation: although salvation is

[1] Roman Catechism, 1566. PT II, ch. 3, Q. 20.

[2] 'Effectus huius sacramenti est, quia in eo datur Spiritus Sanctus ad robur, sicut datus est Apostolis in die Pentecostes, ut videlicet Christianus audacter Christi confiteatur nomen.' *Exultate Deo* (D., 697; M., 235.29).

[3] Trent Sess. 7, can. 9 *de sacr.* (D., 852; M., 304.1; Schaff, II.121).

[4] Synod of Elvira (post A.D. 300). D., 520.

possible without it, provided it be not omitted out of contempt.'[5]

The effect of confirmation takes place, as in all the sacraments, *ex opere operato*. It does not depend on the disposition either of the minister or of the recipient. As a sacrament for the spiritually alive, as it is called, it requires of course for its basis the state of grace attained by baptism. If the sanctifying grace infused by baptism has been lost by some mortal sin, this grace must be recovered before confirmation. This can only be done by means of the sacrament of penance or at least by perfect contrition. Instruction for confirmation, on the contrary, is not an absolute prerequisite for the sacrament. It is part of the 'remoter preparation'.

Even if the indispensable basis, the state of grace, happens inadvertently to be lacking in a confirmation, the indelible character is none the less given. But grace itself is only imparted to the confirmed person when the impediment which hinders its influx is removed. The sacrament, it is said, then comes to life.

2. What Constitutes Confirmation?

It is not altogether clear what constitutes the material of this sacrament. The Union Council of Lyons in 1274 laid it down that the sacrament of Confirmation 'is given by *the imposition of the hands* of the Bishops when they anoint the regenerate'.[6] The Council of Trent contented itself with the rejection of the assertion that 'those who ascribe any virtue to the sacred oil of confirmation' offer an outrage to the Holy Spirit.[7] The Bull *Exultate Deo* is more precise but what it says is meant only as practical guidance. 'The material is chrism made from oil representing purity of conscience, and from balsam signifying the fragrance of good repute, and consecrated by the Bishop.'[8] There are, therefore, two views held. Some theologians regard the laying on of hands, others the anointing, as the material of

[5] *Summa Theol.*, III, Q. 72, I ad 3 (Eng. trans. VOL. II, p. 2424).

[6] 'Per manuum impositionem episcopi conferunt, chrismando renatos.' Union Council of Lyons, 1274 (D., 465).

[7] 'Qui sacro confirmationis chrismati virtutem aliquam tribuunt.' Sess. 7, can. 2 *de conf.* (D., 872; M., 305.13; Schaff, II.125f).

[8] 'Materia est chrisma confectum ex oleo, quod nitorem significat conscientiae, et balsamo quod odorem significat bonae famae, per episcopum benedicto.' *Exultate Deo* (D., 697; M., 235.37).

the sacrament. The olive oil used in the anointing must first have been consecrated by the Bishop. It is applied to the forehead. Among ceremonies still used in the rites are the blow in the face, a sign of participation in Christ's sufferings, and the chrism scarf (*chrismale*).

The formula for the sacrament is: 'I sign thee with the sign of the Cross and I confirm thee with the chrism of salvation in the Name of the Father, etc.'[9] These words are also held to have consecrating power. Roman theology has to admit that there is no such formula in Scripture and indeed 'no formal witness' of any institution of this sacrament by Christ.[10]

The *minister* of the sacrament is the Bishop. This was affirmed by the Council of Trent: 'If anyone says that the ordinary minister of holy confirmation is not the Bishop alone but any simple priest soever: let him be anathema.'[11] This is justified in the Bull *Exultate Deo*, on the ground that tradition tells us that only the Apostles, whose place has been taken by the bishops, imparted the Holy Spirit by the imposition of hands.[12]

The *extraordinary minister* of the sacrament is the priest, provided general Church Law gives him the authority to do this (Cardinals who are not Bishops, Vicars Apostolic, Abbots and so on), or if he holds a special papal dispensation to do so But he must in every case use episcopally consecrated oil.

The *recipients* of the sacrament are baptised Christians over the age of seven.[13] We have already mentioned their disposition. A sponsor must be present at the Confirmation. A sponsor must belong to the same sex as the candidate and must not already have stood sponsor at the latter's baptism.

[9] 'Signo te signo crucis et confirmo te chrismate salutis, in nomine Patris etc.' *Ibid.* (D., 697; M., 235.39).

[10] Bartmann, *Dogmatik*, VOL. II, p. 277.

[11] 'Si quis dixerit, sanctae confirmationis ordinarium ministrum non esse solum episcopum, sed quemvis simplicem sacerdotem: A.S.' Sess. 7, can. 3 *de conf.* (D., 873; M., 305.13; Schaff, II.126).

[12] D., 697; M., 235.42.

[13] Roman Catechism, 1566, PT II, ch. 3, Q. 9 and 18.

CHAPTER 7

THE SACRAMENT OF PENANCE

I. Penance as the Means of Regaining Baptismal Grace

Baptism and penance are often compared. Both are 'sacraments of the dead' (*sacramenta mortuorum*), baptism for those who are spiritually dead in original sin, penance for those who, by mortal sin, have again become spiritually dead. Penance is intended to deliver them from spiritual death and to restore sanctifying grace to them. It is therefore called 'a second plank after the shipwreck of grace lost'.[1] Penance is thus similar to baptism but differs from it because 'unto newness and entireness we are no ways able to arrive by the sacrament of penance, without many tears and great labours on our parts, the divine justice demanding this'.[2] Penance is therefore described as a 'laborious kind of baptism'.[3]

The sacrament brings about the 'restoration of the fallen'.[4] For the lapsed there is always the renewed possibility of justification 'when, God exciting them, through the sacrament of penance they shall have attained to the recovery, by the merit of Christ, of the grace lost'.[5] The effect of the sacrament of penance is '*reconciliation* with God which sometimes in persons who are pious and who receive this sacrament with devotion, is wont to be followed by peace and serenity of conscience, with exceeding consolation of spirit'.[6] Strictly speaking this sacra-

[1] 'Secunda post naufragium deperditae gratiae tabula'. Trent Sess. 6, ch. 14 (D., 807; M., 299.27; Schaff, II.105).

[2] 'Novitatem et integritatem per sacramentum poenitentiae, sine magnis nostris fletibus et laboribus, divina exigente iustitia, pervenire nequaquam possumus.' Trent, Sess. 14 *de sacr. poen.*, ch. 2 (D., 895; M., 311.36; Schaff, II.142f).

[3] 'Laboriosus quidem baptismus.' *Ibid.* [4] 'Lapsi reparatio.' *Ibid.*

[5] 'Excitante Deo per poenitentiae sacramentum merito Christi amissam gratiam recuperare procuraverint.' *Ibid.* Cf. can. 1. (D., 911; M., 317.45; Schaff, II.163f).

[6] 'Reconciliatio . . . cum Deo.' 'Quam interdum in viris piis et cum devotione hoc sacramentum percipientibus conscientiae pax ac serenitas cum vehementi spiritus consolatione consequi solet.' Sess. 14, *de poen.*, ch. 3 (D., 896; M., 312.8; Schaff, II.144).

ment removes the impediment which mortal sin presents and which prevents the influx of grace. This is now able to flow again. As we saw earlier, all the merits previously acquired are revived by the application of this sacrament.

For all baptised persons who have fallen into mortal sin the sacrament of penance is absolutely *necessary for salvation*, just as baptism is for the unregenerate.[7] In an emergency, the desire (*votum*) for this sacrament is sufficient, as, for example, in the case of a priest faced with the duty of saying mass but having previously fallen into mortal sin. The person concerned must submit to the sacrament of penance at the earliest opportunity.

2. What Constitutes the Sacrament of Penance?

There is no real *material* in the sacrament of penance. The Council of Trent states: 'but the acts of the penitent himself, to wit, contrition, confession, and satisfaction, are as it were the matter of this sacrament'[8]; and, since these acts on the part of the penitent are essential to the sacrament, it calls them 'the parts of penance'.[9]

On contrition (*contritio*) the Council of Trent says: it is 'a sorrow of mind and a detestation for sin committed; with the purpose of not sinning for the future'.[10] It distinguishes between 'perfect contrition' (*contritio perfecta*) and 'imperfect contrition' (*imperfecta*). The former is the contrition 'which is perfected by love' (*contritio caritate perfecta*), the latter is called *attritio*, and the Council says of it 'that if with the hope of pardon it excludes the wish to sin, it does not make a man a hypocrite and a greater sinner but is on the contrary a gift of God and an impulse of the Holy Spirit', for it springs 'either from the consideration of the turpitude of sin, or from the fear of Hell and of punishment'.[11] Perfect contrition abhors sin because it is sin against

[7] Sess. 14, ch. 2 (D., 895; M., 311.30; Schaff, II.141f).

[8] 'Sunt autem quasi materia huius sacramenti ipsius poenitentis actus, nempe contritio, confessio et satisfactio.' Sess. 14, ch. 3 (D., 896; M., 312.3; Schaff, II.143).

[9] *Ibid.*

[10] 'Animi dolor ac detestatio est de peccato commisso, cum proposito non peccandi de cetero.' Sess. 14, ch. 4 (D., 897; M., 312.14; Schaff, II.144).

[11] 'Quoniam vel ex turpitudinis peccati consideratione vel ex gehennae et poenarum metu communiter concipitur, si voluntatem peccandi excludat cum spe veniae, declarat non solum non facere hominem hypocritam et magis peccatorem, verum etiam donum Dei esse et Spiritus Sancti impulsum.' Sess. 14, ch. 4 (D., 898; M., 312.33; Schaff, II.145f).

God, *attritio* does so because sin hurts man. Yet attrition is a sufficient disposition for the right reception of the sacrament.[12] When to the quasi-material of the sacrament the form is added, grace is imparted to the penitent. The crude 'attritionism', which regards attrition as the mere fear of punishment, cannot of course appeal to Trent,[13] and was in fact condemned by Innocent XI in 1679. He rejected the proposition: 'It is permissible to hold that *natural* attrition is sufficient if only it is sincere.'[14] But even earlier Alexander VII had said it was not heretical to hold that contrition based on the fear of Hell and punishment need not be joined by a special act of love to God[15]; and Alexander VIII had condemned two Jansenist propositions aimed against attritionism: 'The fear of Hell is not supernaturally inspired'; and, 'Attrition which springs from fear of Hell or punishment, without love for God's mercy is not a good and supernaturally inspired disposition.'[16] Yet many theologians hold that genuine attrition requires at least the beginning of love to God,[17] whereas others continue to regard fear of temporal punishment as a sufficient motive if in it there is also some thought of God, and they support this view by pointing out that Trent cites the Ninevites as an example of such contrition. The whole controversy shows into what straits theology can stray when it fails to look at man strictly in the light of revelation. Man then acquires such independence that the question constantly arises whether what he does satisfies God or whether more is not required. God's Word of grace is not sufficiently authoritative by itself: on the contrary, man's relationship to God is measured primarily by man's capacities and actions. The inward disposition required of man is little enough provided only he submits himself to the judgment and direction of the Roman Church. The forsaking of sin is, of course, part of the good intention required in every case.[18]

If on the other hand a man who has committed mortal sin

[12] *Ibid.* [13] Cf. Sess. 6, can. 3 (D., 813; M., 301.12; Schaff, II.110f).

[14] 'Probabile est, sufficere attritionem naturalem, modo honestam' (D., 1207: M., 389.9). [15] D., 1146.

[16] 'Timor gehennae non est supernaturalis' (D., 1304). 'Attritio, quae gehennae et poenarum metu concipitur, sine dilectione benevolentiae Dei propter se, non est bonus motus ac supernaturalis' (D., 1305).

[17] Bartmann, *Dogmatik*, VOL. II, p. 394.

[18] Trent Sess. 14, ch. 4 (D., 898; M., 312.34; Schaff, II.144f).

has perfect contrition, he is already justified by this, so long as at the same time he desires the sacrament of penance. Contrition alone, however, is not enough.[19] The desire to receive the sacrament must be carried out at the earliest opportunity. But how far is this really necessary, if justifying grace is already acquired by perfect contrition plus a desire for the sacrament of penance? The answer is revealing: the sacrament then produces an increase of grace.

In addition to contrition, *oral confession* of sin (*confessio oris*) must be made to the priest. 'If anyone denies either that sacramental confession was instituted or is *necessary to salvation, of divine right*; or says that the manner of confessing secretly *to the priest alone*, which the Church has always observed from the beginning and does observe, is alien to the institution and command of Christ and is a human invention, let him be anathema.'[20] What is the basis of this necessity for confession to the priest? The Council of Trent says that Christ left behind him as his vicars, priests who should be judges of all mortal sins. To be able to do so, they need to be put in full possession of the facts about these sins. 'For it is manifest that priests could not have exercised this judgment without knowledge of the cause nor could they have observed equity in enjoining punishments, if the said faithful should have declared their sins in general only and not rather specifically one by one. Whence it is gathered that all the mortal sins, of which, after a diligent examination of themselves, they are conscious, must needs be by penitents enumerated in confession, even though those sins be most hidden and committed only against the last two precepts of the Decalogue.'[21]

To the priest must be confessed therefore: (*a*) all mortal sins

[19] *Ibid.*

[20] 'Si quis negaverit, confessionem sacramentalem vel institutam vel ad salutem necessariam esse iure divino, aut dixerit, modum secrete confitendi soli sacerdoti, quem Ecclesia catholica ab initio semper observavit et observat, alienum esse ab institutione et mandato Christi, et inventum esse humanum: A.S.' Sess. 14, can. 6 (D., 916; M., 318.20; Schaff, II.165f).

[21] 'Constat enim, sacerdotes iudicium hoc incognita causa exercere non potuisse, neque aequitatem quidem illos in poenis iniugendis servare potuisse, si in genere dumtaxat, et non potius in specie ac singillatim sua ipsi peccata declarassent. Ex his colligitur, oportere a poenitentibus omnia peccata mortalia, quorum post diligentem sui discussionem conscientiam habent, in confessione recenseri, etiamsi occultissima illa sint et tantum adversus duo ultima decalogi praecepta commissa.' Sess. 14, ch. 5 (D., 899; M., 313.8; Schaff, II.147f).

(we recall here how difficult it is to know whether an offience is a mortal sin or merely a venial one); (*b*) even the most secret mortal sins (if a sin is concealed the whole confession is invalid); (*c*) even those sins which break the last two precepts of the Decalogue (the tenth only, according to the biblical numbering); (*d*) all we remember after a searching examination of our consciences ('*quae memoriae occurrunt*'); (*e*) even the attendant circumstances (which alter the character of a sin)[22]; (*f*) seriously sinful lapses which one does not recall are counted as included in the confession[23]; (*g*) questions asked by the priest during confession are to be answered[24]; (*h*) venial sins need not be mentioned, but can be confessed,[25] in which case the sacrament of penance becomes *per accidens* a 'sacrament of the living'. Oral confession in this far-reaching sense rests, according to Roman doctrine, on a mandate of Christ. Its attendant risks, in view of the required examination of the conscience by the priest, and the temptations to which the questioning by the priest subjects the person making confession, hardly need pointing out.

Satisfaction (*satisfactio operis*). By the sacrament of penance sin is forgiven, but not every punishment remitted. 'If anyone says that God always remits *the whole punishment together with the guilt*, and that the satisfaction of penitents is no other than the faith whereby they apprehend that Christ has satisfied for them; let him be anathema.'[26] What is remitted is the eternal punishment; temporal punishments like 'fastings, prayers, almsgiving, or other works also of piety . . . serve the end that in virtue of the merits of Christ God receives satisfaction'.[27] It is stated explicitly that in determining the appropriate penalty priests should bear in mind 'that the satisfaction which they impose should be not only for the preservation of a new life and a medicine of infirmity, but also for *the avenging and punishing of past sins*'.[28] Even prayer is thus included among these punishments.

[22] *Ibid.* [23] Sess. 14, ch. 5 (D., 900; M., 313.35; Schaff, II.149).

[24] Leo X, *Exsurge Domine*, 1520, against Martin Luther (D., 754; M., 257.45).

[25] Trent Sess. 14, ch. 5 (D., 899; Schaff, II.147f).

[26] 'Si quis dixerit, totam poenam simul cum culpa remitti semper a Deo, satisfactionemque poenitentium non esse aliam quam fidem, qua apprehendunt Christum pro eis satisfecisse: A.S.' Sess. 14, can. 12 (D., 922; M., 319.6; Schaff, II.168). [27] Sess. 14, can. 13.

[28] 'Ut satisfactio, quam imponunt, non sit tantum ad novae vitae custodiam et infirmitatis medicamentum, sed etiam ad praeteritorum peccatorum vindictam et castigationem.' Sess. 14, ch. 9 (D., 905; M., 316.7; Schaff, II.157).

Satisfaction does not have to precede the priest's absolution.[29] The sacrament of penance is validly administered therefore even without satisfaction having been made.

According to the Roman Catechism[30] a *vicarious* satisfaction is possible in the case of temporal penalties for sin. One person can make satisfaction for another, but only of course by intercession.

The *form* of the sacrament 'wherein its force principally consists' is contained in the words spoken by the priest.[31] According to the *Rituale Romanum* they are: 'I absolve you from all punishments and sins, in the Name of the Father and of the Son and of the Holy Ghost, Amen.'[32] This formula is not to be mistaken for the declaration of the Word of forgiveness. The sovereign free encounter between the Word and the sinner is, indeed, expressly denied. It does not fit into Rome's priestly and sacramental institution for salvation. 'If anyone says that the sacramental absolution of the priest is not a *judicial act* but *a bare ministry* of pronouncing and declaring sins to be forgiven to him who confesses—let him be anathema.'[33] The judicial act of absolution is consecratory not declaratory. It must therefore be given orally by a priest to someone actually present. Clement VIII condemned written absolution.[34]

The *minister* of the sacrament is the priest. The Reformers' teaching that every believer can absolve the sin of another was rejected.[35] The reason for this is that in the sacrament the priest acts not simply as priest but also as judge. In this penance differs from baptism: 'It is beyond doubt certain that the minister of baptism need not be a judge, seeing that the Church exercises judgment on no one who has not entered therein through the gate of baptism.' 'For the Lord would have those who have afterwards defiled themselves by any crime . . . to know themselves placed as criminals before this tribunal, so

[29] Alexander VIII, *Errores Iansenistarum*, 1690 (D., 1306ff).

[30] Roman Catechism, 1566, PT II, ch. 5, Q. 61.

[31] Sess. 14, ch. 3 (D., 896; M., 311.42; Schaff, II.143).

[32] 'Ego te absolvo ab omnibus censuris et peccatis in nomine Patris etc.' (*Rituale Romanum*, III, 2, 5).

[33] 'Si quis dixerit, absolutionem sacramentalem sacerdotis non esse actum iudicialem, sed nudum ministerium pronuntiandi et declarandi remissa esse peccata confitenti . . . A.S.' Sess. 14, can. 9 (D., 919; M., 318; Schaff, II.167).

[34] *De absolutione absentis*, 1602 (D., 1088).

[35] Sess. 14, can. 10 (D., 920; M., 318.41; Schaff, II.167f).

that by the sentence of the priests they might be freed, not once, but as often as, being penitent, they should flee thereunto from their committed sins.'[36] Thus, though in emergency baptism it is in order for a layman to take the place of the priest, this is impossible in the sacrament of penance. The only exception is that a priest other than the regular parish priest may receive confession of the dying. In the sacrament of penance the role of the priest is very clearly that of a mediator between God and man, in so far as he uses his own discretion in giving his judgment, and thus controls the effect of the sacrament. It makes little difference that the judgment of certain more atrocious and more heinous crimes (*atrociora quaedam et graviora crimina*) is reserved to the bishops and to the Pope, except when the person desiring the sacrament is at the point of death.[37]

3. The Indulgence

A supplementary word about indulgences. The indulgence is intended for those who have acquired forgiveness by the sacrament of penance and are therefore in a state of grace. The indulgence is a remission of the temporal penalties they still owe, whether these penalties have been appointed by the Church or by God Himself.[38] Indulgences do not remit sins or the guilt of sin. That is what is taught today. When the liturgical formulae speak of 'the forgiveness of all sins', it is explained that this is an inexact way of speaking and that what is meant is not sins but the penalties for sins.

It is a defined dogma that *Christ Himself granted the Church authority* to dispense indulgences, and that '*the use of indulgences*' is '*most salutary* for the Christian people'.[39] The bold assertion

[36] 'Constat certe, baptismi ministrum iudicem esse non oportere, cum Ecclesia in neminem iudicium exerceat, qui non prius in ipsam per baptismi ianuam fuerit ingressus.' Ch. 2 (D., 895; M., 311.26; Schaff, II.142). 'Nam hos, si se postea crimine aliquo contaminaverint . . . ante hoc tribunal tanquam reos sisti voluit, ut per sacerdotum sententiam non semel, sed quoties ab admissis peccatis ad ipsum poenitentes confugerint, possent liberari' (*Ibid.*).

[37] Sess. 14, ch. 7 (D., 903; M., 315.10; Schaff, II.153f).

[38] Cf. the position adopted against the Reform Synod of Pistoia: 'quasi indulgentia praeter nudam remissionem poena canonicae non etiam valeat ad remissionem poenae temporalis pro peccatis actualibus debitae apud divinam iustitiam' (as if an indulgence had no power to remit any temporal punishment for actual sins, required by divine justice, beyond the bare remission of the canonical penalty). D., 1540.

[39] 'Cum potestas conferendi indulgentias a Christo Ecclesiae concessa sit, atque

that indulgences go back to Christ Himself is based on the universal authority which He gave to His disciples, according to Matt. 16 and 18. The indulgence is therefore part of the judicial and not of the sacramental practice of the Church.

The bishops, and above them the Pope, as the principal bearers of the Church's judicial authority, also enjoy the power to grant indulgences. Ecclesiastical Law determines in detail the extent to which bishops may do so. In every case there must be good cause (*iusta causa*) for the indulgence; it must be to the spiritual benefit of the Church and of the recipient. Otherwise it is invalid.

On the part of the recipient a state of grace and the prescribed works of indulgence are required. The indulgence is therefore attached to certain prayers and religious exercises, to objects, places and times of devotion, to fraternities, congregations and so on. For example the Jubilee Indulgence (once every twenty-five years since 1475), first introduced by Boniface VIII during the centenary celebrations in 1300, grants plenary indulgence. The great Portiuncula Indulgence has a similar effect, when anyone, after confession and communion, prays in accordance with the intention of the Lord's Prayer, in the Portiuncula Church at Assisi or in any other Church of the Franciscan order on 2 August.[40] Even the payment of money to obtain an indulgence is not ruled out, since, according to the Council of Trent, permission is explicitly given to bishops when granting indulgences 'diligently to collect alms and gifts of love without any kind of tariff, so that in future all may really see that the Church's heavenly treasury of grace [i.e. the indulgence] is used not for the purpose of gain but in the interests of true religion'.[41]

huiusmodi potestate divinitus sibi tradita antiquissimis etiam temporibus illa usa fuerit: sacrosancta Synodus indulgentiarum usum, christiano populo maxime salutarem et sacrorum Conciliorum auctoritate probatum, in Ecclesia retinendum esse docet.' Trent Sess. 25, *Decretum de indulgentiis* (D., 989; M., 336.27; Schaff, II.205).

[40] Cf. M., 566-70.

[41] 'Indulgentias . . . per ordinarios locorum [i.e. the bishops] adhibitis duobus de capitulo, debitis temporibus populo publicandas esse decernit. Quibus etiam eleemosynas atque oblata sibi caritatis subsidia, nulla prorsus mercede accepta, fideliter colligendi facultas datur, ut tandem coelestes hos ecclesiae thesauros non ad questum, sed ad pietatem exerceri omnes vere intelligant.' Trent Sess. 21, *decr. de reformatione* (M., 322.6).

A distinction is made between plenary indulgence (*indulgentia plenaria*), the remission of all temporal penalties, and partial indulgence (*indulgentia particularis*), the remission of part of these penalties. We have already given examples of plenary indulgence. Strangely enough one can obtain many of them, e.g. the Portiuncula Indulgence mentioned above, several times in succession. What is the advantage, if this indulgence remits all temporal penalties? Answer: to be on the safe side, for some fault may have been incurred in the prescribed exercises. Moreover one can apply the superfluous indulgences to the 'poor souls' in Purgatory, and thereby acquire merit for oneself. The period of time for which a partial indulgence is granted does not mean that the person concerned spends that time less in Purgatory. It means rather that he is remitted a temporal penalty for sin, for which, according to the ancient penitential rules of the Church, he would have had to spend the time indicated in doing penance.[42]

The indulgence can be used *as an intercession for the 'poor souls'* in Purgatory. Anyone wishing to intercede for the dead in this way must, therefore, first acquire the indulgence for himself, and he can then put it at God's disposal on behalf of the dead person. Such an indulgence is not certain, therefore.

The indulgence is possible, according to Roman teaching, because the Church has a Treasury of Grace (*thesaurus ecclesiae*) filled by the superfluous meritorious works of Christ and His saints. Because the Church is a Communion of Saints, those who hold the judicial authority of the Church can make grants to the needy from the Church's treasury, in other words, can grant indulgences. The indulgence thus rests on the Roman doctrine of merit. It presupposes the superfluous merits of the saints and requires from those who seek indulgence similar meritorious works which are prescribed in detail. Those who cannot speak of human merit at all in face of the Christ who is present in His Word, because they see salvation wholly enclosed in Him and in His Work, can literally make nothing of this system of indulgences with its calculated remission of penalties.

[42] 'This means, for example, that an indulgence of 100 days or of one year is the remission of the temporal penalties which in those days would have needed to be expiated before God by a canonical penance lasting 100 days or one year respectively' (M., 565.40).

CHAPTER 8

EXTREME UNCTION

1. Extreme Unction as a Means of Strengthening the Dying

JUST as the sacrament of confirmation completes baptism, so too the sacrament of extreme unction completes penance.[1] To what extent? The Council of Trent declares: 'The thing signified and the effect of this sacrament are explained in the words: "And the prayer of faith will save the sick man, and the Lord will raise him up; and if he be in sins they will be forgiven him" [Jas. 5.15]. For the thing here signified is *the grace of the Holy Ghost*, whose anointing cleanses away sins, if there be any still to be expiated, as also *the remains of sins*, and *raises up and strengthens the soul* of the sick person, by exciting in him a great confidence in the divine mercy; whereby the sick man being supported, bears more easily the inconveniences and pains of his sickness; and more readily resists the temptations of the Devil, who lies in wait for his heel; and in some cases obtains bodily health, when expedient for the welfare of the soul.'[2] The main effect of the sacrament is therefore 'the imparting of grace' to assuage and strengthen the souls of the dying. Then, in certain cases, it also wipes out mortal sins and the remnants of sin. Finally it sometimes effects the healing of the body, if this is expedient for the salvation of the soul. The sacrament is not absolutely necessary for salvation, since it presupposes that habitual grace is present in the sick person, who must therefore,

[1] Trent Sess. 14, *doctr. de sacra. extr. unct.* (D., 907; M., 316.26; Schaff, II.158f).

[2] 'Res porro et effectus huius sacramenti illis verbis explicatur: "Et oratio fidei salvabit infirmum, et alleviabit eum Dominus; et si peccatis sit, dimittentur ei" (Iac. 5.15). Res etenim haec gratia est Spiritus Sancti, cuius unctio delicta, si quae sint adhuc expianda ac peccati reliquias abstergit, et aegroti animam alleviat et confirmat, magnam in eo divinae misericordiae fiduciam excitando, qua infirmus sublevatus et morbi incommoda ac labores levius fert, et tentationibus daemonis "calcaneo insidiantis" (Gen. 3.15) facilius resistit, et sanitatem corporis interdum, ubi saluti animae expedierit, consequitur.' Trent Sess. 14, *doctr. de sacr. extr. unct.*, ch. 2 (D., 909; M., 317.8; Schaff, II.161).

before receiving it, either have received the sacrament of penance or shown perfect contrition. Theologians admit that it remains 'uncertain'[3] whether the sacrament was instituted by Jesus Christ, but not, of course, that Jas. 5.15 refers to prayer for healing and not to a preparation for death.

2. What Constitutes Extreme Unction?

The *material* is 'olive oil blessed by a bishop'.[4] The sick person is to be anointed with this consecrated oil in the following places: 'on the eyes for seeing, on the ears for hearing, on the nose for smelling, on the mouth for tasting and speaking, on the hands for touching, on the feet for walking, on the loins for the desire which is seated there'.[5] The last named is prescribed only in the case of a male. In emergency it is enough to anoint the dying person's forehead.[6]

The *form* of the sacrament consists of the words spoken at the anointing of each part of the body: 'By the holy anointing and by His tender mercy, may the Lord pardon thee whatever sins thou hast committed by sight [hearing, etc.].'[7] If required these words can be reduced to the formula: 'By this holy anointing may the Lord pardon thee all thy sins.'[8]

The *minister* of the sacrament is the *priest*, and he alone. 'If anyone says that the presbyters of the Church whom blessed James exhorts to be brought to anoint the sick are not the priests who have been ordained by a bishop, but the elders in each congregation, and that for this cause a priest alone is not the proper minister of Extreme Unction: let him be anathema.'[9]

[3] Bartmann, *Dogmatik*, vol. ii, p. 427.

[4] 'Oleum olivae per episcopum benedictum.' Trent Sess. 14, ch. 2 (D., 908; M., 317.3; Schaff, ii.160).

[5] 'In oculis propter visum, in auribus propter auditum, in naribus propter adoratum, in ore propter gustum vel locutionem, in manibus propter tactum, in pedibus propter gressum, in renibus propter delectationem ibidem vigentem.' Bull *Exultate Deo*, 1439 (D., 700; M., 237.5).

[6] *Codex Juris Canonici*, henceforth cited as *C.J.C.*, Canon 947. Cf. S. Woywod, *The New Canon Law*, 7th edn. New York 1929, p. 190.

[7] 'Per istam sanctam unctionem et suam piissimam misericordiam indulgeat tibi Dominus, quidquid per visum etc. deliquisti.' *Ibid.*

[8] 'Per istam sanctam unctionem indulgeat tibi Dominus quidquid deliquisti.' Pius X, 1906 (D., 1996).

[9] 'Si quis dixerit, presbyteros Ecclesiae, quos beatus Iacobus adducendos esse ad infirmum inungendum hortatur, non esse sacerdotes ab episcopos ordinatos, sed aetate seniores in quavis communitate, ob idque proprium extremae unctionis

Only the dying are to receive this sacrament[10]: 'It is declared that this unction is to be applied to the sick, but to those especially who lie in such danger as to seem about to depart this life: whence also it is called the sacrament of the departing.'[11] Since the sacrament includes the possibility of healing, it may be administered again if after receiving it the sick person is healed and later becomes mortally sick again.[12] The necessary disposition for receiving the sacrament is the state of grace. If therefore the sick person has committed mortal sin he must first confess or at least show perfect contrition. He is then fit to receive extreme unction.

3. Purgatory (Purgatorium)

The person who has received extreme unction is not thereby ready to enter the Kingdom of God. For even though mortal sins and the remnants of venial sins in him may have been cancelled there still remains in him much guilt to be expiated and also temporal penalties for sin. This is only to be expected because righteousness is not declared to man unconditionally by the Word, but is infused into him as a new capacity to enable him to work at his own perfection. What he fails to achieve in this temporal life he must accomplish after death. The unexpiated guilt and the penalties for sin, which still cling to him, he has to purge away in Purgatory. That was affirmed by the Council of Trent when it explicitly rejected the Reformers' doctrine of the perfect justification of the sinner: 'If anyone says that after the grace of justification has been received to every penitent sinner the guilt is remitted, and the debt of eternal punishment is blotted out, in such wise that there remains *not any debt of temporal punishment* to be discharged either in this world, or in the next in *Purgatory*, before the entrance to the Kingdom of Heaven can be opened to him: let him be anathema.'[13] In 1274 the Council of Lyons had said: 'But if

ministrum non esse solum sacerdotem: A.S.' Trent Sess. 14, can. 4 (D., 929; M., 319.27; Schaff, II.170).

[10] Including the dead up till two hours after their decease.

[11] 'Declaratur etiam, esse hanc unctionem infirmis adhibendam, illis vero praesertim, qui tam periculose decumbunt, ut in exitu vitae constituti videantur, unde et sacramentum exeuntium nuncupatur.' Trent Sess. 14, ch. 3 (D., 910; M., 317.22; Schaff, II.162). [12] *Ibid.*

[13] 'Si quis post acceptam iustificationis gratiam cuilibet peccatori poenitenti ita

they have departed this life in true contrition of heart and in love, before they have made satisfaction by fruits worthy of repentance, their souls are purified after death, by purifying and refining penalties.'[14]

The *sole purpose of the soul's stay in Purgatory* is the payment of penalties for sin, and purification from the guilt of venial sins. It is intended to perfect and glorify the man into whom sanctifying grace was infused by baptism, and who, when this grace was lost by mortal sin, received it again by the sacrament of penance. It means a final change in the man whose transformation began at baptism.

The *purifying* penalties suffered in Purgatory are first of all, a punishment of loss (*poena damni*), i.e. the provisional loss of blessedness, and, secondly, a felt punishment (*poena sensus*). What the departed experience there is usually thought of as material fire in a forecourt of Hell. But in this condition souls have the assurance that they will be perfected and attain salvation. Luther's assertion that 'the souls in Purgatory are not sure of their salvation' was rejected.[15]

The Council of Trent explicitly teaches that by their prayers the faithful can intercede for the poor souls in Purgatory: 'There is a purgatory and the souls there detained are helped by the suffrages of the faithful, but principally by the acceptable sacrifice on the altar.'[16] They can be assisted most effectively, by the application of the sacrifice of the Mass, through the celebration of requiem masses, to come out from Purgatory before their time. On the other hand, the souls there can intercede for those on earth if asked to do so. This is not defined dogma but such an invocation of the dead is not prohibited by the Church.

culpam remitti et reatum aeternae poenae deleri dixerit, ut nullus remaneat reatus poenae temporalis, exsolvendae vel in hoc saeculo vel in futuro in purgatorio, antequam ad regna coelorum aditus patere possit: A.S.' Trent Sess. 6, can. 30 (D., 840; M., 302.33; Schaff, II.117).

[14] 'Quod si vere poenitentes in caritate decesserint, antequam dignis poenitentiae fructibus de commissis satisfecerint et omissis: eorum animas poenis purgatoriis seu catharteriis . . . post mortem purgari' (D., 464).

[15] Leo X, *Exsurge Domine*, 1520 (D., 778; M., 258.34).

[16] 'Purgatorium esse, animasque ibi detentas fidelium suffragiis, potissimum vero acceptabili altaris sacrificio iuvari.' Sess. 25, *decr. de purgatorio* (D., 938; M., 333.4; Schaff, II.198).

CHAPTER 9

THE SACRAMENT OF MARRIAGE

THE four sacraments so far dealt with are means by which grace is received and increased. Marriage and the ordination of priests are sacraments of status. They serve the continuation of the natural and supernatural life respectively.

1. The Effect of the Sacrament of Marriage

The effect of the sacrament of marriage is to establish the marriage bond which permanently binds the partners to one another. It is indissoluble save by death. The question of divorce can only arise on the basis of the *privilegium Paulinum* (1 Cor. 7.12-15), or in the case of a marriage which has been entered into but not yet consummated. Apart from that the Roman Church will accept a separation of the married couple from bed and board, but not a divorce.

The second effect of the sacrament is to increase grace. Pius XI states this positively: this sacrament 'increases in the soul sanctifying grace'[1]; and the Council of Trent, negatively: 'If anyone says that matrimony . . . does not confer grace, let him be anathema.'[2]

Finally the sacrament confers 'special gifts of grace' on the married couple, and 'also gives them the right to obtain the help of actual grace whenever they need it for the discharge of their matrimonial tasks'.[3]

2. What Constitutes the Sacrament of Marriage?

The sacrament of marriage must not be confused with the

[1] Encyclical *Casti connubii*, 1930 (D., 2237; Eng. trans. *Christian Marriage*, London 1959, p. 22).

[2] Sess. 24, can. 1 *de sacr. matr.* (D., 971; M., 330.22; Schaff, II.195).

[3] 'Ius denique iis concedit ad actuale gratiae auxilium toties impetrandum, quotiescumque ad munera huius status adimplenda eo indigent.' *Casti connubii* (D., 2237; Eng. trans, p. 22).

nuptial mass which the Church celebrates. The sacrament of marriage is not the latter but the actual marriage between husband and wife.

The terms employed in Scholastic sacramental doctrine can hardly be applied to the sacrament of marriage. It is said: *the material and form* of the sacrament are the mutually exchanged promises of the two people concerned. 'For marriage the consent of those whose union is involved is sufficient of itself.'[4] The blessing spoken by the priest at the wedding cannot be regarded as the form ('Ego vos . . . coniungo'), since the Council of Trent leaves the use of this formula optional.[5]

Nevertheless marriage is reckoned as a sacrament instituted by Christ, and the contrary view of the Reformers is rejected.[6] Hence the acts of marriage are good and even meritorious, when they are done in accordance with the intention of marriage.

The *minister* of the sacrament is each of the two persons consenting to the marriage covenant, and not the priest in whose presence the marriage vows must be made, according to the rule laid down by the Council of Trent: 'in the presence of the authorised priest . . . and two or three witnesses'.[7] Otherwise the marriage vows and therefore the marriage itself are invalid. This condition was mitigated by Benedict XIV in 1741 for marriages between non-Catholics and also for mixed marriages, in certain countries.

For the valid reception of the sacrament it is essential that the two parties should have been baptised and that there should be no impediments to the marriage. A distinction is made between 'prohibitive impediments' (*impedimenta impedientia*), which render a proposed marriage not invalid but impermissible, and 'divisive impediments' (*impedimenta dirimentia*) which render marriage invalid. The most important of the first kind of impediment is *mixta religio*, and therefore mixed marriages between Catholics and non-Catholics.[8] The 'divisive

[4] 'Sufficiat ad matrimonium solus consensus illorum, de quorum quarumque coniunctionibus agitur.' Innocent III, *Cum apud sedem*, 1198 (D., 404).

[5] Sess. 24, *decr. de ref. matr.* (M., 332.1).

[6] Sess. 24, can. 1.

[7]. 'Praesente parocho . . . et duobus vel tribus testibus.' Sess. 24, *decr. de ref. matr.* (M., 332.9).

[8] *C.J.C.*, can. 1061-4 (M., 550.35). Cf. S. Woywod, *The New Canon Law*, pp. 214f.

impediments' include difference of religion (*cultus disparitas*), therefore marriages between Catholics and non-Christians. Under certain circumstances the Church can grant dispensations from many impediments to marriage. It claims this right on the ground that marriage is a sacrament. This right is at the disposal of the Pope or the bishops.

For the effective reception of the sacrament a state of grace is necessary. Hence the parish priest must exhort the parties to the marriage to go to confession and to take communion beforehand.[9]

Despite the fact that marriage is counted as a sacrament, the celibate state is regarded by the Roman Church as a higher one. The contrary view of the Reformers was rejected by the Council of Trent: 'If anyone says that the marriage state is to be placed above the state of virginity or of celibacy, and that it is not more blessed to remain in virginity or in celibacy, than to be united in matrimony: let him be anathema.'[10] It is appropriate to recall here what was said about the Roman view of merit and works of supererogation when we discussed the doctrine of justification.[11]

[9] *C.J.C.*, can. 1033. Cf. Woywod, *op. cit.*, p. 209.

[10] 'Si quis dixerit, statum coniugalem anteponendum esse statui virginitatis vel coelibatus et non esse melius ac beatius manere in virginitate aut coelibatu, quam iungi matrimonio: A.S.' Sess. 24, can. 10, *de sacr. matr.* (D., 980; M., 331.4; Schaff, II.197).

[11] See above, p. 64f.

CHAPTER 10

THE SACRAMENT OF ORDINATION

1. The Effect of this Sacrament

As the Council of Trent emphasises, the ordination of priests is indubitably one of the seven sacraments of the Roman Church.[1] The person to whom it is administered does not merely receive a task, something happens to him. He becomes part of the stream of grace which flows down from the Apostles to everyone holding priestly office, and through them pours out its floods of grace upon mankind. 'If anyone says that, by sacred ordination, the Holy Ghost is not given; and that vainly therefore do the bishops say: Receive ye the Holy Ghost; or that a character is not imprinted by that ordination; or that he who has once been a priest can again become a layman; let him be anathema.'[2]

The sacramental grace given in ordination is chiefly the indestructible mark of a priest (*character indelebilis*). This mark consists of the 'power to consecrate and offer the true body and blood of the Lord, and to forgive and retain sins'.[3] The Council of Florence could therefore say that this sacrament produces an 'increase of grace so that a person may become fit to serve [at the altar]'.[4] The person concerned thus has an authority which raises him absolutely above other men. He is not a brother among brethren, as the Barmen Declaration described all members of the Church under Christ their Head. According to Roman doctrine there is a clear dividing line between the clergy and the laity. 'The manifestation of the Spirit for the common good' (1 Cor. 12.7) is given not to each member but

[1] Trent Sess. 23, ch. 3 (D., 959; M., 327.10; Schaff, II.188).

[2] 'Si quis dixerit, per sacram ordinationem non dari Spiritum Sanctum, ac proinde frustra episcopos dicere: "Accipe Spiritum Sanctum"; aut per eam non imprimi characterem, vel eum qui sacerdos semel fuit, laicum rursus fieri posse: A.S.' Sess. 23, can. 4 (D., 964; M., 328.6; Schaff, II.191f).

[3] Sess. 23, can. 1 (D., 961; M., 327.42; Schaff, II.191).

[4] *Exultate Deo* (D., 701; M., 237.20).

only to the priests, who mediate the stream of salvation to men. Without them no one—if we except children dying after emergency baptism—can be saved. The priesthood therefore is quite fundamental to the Roman Church and to its view of the transmission of salvation.

The character received in the sacrament always remains intact, even when the person concerned has been reduced to the status of a layman by Papal rescript or degradation,[5] as a punishment. In this case he is forbidden to exercise the power to consecrate, which is and remains his. His obligation to celibacy also remains.

2. What Constitutes the Sacrament of Ordination?

In the current view, the *material* of this sacrament is the laying on of hands, performed by the bishop. The Bull *Exultate Deo*, which gives further information about this, ranks, as we said earlier, only as pastoral instruction, simply describing the rite customary in the Western Church at that period, without any intention of defining the matter dogmatically. The handing over of a chalice filled with wine, and of the paten with the oblations, after the ordination, is regarded as a mere ceremony and not as the material of the sacrament.

The case is the same with the *form* of the sacrament. Contemporary theologians regard the prayers offered during the laying on of hands as the form of the sacrament.

'The ordinary *minister* of this sacrament is the bishop.'[6] This statement has dogmatic force in view of what was said by the Council of Trent: 'If anyone says that bishops are not superior to priests; or, that they have not the power of confirming and ordaining; or that the power which they possess is common to them and to priests . . . let him be anathema.'[7] The same canon also states that for this reason all who have received their commission to the priestly office from elsewhere have an invalid ordination.

[5] *C.J.C.*, can. 2305. Cf. Woywod, *The New Canon Law*, p. 375.

[6] D., 701; M., 237.20.

[7] 'Si quis dixerit episcopos non esse presbyteris superiores; vel non habere potestatem confirmandi et ordinandi, vel eam, quam habent illis esse cum presbyteris communem . . . A.S.' Sess. 23, can. 7 *de sacr. ord.* (D., 967; M., 328.13, Schaff, II.192).

The bishop retains his power to ordain even if he should leave the Roman Church. Ordinations conferred by him then are sacramentally effective but void in law (*de iure*).

Every baptised male can receive this sacrament, if he wishes to receive it, and if there are no impediments to ordination. The recipient must be in a state of grace, since ordination is a 'sacrament of the living', and must already have received consecration to the minor orders.

The Council of Trent names *seven orders*, four minor and three major. The four minor orders (*ordines minores*) are: the office of porter (*ostiarius*), of lector (*lector*), of exorcist (*exorcista*), and of acolyte (*acolythus*). The consecrations to these offices do not have sacramental character. The major orders (*ordines maiores*) are: the sub-diaconate (though consecration to this is not sacramental either), the diaconate, and the priesthood.[8] Today the episcopate is usually added as an eighth order, breaking the seven-fold scheme. Only the consecrations to the diaconate and to the priesthood are regarded as sacramental. Today consecration to the episcopate is also generally regarded as sacramental. Consecration to the diaconate is a preliminary step towards priestly consecration. The consecration of the bishop is regarded either as part of priestly consecration or as its completion and, in that case, as one which establishes a special order. The conferring of episcopal consecration is reserved to the Pope, but he can allow himself to be represented by a bishop and two assistants.

The rules of the Council of Trent, requiring an interval of time between the giving of each of the minor consecrations, and the lapse of a year[9] between these and the sub-diaconate, are no longer observed. The minor orders play no part at all. Their functions are mostly performed by boys (mass servers). The consecrations to them are given together and the bishops can dispense with the time interval between the subsequent consecrations. The normal canonical age for ordination to the priesthood is twenty-four.

From the sub-diaconate onwards, however, *celibacy* is compulsory. No one in major orders, therefore, can contract a

[8] Sess. 23, ch. 2 (D., 958; M., 327.4; Schaff, II.187).
[9] Sess. 23, *decr. de reform.*, can. 11f (M., 329.5).

valid marriage,[10] but the Pope can accept for ordination to the priesthood someone who is already married, as recently happened in a case in Germany. For the Churches of the Eastern rite, who are in communion with Rome, the arrangement whereby persons already married may be ordained to the priesthood is accepted completely.

The priest furthermore is obliged to say the *Breviary prayers* each day at the appointed hours. He can however be partly or even completely relieved of this obligation. With the minor consecrations the *tonsure* is given as a sign of office.

[10] *C.J.C.*, can. 1072 (M., 551.32). Cf. Woywod, *The New Canon Law*, p. 217.

CHAPTER II

THE SACRAMENT OF THE EUCHARIST AND THE SACRIFICE OF THE MASS

1. The Effect of the Eucharist

THE sacrament to which we now turn forms the climax of Roman Catholic worship. It is the chief reason for the existence of the priesthood, which, though not derived from but existing independently of the Mass, is nevertheless essentially directed to this, the heart of worship in the Roman Church.

It is all the more astonishing to find that this sacrament has no exceptional effect on the individual believer. The Bull *Exultate Deo* does indeed describe its effect as the '*union of man with Christ*',[1] and the Catechisms also stress this. But the document mentioned continues, with striking bathos: 'But when man is joined by grace to the body of Christ and united with its members it follows that by the worthy reception of this sacrament *grace is increased*; and every effect that natural food and drink have on the physical life, maintaining, increasing, renewing and rejoicing it, this sacrament has on the spiritual life.'[2] The Council of Trent speaks in similar terms: 'And He willed also that this sacrament should be received as *the spiritual food of souls*, whereby may be fed and strengthened those who live with His life . . . and as an *antidote* whereby we may be freed from daily faults, and be preserved from mortal sins.'[3] The sacra-

[1] D., 698.

[2] 'Et quia per gratiam homo Christo incorporatur et membris eius unitur, consequens est, quod per hoc sacramentum in sumentibus digne gratia augeatur; omnemque effectum, quem materialis cibus et potus quoad vitam agunt corporalem, sustentando, augendo, reparando et delectando sacramentum hoc quoad vitam operatur spiritualem.' *Exultate Deo* (D., 698; M., 236.33).

[3] 'Sumi autem voluit sacramentum hoc tanquam spiritualem animarum cibum, quo alantur et confortentur viventes vita illius . . . et tanquam antidotum quo liberemur a culpis quotidianis et a peccatis mortalibus praeservemur.' Sess. 13, ch. 2 (D., 875; M., 306.30; Schaff, II. 128).

ment of the Eucharist is not of decisive importance for the individual. The sanctifying grace which he already has by baptism is increased by receiving the Eucharist, or communion as it is commonly called. But other sacraments such as confirmation and marriage also bring about this increase of grace. And though the catechisms do teach that 'the holy communion is the real partaking of the body and blood of Jesus Christ', the emphasis is not placed on this in the documents so far quoted. Indeed, in the Bull mentioned above, which has no dogmatic status of course, it is the grace increased by this sacrament which effects the ingrafting of man into Christ. To this positive effect a negative one is added: by this sacrament the communicant receives an '*antidote*' *against ordinary venial sin* and a *prophylactic against mortal sins*. Finally he receives in the Eucharist a *pledge of eternal life*.[4]

On the other hand, the Eucharist does not guarantee the forgiveness of all sins. Mortal sins can only be absolved by the judicial sentence of the Church within the context of the sacrament of penance. The opposite view of Luther was rejected: 'If anyone says either that the principal fruit of the most holy Eucharist is the remission of sins, or that other effects do not result thereform, let him be anathema.'[5] If that were the case, if the Eucharist were a gracious encounter between the sinner and Christ Himself, then the Church's judicial activity in the sacrament of penance would be beside the point, in fact the whole system of judicial priesthood in the Roman Church would collapse. All that remains, therefore, even for this sacrament, which imperatively requires Christ's gracious encounter with man, is for it to increase the already flowing stream of grace and so to unite man with Christ. The sinner cut off from the stream of grace by mortal sin, however, can only be helped by priestly absolution after confession.

2. What Constitutes the Sacrament of the Eucharist?

The *material* of the sacrament was defined as follows in the Bull *Laetentur coeli* (1439): 'The body of the Lord is properly pre-

[4] *Ibid.*

[5] 'Si quis dixerit, vel praecipuum fructum sanctissimae Eucharistiae esse remissionem peccatorum, vel ex ea non alios effectus provenire: A.S.' Sess. 13, can. 5 (D., 887; M., 309.21; Schaff, II.137).

pared in leavened or unleavened wheaten-bread, and the priests must prepare the Lord's body in one way or the other, each in accordance with the custom of his Church be it the Western or the Eastern.'[6] In *Exultate Deo* it is stated: 'The material is wheaten bread and wine from the vine.'[7] Wheaten bread and genuine wine are therefore absolutely essential for the sacrament. Only in respect of the kind of wheaten bread was any deviation permitted to the Greeks.

As for the *form*, we read: the form of this sacrament is 'the words of the Saviour with which He performed this sacrament; for the priest performs this sacrament by speaking in the person of Christ'.[8] This was confirmed by the Council of Trent: 'And this faith hath ever been in the Church of God, that, *immediately after the consecration*, the veritable body of our Lord, and his veritable blood . . . are under the species of bread and wine, by the force of the words.'[9] That is to say the sacrament becomes what it is intended to be, not by the words of prayer offered during the celebration but by the priest's repetition of Christ's words of institution. The priestly consecration can be performed *only in the context of the whole sacrament* and on both elements at the same time. It is not permissible, therefore, to consecrate bread in an emergency for the purpose of providing viaticum for the dying: 'It is forbidden, even in extreme cases of necessity, to consecrate one species without the other, or both, outside the celebration of the Mass.'[10]

The *minister* of the sacrament is *the priest alone*. This in fact is the essence of the priest's authority, that he can prepare and offer the body and blood of Christ. 'If anyone says that by those words, Do this for the commemoration of me [Luke 22.19], Christ did not institute the Apostles priests; or, did not

[6] Pope Eugenius IV: 'In azymo sive fermentato *pane triticeo* corpus Christi veraciter confici, sacerdosque in altero ipsorum domini corpus conficere debere, unumquemque scilicet iuxta suae Ecclesiae sive occidentalis sive orientalis consuetudinem' (D., 692; M., 234.9).

[7] D., 698; M., 236.15.

[8] *Ibid.* 'Sunt verba Salvatoris, quibus hoc confecit sacramentum, sacerdos enim in persona Christi loquens hoc conficit sacramentum.'

[9] 'Semper haec fides in Ecclesia Dei fuit, statim post consecrationem verum Domini nostri corpus verumque eius sanguinem sub panis et vini specie . . . exsistere . . . ex vi verborum.' Sess. 13, ch. 3 (D., 876; M., 307.2; Schaff, II.129).

[10] 'Nefas est, urgente extrema necessitate, alteram materiam sine altera aut etiam utramque, extra Missae celebrationem, consecrare.' *C.J.C.*, can. 817. Cf. Woywod, *The New Canon Law*, p. 165.

ordain that they and other priests should offer His own body and blood: let him be anathema.'[11] The priest must also have the proper intention, i.e. the intention to pronounce the words of institution as the Church understands them.[12]

Anyone in a state of grace can profitably receive the sacrament. This includes children, therefore, if baptised. Confirmation is not essential. The Reformers' view that faith alone is sufficient for right reception was rejected: 'If anyone says that faith alone is a sufficient preparation for receiving the sacrament of the most holy Eucharist, let him be anathema; . . . this holy Synod declares that *sacramental confession*, when a confessor may be had, *is of necessity to be made beforehand*, by those whose conscience is burdened with mortal sin, how contrite so ever they may think themselves.'[13] Believing surrender to the present Christ is not sufficient for the forgiveness of all sins. Anyone wishing to be rid of these may not flee to Christ, but must betake himself to the priest to whom Christ's authority in this matter has been transferred.

Nevertheless the sacrament of the Eucharist is ranked above all the rest: 'The other sacraments have then first the power of sanctifying when one uses them, whereas, in the Eucharist, before being used, there the Author of Sanctity is Himself present.'[14] *Christ Himself is present* in the Eucharist, quite apart from whether a communion follows or not, and, indeed, the whole Christ, His humanity and His Divinity: 'If anyone denies that, in the sacrament of the most holy Eucharist, are contained truly, really, and substantially, the body and blood together with the soul and divinity of our Lord Jesus Christ, and consequently the whole Christ, . . . let him be anathema.'[15]

[11] 'Si quis dixerit, illis verbis: "Hoc facite in meam commemorationem" Christum non instituisse Apostolos sacerdotes, aut non ordinasse ut ipsi aliique sacerdotes offerrent corpus et sanguinem suum: A.S.' Trent Sess. 22, can. 2 (D., 949; M., 324.35; Schaff, II.184).

[12] Innocent III, 1208 (D., 424).

[13] 'Si quis dixerit, solam fidem esse sufficientem praeparationem ad sumendum sanctissimae Eucharistiae sacramentum: A.S. . . . declarat ipsa sancta Synodus, illis, quos conscientia peccati mortalis gravat, quantumcunque etiam se contritos existiment, habita copia confessoris necessario praemittendam esse confessionem sacramentalem.' Trent Sess. 13, can. 11 (D., 893; M., 309.35; Schaff, II.139).

[14] 'Reliqua sacramenta tunc primum sanctificandi vim habent, cum quis illis utitur: at in Eucharistia ipse sanctitatis auctor ante usum est.' Sess. 13, ch. 3 (D., 876; M., 306.41; Schaff, II.129).

[15] 'Si quis negaverit in sanctissimae Eucharistiae sacramento contineri vere, realiter et substantialiter, corpus et sanguinem una cum anima et divinitate

According to Roman doctrine Christ's presence is brought about because the priest utters the words of institution and so changes the bread and the wine completely into the body and blood of our Christ. This is a dogma defined by the Council of Trent: 'If anyone says that in the sacred and holy sacrament of the Eucharist, the substance of the bread and wine remain conjointly with the body and blood of our Lord Jesus Christ, and denies that wonderful and singular conversion of the whole substance of the bread into the body, and of the whole substance of the wine into the blood—the species only of the bread and wine remaining . . . let him be anathema.'[16] The realisation of Christ's presence by the conversion of the substance of the sacramental signs is called by the Roman Church '*transubstantiation*'.[17] In the same passage 'consubstantiation' is explicitly rejected. Still less is there any question of 'impanation', i.e. any inclusion of Christ's body in the bread, as was affirmed on the Lutheran side. After the conversion bread and wine are no longer there. It should be noted too that the whole substance is changed, materially and formally. All that remains is the physically perceptible form (*species*) of bread and wine, appearance, taste, smell, etc.

Also of importance for the Roman doctrine of Christ's presence in the sacrament of the Eucharist is the assertion of *concomitance*. This means that, not because of the words of institution certainly but because of the natural and supernatural bond which unites Christ's body and blood, His divinity and His humanity, the whole Christ is under each element of the sacrament, indeed even under the divided portions of one element. The Council of Trent states that after the change in the Eucharist there are present: 'the body indeed under the form of bread and the blood under the form of wine, by the force of words; but the body itself under the species of wine and the blood under the species of bread and the soul under both, by the force of that natural connexion and concomitancy (*vi*

Domini nostri Iesu Christi, ac proinde totum Christum . . . A.S.' Sess. 13, can. 1 (D., 883; M., 309.7; Schaff, II.136).

[16] 'Si quis dixerit, in sacrosancto Eucharistiae sacramento remanere substantiam panis et vini una cum corpore et sanguine Domini nostri Iesu Christi, negaveritque mirabilem illam at singularem conversionem totius substantiae panis in corpus et totus substantiae vini in sanguinem, manentibus dumtaxat speciebus panis et vini . . . A.S.' Sess. 13, can. 2 (D., 884; Schaff, II.136f).

[17] *Ibid.*

naturalis illius connexionis et concomitantiae) whereby the parts of Christ, our Lord, who hath now risen from the dead to die no more, are united together; and the divinity furthermore on account of the admirable hypostatical union whereof with His body and soul. Wherefore it is most true, that as much is contained under either species as under both.'[18] That the whole Christ is present also '*separatione facta*', after the fraction, in every part, and therefore in every crumb of bread and drop of wine, was stated in Canon 3.[19] This doctrine justifies the *communio sub una*, the withholding of the cup from the laity, practised by the Roman Church lest otherwise any portion of Christ's blood be split and dishonoured. In opposition to John Hus, the demand that the cup be given to the laity was branded by the Council of Constance (1415) as heretical.[20] The Council of Trent confirmed this in opposition to the Reformers: 'If anyone says that, by the precept of God, or by necessity of salvation, all and each of the faithful of Christ ought to receive both species of the most holy sacrament of the Eucharist: let him be anathema.'[21]

Even more serious and far-reaching is the Roman doctrine of the *permanence* of Christ's eucharistic presence. By the priestly change the body and blood of Christ are present in the Eucharist and they *remain there*, in the event of their not being consumed. According to Church law, in the case of the blood this must always be done; not so in the case of the body. This must be carefully reserved and can be given to the sick.[22] The contrary Lutheran view that Christ's body and blood are present only during the use of them (*in usu*), was rejected: 'If anyone says that after the consecration is completed, the body and blood of our Lord Jesus Christ are not in the admirable sacrament of the Eucharist, but [are there] only during the use, whilst it is being taken, and not either before or after; and that, in the hosts, or consecrated particles, which are reserved or which

[18] Sess. 13, ch. 3 (D., 876; M., 307.5; Schaff, II.129f).

[19] D., 885; M., 309.15; Schaff, II.137.

[20] Council of Constance, 1415, Sess. 13 (D., 626).

[21] 'Si quis dixerit, ex Dei praecepto vel ex necessitate salutis omnes et singulos Christi fideles utramque speciem sanctissimi Eucharistiae sacramenti sumere debere: A.S.' Trent Sess. 21, can. 1, *de communione sub utraque* (D., 934; M., 321.20; Schaff, II.174).

[22] Trent Sess. 13, can. 7 (D., 889; M., 309.27; Schaff, II.138).

remain after communion the true body of the Lord remaineth not, let him be anathema.'[23]

From this doctrine the *worship of the host* necessarily follows. The reason is that the Eucharist, unlike the other sacraments, 'not only causes grace but permanently contains the Author of grace Himself'.[24] If the body of Christ is still present after the Eucharist then it must be treated as such. As a result it becomes possible to exhibit and carry it about, as happens in the Corpus Christi processions of the Roman Church. This custom was introduced in 1264 by Pope Urban IV 'in order above all to shake the foolish incredulity of the heretics'.[25] Attached to the procession in demonstration against the heretics, there is an 'exposition of the sacrament' lasting eight days, during which period the 'visit to the Holy of Holies' is to be paid. Roman Catholics kneel down before the host and worship it, in accordance with Roman dogma: 'If anyone says that in the holy sacrament of the Eucharist, Christ the only-begotten Son of God is not to be adored with the worship, even external of latria; and is, consequently, neither to be venerated with a special festive solemnity, nor to be solemnly borne about in procession, according to the laudable and universal rite and custom of holy Church; or is not to be proposed publicly to the people to be adored, and that the adorers thereof are idolaters: let him be anathema.'[26] It is said that it is one and the same Christ who is also worshipped in other ways, 'only His modes of presence are different'.[27] But that is just the point! Our fathers regarded this mode of presence, in which the risen Lord is simply there under the form of bread, and remains there and

[23] 'Si quis dixerit, peracta consecratione in admirabili Eucharistiae sacramento non esse corpus et sanguinem Domini nostri Iesu Christi sed tantum in usu, dum sumitur, non autem ante vel post, et in hostiis seu particulis consecratis quae post communionem reservantur vel supersunt, non remanere verum corpus Domini: A.S.' Sess. 13, can. 4 (D., 886; M., 309.17; Schaff, II.137).

[24] 'Non modo gratiam gignit sed ipsum gratiae auctorem stabili modo continet.' Pius XII, *Mediator Dei*, 1947 (Eng. trans. *Christian Worship*, London 1957, § 139, p. 53).

[25] M., 203.38.

[26] 'Si quis dixerit, in sancto Eucharistiae sacramento Christum unigenitum Dei Filium non esse cultu latriae etiam externo adorandum atque ideo nec festiva peculiari celebritate venerandum, neque in processionibus secundum laudabilem et universalem Ecclesiae sanctae ritum et consuetudinem solemniter circumgestandum vel non publice, ut adoretur, populo proponendum, et eius adoratores esse idololatras: A.S.' Trent Sess. 13, can. 6 (D., 888; M., 309.23; Schaff, II.137).

[27] Bartmann, *Dogmatik*, VOL. II, p. 315.

can be handled, exhibited and carried about in procession, as the diminution of the Risen One into an idol. The Heidelberg Catechism described the Mass as 'an accursed idolatry'[28] because in it Christ is worshipped under the form of bread and wine. Luther's verdict was no milder.[29] Here if anywhere, it is very significant that Rome can produce no scriptural warrant at all in support of its doctrine.[30] Such a Christ is unknown to Scripture.

3. The Reality and Nature of the Sacrifice of the Mass

The doctrine of the Eucharist culminates in the claim that the body and blood of Christ prepared by the priest are offered to God as a sacrifice: 'If anyone says that in the Mass a true and proper sacrifice is not offered to God; or what is offered is nothing else but that Christ is given us to eat: let him be anathema.'[31] It is also said of the Apostles 'that they and other priests offered His body and His blood'.[32] There is in the Church therefore, according to Roman dogma, a sacrifice which is being offered continually, and this sacrifice consists of the body and blood of Christ. As biblical proof texts for this are cited: Gen 14.18, the story of Melchisedek; Mal 1.10f, a passage which speaks of the pure sacrifice which is offered in every place; and, finally, the words of institution themselves, which, while referring to the sacrifice on the Cross, do not mean that the Lord's Supper itself is a sacrifice.

This sacrifice is a 'true and proper' one and, indeed, must be essentially the same as the sacrifice of Jesus Christ on the Cross: 'For *the victim is one and the same*, the same now offering by the ministry of priests who then offered Himself on the Cross, the manner of offering alone being different.'[33] In both cases the

[28] Q. 80.

[29] 'In addition to all this, this dragon's tail, the Mass, has begotten a numerous vermin brood of manifold idolatries.' Smalcald Articles, Art. II, Of the Mass (*Bekenntnisschriften* (*Luth.*), p. 419, 18; *Concordia*, p. 138).

[30] Bartmann, *Dogmatik*, VOL. II, p. 315.

[31] 'Si quis dixerit, in Missa non offerri Deo verum et proprium sacrificium, aut quod offerri non sit aliud quam nobis Christum ad manducandum dari: A.S.' Trent Sess. 22, can. 1, cf. can. 2 (D., 948; M., 324.33; Schaff, II.184).

[32] Sess. 22, can. 2 (D., 949; M., 324.33; Schaff, II.184).

[33] 'Una enim eademque est hostia, idem nunc offerens sacerdotum ministerio, qui se ipsum tunc in cruce obtulit, sola offerendi ratione diversa.' Sess. 22, ch. 2 (D., 940; M., 323.14; Schaff, II.179).

victim is the same, namely Christ Himself: 'in this divine sacrifice which is celebrated in the Mass, that *same Christ* is contained and immolated in an unbloody manner who once offered himself in a bloody manner on the altar of the Cross'.[34]

The essential equivalence of the sacrifice of the Mass with the sacrifice on the Cross is held therefore to consist in the fact that in both instances *Christ Himself offers* the sacrifice. He offered Himself on the Cross and through the ministry of the priest, He offers Himself in the Mass.

The assertion that the sacrifice of the Mass is essentially one with the death on the Cross is explained in this way: the sacrifice of the Mass is a real setting forth (*repraesentatio*) of the sacrifice of the Cross. What was done historically once only, is made present in a sacramental way in the Mass: 'a sacrifice whereby that bloody sacrifice once to be accomplished on the Cross, might be *represented*, and *the memory thereof remain* even unto the end of the world'.[35] We are not to think of it, however, as a mere picture and a mere memorial of the Cross,[36] but in remembrance *the sacrifice of Christ really takes place there on the altar:* 'He instituted the new Passover [to wit] *Himself to be immolated, under visible signs*, by the Church through [the ministry of] priests, *in memory* of His own passage from this world unto the Father.'[37] Bartmann says: 'The Cross and all that it means is really set up, upon our altars. Every altar becomes Golgotha.'[38] Not surprisingly, therefore, many theologians speak of a 'repetition' of the sacrifice of the Cross and the Roman Catechism of a 'renewal' of this sacrifice. In his Encyclical *Mediator Dei* Pius XII uses the Tridentine expression 'represent' (*repraesentare*).[39]

As well as this essential equivalence there is, of course, an

[34] 'In divino hoc sacrificio, quod in Missa peragitur, idem ille Christus continetur et incruente immolatur, qui in ara crucis semel se ipsum cruente obtulit.' *Ibid.*

[35] 'Sacrificium quo cruentum illud in cruce peragendum, repraesentaretur eiusque memoria in finem usque saeculi permaneret.' Sess. 22, ch. 1 (D., 938; M., 322.32; Schaff, II.177).

[36] Not a '*nuda commemoratio*'. Sess. 22, can. 3 (D., 950; M., 324.37; Schaff, II.185).

[37] 'Novum instituit Pascha se ipsum ab Ecclesia per sacerdotes sub signis visibilibus immolandum in memoria transitus sui ex hoc mundo ad patrem.' Sess. 22, ch. 1 (D., 938; M., 322.33 Schaff, II.177f). Cf. Encyclical *Mediator Dei* (Eng. trans. § 72, pp. 32f).

[38] *Dogmatik*, VOL. II,, p. 354.

[39] *Mediator Dei* (Eng, trans. § 71, p. 32).

unessential difference between the sacrifice of the Cross and the sacrifice of the Mass, and even 'the manner of the sacrifice' differs in two respects. Firstly, Christ offers Himself now 'by the ministry of the priests'. By their ordination to the priesthood He has given these authority 'to act *by the power of Christ Himself and in His name*. And therefore when he exercises his priestly power he as it were "lends Christ his tongue and gives Him the use of his hand".'[40] Only the priest can do that. The idea of a concelebration in which the congregation also participates, was rejected by Pius XII as an error.[41] 'The people . . . can in no way possess the priestly right.'[42] In other words, the representation of Christ as the one sacrifice, by the utterance of the words of conversion, has been committed into the power of the priest alone. In the offering of this sacrifice to the glory of God, which then follows, the laity present also share,[43] 'inasmuch as they unite their sentiments of praise, entreaty, expiation, and thanksgiving with the sentiments or intention of the priest, in order . . . that in the very oblation of the victim those sentiments may be presented to God the Father also by the priest's external rite'.[44] The people do not join with the priest in the performance of the visible liturgical action. Secondly, the sacrifice of the Mass differs from the sacrifice of the Cross in that an unbloody sacrifice is offered in the Mass.[45] Christ had once to suffer the bloody death, but now, 'by reason of the glorious condition of His humanity', death no longer has any power over Him.[46] 'But the Eucharistic species under which He is present, symbolise the violent separation of His body and blood, and so a commemorative showing forth of His death is repeated in each Mass, because by distinct representations Christ Jesus is signified and shown forth in the state of victim.'[47]

The *Communion* is not essential to the Mass; it serves only to complete it. But the priest's communion is sufficient to do this;

[40] 'Operandi virtute ac persona ipsius Christi. Quamobrem actione sua sacerdotali Christo quodammodo linguam suam accommodat, manum porrigit.' *Mediator Dei* (Eng. trans. § 73, p. 33). [41] *Op. cit.* (Eng. trans. §§ 86ff, p. 38).

[42] *Op. cit.*, § 88. [43] *Op. cit.* (Eng. trans. § 96, p. 40).

[44] 'Sed idcirco quod sua vota laudis, impetrationis, expiationis gratiarum actionis una cum votis seu mentis intentione sacerdotis, immo Summi ipsius Sacerdotis, eo fine coniungit, ut eadem in ipsa victimae oblatione, externo quoque sacerdotis ritu, Deo Patri exhibeantur.' *Op. cit.* (Eng. trans. § 98, p. 41).

[45] Trent Sess. 22, ch. 2 (D., 940; M., 323.9; Schaff, II.179).

[46] Pius XII, *Mediator Dei* (Eng. trans. § 74, p. 33). [47] *Ibid.*

that of the people is not necessary, even though it is strongly urged.[48] The Council of Trent therefore defended private masses said by a priest alone without the presence of the people, which the Reformers branded as 'corner-masses'. 'But whenever this does not happen [i.e. that faithful are present] the Synod does not for that reason condemn as private and unlawful but approves of and therefore commends those masses in which the priest alone communicates sacramentally; since those masses also ought to be considered as *truly common*: partly because the people communicate spiritually thereat, partly also because they are celebrated by a public minister of the Church, not for himself only but for all the faithful who belong to the body of Christ.'[49] This was expressly confirmed by Pius XII: 'It is in no way necessary that the people should ratify what has been done by the sacred minister.'[50] It is, of course, an ecclesiastical rule 'that no priest should go to the altar without a server who shall serve and answer him'.[51]

4. The Effect of the Sacrifice of the Mass

Against the Reformers, the Council of Trent affirmed the *propitiatory power of the sacrifice* of the Mass: 'If anyone says that the Sacrifice of the Mass is only a sacrifice of praise and of thanksgiving: or that it is a bare commemoration of the sacrifice consummated on the Cross, but not a propitiatory sacrifice: or that it profits him only who communicates; and that it ought not to be offered for the living and the dead, for sins, penalties, satisfactions, and other necessities; let him be anathema.'[52] This does not mean that it is this propitiation itself, but rather

[48] *Op. cit.* (Eng. trans. § 123, p. 48).

[49] 'Nec tamen, si id non semper fiat, propterea missas illas in quibus solus sacerdos sacramentaliter communicat, ut privatas et illicitas damnat, sed probat atque adeo commendat, si quidem illae quoque Missae vere communes censeri debent, partim quod in eis populus spiritualiter communicet partim vero, quod a publico Ecclesiae ministro non pro se tantum, sed pro omnibus fidelibus, qui ad Corpus Christi pertinent, celebrentur.' Sess. 22, ch. 6 (D., 944; M., 324.4; Schaff, II.182). Cf. can 8 (D., 955; M., 325.4; Schaff, II.185f).

[50] *Mediator Dei* (Eng. trans. §101, p. 42).

[51] *C.J.C.*, can. 813. Cf. Woywod, *The New Canon Law*, p. 164.

[52] 'Si quis dixerit, Missae sacrificium tantum esse laudis et gratiarum actionis aut nudam commemorationem sacrificii in cruce peracti non autem propitiatorium; vel soli prodesse sumenti neque pro vivis et defunctis, pro peccatis, poenis, satisfactionibus et aliis necessitatibus offerri deberi: A.S.' Sess. 22, can. 3 (D., 950; M., 324.37; Schaff, II.184f). Cf. *Mediator Dei* (Eng. trans. § 77, p. 34).

that it applies the saving power of the Cross to the forgiveness of daily sins.[53] 'The fruits of the bloody sacrifice are received most plentifully through this unbloody one.'[54]

That applies of course only within definite limits. The sacrifice of the Mass cancels only venial sins, temporal punishments, and required reparations. For the remission of mortal sins, it creates, as it were, the condition: 'Appeased by the offering of this sacrifice, the Lord gives grace and the gift of penitence, and He forgives crimes and sins however grievous they may be.'[55] God, who has been reconciled by the offering of the sacrifice of the Cross in the Mass, makes it possible for the person guilty of mortal sin to return to a state of grace by the sacrament of penance.

The *recipient* of the fruit of the sacrifice of the Mass is first of all the *celebrant* himself. He receives a quite special benefit (*fructus specialissimus*). Next, those *communicating* at the Mass receive a special fruit (*fructus specialis*), and, indeed, *all the faithful* everywhere receive a general fruit (*fructus generalis*). Finally, those *for whom the priest says a Mass*, bringing them before God by the intention of the Mass, receive an imparted fruit (*fructus ministerialis*).[56] Any member of the Church can be remembered in this way: those still living or those already departed, 'who are not yet fully purified'.[57] Indeed since the sacrifice of the Mass is an intercessory sacrifice it can be applied to *all men* without exception, so long as it has their conversion in view. This happens solemnly and publicly every Good Friday.

The Council of Trent also upheld the view that the Mass can be offered *in honour of the Saints*: 'If anyone says it is an imposture to celebrate Masses in honour of the Saints and for obtaining their intercession with God, as the Church intends; let him be anathema.'[58] The comment is added, however, 'that

[53] Trent Sess. 22, ch. 1 (D., 938; M., 322.33; Schaff, II.177).

[54] Sess. 22, ch. 2 (D., 940; Schaff, II.179f).

[55] 'Huius quippe oblatione placatus Dominus gratiam et donum poenitentiae concedens crimina et peccata etiam ingentia dimittit.' *Ibid.*

[56] Cf. D., 1530.

[57] Trent Sess. 22, ch. 2 (D., 940; M., 323.19; Schaff, II.179f).

[58] 'Si quis dixerit, imposturam esse, Missas celebrari in honorem Sanctorum et pro illorum intercessione apud Deum obtinenda, sicut Ecclesia intendit: A.S.' Sess. 22, can. 5 (D., 952; M., 324.42; Schaff, II.185).

the sacrifice is not offered to them but unto God alone who crowned them.'[59]

Clearly, the impressive statements made by the Roman Church about the presence of Christ's sacrifice in the Mass, once again offer in fact too little. The all-sufficient sacrifice of Christ is represented in the Mass and yet the believer in Christ still needs other helpers to intercede for him with God. What kind of Christ is that, and what power has His sacrifice if man still needs other mediators?

Indeed, what kind of Christ is this, who can be made present by a priest in virtue of an invested authority? We said earlier that our fathers saw here a degradation of the living Lord to the status of an idol. Certainly, in the Mass, it is not the Jesus Christ of whom the Barmen Declaration bore witness that he 'acts presently as Lord in Word and Sacrament by the Holy Spirit'. This Christ is 'prepared' by no priest, but is everywhere present where two or three are gathered together in His name (Matt. 18.20).

[59] Sess. 22, ch. 3 (D., 941; M., 323.22; Schaff, II.180).

CHAPTER 12

MARIOLOGY

THE significance attached by the Roman Church to the person and work of Jesus Christ becomes an urgent question when, in conclusion, we examine the role assigned to the mother of Jesus.

1. THE PRIVILEGES OF THE MOTHER OF GOD

It is Roman dogma that Mary was not only a virgin when Jesus was born but also remained a virgin ever afterwards. 'She continued always in spotless virginity, before the birth, during the birth, and for ever after the birth.'[1] Roman theologians evade the New Testament statement that Jesus had brothers and sisters, by the explanation that 'brother' is used here in the broader sense of 'relative'.

In his Bull *Ineffabilis Deus* of 8 December 1854, Pius IX proclaimed as a dogma Mary's freedom from the stain of original sin: 'We define that the doctrine which holds that the most blessed Virgin Mary was, in the first instant of her conception, by the singular grace and privilege of Almighty God, with regard to the merits of Jesus Christ the Saviour of the human race, *preserved free from every stain of original sin*, has been revealed by God and therefore is to be firmly and constantly believed by all the faithful.'[2] This doctrine of the immaculate conception of Mary makes no statement about the parents' part in the conception but only about their child.

[1] 'Perstitisse semper in virginitatis integritate, ante partum, scilicet, in partu et perpetuo post partum.' Paul IV, Const. *Cum quorundam*, 1555 (D., 993). This first became dogma at the Lateran Council of 649 (D., 256).

[2] 'Definimus, doctrinam, quae tenet, beatissimam Virginem Mariam in primo instanti suae conceptionis fuisse singulari omnipotentis Dei gratia et privilegio, intuitu meritorum Christi Iesu Salvatoris humani generis, ab omni originalis culpae labe praeservatim immunem, esse a Deo revelatam atque id circo ab omnibus, fidelibus firmiter constanterque credendam' (D., 1641; M., 447.11; Schaff, II.211f).

By special divine privilege the soul of Mary possessed sanctifying grace from the very beginning. She received this grace in view of the merits of Jesus Christ. It is therefore said that even Mary was redeemed by Christ. But she received this grace before she came into the world 'so that she was not purified from sin' but 'protected' from it.[3] This doctrine has far-reaching consequences. If Mary had been free from original sin then she could not have brought Jesus into the world as one who Himself bore our sinful flesh. Jesus' solidarity with sinful humanity is thereby endangered and with it the whole work of redemption.

The definition of the bodily assumption[4] of Mary by Pius XII on 1 November 1950 was simply a natural consequence of his predecessor's doctrinal definition, just quoted. Mary's bodily assumption to Heaven, celebrated in the Roman Church since the sixth century on 15 August lies in fact, as Bartmann rightly says, 'at the logical terminus of the main Marianic dogma'.[5] Since death is the wages of sin, the sinless one could not remain in death, and so it is now regarded as revealed dogma that 'the immaculate Mother of God, Mary ever virgin, was . . . assumed body and soul to the glory of Heaven'.[6]

It must further be noted that, in the view of the Roman Church, this legendary Mary, in virtue of a divine privilege of grace, never once sinned during the whole course of her life. The Council of Trent states this incidentally: 'No one can completely avoid sin during his lifetime *except by a special privilege from God*, as the Church holds in regard of the Blessed Virgin',[7] 'of such a kind that a greater purity cannot be imagined, except that of God Himself'.[8]

It is not surprising that a special reverence is due to this Mary beyond that which is owed to the Saints, namely, not

[3] Bartmann, *Dogmatik*, VOL. I, p. 430.

[4] For literature see H. Hermelink, 'Das Dogma von der leiblichen Himmelfahrt' in *Kirche in der Zeit*, 1950, pp. 273ff. Cf. also G. Miegge, *The Virgin Mary*, London 1955, pp. 83ff, and the books there cited.

[5] Bartmann, *Dogmatik*, VOL. I, p. 444.

[6] Constitution *Munificentissimus Deus*, 1950 (Eng. trans. *Assumpta est Maria*, London 1951, p. 16).

[7] 'Nisi ex speciali Dei privilegio quemadmodum de beata Virgine tenet Ecclesia.' Trent Sess. 6, can. 23 (D., 833; M., 302.15; Schaff, II.115).

[8] Pius XI, Encyclical *Lux veritatis*, 1931 (*Heilslehre der Kirche, Dokumente von Pius IX bis Pius XII*, Freiburg 1933, p. 473).

δουλεῖα but ὑπερδουλεῖα. This is expressed in a cycle of Marian festivals, recalling the sequence of festivals in honour of Christ Himself: 2 February, Purification of the Blessed Virgin Mary (Candlemas); 25 March, Annunciation of the Blessed Virgin Mary; 15 August, Assumption of the Blessed Virgin Mary; 8 September, Nativity of the Blessed Virgin Mary; 8 December, Immaculate Conception of the Blessed Virgin Mary. In addition there are ten lesser Marian festivals.

2. Mary's Place in the Work of Redemption

Christ's redemptive work is already threatened by the doctrine of the person of Mary. This threat becomes still more evident when we hear of the actions which the Roman Church assigns to her. Here we come to the heart of the matter. Here, the gulf which separates Rome from the Church of the Gospel becomes quite visible. We may preface our remarks by citing two witnesses who demonstrate this and are for that reason referred to by Karl Barth in his *Dogmatics*.[9] In his *Summa theologica*, Thomas Aquinas says: 'The Blessed Virgin is said to have merited to bear the Lord of all; not that she merited His Incarnation, but because by the grace bestowed upon her she merited that grade of purity, which fitted her to be Mother of God.'[10] Here it is taught that what is true of every man is true of Mary; namely, that he is capable by prevenient grace of fitting himself to receive justifying and sanctifying grace. Barth rightly says: 'The creature blessed in virtue of its acquiescence is the real object of Mariology.'[11] Eric Przywara has confirmed this view by saying: 'According to the Catholic doctrine of the *analogia entis*, there exist possibilities for a genuinely incarnational cosmos, inclusive of body and soul, society and individual, because these in their totality are "open" towards God. From the standpoint of the Catholic *analogia entis*, creation in its totality is the vision which in the parables looks beyond all parables to the incomparable God, and is the receptive readiness for Him: "Behold the handmaid of the Lord! Be it unto

[9] *Church Dogmatics*, VOL. I, 2, p. 144.

[10] 'Beata Virgo dicitur meruisse portare Dominum omnium, non quia meruit ipsum incarnari sed quia meruit ex gratia sibi data illum puritatis et sanctitatis gradum, ut congrue possit esse mater Dei.' *Summa Theol.*, III, Q. 2, art. ii ad 3 (Eng. trans. VOL. II, p. 2043*r*).

[11] *Church Dogmatics*, VOL. I, 2, p. 144.

me according to thy Word." '[12] It can be truly said that, in Mariology, Rome's understanding of the basic relationship of man to God becomes manifest. Here in Mary we are confronted by man as Rome understands him.

Since the sixteenth or the seventeenth century Roman theologians have referred to Mary as the co-worker in redemption (*co-operatrix in redemptione*) or Co-redemptress (*corredemptrix*).[13] Benedict XV said of her: 'Thus she suffered with her suffering and dying Son and virtually died with Him. Thus for the salvation of men she renounced her motherly privileges in relation to her Son, and to appease the divine justice offered her Son, so far as that pertained to her, so that one can justly say that with Christ, *she herself redeemed* mankind.'[14] Pius XII expressed himself similarly and more explicitly in the Encyclical *Mystici corporis*.[15] And Pius X very significantly distinguished Mary's saving work from that of Jesus Christ: 'Since Mary surpasses all in holiness and inward unity with Christ and since she was associated by Christ for the work of human salvation, she merits for us *de congruo*, as it is said, what Christ has merited *de condigno*.'[16] This active participation of Mary in the work of redemption begins with the Incarnation, which she believed and served, and ends with her subjective joint-sacrifice on the Cross. Many theologians still have reservations about the title 'Co-redemptress', as being open to misinterpretation and also because Mary's share in the redemptive work can only be a mere co-operation and a ministerial one at that. But recent papal statements make it clear whither this development is leading, and, indeed, must lead given the premises of Roman theology.

If Mary thus co-operates with God in the work of salvation, the same applies to the communication of salvation to men. Pius XI called her 'Mediatrix of our reconciliation with God'.[17]

[12] *Religionsphilosophie katholischer Theologie* (Eng. trans. *Polarity*, Oxford 1935, p. 73). [13] D., 1978 *a*, note 2.

[14] Benedict XV in the Encyclical *Inter sodalicia*, 1918: 'Ita cum Filio patiente et moriente passa est et paene commortua, sic materna in Filium iura pro hominum salute abdicavit placandaeque Dei iustitiae, quantum ad se pertinebat, Filium immolavit, ut dici merito queat, ipsam cum Christo humanum genus redemisse' (*ibid.*). [15] D., 2291 (Eng. trans. § 110, pp. 67f).

[16] 'Quoniam universis sanctitate praestat coniunctioneque cum Christo atque a Christo ascita in humanae salutis opus, "de congruo" ut aiunt, promeret nobis, quae Christus "de condigno" promeruit.' Encycl. *Ad diem*, 1904 (D., 1978 *a*).

[17] Encyclical *Miserentissimus Redemptor*, 1928 (*Heilslehre der Kirche*, p. 147).

Pius IX, who defined the immaculate conception, had already said: 'Our salvation is based upon the holy Virgin . . . so that if there is any hope and spiritual healing for us we *receive it solely and uniquely from her*.'[18] For Christ 'who is the only Mediator between God and Man, wished to have His mother beside Him as the intercessor for sinners and as the dispenser and mediatrix of grace'.[19] Thus it is she who causes the stream of grace to flow, not directly of course, but indirectly by her intercession: 'She too it was who by her most powerful intercession obtained for the new-born Church the prodigious Pentecostal outpouring of that Spirit of the divine Redeemer, who had already been given on the Cross.'[20] Hence she is the 'Mediatrix of all graces'[21] or 'the spiritual mother of all members of Christ'.[22] Theologians today say that the following points still need 'clarification': '(1) How she mediates all graces, and (2) what the basis in revelation is for this mediation.'[23] But how long will they be allowed to ask such critical questions? The cult of the beloved Lady, the human being who co-operates in the work of redemption, increasingly pushes the Redeemer Himself and His work into the shadows.[24]

3. The Worship of Images of Mary

Our account of Mariology would be incomplete without at least a brief word about images of Mary and the worship of them. We know that the Council of Trent taught that all images, including those of Mary, should be honoured '*not that any divinity or virtue is believed to be in them* . . . but because the honour which is shown them is referred to the prototypes which

[18] Encyclical of 2 February 1849, quoted from Chambon, *Maria, die Herbstreife eines Menschenkults*, Essen 1950, p. 25.

[19] 'Qui unus cum sit mediator Dei et hominum suam sibi matrem adsciscere voluit peccatorum advocatam gratiaeque ministram ac mediatricem.' Pius XI, *Miserentissimus Redemptor* (*Heilslehre der Kirche*, p. 147).

[20] 'Ipsa fuit, quae validissimis suis precibus impetravit, ut Divini Redemptoris Spiritus, iam in cruce datus, recens ortae Ecclesiae prodigialibus muneribus Pentecostes die conferretur.' Pius XII, *Mystici corporis* (D., 2291; Eng. trans. § 110, p. 67).

[21] 'Universorum munerum dispensatrix.' Pius X, *Ad diem* (D., 1978 *a*).

[22] 'Omnium membrorum Christi sanctissima genetrix.' Pius XII, *Mystici corporis* (D., 2291; Eng. trans. p. 67).

[23] Bartmann, *Dogmatik*, VOL. I, p. 442.

[24] Pius XII even ventured to apply to Mary the saying of Jesus in Matt. 11.28: 'Come unto me . . .'. Encyclical, *Le Pèlerinage de Lourdes*, 1957 (Eng. trans. § 20, p. 15).

those images represent'.[25] This principle applies also to the so-called 'grace images': 'There is no causal connexion at all between the image in itself and any possible favour granted.'[26] But then it is not easy to understand how it is permissible for the various 'grace images' of Mary sometimes to acquire special celebrity for particular healing powers, so that the honouring of one image promises freedom from barrenness, the honouring of another freedom from some other misfortune. It is further hard to understand why tiny replicas are brought into contact with the 'grace image' and when the place of contact has been marked returned to the faithful.[27] Finally, the Council of Trent's theory conflicts with the tolerance shown by Rome to the swallowing of pictures of Mary as a means of healing 'provided only that precaution is taken against all superstition and the danger of falling into it'.[28] The image of Mary has almost become a 'sub-hypostasis of the Queen of Heaven'.[29]

The doctrine of the Mediatrix is placed in a still clearer light by the devotion offered to her, the cult of her image and by the places where she is supposed to have appeared to men. Mary represents the creature and its readiness for supernatural life, *analogia entis*. 'Grace does not destroy nature but perfects it.'[30]

[25] 'Non quod credatur inesse aliqua in iis divinitas vel virtus, . . . sed quoniam honos, qui eis exhibetur, refertur ad prototypa, quae illa repraesentant.' Sess. 25 (D., 986; M., 334.5; Schaff, II.201f).

[26] Bartmann, *Dogmatik*, VOL. II, p. 205.

[27] Chambon, *Maria*, p. 15.

[28] In keeping with this is the tolerance still shown today in Spain, for example, of the pictures of Mary on so many postage stamps. But this should not surprise us in view of the fact that even in the recent papal Encyclical *Le Pèlerinage de Lourdes*, the miraculous power of an image of Mary is extolled (Eng. trans. § 4, p. 5).

[29] Chambon, *Maria*, p. 15.

[30] 'Gratia non tollit naturam sed perficit.' Thomas Aquinas, *Summa Theol.*, I, Q. I, 8 ad 2. (Eng. trans. VOL. I, p. 6.)

II

THE GOSPEL AND THE ORTHODOX CHURCH

INTRODUCTION

We now ask how the Orthodox Church interprets and communicates the Gospel of Jesus Christ. This question is not easy to answer, since Orthodoxy acknowledges no infallible teaching authority and, in other respects too, presents a much less uniform appearance than Roman Catholicism. There is a large group of separate Orthodox National Churches, uncoordinated by any single organisation, and also with widely different views on many questions.

An historical approach would have necessitated dealing with the Orthodox Church first and only then with the Roman Church, since, after the separation from Rome (final in 1054), Orthodox Christendom had no part in the rich development undergone by the Western Church, and has remained in much the same condition down to the present day. As we said earlier, our reason for choosing a different course and only now turning our attention to the Orthodox Church, is a practical one. The Roman Church has tended increasingly to seal itself off from the Gospel, so that we are bound to ask, in all seriousness, whether it is not in fact another Gospel which is being preached there. All we can rightly learn from Rome is how not to be the Church. With the Orthodox Church, the case is different. In an encyclical addressed to 'all the Churches of Christ' in January 1920, the Church of Constantinople was the first Church to make an official proposal 'to bring about an alliance and union of Churches' which would, as the Patriarch's covering letter suggested, match the then newly founded League of Nations. Of fundamental importance was the appeal the encyclical made to the Churches 'no longer to look upon each other as distant strangers but as relatives belonging to the family of Christ, "as fellow heirs, members of the same body, and partakers of the promise in Christ Jesus through the Gospel" [Eph. 3.6]'.[1]

[1] W. A. Visser't Hooft, the General Secretary of the World Council of Churches,

Since the World Conference of Churches on 'Life and Work' at Stockholm in 1925 and that on 'Faith and Order' at Lausanne in 1925, a considerable section of Orthodox Christendom has, consistently with this attitude, been in vital touch with the rest of non-Roman Christendom, and, since the formation of the World Council of Churches at Amsterdam in 1948, even in official connexion with it. The Orthodox representatives at the Edinburgh Conference in 1937 declared: 'In spite of all our differences, our common Lord and Master is *One*—Jesus Christ who will lead us to a more and more close collaboration for the edifying of the body of Christ.'[2] This submission to our common Lord, as well as the desire for brotherly co-operation, brings the Orthodox Church very close to the other non-Roman Churches.[3]

referred to this Encyclical and its importance at the meeting of the Council at Rhodes in 1959, the first ever to be held in an Orthodox country. (*Ecumenical Review*, XII, pp. 70ff. The text of the Encyclical is given there, pp. 79-82.) See also S. C. Neill in *A History of the Ecumenical Movement*, edd. R. Rouse and S. C. Neill, London 1954, p. 446; and N. Zernov, *ibid.*, p. 654. TR.

[2] *The Second World Conference on Faith and Order*, ed. Leonard Hodgson, Edinburgh 1937, p. 157.

[3] Cf. also the official report of the first meeting between delegates of the Russian Orthodox Church and those of the World Council, in Utrecht, August 1958: 'The basis which enabled us to meet was our brotherhood in Christ.' *Ecumenical Review* XI (1958), p. 79.

CHAPTER I

THE SOURCES

1. Holy Scripture and Tradition

'THE Orthodox Church acknowledges the *Divine Revelation*, contained in Holy Scripture, and in the holy Tradition of the Church, as the source and basis of the truths to be believed.'[1]

Originally the revelation had been handed down exclusively by oral tradition, but was subsequently in part written down.[2] Understood in this way the tradition is equivalent to the Gospel.[3] With this sense in mind, the Orthodox Conference at Moscow in 1948 reaffirmed its adherence to an older statement: 'We shall hand on unaltered to future generations the Holy Faith which we ourselves have received'.[4] With its strong emphasis on the word 'unaltered', this formula has quite a Reformation ring about it. The Orthodox Church regards itself as the guardian and trustee of the deposit of faith committed to its care, or of the Tradition, as it is also called.[5] A modern theologian writes: 'It is an undeniable fact . . . that we in the Church stand on the firm rock of Apostolic Tradition. If we were to quit the solid ground of this gracious reality, we should simply be abandoning the Church. It would mean we had already changed Christianity into a speculative doctrine, into a game of gnostic fantasy, a subjective dream.'[6]

The term 'tradition' is also used, however, in a narrower sense, as for example in the quotation at the beginning of this

[1] Metropolitan Seraphim, *Die Ostkirche*, Stuttgart 1950, p. 31.

[2] K. Dyobouniotes, in *Ekklesia, Eine Sammlung von Selbsdarstellungen der christlichen Kirchen*, ed. F. Siegmund Schultze, VOL. x, Leipzig 1939, p. 55.

[3] Cf. the excerpts from the *Commonitorium* of Vincent of Lerins given in L. Müller's fine essay 'Die Bedeutung der Tradition in des orthodoxen Theology und Kirche', in *Kirche und Kosmos*, Orthodoxie und evangelisches Christentum, No. 2. Witten 1949, p. 82.

[4] *Dokumente der orthodoxen Kirchen, zur ökumenischen Fragen*, No. 1, Witten 1949, p. 36.

[5] Cf. 2 Tim. 1.14.

[6] Kartaschov, as quoted by L. Müller in *Kirche und Kosmos*, p. 82.

chapter. 'How is divine revelation spread among men and preserved in the true Church?' asks the Russian Philaret in his catechism. Answer: 'By two channels, *holy tradition* and *Holy Scripture*.'[7] Whereas this catechism is careful to show that Scripture and tradition are in essential agreement, a modern Greek theologian says that 'Apostolic tradition is not just an interpretation of the divine revelation contained in the New Testament, but is also an addition'. He therefore holds that there are 'two equally valuable sources of doctrine'.[8] A modern Russian theologian, on the other hand, puts the position more carefully: 'Holy Scripture is the source of doctrine for every Christian Church, but the existence of Holy Scripture has itself been conditioned by the holy tradition.'[9]

Holy Scripture is generally accorded a unique status. This was done, for example, in the discussions between the Anglicans and the representatives of the Ecumenical Patriarch.[10] The biblical authors are regarded as inspired by the Holy Spirit, but not the holy fathers of the Church. The latter were simply illuminated by God 'to explain by the power of reason the truths already given'.[11] The important place of the Bible in Russian Christianity is well known. In the official Russian Catechism, Philaret says that through it 'divine revelation is preserved more exactly and unchangeably. In Holy Scripture we read the words of the Prophets and Apostles precisely as if we were living with them and heard them.'[12] By Holy Scripture the Catechism means the books of the Old and New Testaments, without the Apocrypha. In the eighteenth century there were, however, two Synods of Constantinople which described the apocryphal books as canonical. The same applies to the *Confessio Dosithei* of 1672, which was approved by all the Patriarchs. Present-day theologians are not unanimous on this question.

The *tradition* which, alongside Holy Scripture, is authoritative for the belief of Orthodox Christians, is today only in

[7] Q. 16. Schaff, II.448.
[8] K. Dyobouniotes, in *Ekklesia*, VOL. X, p. 55. Cf. also p. 143.
[9] Doktussov, 'Die Orthodoxie', in *Kirche in die Zeit*, X (1955), p. 224 *b*.
[10] *Ekklesia*, VOL. X, p. 142.
[11] Doktussov, in *Kirche in die Zeit*, X (1955), p. 226 *a*.
[12] Q. 22. Schaff, II.449.

part clearly defined and recognised by all. It includes the doctrinal decisions of the *seven Ecumenical Councils*: Nicea (325, for the *homoousia* of the Son, against Arius), Constantinople (381, for the divinity of the Holy Spirit), Ephesus (431, for the unity of the God-man, against Nestorius), Chalcedon (451, against the monophysitism of Eutyches), Constantinople II (553, against Origen), Constantinople III (680, for two wills in Christ and the subordination of the human will to the divine will, against the Monothelites), Nicea II (787, for the veneration of images), and, usually, the Quinisext, so called because it was regarded as completing the fifth and sixth Councils (692, list of witnesses to the tradition in Canon 2, recognition of the Synod of Carthage 418, regulations for example about fasting, marriage of priests, the equality of the Bishop of Byzantium with the Pope). Along with Holy Scripture, the decisions of these Councils form the absolute basis of the doctrine and practice of the whole of Orthodox Christendom. It should be remembered, however, that these Councils 'established no new doctrines not already contained in the revelation'.[13] Keeping as it does to the agreed Christian witness of the first eight centuries, the Orthodox Church regards itself as the ancient Church and sees in the innovations of other Christian communions a departure from the ancient heritage.

One witness, of course, stands out from this basic tradition and is given priority over the others, namely, the so-called Nicaeno-Constantinopolitan Creed, 'a baptismal symbol, probably based on a Jerusalem original, with Nicene phrases added, which somehow found its way into the official acts of the first Council of Constantinople and in time completely displaced the original creed of Nicea'.[14] This Nicaeno-Constantinopolitan Creed (without the *filioque* clause, of course) is the *essential Confession of Faith* (*σύμβολον τῆς πίστεως*) of Orthodoxy. It is the distinctive feature of Orthodox Christianity and, as such, not only the rule of all doctrine and instruction but above all, the heart of Orthodox worship. Of the other two ancient creeds that still retain their position in the West, only the Athana-

[13] Doktussov, in *Kirche in die Zeit*, x (1955), p. 224 *a*.

[14] Loofs, *Symbolik*, pp. 33ff. Cf. J. N. D. Kelly, *Early Christian Creeds*, ch. X, esp. pp. 310ff.

sian has been accepted within the Orthodox Church, here and there.

The *Apostolic Fathers* and the *recognised theologians* of the Church also bear witness to the tradition. John Damascene (*d.* 753) occupies a special place among the accepted theologians because the third section of his work *Πηγὴ γνώσεως* ('Fount of Knowledge') provides a classic statement of Greek theology.[15] Nevertheless, as we have seen, these teachers simply 'explain . . . the truths already given'.

The *liturgical books* of the Church, especially the *Euchologion* containing the order of the Mass, and the formularies for the other Church sacraments and ceremonies, rank as indispensable sources of the tradition. The most important liturgy is that of Chrysostom.[16] In these texts, it is held, 'the faith of the ancient Church has been preserved'. That is why Heiler can say: 'For the Orthodox Church, the mediation of grace through the sacraments, the changing of the bread and wine into the body and blood as well as the sacrificial character of the Eucharist, the apostolic succession of bishops and priests, the reverencing and invocation of the Mother of God and of the saints, the efficacy of prayers for the departed, are all obligatory norms of belief, even though they have never been defined as dogma by any Council.'[17]

It was misleading when Kimmel published later documents of the fifteenth and sixteenth centuries in a book bearing the title *Libri Symbolici ecclesiae orientalis*. In his account of the 'source and basis of Orthodox belief', Metropolitan Seraphim does not mention them at all.[18] A modern Greek theologian also writes: 'Misled by false analogies, a few theologians have wrongly described these confessional documents and even the acts of these Synods as the symbolic books of the Orthodox Church, whereas both in form and content they lack the characteristics of such books. Written in a decadent age they are not free from heretical tendencies, nor do they always

[15] See F. Kattenbusch, 'John of Damascus', in *New Schaff-Herzog*, VOL. VI. A translation of Part III of the *Fount of Knowledge* is given in Nicene and Post-Nicene Fathers, 2nd Series, VOL. IX, New York 1890-1900.

[16] Eng. trans. *The Orthodox Liturgy*, London 1939. Greek texts in E. F. Brightman, *Liturgies Eastern and Western*, Oxford 1896. VOL. I.

[17] F. Heiler, *Urkirche und Ostkirche*, Münich 1937, p. 190.

[18] Seraphim, *Die Ostkirche*, pp. 31f.

accurately state the Orthodox standpoint. They also contain misinterpretations and contradictions.'[19]

The most important of them is the *Confessio orthodoxa*[20] composed in Latin in 1640 at the suggestion of Peter Mogilas, the Metropolitan of Kiev. This doctrinal statement is in the form of a catechism defending the Orthodox faith against the Calvinistic teachings of Cyril Lucaris,[21] the recently executed Patriarch of Constantinople. Lucaris had at one time actually been in Geneva, and in 1629, during his stay there, had as Patriarch published his *Orientalis confessio Christianae fidei*, consisting of eighteen doctrinal articles and four questions.[22] This, when translated into Greek, met with strong opposition on all sides. The *Confessio orthodoxa*, on the other hand, was approved by the four Orthodox patriarchs. In 1672, the Jerusalem Patriarch Dositheus persuaded a Synod to adopt yet another anti-Lucaris confession, the *Confessio Dosithei*[23] as it is called, which refuted Cyril's Confession section by section. This Confession is embedded in a memorandum of the Synod itself entitled *'Ασπίς ὀρθοδοξίας*.[24] For some time these two Confessions of Mogilas and Dositheus were regarded as authoritative statements of Orthodox belief. These seventeenth-century statements, however, were strongly influenced by Roman Scholasticism, and the more this has been recognised the more their trustworthiness has been questioned. They no longer have any normative significance nowadays.[25]

Kimmel's collection also includes the confession which the

[19] D. Balanos, in *Ekklesia*, VOL. X, p. 45.

[20] Greek and Latin texts in Schaff, II.275-400.

[21] On Cyril Lucaris see Schaff, I.54-57; Florovsky in *History of the Ecumenical Movement*, edd. Rouse and Neill, pp. 183ff; G. A. Hadjiantoniou, 'Cyril Lucaris the Greek Reformer', in *Reformed and Presbyterian World* XXVI (1960), pp. 3-14. Dr Hadjiantoniou has written a full-length study of Lucaris, an English version of which was published as *Protestant Patriarch, The Life of Cyril Lucaris, Patriarch of Constantinople*, Richmond, Va. 1961.

[22] E. J. Kimmel, *Libri symbolici ecclesiae orientalis*, henceforth cited as *Libri symbolici*, Jena 1843-50, pp. 24-44; J. Michalescu, *Die Bekenntnisse und die wichtigsten Glaubenszeugnisse der griechisch-orientalischen Kirche*, henceforth cited as *Bekenntnisse und Glaubenszeugnisse*, Leipzig 1904, pp. 29-122. Summary in Schaff, I.56f.

[23] Kimmel, *Libri symbolici*, pp. 425-74; Michalescu, *Bekenntnisse und Glaubenszeugnisse*, pp. 160-81; Schaff, II.400-44, Summary in I.62-67.

[24] Kimmel, *Libri symbolici*, pp. 325-488; Michalescu, *Bekenntnisse und Glaubenszeugnisse*, pp. 126ff. See Schaff, I.61, n. 1.

[25] Cf. Seraphim, *Die Ostkirche*, p. 18f, and the writers quoted by Heiler, *Urkirche und Ostkirche*, pp. 192f.

Patriarch Gennadius wrote out for the Sultan in 1453 after the fall of Constantinople,[26] as well as the private confession of Metrophanes Kritopulos, a friend of Cyril Lucaris, composed during a stay in Helmstedt for the Lutheran theologians there.[27] But neither of these documents attained credal status.

More important still are the *Catechisms*, especially the 'Longer Catechism' composed by Philaret, the Metropolitan of Moscow, in 1839 and adopted by the Holy Synod.[28]

2. The Church as the Interpreter of Tradition

It would be wrong to infer, from what has so far been said about Scripture and tradition, that the Orthodox Church regards itself merely as the custodian of the doctrines set down in Scripture and in the documents just mentioned. 'It is naive to imagine that the only duty of Orthodoxy is to record and preserve the ancient tradition intact.'[29] We recall that the Orthodox Church also employs the term 'tradition' in the sense of 'divine revelation'. That is to say, the Orthodox Church regards itself primarily as 'the guardian of the divine revelation'.[30] As such, it influenced the formation of Holy Scripture. The various books of the Bible came to form the Canon because the Church recognised them as authentic testimony to revelation. The Church lent its own authority to the written witnesses of the tradition. This function of the Church is, however, a continuing one. As the custodian of divine revelation the Church can authorise doctrines even today. 'Scripture is external, tradition is external, only the Holy Spirit of God is internal.'[31] This Spirit dwells in the Church. On the basis of this conviction, a modern theologian can even say: 'The life of the Church is the continuing

[26] Kimmel, *Libri symbolici*, pp. 11-20; Michalescu, *Bekenntnisse und Glaubenszeugnisse*, pp. 17-20. The conclusion of this confession (chs. 13-20) is spurious, as is also a dialogue attributed to Gennadius (Kimmel, *Libri symbolici*, pp. 1-10; Michalescu, *Bekenntnisse und Glaubenszeugnisse*, pp. 255-61). See Schaff, I.46-50.

[27] Kimmel, *Libri symbolici*, Append., pp. 1-123; Michalescu, *Bekenntnisse und Glaubenszeugnisse*, pp. 186-252. See Schaff, I.52f.

[28] In Philaret, *Geschichte der Kirche Russlands*, Frankfurt 1872, VOL. II. An English translation of the Longer Catechism is given in Schaff, II.445-542. See also Schaff, I.71-73.

[29] Kartaschov, as quoted by L. Müller, in *Kirche und Kosmos*, p. 95.

[30] Seraphim, *Die Ostkirche*, p. 33.

[31] Chomiakov, 'Die Einheit der Kirche' in *Östl. Christentum*, II.6, as quoted by Heiler, *Urkirche und Ostkirche*, p. 187.

revelation of the fullness of truth invested in her.'[32] Because of the indwelling Spirit the Church can always interpret divine revelation afresh. The Church's life is the unfolding of the divine truth entrusted to her.

That is not to say that everything in the Church's life expresses the divine truth. Every individual member of the Church, whether priest or layman, can err. It is the Church 'as a whole' which is 'infallible'.[33] This does not mean that only an Ecumenical Council can declare the divine truth with authority. 'The Church as a whole can reject a supposedly ecumenical synod (e.g. the Robber Synod).'[34] There is no formal characteristic by which to identify what is in accordance with the divine truth. 'Even a doctrine defined by a Council becomes a dogma only when it has been accepted as such by the Ecumenical Church.' 'The decisive factor therefore is the *consensus ecclesiae*.'[35] The Orthodox Patriarchs told Pius IX in 1848: 'With us, neither the Patriarchs nor the Synods can introduce innovations, because the custodian of religion is the body of the Church itself, namely, the whole community, which desires its faith to be preserved always and unalterably in accord with its fathers.'[36] Ecumenical Synods are infallible only as they agree with this consensus. They have therefore only a derived infallibility. The Church as a whole, on the other hand, has decisive authority even apart from Synods. What is 'accepted by the mind of the Church as a whole' ranks as dogma, therefore.[37] Theology's task is to test whether or not this is so in the case of any particular doctrine.

Orthodox theologians show evident signs of discomfort under the burden this task imposes on them.[38] Yet the obvious and almost inevitable solution, namely, to call in the aid of an infallible teaching office, is firmly rejected, not merely in the form of Papalism but even in that of Conciliarism. That is a good and hopeful sign. But is the Orthodox Church wise thus to make a virtue of necessity and to rely on the 'instinct of the

[32] Bulgakov in *Procès-verbal du Ier congrès de théologie orthodoxe,* Athens 1936, p. 19, as quoted by L. Müller in *Kirche und Kosmos,* p. 96.

[33] Dyobouniotes in *Ekklesia,* VOL. X, p. 55.

[34] *Op. cit.,* p. 56.

[35] Seraphim, *Die Ostkirche,* p. 33.

[36] Heiler, *Urkirche und Ostkirche,* p. 218.

[37] Dyobouniotes, in *Ekklesia,* VOL. X, p. 55.

[38] *Op. cit.,* pp. 57f.

whole'?[39] Would it not be better to keep to the words of the prophets and apostles, which we can read 'as if we were living with them and listening to them'?[40] Must not the Church continually let these men, who saw and heard the Lord, bear witness to her concerning Jesus Christ, instead of courting the danger of listening merely to the sound of her own voice, the voice of the conscience of the whole Church?

[39] Kartaschov as quoted by L. Müller in *Kirche und Kosmos*, p. 97.
[40] Philaret, *Longer Catechism*, Q. 22 (Schaff, II.449).

CHAPTER 2

THE ORTHODOX VIEW OF THE CHURCH

THE Russian theologian Florovsky begins his contribution to the Amsterdam volume on the nature of the Church by saying that there is *no formal definition* of the Church '*which could claim any doctrinal authority*'.[1] Without exception the usual definitions all bear the imprint of their times. The position is thus very similar to that of Roman Catholicism, only much more open because Orthodoxy firmly rejects the dogma defined by the Vatican Council. That fact is of the greatest importance for the doctrine of the Church.

The Orthodox Church nevertheless makes it quite clear what it believes the Church to be. Already in the previous chapter we saw that the Church is the custodian and interpreter of the tradition, so it is appropriate that, with this description in mind, we should at once listen to further statements of Orthodox theologians giving their view of the Church.

1. THE CHURCH AS A SACRAMENTAL SOCIETY

'In Orthodoxy the Church is neither an institution nor a collective [by this is meant: a collection of individual believers]. It is essentially a life, more precisely, a divine-human life, the continuation of the life of Christ, in believers who are in communion with Christ, and by the power of the Holy Spirit.'[2] Thus the Church is frequently described in Pauline terms as the body of Christ, and 'the fullness of him who fills all in all' (Eph. 1.23). These last words are taken to mean that the Church as Christ's body fills out Christ Himself. In support of this, Florovsky appeals to Chrysostom: 'Observe how he [i.e. St

[1] G. Florovsky, 'The Church—her Nature and Task', in *Universal Church*, p. 43. Cf. H. Alivisatos in *The Nature of the Church*, ed. R. N. Flew, London 1952, p. 41.
[2] Seraphim, *Die Ostkirche*, p. 64.

Paul] introduces Him as having need of all the members. This means that only then will the Head be filled up, when the body is rendered perfect, when we are all together, co-united and knit together.' This modern theologian concludes from this that the Church is 'an extension and the "fulness" of the Holy Incarnation'. He even ventures the dangerous statement: 'The Incarnation is being completed in the Church.'[3]

This completion of the Incarnation took place in principle at Pentecost, when 'once for all' the Holy Spirit entered into the world redeemed by Christ. What happened then was a kind of renewed Incarnation. The place in the world where the Spirit took up residence was the Church. Christ baptised it with the promised baptism of fire, when He sent down the Spirit upon it from the Father, and thus incorporated the faithful into His body. What happened then continues to happen in the Church since then, by means of the sacraments. 'The sacramental life of the Church is the continuation of Pentecost.'[4] And since it was Christ Himself who then returned to His own in the Spirit, so too He now dwells, 'in a sacramental way', in the Church which is His body. The final reality for which the Church longs is thus already in her midst now. Therefore the Church as a sacramental society is also an eschatological society. In the Church 'the ultimate is being realised within the stream of historical happenings and events'.[5] It '*is*' in fact an organism of Divine grace.

The sacramental character of the Church is also to the fore when we ask about its *task*. Florovsky actually says that this consists in preaching the Gospel—where on the Roman side do we ever hear anything like that? The Church has to bear witness to the new life in Christ by word and deed. But this activity must aim 'to introduce' men 'into the New Reality . . . through their faith and repentance'. To this end 'the ministry of the Word is completed in the ministry of the Sacraments.'[6]

2. The Hierarchy

According to Orthodox doctrine, the Holy Spirit poured out at

[3] Florovsky, in *Universal Church*, p. 50.

[4] *Op. cit.*, p. 48. [5] *Op. cit.*, p. 54.

[6] *Op. cit.*, p. 55. Cf. Alivisatos in *The Nature of the Church*, ed. Flew, p. 53: 'The means to bring about this purpose of the Church are Word and Sacraments.'

Pentecost has been transmitted from the Apostles to their successors right down to the present day by the laying on of hands. 'Pentecost is continued and made permanent in the Church by means of the Apostolic Succession.'[7] The latter is of the essence of the Church, therefore. It is the mystical bond which secures the Church's unity. Apostolic succession is a charismatic principle rather than a principle of Church Law. It becomes especially clear at this point that, unlike the Roman Church, Orthodoxy regards itself not as a judicial institution but as a charismatic organism.

The successors of the Apostles, *the bishops*, certainly have the supreme authority here on earth; but this is essentially a sacramental authority, not a judicial one. As the authentic vessels of the Holy Spirit, bishops alone have the power to ordain priests and to perform those sacramental acts not entrusted to the priest. Without the bishops there is no spiritual office in the Church.[8] They are therefore the instruments of the Church's unity, beyond the bounds of the regional Churches which together make up the whole Orthodox Church. Indeed, they link their Churches both with the past and with the future.

The *priests* ordained by the bishops secure the unity of each local Church by celebrating the Eucharist, since the Lord Himself is present in the Eucharistic meal. There is, therefore, no upbuilding of the Church without the priests and no unity of the Church without the bishops. Yet only together with the laity do these constitute the organism of the Church. 'Clergy and laity make together the fullness (*pleroma*) of the Church and the expression of its authority through the conscience of the Church.'[9] All believers have the same dignity. They are all members of Christ's body, it is only their functions that differ.

The Orthodox Church acknowledges only one Head, Jesus Christ. 'There cannot be another Head, since every body can have only one head.'[10] This argument, based not on the nature of Christ but on the nature of the body, is significant. It shows the extent to which the Orthodox view of the Church is dominated by the idea of an organism. As the Head of the body,

[7] Florovsky, in *Universal Church*, p. 51.
[8] Anglican Conversations with the Orthodox, *Ekklesia*, VOL. X, p. 141.
[9] Alivisatos in *The Nature of the Church*, ed. Flew, p. 53.
[10] Seraphim, *Die Ostkirche*, p. 67.

Christ Himself is also '*the only true Minister of the Church.* All others are but stewards of His mysteries.'[11] The Patriarchs of the regional Orthodox Churches are not the heads of these Churches. They have merely a position of honour among the other bishops. Each patriarch is *primus inter pares*. Contemporary theologians go so far as to say: 'The Eastern Church recognises no formal juridical authority. For her, Christ, the apostles, the Church Councils are not "authority". There is no question here of authority, but of an infinite stream of the life of grace, which has its source in Christ.'[12] The Orthodox Church, which points so positively to Jesus Christ as the only Head of the Church, therefore rejects vigorously the Roman dogma of the Pope's episcopal authority over the whole Church, and of his infallibility. Even today she would still, of course, give the Pope a position of honour above the other Patriarchs in accordance with the ancient canons, if the Pope renounced his unwarranted claim.

3. The Marks of the Church

Orthodox Christendom believes, in the words of its Creed, that the Church is the One, Holy, Catholic, and Apostolic Church. It is *one* because Christ as the sole Head can have only one body, and His body is held together by the one ministry which in Christ's stead dispenses the mysteries. It is *holy*, because Christ has sanctified men and imparted among them the grace of the Holy Spirit. The Church is *catholic* because in it the many are joined together into a unity in Christ. 'Catholicity is therefore a qualitative not a quantitative characteristic of the Church.'[13] 'It is the Ecumenical Church not merely in the totality of all its members, of all local Churches, but everywhere and always, in every local Church, in which the Lord Himself is present, and where the Heavenly powers serve Him.'[14] Finally, the Church is *apostolic* because the Apostolic succession and tradition is in force in it.

The Church is *visible* and *invisible*. Visible because it includes

[11] Florovsky in *Universal Church*, p. 52.

[12] N. Arseniev, *Ostkirche und Mystik*, 1924, p. 30 as quoted by Heiler, *Urkirche und Ostkirche*. Eng. trans. *Mysticism and the Eastern Church*, tr. A. Chambers, London 1926, p. 60.

[13] Seraphim, *Die Ostkirche*, p. 72.

[14] Florovsky, as quoted by Seraphim, *op. cit.*, p. 69.

Christians on earth, invisible because it also includes those in Heaven. It is also invisible as the mystical body of Christ, and visible in its hierarchical order and worship. 'But even these visible aspects and features of the Church express what is essentially invisible—the grace and power of the Holy Spirit and the life of grace produced by Him in the Church as the mystical body of Christ.'[15]

The Orthodox Church is the one holy, catholic, apostolic Church emerging visibly in its hierarchy and mysteries. Strictly speaking, therefore, all other Christians stand outside the Church of Christ. This view has been maintained down to our own day.[16] But other views are expressed. One important factor in assessing other Churches is whether the Church in question has retained the Apostolic Succession or not. There are accordingly 'degrees of separation from the Church'.[17] It is noteworthy that the Moscow Conference of 1948, while condemning the Papacy, did not condemn the Roman Church as such, and that it also rejected the Ecumenical Movement in its present form, though not Protestantism as such.[18] Views showing a really ecumenical breadth of judgment have also been expressed. One such was the official view of the Ecumenical Patriarch who, in 1920, addressed an encyclical 'to all Churches of Christ in all countries', in which he explained his attitude to other Churches and used the apostle's picture of the body with many members in which one serves the others and furthers the growth of the whole body. One section of Orthodox Christendom has translated this into action by joining the World Council of Churches. Their delegates united with those from other Churches at Amsterdam in 1948, in declaring 'that notwithstanding our divisions we are one in Jesus Christ'[19]; and at Evanston in 1954 representatives of the Ecumenical Patriarch greeted the second Assembly of the Council with the affirmation

[15] Seraphim, *op. cit.*, p. 74.

[16] See quotations in Heiler, *Urkirche und Ostkirche*, pp. 224f.

[17] Bulgakov in *Procès-verbal du Ier congrès de théologie orthodoxe*, p. 19, as cited by L. Müller, in *Kirche und Kosmos*, p. 96.

[18] *Dokumente der orthodoxen Kirchen zur ökumenischen Fragen*, No. 1, Witten 1949, pp. 35-41. The attitude of the Russian Church to the World Council is now beginning to change. See above, p. 122, n.3.

[19] See World Council of Churches, Amsterdam Assembly Series, VOL. V, *Official Report*, ed. W. A. Visser't Hooft, p. 51.

that the unity of Christendom does not necessitate an absolute uniformity but is compatible with a diversity of rites and practices.[20]

Words such as these are basically and encouragingly different from those heard from the Roman side. Nevertheless, at world conferences of Churches at all levels, we have been conscious of the divisions still existing between the Churches.

The questions we must put to Orthodox theologians are these. Does not their view of the Church dissolve the events of Christmas and Pentecost into an historical process? Do we not have to make a much clearer distinction between the Incarnate *Logos* and the Church as His body? Is the Holy Spirit still in fact the third Person of the Trinity if He enters into the sacramental life of the Church in the way described? Does the Orthodox view of the Church as an organism composed of the hierarchy and the laity do justice to the Pauline conception of the Church as the body of Christ, in which each member serves the others? Is it not Paul's view rather, that all Christians are 'spiritual', endowed and called by Christ in this way in order to minister to the others? The Church's ministry can indeed be described as the bond of unity but only in the Pauline sense that no member has everything but each needs the ministry of the other members (cf. 1 Cor. 12).

This Pauline view of the ministry, which is certainly incompatible with the idea of apostolic succession, was maintained by Calvin. According to the testimony of the apostle, the stream of the Spirit is broader and more varied and His action in the distribution of the gifts of grace incomparably freer than the scheme of apostolic succession allows. It is in line with Paul to affirm that 'in all the variety of ministry and gifts each holds its promise and authority directly from the Church's Lord'.[21] Nevertheless, it does not seem hopeless to discuss these questions with a Church that emphasises as strongly as the Orthodox Church does the fact that the Church has only one Head, namely Christ.

[20] World Council of Churches, *Evanston Assembly* 1954, Report, London 1954.

[21] Düsseldorf Theses, No. 13: *Bekenntnisschriften und Kirchenordnungen*, ed. Niesel, p. 328.

CHAPTER 3

REDEMPTION

1. The Incarnation of God

Almost all the Councils regarded by the Orthodox Church as Ecumenical deal with Christology. It is thus no accident that, as we saw, Christ plays a decisive role in the Orthodox view of the Church. Even the Nicene doctrine of the Trinity had a Christological purpose. The doctrinal decisions of the first seven centuries were attempts to state correctly the mystery of the Incarnation of the *Logos*, which is for the Eastern Church the supreme mystery.

The characteristic feature of Orthodox Christology is clear from the correction which appears in some Greek manuscript versions of the Creed of Chalcedon (451): 'We confess one and the same Christ . . . consisting *from* [instead of 'in'] two natures, without confusion, without change, without division, without separation.'[1] This version of the text was not, of course, officially recognised, but the following Council, Constantinople II (553), interpreted the Chalcedonian formula in a monophysite direction: the two natures of the Redeemer are to be distinguished 'only in thought'.[2] It is their unity which is stressed. It can therefore be said: 'The Orthodox belief is that the human nature was deified in Christ as a result of the hypostatic union with the Divine nature.'[3] This means not that the human nature has been changed but that it has become inseparably one with that of the Logos.

2. The Deification of Man

The purpose of the mission of God's Son is that all men should share what was imparted to the human nature of the *Logos*:

[1] *ἕνα καὶ τὸν αύτον Χριστὸν . . . ἐκ δὺο φύσεων ἀσύγχυτως, ἀτρέπτως, ἀδιαιρέτως, ἀχωρίστως γνωριζόμενον.* D., 148, p. 71, n. 1. Cf. Schaff, II.62 and 64, n. 4.

[2] D., 219.

[3] Seraphim, *Die Ostkirche*, p. 45.

'He became man in order that we should become divine.'[4] In those few words, Athanasius formulated the fundamental faith of the Orthodox Church.[5] It is emphasised, of course, with John Damascene that this deification comes about 'by participation in the Divine illumination' and 'not by any transformation into the Divine essence'. But it was surely going too far when Simon the New Theologian (*d.* 1041) wrote: 'When the Christian receives the grace of the Holy Spirit and thus becomes a partaker of the Divine nature in our Lord Jesus Christ, he is transformed and changed by His power into a quasi-divine condition.' Seraphim takes this to mean that 'while still remaining human, man is filled and permeated by God'.[6] Since the effect of deifying grace depends on the extent of man's union with Christ, this deification, though not yet a realised fact for most men, is nevertheless a real possibility, given to all men.[7] The statement in the Creed that the Incarnation took place 'for our salvation' was and still is understood in this sense.

But these words of the Creed have also prompted other views, making use of the biblical accounts of Christ's saving work. The Creed itself points in this direction by its emphasis on the Crucifixion of Christ. John Damascene, the classical exponent of Orthodox theology, interprets Christ's work as essentially *an expiatory sacrifice offered to God* and not as a ransom paid to the Devil, as most of the Greek theologians do. Here too, Russian theology tried to free itself from the Anselmian influences which had intruded, on the ground that Anselm's doctrine of satisfaction owed too much to legal concepts. Christ 'on the Cross manifested supreme sacrificial love' and 'in the name of this love God pardoned men'.[8] The Cross of Christ is viewed in the light of Easter morning. Only with the Resurrection is Christ's redeeming work completed. Orthodoxy therefore regards the Easter miracle as 'the foundation of Christianity'.[9] Heiler praises Orthodox theology because it consistently 'keeps silence about the mystery of the Resurrection and humbly entrusts it to the worshipping Church'.[10] The celebration of Easter is the most impressive of all the Orthodox services. It is

[4] αὐτὸς γὰρ ἐνανθρώπησεν, ἵνα ἡμεῖς θεοποιηθῶμεν. Athanasius, *De incarnatione*, 54 (Migne, P.G., vol. xxx, col. 192). [5] Seraphim, *Die Ostkirche*, p. 55.
[6] *Ibid.* [7] Seraphim, *op. cit.*, p. 56. [8] Seraphim, *Die Ostkirche*, p. 54.
[9] *ibid.* [10] Heiler, *Urkirche und Ostkirche*, p. 205.

said with some truth that a man only understands the Orthodox Church when he has taken part in this service, filled as it is with the joy of Easter to a greater extent than in any other Church.

3. Man as the Object of Redemption[11]

Man did not come from God's hands in the condition from which God redeems him by sending His Son. By His act of creation 'God made man innocent, upright, good, happy, care-free, enjoying every virtue, endowed with every blessing, as it were a second world, a microcosm in the macrocosm, a spectator of the visible creation, with knowledge of the invisible creation, . . . a being at once earthly and heavenly, temporal and immortal'.[12] 'By being turned Godwards and by his participation in the Divine illumination he was deified without becoming equal to God in essence.'[13] From the beginning man was created in order 'that he should know God, love and glorify Him, and so be happy for ever'.[14] Unlike Roman doctrine, Orthodox theology knows nothing of man apart from God, nor of any piecemeal elevation of man by additional gifts of divine grace (*dona superaddita*). This mechanical conception of man is missing even from the *Confessio Orthodoxa*.[15]

By his disobedience, the first man fell from God and as a result lost what he had possessed in his 'deified state', i.e. his exemption from suffering and death, and his knowledge of the spiritual world. According to Rom. 5.12, in Adam all men sinned and, from him, inherited *original sin*.[16] More than that we are not told. Because it holds a creationist[17] view of the human soul, Orthodox doctrine cannot find room for original sin in the strict sense, but regards it as consisting essentially in the sensuality and mortality which mankind has inherited from

[11] See further . 1951 Conference of Protestant and Orthodox theologians on the doctrine of man, in *Evangelische Theologie*, II (1951-52), Nos. 7 and 8.

[12] John Damascene, II, 12, as quoted by Seraphim, *Die Ostkirche*, p. 40

[13] John Damascene, II, 30, as quoted by Heiler, *Urkirche und Ostkirche*, p. 40.

[14] Philaret, Longer Catechism, Q. 120 (Schaff, II.464).

[15] Orthodox Confession, Q. 23 (Kimmel, *Libri symbolici*, VOL. I, pp. 84ff; Michalescu, *Bekenntnisse und Glaubenszeugnisse*, p. 39, Schaff, II.301f).

[16] Synod of Carthage 418, recognised by the Quinisext (M., 65, 39ff).

[17] Creationism is the doctrine that 'each individual soul originates in a divine creative act, an immediate *creatio ex nihilo*', as against Emanationism, the view that the human soul is an emanation of the divine substance, and Traducianism, the view that the soul originates in the act of conception. See K. Barth, *Church Dogmatics*, VOL. III, 2, pp. 573f.

Adam. 'Adam was changed from an immortal being into a mortal one, and came under the bondage of death. When in this fallen condition he begot children, these too became mortal as the offspring of a mortal being. So we have inherited the curse which fell upon Adam.'[18] The *consequences of Adam's sin* were transmitted to men.[19] Man has retained his freedom, although impaired, and his reason, though darkened. Hence the denial that 'everything good in fallen man comes from grace alone'.[20] Yet the good which remains in man, by itself cannot save him 'since salvation is God's gift'.[21]

4. The Appropriation of Redemption

'Man's salvation is a *Divine-human process*.'[22] This statement shows that the Orthodox view of the appropriation of salvation is synergistic. God and man co-operate. Man cannot, of course, take the first step. He needs the grace of the Holy Spirit to impel him.[23]

This is the proper place to say a word about the Orthodox doctrine of the *Holy Spirit*. This doctrine is one of the main points in dispute between the Orthodox and Roman Churches. The Eastern Church did not experience the development which in the West led to the Augustinian form of the doctrine. It kept to the original text of the creed, whereas, after hesitating for centuries, Rome altered this text to read that the Holy Spirit proceeds 'from the Father *and* the Son' (*a patre filioque*).[24] Apart from the 'non-theological' factors and motives which played some part in this controversy, the main anxiety of the Orthodox Church was that the Western form of the doctrine suggested two sources in the Godhead, and so endangered the Divine Unity.[25] A co-operation of the Son in the procession of the Spirit was

[18] Anastasius Sinaita (640-700), *Quaestiones*, 143. (Migne, P.G., vol. lxxxix, col. 796) as quoted by Heiler, *Urkirche und Ostkirche*, p. 201.

[19] Cf. Verkhovsky in *Evangelische Theologie*, xi, p. 318: 'The view which legalistically attributes Adam's guilt to all his descendants is alien to Orthodoxy. In the broad sense, original sin is not Adam's sin itself but rather its consequences.'

[20] Verkhovsky, *op. cit.*, p. 325.

[21] Dyobouniotes, in *Ekklesia*, vol. x, p. 64.

[22] Seraphim, *Die Ostkirche*, p. 59.

[23] Dyobouniotes, in *Ekklesia*, vol. x, p. 64.

[24] D., 86; M., 56.41. First adopted at the Synod of Toledo (589) but not officially binding on the whole Church until Benedict VIII (1012-24) who introduced the singing of the Creed in the Mass. On the '*filioque*' see Kelly, *Early Christian Creeds*, pp. 358ff.

[25] Dyobouniotes, in *Ekklesia*, vol. x, p. 59.

recognised even at the time of the Cappadocian Fathers.[26] This co-operation was kept quite distinct from the temporal mission of the Spirit, which takes place through the Son.

What is the significance of this peculiarity of Orthodox doctrine? E. F. K. Müller writes: 'Much more closely than appears at first sight, this characteristic is bound up with the distinctively Greek type of piety, in which the Holy Spirit plays a far greater part than in Western Catholicism. In the mysteries operated by the Spirit, the Christian comes, in some sense, into direct touch with God. The historical revelation in the person of Christ is of less moment to him than the divine power present in the mysteries.'[27] We must in fact ask whether Orthodox theology, when speaking of the Holy Spirit, does not ignore the Mediator of revelation[28] and assert a direct relation between believers and the Divine. Such a conception of the activity of the Spirit, which as it were bypasses the Incarnate Son, is intelligible enough on the basis of the Orthodox view of the inner-trinitarian relationship of the Spirit to the Father, but quite unacceptable to a theology which keeps strictly to the revelation of God in Jesus Christ. The doctrine of the Trinity is not there to undergird a mysticism of being with a Christian colouring. On the contrary it is intended to bear witness to the fact that in Jesus Christ it is God Himself who comes to meet us.

We now come back to the Orthodox doctrine of the appropriation of redemption. Since fallen man has retained his freedom he can either accept God's call or reject it. The appropriation of redemption is God's gift, yet man can refuse even God.[29] 'The grace which comes from above is not given to one who makes no effort. On the contrary, there must be a combination of two things: human effort and the help which by faith comes from above to complete the virtue.'[30] The Holy Spirit works in man a process of transformation in which man co-operates. There takes place that deification of man referred to earlier.

[26] Cf. Heiler, *Urkirche und Ostkirche*, p. 195. [27] Müller, *Symbolik*, p. 220.

[28] Florovsky's plea for a Christological rather than a Pneumatological view of the Church is therefore welcome: 'She is not an incarnation of the Holy Ghost.' *Universal Church*, p. 53. [29] Dyobouniotes, in *Ekklesia*, VOL. X, pp. 64f.

[30] Basil, *'Ασκητικά Const. monast.*, 15 (Migne, P.G., VOL. XXXI, col. 1377), as quoted by Heiler, *Urkirche und Ostkirche*, p. 210.

The Protestant teaching of Cyril Lucaris compelled Orthodox theology to turn its attention also to the doctrine of the sinner's *justification*. But Orthodoxy continues to regard this justification as a 'gradual development' and 'links sanctification with it as the development and extension of justification'.[31] It is certainly not taken to mean that Jesus Christ Himself is 'God's declaration of the forgiveness of all our sins'[32] and that in Him we ourselves are really righteous and able to stand in God's presence, but rather that man is gradually made righteous by infused grace, or, what amounts to the same thing, is transformed into a 'quasi-divine condition'.

All this appears in a different light of course, when we remember, as we should, the following points:

(1) Orthodox, and especially Russian, theology is aware that man remains a *sinner* in the presence of God. 'Who are they that hunger and thirst after righteousness?' asks Philaret in his Catechism. Answer: 'They who while they love to do good yet count not themselves righteous, nor rest on their own good works, but acknowledge themselves sinners and guilty before God; and who, by the wish and prayer of faith, hunger and thirst after the justification of grace through Jesus Christ, as after spiritual meat and drink.'[33]

(2) In the Orthodox Church great importance is attached to *personal faith*. The daily morning prayer provides a good example of this: 'O my Saviour, by Thy grace deliver me; for if it were Thy will to save me according to my works, that would be neither grace nor gift but only a burden. Thou hast said: "He that believeth in me shall live." . . . Since, then, it is faith in Thee that saves, behold: "I believe," therefore save me! . . . O, my God, let my faith be counted to me for works. Do not ask me from my own strength for the works which should justify me, but let this my faith be all-sufficient, let it answer for me, let it make me a partaker of Thine eternal glory.'[34]

(3) It is very significant that in Orthodox theology there is no trace of the *idea of merit* so characteristic of Roman theology. There is not even a doctrine of supererogatory works (*opera*

[31] Dyobouniotes, in *Ekklesia*, vol. x, p. 66.
[32] Barmen Thesis No. 2.
[33] Philaret, Larger Catechism, Q. 457 (Schaff, II.516).
[34] Seraphim, *Die Ostkirche*, pp. 59f.

supererogatoria). On the contrary, the Sermon on the Mount is the standard for the life of all Christians and not just a stimulus to extraordinary acts and rewards. At the end of the Russian Catechism we read: 'What caution do we need when we seem to ourselves to have fulfilled any Commandment? Answer: We must then dispose our hearts according to the words of Jesus Christ: "When ye shall have done all those things which are commanded you, say, we are unprofitable servants, we have done that which was our duty to do." '[35]

These are biblical echoes which we do not hear in Roman theology. They appear to suggest that it would not be impossible for Orthodox theology to re-examine its entire doctrine of the appropriation of salvation in the light of such insights.

[35] Philaret, Larger Catechism, Q. 611 (Schaff, II.542).

CHAPTER 4

THE DOCTRINE OF THE SACRAMENTS

1. General

The Redemption won by Christ is applied to men by means of the sacraments or—as Orthodox theologians prefer to say—by the mysteries which the Church administers. The great mystery of the past, namely the Incarnation of the *Logos*, is at work in the mysteries of the present, deifying man. The sacraments are therefore *means of grace* instituted by Christ. 'The faithful are united with God in the mysteries in which the higher divine world manifests itself; by the power of the Holy Spirit, these mysteries transform men and create a new being and a new life in Christ. This new being is the change into the divine likeness by grace; the new life is the beginning, the foretaste of eternal life.'[1] This is stated more succinctly in Philaret's Catechism: 'A mystery or sacrament is a holy act through which grace, or, in other words, the saving power of God, works mysteriously upon man.'[2]

There is no official doctrine of the sacraments in the Orthodox Church. It was only when compelled to meet the Calvinist views of Cyril Lucaris that the Orthodox Church developed a sacramental doctrine of its own, by drawing heavily upon medieval scholasticism. Here as elsewhere attempts have been made to shake off these bonds.

The view that there are *seven sacraments* began to be general in the Orthodox Church perhaps from the time of the Union Council of Lyons (1274). Previously there was no clear agreement about their number. John Damascene, for example, referred to two only: Baptism and Eucharist.[3] This is no longer

[1] Seraphim, *Die Ostkirche*, p. 78.

[2] Larger Catechism, Q. 284 (Schaff, II.490).

[3] John Damascene, *De fide orthodoxa*, IV.9, 13.(Migne, P.G., VOL. XCIV, cols. 1117ff, 1136ff.) As quoted by Heiler, *Urkirche und Ostkirche*, p. 240.

held to be true and attempts have been made to prove that he recognised other sacraments as well.[4] But even today the Orthodox accept Baptism and Eucharist as the chief sacraments because of the importance of their saving effects.[5] Baptism and Eucharist manifest and seal Christian 'togetherness' in the Church.[6]

Although, under Roman Catholic influence, the view that the sacraments work 'of necessity' (ἐξ ἀνάγκης)—a phrase recalling the Roman '*ex opere operato*'—has arisen in the Orthodox Church [7] and is still maintained even today,[8] it is, on the other hand, also stoutly contested. Florovsky says for example, 'Sacraments must be "worthily" received indeed; therefore they cannot be separated or divorced from the inner effort and spiritual attitude of believers. Baptism is to be preceded by repentance and faith. A personal relation between an aspirant and his Lord must be first established by the hearing and the receiving of the Word, of the message of Salvation.'[9] Zankov too, bluntly says: 'The Orthodox Church knows of no "*opus operatum*".'[10]

2. Baptism

Baptism is the basic sacrament of the Orthodox Church. 'It is at once the door into the Holy Church and into the Kingdom of God.'[11]

Baptism is administered to the candidate by a *threefold immersion* in water. Only in the case of those who are sick is sprinkling with water permissible instead of immersion. The formula used at baptism is: 'The servant of God A. B. is baptised in the Name of the Father and of the Son and of the Holy Ghost.'[12]

The *effect* of baptism is to create 'a new being'.[13] It causes

[4] Dyobouniotes, in *Ekklesia*, VOL. x, p. 68.
[5] Anglican Conversations with the Orthodox, *Ekklesia*, VOL. x, p. 144.
[6] Florovsky, *Universal Church*, p. 47.
[7] Confessio Dosithei, xv (Kimmel, *Libri Symbolici*, p. 450; Michalescu, *Bekenntnisse und Glaubenszeugnisse*, p. 169; Schaff, II.422).
[8] Dyobouniotes, in *Ekklesia*, VOL. x, p. 68.
[9] Florovsky, in *Universal Church*, p. 47.
[10] S. Zankov, *The Eastern Orthodox Church*, trans. D. A. Lowrie, London 1929, p. 113. [11] Seraphim, *Die Ostkirche*, p. 80.
[12] Cf. R. French, 'The Services of the Eastern Orthodox Church', in *Liturgy and Worship*, edd. W. K. Lowther, Clarke and C. Harris, London 1947, p. 843.
[13] Seraphim, *Die Ostkirche*, p. 82.

regeneration, i.e. the believer 'dies to the carnal life of sin and is born again of the Holy Ghost to a life spiritual and holy'.[14] In baptism the baptised person becomes 'a member of the mystical body of Christ'.[15]

Many theologians emphasise that faith is essential for the *right reception* of baptism. We saw earlier how Florovsky stressed that a personal relationship must first be established between the candidate and his Lord. 'And again,' he goes on, 'an oath of allegiance to God and His Christ is a prerequisite and indispensable condition of the administration of the sacrament (the first meaning of the word "*sacramentum*" was precisely "the military oath"). A catechumen is already enrolled among the brethren on the basis of his faith.'[16] Even the Greek theologian Dyobouniotes says that the regeneration taking place in baptism 'needs to be appropriated and developed in order to become personal'.[17] That says less but represents an improvement on the unqualified Roman assertion that baptism is effective simply by being administered.

Since acceptance of baptism is 'the condition for salvation for all who know of this obligation',[18] the Orthodox view is that even infants are to be baptised. There is no agreed view about the destiny of infants dying unbaptised. The more charitable view is that these infants come to share 'a relative beatitude'.[19]

Baptism is administered by the priest or bishop. In emergency it can be administered by a layman of either sex.[20] When the baptised person is well again, however, the ceremonies attached to baptism are to be carried out by a priest.

On the question of the validity of baptisms administered by non-Orthodox Christians no clear answer is given by the tradition of the Orthodox Church. Whereas for a long time it used to be the custom to rebaptise baptised heretics and even Roman Catholics, baptism which has been properly administered is now generally accepted.[21]

[14] Philaret, Longer Catechism, Q. 288 (Schaff, II.491).
[15] Seraphim, *Die Ostkirche*, p. 82. [16] Florovsky, in *Universal Church*, p. 47.
[17] Dyobouniotes, in *Ekklesia*, VOL. X, p. 69.
[18] Seraphim, *Die Ostkirche*, p. 81.
[19] Dyobouniotes, in *Ekklesia*, VOL. X, p. 69.
[20] Orthodox Confession, CIII (Kimmel, *Libri symbolici*, p. 174; Michalescu, *Bekenntnisse und Glaubenszeugnisse*, p. 70; Schaff, II.376ff).
[21] Zankov, *Eastern Orthodox Church*, p. 82.

3. CHRISMATION (CONFIRMATION)

Immediately after Baptism the baptised person is anointed with holy oil. One difference from the Roman Church is that this sacrament may be administered by any priest. He anoints the forehead, eyes, nostrils, mouth, ears, breast, hands, and feet with the consecrated oil, each time saying: 'The seal of the gift of the Holy Spirit. Amen.'[22]

In the Orthodox view this sacrament was originally administered after baptism by the laying on of the Apostles' hands. But when in time the number of the Apostles became insufficient for this to be done, the imposition of the hands was replaced by the anointing with holy oil, which any priest was qualified to perform.[23] Orthodoxy regards the anointing of Christ with the Holy Spirit immediately after His baptism as the prototype of this anointing.

According to ancient Church Law the consecration of the oil is the prerogative of each bishop. Later this right came to be restricted to the Ecumenical Patriarch alone; more recently it has belonged to all the Patriarchs of the autocephalous Churches. The Greek Church alone still preserves its ancient ties with Byzantium by obtaining the consecrated oil from the Ecumenical Patriarch. The chrism is olive oil, mixed with a variety of fragrant substances, representing the manifold gifts of the Holy Spirit. The oil is prepared once every seven years during Holy Week, the consecration taking place on Maundy Thursday. The words spoken at the consecration are important 'Send down Thy most Holy Spirit upon this oil. Make it become a kingly unction, a spiritual unction, to preserve life and to sanctify soul and body, and show the same by the descent of Thy Holy and Adorable Spirit as a garment of immortality, a seal of perfection.'[24] This sounds like a prayer for the Holy Spirit to enter into the oil. Heiler points out that the change in the eucharistic bread was already compared by Cyril of Jerusalem with the change in the oil of chrism: 'Just as the Eucharistic bread is no longer ordinary bread after the invocation of

[22] Cf. R. French in *Liturgy and Worship*, edd. Clarke and Harris, p. 843.
[23] Dyobouniotes, in *Ekklesia*, VOL. x, p. 69.
[24] Seraphim, *Die Ostkirche*, p. 83.

the Holy Spirit, but is Christ's body, so this holy oil, after the invocation, is no longer ordinary oil but a gift of Christ and of the Holy Spirit, having become so by the Divine presence.'[25] The *effect* of the Sacrament is 'that the baptised believer, when anointed with holy chrism on certain parts of the body in the name of the Holy Ghost, receives the gifts of the Holy Ghost for growth and strength in spiritual life'.[26] By the anointing with chrism, therefore, baptism is completed. That is also evident from the fact that when other Christians are received into the Orthodox Church this anointing at least is administered to them. Only in this way can one become a fully qualified member of the Church.

The question is whether by this ceremony Orthodoxy does not diminish the force and completeness of the promise of baptism, and endanger the freedom of the Gospel by making the complete efficacy of the Gospel message depend upon a rite which, as she herself admits, is not in the strict sense apostolic?

Confirmation is not regarded as absolutely unrepeatable as it is in the Roman Church. The lapsed are anointed again when they are restored.

4. The Eucharist

The most sublime of all 'the mysteries of the present' is that of the Eucharist. In baptism it is held that Christ has communion with believers by His power (κατὰ δύναμιν) but in the Eucharist by His substance (κατ' οὐσίαν).[27] Dyobouniotes says: 'The Holy Supper is the sacrament by which he who consumes the elements of bread and wine, consecrated and changed by the priest into the body and blood, partakes of the body and blood of Christ Himself for the forgiveness of sins and eternal life.'[28]

Much more so than in the Roman Church, this sacrament is a *communion with the present Lord Jesus Christ*. 'The keynote of this mystery,' says Zankov, 'is the basic mood of the early

[25] Cyril of Jerusalem, *Cat. Myst.*, 3.3 (Migne, P.G., vol. xxxiii, cols. 1089, 1091), as quoted by Heiler, *Urkirche und Ostkirche*, p. 249.

[26] Philaret, Longer Catechism, Q. 307 (Schaff, ii.494).

[27] Theophilus, ταμεῖον, 1780, p. 35, quoted from Loofs, *Symbolik*, p. 147.

[28] Dyobouniotes, in *Ekklesia*, vol. x, p. 70.

Church: "Yea come, Lord Jesus! Marana tha!—Yea come, and give us Thy fullness and Thy Self." '[29] Only when we realise this do we really understand what the Eucharist means in the Orthodox Church. Throughout it is an *action*, a drama, which begins to be enacted at the altar behind the iconostasis in the actions of the priest and his deacon, who then proceed from the altar through the doors into the place where the congregation stands and from thence back again to the altar.[30] The invasion of time by eternity is thus made clear to the people. The Orthodox Church has preserved a sense that the Christian revelation has the character of an event. She therefore celebrates no private masses. For her the Eucharist is 'the mystical-symbolic interpenetration of Heaven and earth, of God and man, of Christ and the Church'.[31] 'The profoundest gift of grace in the holy Eucharist is . . . living communion with the Lord Jesus Christ and with the Holy Spirit, which in and by itself is the supreme blessing and the greatest happiness.'[32] That sounds very different from the Roman assertion that, by the

[29] Zankov, *The Eastern Orthodox Church*, p. 115.

[30] The Orthodox Liturgy falls into three parts, the preparation (*proskomidia* or *prothesis*), the liturgy of the catechumens, and the liturgy of the faithful. In the first, the elements are prepared for the Eucharist. In the second, the main feature is the 'Little Entrance'. The priest and the deacon, carrying the Book of the Gospels, move from the altar in the chancel, through the north door of the iconostasis into the nave, where the congregation stands waiting. This Little Entrance represents the Lord's coming in His Word. When the lector has read the Epistle and the deacon the Gospel, the Longer Litany, i.e. the litany of fervent supplication known as the prayer of Chrysostom, is recited. The third part consists of the 'Great Entrance', when the priest and deacon once again enter the nave through the north door, carrying the prepared elements, and then return to the chancel behind the iconostasis through the centre door, the 'royal door'. This represents the sacramental coming of Christ into the midst of His people. After the offertory of the holy gifts, the recital of the Nicene Creed, and many hymns and prayers, the centre door of the iconostasis is closed, so that the mystery may reach its climax. Then the words of institution are read aloud at the altar, and, in the epiclesis, the power of the Holy Spirit is invoked for the priest and the elements. The commemoration of the faithful departed and the prayer of preparation for communion follow. When the priest and deacon have partaken, the royal door is opened again, the sacramental gifts are taken out to the congregation—which is thereby reminded of Christ's reappearance after His resurrection—and those who wish to communicate come forward to receive the bread and wine, Christ's body and blood, given to them in a spoon. Immediately after this, the elements are returned to the chancel since Christ, after His resurrection appearances, ascended at once into Heaven. In the whole of this service the priest is in no way assigned the prominence given him in the Roman Mass. See *The Orthodox Liturgy*, pp. vii-xiv; E. Molland, *Christendom*, London 1959, pp. 28-34; E. Underhill, *Worship*, London 1937, pp. 262-70; R. M. French, *The Eastern Orthodox Church*, London 1961, pp. 114-22.

[31] Zankov, *Eastern Orthodox Church*, p. 115.

[32] Seraphim, *Die Ostkirche*, p. 90.

Mass, grace is increased in those who communicate. All other blessings spring from communion with Christ, above all the forgiveness of sins and the hope of eternal life. Communion with Christ also creates the communion of believers with one another.[33]

That the consecrated gifts, bread and wine, are the *true body and blood of Christ*, must be regarded as a dogma of the Orthodox Church. As to the mode and manner in which this happens there are only theological opinions.[34] The doctrine of transubstantiation came into Orthodox theology from Thomas Aquinas and was then accepted in detail (in the *Confessio orthodoxa* and the *Confessio Dosithei*) during the controversy with Cyril Lucaris. In recent times, it has been rejected for various reasons. Coming into favour again is the doctrine of the ancient Greek Fathers which affirms *a change of the whole bread and wine* into the body and blood of Christ.[35] 'If you ask how this comes about,' says John Damascene, 'be content to be told that it does so by the Holy Spirit, in the same way that the Lord also took from the Virgin Mary the flesh which subsisted in Him. We know simply that God's Word is true and effective and can do all things, but the mode and manner is utterly incomprehensible. Yet this at least can certainly be said: as bread by eating, and wine and water by drinking are changed naturally into the body and blood of him who eats and drinks, becoming no different body from that which was there before, so too, the consecrated bread, wine, and water, are changed supernaturally by the invocation and descent of the Holy Spirit into the body and blood of Christ, so that there are no longer two things but one and the same.'[36] Chomiakov rejects the Roman doctrine of transubstantiation because it turns the supreme Christian mystery into an 'atomistic chemical miracle'.[37] 'Orthodox theological statements on this question within the past few decades have made it clear that this doctrine has never been a dogma of the Orthodox Church.'[38]

[33] John Damascene as quoted by Seraphim, *Die Ostkirche*, p. 88.

[34] Zankov, *Eastern Orthodox Church*, p. 117.

[35] Dyobouniotes, in *Ekklesia*, VOL. X, p. 70.

[36] John Damascene, *De fide orthodoxa*, IV, 13 (Migne, P.G., VOL. XCIV, cols. 1145ff), as quoted by Heiler, *Urkirche und Ostkirche*, p. 252.

[37] Zankov, *Eastern Orthodox Church*, p. 117. [38] *Ibid.*

In the Liturgy of Chrysostom, after reciting the words of the institution, the priest prays: 'Send down Thy Holy Spirit upon us and these gifts . . . and make this bread into the precious body of Thy Christ! and the contents of this cup the precious blood of Thy Christ, changed by Thy Holy Spirit!'[39] The change is, therefore, brought about by the Holy Spirit *in response to the invocation* and not by the recital of the words of institution, as in the Roman Mass. This opinion is shared even by the two Romanising Confessions of the seventeenth century.[40] The words of institution have nevertheless been accorded great significance from very early times, as Heiler has shown[41]; indeed the view of more recent Russian theology is that, together with the epiclesis, they form 'an indivisible unity'. In answer to the question: which is the most important action in the Eucharist? the Russian Catechism says: 'The utterance of the words which Jesus spake in instituting the Sacrament, . . . and after this the invocation of the Holy Ghost, and the blessing the gifts . . . because at the moment of this act the bread and wine are changed.'[42]

From the *reservation* of the elements left over from a Eucharist it follows that it is generally believed in the Orthodox Church that the consecrated elements remain Christ's body and blood even when the service is over. This reservation is made for the communion of the sick and for weekday services during seasons of fasting. The *Confessio Dosithei* insists on the reserved sacrament receiving the reverence due to God.[43] But in the Orthodox Church it is not usual to do this except during worship. From the sacrament reserved for the cases mentioned, we must distinguish the *eulogia*, pieces of bread sanctified, but not consecrated, during the Eucharist, which the communicants take home for their relatives.

We should notice too that in the Eucharist the Eastern Church uses leavened wheaten-bread and red wine mixed with

[39] Seraphim, *Die Ostkirche*, p. 86. Cf. *Orthodox Liturgy*, pp. 72f.

[40] Orthodox Confession, CVII (Kimmel, *Libri symbolici*, p. 180; Michalescu, *Bekenntnisse und Glaubenszeugnisse*, p. 72; Schaff, II.381ff). *Confessio Dosithei*, XV (Kimmel, *Libri symbolici*, p. 451; Michalescu, *Bekenntnisse und Glaubenszeugnisse*, p. 169; Schaff, II.422).

[41] Heiler, *Urkirche und Ostkirche*, pp. 259ff.

[42] Philaret, Longer Catechism, Q. 338-9 (Schaff, II.497).

[43] *Confessio Dosithei*, XVII (Schaff, II.427ff). Cf. also *Orthodox Confession*, LVI (Schaff, II.335f).

water, recalling the blood and water which flowed from Jesus' side.

The Communion is made in *both kinds*, and this indeed, as it is held, on the basis of Christ's commandment. Even the *Confessio orthodoxa* states that.[44] Only to little children is the sacrament given merely in the form of wine, at their first communion immediately after baptism and anointing.

We must also regard as a dogma the belief that the Eucharist is an unbloody sacrifice of praise, thanksgiving, prayer and atonement. There is no universally binding doctrine concerning the details 'especially as to the real nature of the eucharistic sacrifice'.[45] Zankov's opinion is that the view of Orthodox theology approximates most closely to that held by the early Church Fathers 'that . . . the offering of the body and blood of Christ' is to be understood 'chiefly in the symbolic sense'.[46] Yet a Synod of Constantinople in 1156 rejected the view that it merely commemorated the sacrifice on the Cross.[47] Greek theology firmly held to the view of the Eucharist as an expiatory sacrifice 'offered to God on behalf of the living and the dead', in the sense, of course, that it 'serves the distribution of the fruits of the sacrifice made on the Cross and our appropriation of them'.[48] Russian theologians continue to regard it as a sacrifice but have abandoned the idea of a propitiatory sacrifice. According to Zankov, the questions still open are: '*What* is offered in the Eucharist, the gifts of Christians (the elements) or Christ Himself? *Who* sacrifices, Christ (sacrificing Himself) or the priest, or the Church or the Communion, the body of the faithful? Or *to whom* is it offered, to God the Father or to the God-man Christ?'[49]

Agreement is confined to the *purpose*. The Eucharist is offered 'for the whole Church, the earthly and the heavenly, for the living and the dead, for all Christians, for everyone'.[50] For all these the Eucharist has 'redemptive and sanctifying power'.[51]

[44] Orthodox Confession, CVII (Kimmel, *Libri symbolici*, pp. 181f; Michalescu, *Bekenntnisse und Glaubenszeugnisse*, pp. 72f; Schaff, II.381ff).
[45] Zankov, *Eastern Orthodox Church*, p. 115. [46] *Op. cit.*, p. 116.
[47] Heiler, *Urkirche und Ostkirche*, p. 265.
[48] Dyobouniotes, in *Ekklesia*, VOL. X, pp. 70f.
[49] Zankov, *Eastern Orthodox Church*, pp. 115f.
[50] *Op. cit.*, p. 116. [51] Seraphim, *Die Ostkirche*, p. 91.

5. Penance

'Penance is a sacrament in which he who confesses his sins is, on the outward declaration of pardon by the priest, inwardly loosed from his sins by Jesus Christ Himself.'[52] In this sacrament a marked difference is evident between the Orthodox Church and Rome. That can be seen even from the definition just quoted.

Part of the sacrament of penance is the oral confession of all actual sins to the priest. In this confession there is no detailed examination of conscience as in the Roman Church. What is expected in it is genuine penitence and not just a contrition based on mere fear of punishment (*attritio*). The Russian Catechism requires of the person making confession: 'contrition for his sins, with a full purpose of amendment of life, faith in Jesus Christ, and hope in His mercy'.[53] These are genuine biblical tones.

Important too is the fact that furthermore it is not the priest who forgives sins. *God Himself forgives them.*[54] The priest is simply His instrument for this. Hence in the Greek Church the forgiveness of sins is pronounced in the form of a prayer. This rests on ancient tradition. Likewise the Russian Catechism regards the action of the priest as a declaration of forgiveness.

A Greek theologian says that this is in keeping with 'the spirit of the Orthodox Church which never exalts the clergy above the laity'.[55] We are bound to ask why then are the hearing of confession and the declaration of forgiveness restricted to the priest? Does not the further step have to be taken of conceding authority to every Christian? Whereas in ancient times even lay monks heard confessions as spiritual advisers, today the episcopally ordained priest is regarded as the only authorised minister of this sacrament. He imparts forgiveness by the laying on of hands. Confessional boxes are unknown in the Orthodox Churches. The priest acts not as a judge but as a helpful physician.

This also finds expression in the fact that he imposes *no*

[52] Philaret, Longer Catechism, Q. 351 (Schaff, II.500).
[53] *Op. cit.*, Q. 353 (Schaff, II.500).
[54] Zankov, *Eastern Orthodox Church*, pp. 118f, 87.
[55] According to Heiler, *Urkirche und Ostkirche*, p. 268.

penalties on the person making confession. He can, of course, impose ἐπιτίμια on the penitent if he thinks fit. These include such religious exercises as prayers, fasting and the like. They are not so much 'punishments' as rather aids to assist him to subdue 'sinful habit'.[56] It cannot be otherwise since Orthodoxy has not adopted the Roman doctrine of satisfaction. In the sacrament of penance not only sins but also, in contrast to the Roman dogma, *the penalties for sin are completely blotted out*, so complete is the effect of this sacrament.

Hence 'the Orthodox Church also rejects the Roman view of indulgences and the treasury of superfluous good works, supposed to have been acquired by the saints and to be applicable to other men'.[57]

6. Ordination

Ordination is the 'sacrament, in which the Holy Ghost, by the laying on of the Bishop's hands, ordains them that be rightly chosen, to minister sacraments, and to feed the flock of Christ'.[58]

The laying on of hands together with the prayers offered during this act constitute the sacrament. This again shows the attitude of the Orthodox Church: it repudiates any suggestion of mechanical efficacy in the sacraments.

The right to ordain belongs only to bishops as the successors of the Apostles. As a rule ordination to the episcopate is performed by several bishops.

The Orthodox hierarchy, which is regarded as instituted by Christ, falls into three grades: diaconate, presbyterate, and episcopate. So too the grace of the sacrament 'which is single' 'is distributed in stages'.[59] 'Thus the bishop is preeminently the preacher of the truth,[60] who celebrates the sacraments and

[56] Philaret, Longer Catechism, Q. 356 (Schaff, II.500). Cf. also Dyobouniotes in *Ekklesia*, VOL. X, p. 71. [57] Dyobouniotes, *loc. cit.*

[58] Philaret, Longer Catechims, Q. 357 (Schaff, II.501).

[59] Dyobouniotes, in *Ekklesia*, VOL. X, p. 72.

[60] What applies chiefly to the bishop also applies, therefore, to the priest. Roman theology would not describe the priestly office in that way. In the Orthodox Church the sermon is not an indispensable part of Christian worship, though there have been times when it played an important role. We need only recall John Chrysostom (345-407). In ancient times priests who neglected preaching were punished. It is a striking fact that preaching has recently become much more frequent in the Russian Church. Cf. Martin Niemöller's account of his visit to Moscow, in *Die Stimme der Gemeinde*, 1952, p. 38; cf. also E. Schlink, 'The ecumenical contribution of the Russian Orthodox Church', in *Scottish Journal of*

rules the Church.' Apart from ordination and the consecration of the chrism oil, the priest does all that too, but is subordinate to the bishop. The deacon assists them both, 'but has no authority to preach, administer the sacraments or rule the Church'.[61] Ordination to the priesthood is a single sacrament with a threefold sacramental action, each part of which is complete in itself. The minor orders of ministry are still retained in the Orthodox Church. They receive a consecration but no imposition of hands.

Only an unmarried priest may be consecrated bishop, but a man can become a priest or a deacon whether he is married or single. After ordination none may contract a marriage.

Ordination cannot be repeated. The Supreme Russian Synod in 1868 decided otherwise. It declared that priests who are deposed or who relinquish holy orders, lose the gift of ordination. On this view, therefore, ordination does not confer any *character indelebilis*.[62] There is no uniform Orthodox attitude to those ordained by schismatics or heretics. Even into the nineteenth century Roman Catholic priests were re-ordained when received into the Orthodox Church, but nowadays even Old Catholic and Anglican ordinations are widely accepted.

We must not forget that the idea of the universal priesthood of all believers plays an important part in the Orthodox Church.[63] It finds expression even at ordination to the priesthood, when the congregation shows its approval by acclamation.[64] Priests and laymen have the same dignity.[65] All the cells of an organism 'are equal as such and yet differentiated by their functions'.[66] It is the function of those who are ordained,

Theology, XII (1959), p. 47: 'there has recently been more preaching in Church services than there used to be.'

[61] Dyobouniotes, in *Ekklesia*, VOL. X, p. 72.

[62] Cf. also Zankov, *Das orth. Christentum*, p. 108.

[63] Even in Orthodox Confession, CVIII (Kimmel, *Libri symbolici*, pp. 185f; Michalescu, *Bekenntnisse und Glaubenszeugnisse*, pp. 73f; Schaff, II.386).

[64] In Alexandria in ancient times, according to a document seen by Professor Hamilcar Alivisatos of Athens, the congregation even shared in the actual ordination itself. The ordaining minister would place his right hand on the ordinand, and with his left grasp the hand of the priest standing beside him at the altar. This priest in turn grasped the hand of the nearest member of the congregation and so on, until, at the very moment of laying on of hands, a complete chain of hands was formed. *Publications de l'Institut d'Études Orientales de la Bibliothèque Patriarcale d'Alexandrie*, 1953, No. 2.

[65] Florovsky, in *Universal Church*, p. 52. See also p. 113 above.

[66] *Ibid.*

as stewards of Christ's mysteries to stand '*for* Him *before* the community'.[67]

7. Marriage

Like the Roman Church, the Orthodox Church considers marriage to be a sacrament, on the basis of Eph. 5.31f. But unlike Rome, it regards the sacrament as given, not in the agreement (*consensus*) of the two partners but in the blessing of them by the priest and in the coronation which follows, i.e. the garlanding, which is accompanied by appropriate words. The sacrament consists in the wedding by the priest. In this the latter prays for the grace of the Holy Spirit: 'O Lord, stretch forth now Thy hand from Thy Holy dwelling place and bind together this Thy servant . . . and this Thine handmaid . . . for by Thee the wife is joined to her husband.'[68] Strictly speaking therefore, in this sacrament too it is God Himself and not the priest who is 'the priestly ministrant of marriage mystical and pure'.[69]

In contrast to Rome, the Orthodox Church regards marriage as dissoluble. In the ancient canons, of course, the only accepted ground for this was the adultery of one of the partners. State recognition of the Church resulted in the Church's adoption of a more lax civil marriage code and the Church regards divorce as permissible in many cases, and blesses second and even third marriages. In these cases, however, prayer is offered at the wedding for the forgiveness of the sin of the second marriage.[70] The Church regards such a marriage as not 'a divinely willed marriage' but 'a consequence of sinful human nature'.[71]

8. Holy Unction[72]

On the basis of Mark 16.18 and Jas. 5.14f the Orthodox Church practises the sacrament of holy unction, in which 'while the body is anointed with oil, God's grace is invoked on the sick, to heal him of spiritual and bodily infirmities'.[73] The sacrament is not intended for the dying, as in the Roman Church. It is

[67] *Ibid.* [68] Seraphim, *Die Ostkirche*, p. 92.
[69] *Op. cit.*, p. 93. Cf. R. French, in *Liturgy and Worship*, edd. Clarke and Harris, pp. 844f. [70] Seraphim, *Die Ostkirche*, p. 94. [71] *Op. cit.*, p. 93.
[72] Cf. R. French, in *Liturgy and Worship*, edd. Clarke and Harris, pp. 845f.
[73] Philaret, Longer Catechism, Q. 364. (Schaff, II.502.)

usually preceded by confession. Those receiving it are the *sick in body or in soul*; usually, too, the sick person's family even though they are in good bodily health. The anointing is performed with twigs dipped in oil and applied to the forehead, nose, cheeks, mouth, breast, hands back and front. It is *administered by seven priests*. Only in emergency is one sufficient. The oil mixed with wine or water is consecrated by the priest himself during the ceremony: 'Send down Thy Holy Spirit and sanctify this oil and make it for this Thy servant to be anointed therewith, the perfect remission of his sins.'[74] During the anointing the priest prays: 'Heal also Thy servant from the spiritual and bodily ills that afflict him.'[75] The anointing effects 'the healing of bodily sickness and the forgiveness of sins, and even the sins of those from whom the bodily sickness was caught'.[76] The sacrament can be repeated as often as necessary.

[74] Seraphim, *Die Ostkirche*, p. 95. [75] *Ibid.*
[76] Dyobouniotes, in *Ekklesia*, VOL. X, p. 73.

CHAPTER 5

THE MYSTERY OF THE HOLY IKONS

IMMEDIATELY after his account of the Orthodox doctrine of the sacraments, Seraphim adds a chapter on the mystery of the holy ikons. For in Orthodoxy, pictures of our Lord, of Mary and the Saints, have a position similar to that of the sacraments. Seraphim says: 'In the ikon . . . nature and super-nature, here and the beyond, world and God, are linked together. The ikon links believers with the higher world, with the Heavenly Church of the transfigured and glorified saints; it does not just point to an eternal world beyond, but is also a bond with the eternal, for *in the ikon the beyond and the here are present*, and the here shares in the beyond.'[1]

'The image is not to be separated from the original,' says Seraphim; 'a mystical bond unites them. The image shares the nature of the original and the original is present in the image and reveals itself in it. There is a mystical unity of being between what is depicted, and the ikon itself; the former inhabits the ikon.'[2] According to John Damascene the images are not merely picture-books for the uneducated, but 'material laden with Divine energy and gracious power'.[3] To such lengths does this theologian go in his defence of the cult of ikons. The seventh Ecumenical Council (Nicea 787), which relied on his teaching, did not adopt this proposition, however, while Rome rejected it in theory at the Council of Trent, though confirming it in practice by the reverence it shows to 'grace pictures'. In support of the view that the Orthodox Church still accepts the position of John Damascene, Seraphim appeals to what is said in the liturgy. Each year, on the Feast of Orthodoxy, when the Church celebrates the victory over the iconoclasts, it is con-

[1] Seraphim, *Die Ostkirche*, p. 98. [2] *Op. cit.*, pp. 97f.
[3] John Damascene, as quoted by Heiler, *Urkirche und Ostkirche*, p. 293.

fessed: 'Not before powerless idols do we believers prostrate ourselves. . . . No! . . . from it we draw the grace of salvation.' It is still open to question whether that last sentence really refers to the external image. But no other interpretation seems possible when we learn that 'in the Rite for the consecration of the ikons, the Orthodox Church prays God to send down the grace of the Holy Spirit upon the ikons, thereby giving them miraculous power, e.g. to heal the sick and to exorcise the demons'.[4] By the blessing, the image wrought by the craftsman becomes what it is meant to be, a means of salvation.

Yet even the style of painting must make it clear that the images depict beings from the heavenly world. The ikons are not realistic paintings but portray flat, unreal figures, whose colours, and gold and silver garments, are meant to indicate that the persons they represent belong to the eternal world. Statues and crucifixes are therefore rejected. To this extent, not only Rome but many modern Protestants too could learn something from Orthodoxy. 'By the very fact that the ikon is a representation or material picture of a transfigured world . . . into which the person depicted has entered, it lifts the beholder into the divine world.'[5]

The regulations of the Nicene Council of 787 are, of course, accepted: 'The actual worship is paid not to the image but to the person the image represents. The images are intended to awaken a longing for the originals.'[6]

In the Orthodox view, the justification for pictures of Christ and the saints is already found in the Incarnation itself. 'The Incarnation of the *Logos* makes possible a pictorial representation of the Divine, which in and for itself is invisible and transcendent.'[7] This applies to the saints as well because, by their communion with Christ, they have become 'partakers of the Divine nature'. Ikons depicting them are justified because they are copies of this 'divinised humanity' of the saints.[8]

One can only wish that the attitude of Orthodox theology in this matter were really Christocentric. It would then see itself compelled to find its way back to the attitude of the ancient

[4] Seraphim, *Die Ostkirche*, p. 98. [5] *Op. cit.*, p. 97.
[6] D., 302; M., 116. Cf. Bettenson, *Documents*, pp. 129f.
[7] Seraphim, *Die Ostkirche*, pp. 95f. [8] *Ibid.*

Greek Fathers towards images.[9] Later Orthodox theologians have overlooked the fact that the hypostatic union of the *Logos* with human nature was a unique event. Hence the statement that 'the holy ikon is, so to speak, a continuation of the Divine Incarnation, and reveals the invisible hidden divinity, just as Christ's body did',[10] rests on an error which strikes at the foundation of all theology. The Incarnation of the *Logos* can only be attested and believed, in obedience to Christ's command, by means of the word and sacramental signs which He instituted. It can never be imitated, because the form of the picture can never succeed in containing the *Logos*. Obviously there is some awareness of this truth. Otherwise there would not be so great an emphasis on the blessing of the ikon. This act is apparently thought of as connected with the assumption of flesh by the *Logos* from Mary. But this challenges the uniqueness of God's manifestation in the flesh. Confronted by the worship of images, a Christocentrically based theology does not find it adequate to say merely that there are 'certain abuses among uninstructed people'.[11] The images themselves and the worship of them must be decisively rejected. The worship of images conflicts with the true and unique Incarnation. Moreover it represents an unwarrantable rival to the sacraments in which Christ Himself has given us, along with the spoken word of preaching, the picture He wishes His own to use to assure us of His presence.

[9] Cf. Second Helvetic Confession, ch. IV. (See below, p. 223, note 78).
[10] Seraphim, *Die Ostkirche*, p. 96.
[11] H. S. Alivisatos, in *Ekklesia*, VOL. X, p. 94.

CHAPTER 6

THE VENERATION OF MARY AND THE SAINTS

THE veneration of Mary occupies as important a place in the Orthodox Church as it does in the Roman. This reverence is due to her as the *Mother of God* and *Perpetual Virgin*.[1] The Eastern Church also celebrates the feast of the Immaculate Conception, but understands this somewhat differently from Rome. The Orthodox Church is thinking simply of the miraculous conception by elderly parents, and not of any preservation of Mary from original sin. In the Orthodox view even the Mother of God *shared in original sin*.[2] Many theologians stress the fact that "only Christ is sinless."[3] Yet the view that Mary ascended bodily into Heaven arose in the Eastern Church and was first celebrated there in the fifth century, though it was never made into a dogma. For, although this view is a very ancient one, in answer to the 1950 Papal definition it was affirmed that the ascension of Mary 'neither rests on any revealed fact, nor is it evident from any text of Scripture'.[4]

The official teaching of the Orthodox Church about Mary hardly goes beyond the statements of the Evangelical confessions of faith. We hear nothing in Scripture about her 'perpetual virginity', and must also reject all the other speculations dreamed up by the theologians. It sounds ominous however when Seraphim thinks he can say that the Virgin Mary 'co-operated in Christ's saving work'.[5] 'Because she had received God's Son into her womb and thus became bound to the Divine nature'—that is his basis for the assertion—'she renewed not

[1] Ephesus, 431 (D., 113; M., 72.25. Bettenson, *Documents*, p. 65, 1; *De fide et symbolo*, ed. C. A. Heurtley, with an Eng. trans., Oxford 1889, p. 196, trans. p. 174). Constantinople II, 553 (D., 214; Bettenson, *Documents*, p. 126, 2).

[2] Dyobouniotes, in *Ekklesia*, VOL. X, p. 59.

[3] Chomiakov, *Östliche Christentum*, VOL. II, p. 22.

[4] P. Kovalevsky, in *Ecumenical Press Service*, 1950, No. 44.

[5] Seraphim, *Die Ostkirche*, p. 47.

only herself but also the whole world of which she was the representative.'[6] Happily, this view, which points disturbingly in the direction of Rome, finds no support in the liturgical texts cited by Seraphim.

As in the Roman Church, so too in the Orthodox, the veneration of Mary takes precedence over the veneration of the saints. Of these there is a vast number. But in spite of the large part that saints play in Orthodox worship, little attention has been given to them in theology. The only dogma, as in the Roman Church, is that the saints may be invoked to pray to God for believers.[7]

Reverence is also paid to the relics of saints. It is thought that the abounding grace of the saints is so powerful that it manifests itself through their relics and works miracles: 'The grace that the saints have received from Christ is boundless, so that thanks to the divine power their relics unceasingly work miracles and heal incurable diseases for those who in faith invoke their names.'[8] If this statement is to be taken seriously it means that there has been a second incarnation of the Divine in the saints. The deification expected by the Orthodox Church has been so completely realised in the saints that even their bodily remains still contain the divine. Such a view would impair the Gospel of the absolute uniqueness of the Incarnation of the *Logos* in Jesus Christ.

[6] *Ibid.*

[7] Nicea II, 787, Act. 6 (*Sacrorum Conciliorum nova, et amplissima collectio, in qua praeter ea quae P. Labbeus et G. Cossarteus . . . in lucem edidere, ea omnia insuper suis in locis exhibentur, quae Joannes Dominicus Mansi evulgavit*, etc. VOL. XIII, Florence 1767, p. 203).

[8] Service for the commemoration of the saints, as quoted by Seraphim, *Die Ostkirche*, p. 99.

CHAPTER 7

ESCHATOLOGY

1. The Intermediate State after Death

The Orthodox Church, unlike Rome, knows of no purgatory as a temporary abode for the souls of the faithful departed, and also rejects the idea that after death these faithful departed must still expiate temporal punishments for sin. Both ideas are contrary to Scripture and tradition.[1] The Eastern Church holds that after death men experience a *provisional judgment* on the basis of their faith and works. The souls enter Heaven or Limbo. There they see their future reward or punishment, and thus in anticipation enjoy blessedness or suffer anguish. The faithful still on earth are able to ask God's pardon for the souls already in Hell. The destiny of these can be changed but only by God's mercy.

Since souls after death have not yet reached their ultimate goal, the Eastern Church believes in offering the eucharistic gifts on behalf of all believers and saints who have fallen asleep. The Liturgy of Chrysostom says: 'We offer this reasonable service also for all those who have fallen asleep, for our forefathers and fathers, for Patriarchs, Prophets, Apostles . . . for Martyrs and Virgins and for every righteous spirit made perfect in faith.'[2] For even the vision of God granted specially to the saints after death, still does not mean the perfection of their souls.

2. The Return of Christ

Only the return of Christ brings with it the second and final judgment on all men, the dead and the living. This judgment presupposes the resurrection of the bodies of the dead and the

[1] This is stated even in the Orthodox Confession, I, Q. LXVI (Kimmel, *Libri symbolici*, p. 136; Michalescu, *Bekenntnisse und Glaubenszeugnisse*, p. 57; Schaff, II.345f).

[2] Seraphim, *Die Ostkirche*, p. 101.

reunion of their souls with their bodies in Heaven or in Limbo. The second judgment also is determined by men's faith and works. It assigns eternal reward and eternal punishment for men, soul and body, whereas the provisional reward and punishment given in the first judgment applied only to the soul.

3. The Eschatological Attitude of the Eastern Church

The Eastern Church not only holds definite views about Christ's return and the completion of His redeeming work in men; its whole attitude is strongly directed towards the last things. Zankov says: 'Perhaps more than any other branch of Christianity, Orthodoxy has retained the eschatological character of the Church of the first Century.'[3]

This outlook comes to expression in the fact that Orthodox worship rests upon and culminates in the Easter festival. Over and over again in the Easter celebrations, beginning at midnight and reaching their climax in the Eucharist of Easter Day, the rapturous words of priest and people glorify Christ's Resurrection.[4] This jubilation is echoed in every Eucharist throughout the whole year. 'Thus at the deepest level, for the Orthodox Church the whole year is Easter, an anticipation of the Eternal Easter in Heaven.'[5] Yet it is not forgotten that it is the One who was crucified who has overcome death. In the Easter festival this comes out continually. We can learn much, therefore, from the Eastern Church about the eschatological character of the Lord's Supper, and how to celebrate it as the festive meal which it was in the primitive Church (Acts 2.47).

The form and manner of Orthodox worship, celebrated in Churches whose walls are adorned with ikons, is meant to express the conquest of time by eternity. 'The whole system of the ikons, with the Pantocrator at the head, surrounded by the Prophets, Apostles and Saints, is a symbolic unity, representing the Church Triumphant, while it is completed by the living congregation of clergy and people, representing the Church Militant. Thus the whole Church, visible and invisible, is assembled in the presence of the Most Holy Trinity, praying

[3] Zankov, *Eastern Orthodox Church*, p. 63.
[4] Cf. Heiler, *Urkirche und Ostkirche*, pp. 352ff.
[5] *Op. cit.*, p. 355.

and praising together in a mystical communion.'[6] 'Yet there is no inclination to understand by this term [i.e. Kingdom of God] the externals of the Christianity at present in the world, but on the other hand, neither is it considered so unimportant as to be left completely out of account.'[7]

Anyone wishing to criticise Orthodox worship and the interpretation placed upon it, questioning whether it really expresses the authentic biblical hope of redemption, and not rather an impermissible cultic anticipation of the Consummation, must listen to the answer given by the theologians of this Church. The Orthodox Christian, 'more easily than the Western Christian, can renounce everything . . . in order to save his soul for eternity, in order to go forth to meet the returning Christ'.[8] In other words, what happens in Orthodox worship has real implications for the daily life and practice of individual Christians. This eschatological outlook of the Eastern Church also expresses itself in an ethic directed to the End in definite ways. F. M. Dostoievsky made this plain in memorable fashion in his fantastic story, *The Dream of a Strange Man*.[9] Here is the deepest reason for the Orthodox Church's reserve in face of the attempts of other Churches to accept political and social responsibility in the world. 'For the ideal of Orthodoxy is in fact not the civilisation of man and the world but their transfiguration.'[10] This statement shows, of course, that here one false thesis has been rejected in favour of another which is no better. Certainly civilisation cannot be the concern of a Church under the Gospel, nor a transfigured world either, but only Christ, who is nevertheless 'God's mighty claim upon our whole life' through whom 'we obtain joyful deliverance from the godless bondage of this world for the free grateful service of His creatures'.[11] The monk is just as questionable a figure as the liberal Protestant advocate of civilisation. In face of both, we have to ask whether Christ is really being taken seriously as Saviour and Lord.

[6] Alivisatos, in *Ekklesia*, VOL. X, p. 95.
[7] Zankov, *Eastern Orthodox Church*, p. 64.
[8] Seraphim, *Die Ostkirche*, p. 110.
[9] F. M. Dostoievsky, *The Diary of a Writer*, trans. Boris Brasol, London 1949, VOL. II, pp. 672-90.
[10] Seraphim, *Die Ostkirche*, p. 110.
[11] Barmen Thesis, No. 2.

III

THE GOSPEL AND THE CHURCHES OF THE REFORMATION

INTRODUCTION

WE now turn to the Churches of the Reformation. In respect of these too, the question that concerns us is how they have interpreted and communicated the Gospel. At the very outset of this enquiry we recalled how, in our own days, members of the Lutheran, Reformed, and United Churches in Germany came together at Barmen in 1934 to confess Jesus Christ as 'the One Word of God which we have to hear and which we have to trust and obey in life and in death'. At that time the Synod resolved 'to transmit this Declaration to the Confessional Conferences [of the Synod] in order that they may work out interpretations of it on the basis of their Confessions'.[1] A few years later, in 1937, a commentary on the Barmen Declaration, entitled *Consensus de doctrina evangelii* was submitted to the Synod of the Evangelical Church of the old Prussian Union, meeting at Halle. In the final section of this document, the official Reformation Confessions were subjected to a critical examination.[2] That is exactly what is proposed in what follows. We shall compare the testimony borne in our own times with the Confessions of Faith drawn up at the time of the Reformation. That was essentially our purpose in the first two sections, when the Roman and Orthodox Churches were questioned about their testimony to the Gospel. But now this question is to be put to the Churches in which we have our own roots, and whose confessional statements therefore affect us differently from the dogmas of Rome and the East. As we listen, test and comment we have a special responsibility to see that a legitimate loyalty to the affirmations of our fathers does not degenerate into misguided prejudice.

Prejudice here can take several forms. On the one hand, it can take the form of a narrow attachment to the confession

[1] Minutes (*Synodalbericht*) p. 28. Cf. *The Significance of the Barmen Declaration*, London 1943, p. 10

[2] *Abendmahlsgemeinschaft?* (Intercommunion?) 2nd edn. Munich 1938, pp. 174ff.

made by our fathers. On the other hand, it can also take the form of a new doctrinal legalism, bearing the label 'Barmen', which pays no attention to the Reformation confessions at all. The division between the Churches of the Reformation cannot be ignored. When we on the Continent speak of this division we usually have in mind the gulf which exists between the Lutheran and Reformed Churches. But this is a very superficial and parochial view of the situation. From the standpoint of certain countries like Germany, it is an understandable view but, nevertheless, a mistaken one. The two contending Continental brothers must not overlook the fact that a large Methodist Church and a large Baptist Church also arose out of the Reformation. And anyone tempted to dismiss these as merely extremist movements on the fringe of the Reformation, need only be reminded of the existence of the Anglican Church, to realise that the Lutheran and Reformed Churches are not the only ones proclaiming the Gospel to the world on the basis of the Reformation. The Ecumenical Movement has helped to shake the complacency even of the Churches of the Reformation. It is as well to remember from the outset that the Reformation gave rise to variously formed Churches each of which seeks in its own way to proclaim the Gospel. Recognising this, let us turn first of all to the testimony of the Lutheran and Reformed Churches.

PART A. THE LUTHERAN AND REFORMED PRESBYTERIAN CHURCHES

1. Efforts to Reach Agreement

The points of agreement and disagreement between these two branches of the Reformation movement were first set out in 1529 (2-4 October) at the Marburg Colloquy between Luther and Zwingli. Luther submitted a proposed agreement in which some existing doctrinal propositions, subsequently called the Schwabach Articles, were summed up in fifteen Articles on God, the Person of Christ, the Work of Christ, Original Sin, Redemption, Faith, Justification, Preaching, Baptism, Good Works, Confession, Civil Government, Tradition, Infant Baptism, and the Lord's Supper.[1] No agreement was reached on Article 15. It is however, worth noticing that the difference over the doctrine of the Lord's Supper was not taken to imply concealed disagreement in the other articles as well. Doctrinal arithmetic of this sort was reserved for more recent times.

It is not our concern to offer an account of the further efforts in this direction. But we must at least mention three men of Reformation times who laboured strenuously to overcome the disagreements which emerged: Bucer in Strasbourg, Calvin and Beza in Geneva. Calvin's *Institutio* is an eirenical Dogmatics, which, without concealing differences, attempts to secure an agreed doctrine in spite of them.

In Poland in the year 1570 agreement was even reached for a time between the Lutherans, the Reformed, and the Bohemian Brethren, in the so-called Consensus of Sendomir. Here again, the doctrine of the Lord's Supper proved to be the difficulty which threatened to wreck the proceedings: 'We agree in believing and confessing that the substantial presence of Christ [the Lutheran Gliczner had suggested: 'the flesh of Christ'] is

[1] *Bekenntnisschriften* (*Luth.*), pp. 51ff. Cf. Schaff, I.212, n. 1, 228, n. 2.

not merely represented in the Lord's Supper but that the Lord's body and blood is truly made present, distributed and imparted to those who communicate, since, in accordance with the nature of sacraments symbols of the thing itself are present which are by no means empty.'[2]

At the Leipzig Colloquy in 1631 theologians from both sides discussed the Augsburg Confession. They were unable to reach full agreement about Article 3: *De filio Dei.* Their agreements and differences in the doctrine of the Person of Christ were specified.[3] The same thing happened with Article 10 on the Lord's Supper. The main points in the Lutheran doctrine which proved unacceptable to the Reformed representatives were: the eating with the mouth (*organo oris*), and the eating by the unworthy (*manducatio indignorum*).[4] If Melanchthonian ideas made agreement possible at Sendomir, authentic Lutheran doctrine made it impossible at Leipzig.

When at the beginning of the nineteenth century the Union was introduced into various regional Churches in Germany,[5] differences were glossed over even in those cases where doctrinal unity was sought, and a common confession was actually drawn up. Thus for example the Palatinate Deed of Union stated: 'Points of doctrine previously in dispute have for carefully considered reasons been set aside by a view which is in agreement with the clear statements of the Gospel.' 'In accordance with this the Protestant Evangelical Christian Church declares that the Holy Supper is a feast in memory of Jesus and [a feast] of the most blessed communion with the Redeemer who, for us men, was given up to death, raised again from the dead, and

[2] 'Convenimus, ut credamus substantialem praesentiam Christi non significari duntaxat, sed vere in coena eo vescentibus repraesentari distribui et exhiberi corpus et sanguinem domini, symbolis adiectis ipsi rei, minime nudis: secundum sacramentorum naturam.' *R.E.*, VOL. XVIII, p. 217; H. A. Niemeyer. *Collectio confessionum in ecclesiis reformatis publicatarum*, Leipzig 1840, p. 554. See B. J. Kidd, *Documents illustrative of the Continental Reformation*, Oxford 1911, henceforth cited as *Documents*, p. 659. On the *Consensus Sendomiriensis*, see H. W. Erbkam in *New Schaff-Herzog*, VOL. X, pp. 356f; E. A. Payne, in *Intercommunion*, edd. D. Baillie and J. Marsh, London 1952, p. 86; J. T. McNeill in Rouse and Neill, *History of the Ecumenical Movement*, pp. 62f. Schaff, 1.586f, gives a short account and summary.

[3] Niemeyer, *Collectio confessionum*, pp. 657f. On the *Leipzig Colloquy* see A. Hauck in *New Schaff-Herzog*, VOL. VI, pp. 445f, and Schaff, 1.558f.

[4] Niemeyer, *Collectio confessionum*, p. 663.

[5] On the Union of 1817 see H. R. T. Brandreth in Rouse and Neill, *History of the Ecumenical Movement*, pp. 286ff.

taken up to His Father and theirs, and who is with them always even to the end of the world.' 'Respecting the earlier Church doctrines of predestination and gracious election, the Protestant Evangelical Christian Church bases its conviction that God has destined all men to blessedness and does not withhold from them the means of attaining the same, on the words of the New Testament in 1 John 4.16, 1 Tim. 2.4-6, and 2 Pet. 3.9.'[6] That of course was no solution of the problems left in abeyance.

Just before the Second World War, the Confessing Church of the old Prussian Union attempted to define and clarify the main issue at stake between the Lutherans and the Reformed. The Confessional Synod of Halle declared in 1937: 'The differences still existing between us in the doctrine of the Holy Supper concern the mode and form in which the Lord gives Himself in the Supper. They do not touch the fact that the gift in the Supper is the Lord Himself.'[7] This affirmation was attacked by Lutherans of a different stamp. Nevertheless the Halle decision represents a milestone on the road to agreement between the two confessions.

Of even greater importance for the mutual relationship of the two confessions is the fact that, previously to this, it had already been possible at Barmen in 1934 for Lutheran and Reformed Christians to express their common faith in six theological propositions. The differences were not thereby settled but retired into the background, since the Church was required to confess its faith at a different point. At this point, Lutherans and Reformed showed themselves joint witnesses of Jesus Christ, by an utterance which, as they confessed, God had placed in their mouth. It matters little whether we say that by so doing they proved themselves to be one Church, or whether we would regard such a statement as exaggerated. At all events, the two previously divided confessions rendered together the service to which the Church is summoned. That was a miracle before our very eyes. The fact that many today are emphasising the differences between Lutheran and Re-

[6] E. F. K. Müller, *Die Bekenntnisschriften der reformierten Kirche*, Leipzig 1903, pp. 871f.

[7] W. Niesel, *Um Verkündigung und Ordnung der Kirche, Die Bekenntnissynoden der Ev. Kirche der alt. pr. Union 1934-1943*, Bielefeld 1949, p. 37. Cf. W. Niesel in *Intercommunion*, edd. Baillie and Marsh, pp. 283f.

formed is simply a sign that the Church once more has time on its hands to be concerned with itself. It no longer stands hard pressed between its enemies and the Lord Jesus Christ, and is thus in danger of forsaking its role as witness. It is essential to keep this danger of a false detachment clearly before us as we approach the question how the Lutheran and Reformed Churches bear witness to the Gospel.

2. Some Assessments of the Doctrinal Differences

Apart from these conversations between the Lutheran and the Reformed, the most important of which have just been mentioned, already in Reformation times a whole body of controversial writings existed, especially on the doctrine of the Lord's Supper. Since we do not intend to offer a history of the theological debate between the two confessions we will simply refer to a few modern assessments of the main point at issue between them.

Max Goebel, in *Die religiöse Eigentümlichkeit der lutherischen und reformierten Kirche* ('*The Religious Character of the Lutheran and Reformed Churches*'), 1837, saw the starting-point for Lutheran doctrine in its material principle, i.e. its view of justification by faith alone, and the starting-point for Reformed doctrine in its formal principle, its view of Holy Scripture as the norm for the whole Christian life, 'or, what amounts to the same thing, the striving to glorify God by absolute submission to His Word, as against all other, human commandments'.[8] Clearly there is some truth in this observation. On the Lutheran side the doctrine of justification is always made the starting-point for everything else (e.g. by Elert and Sasse). But how far is it possible to describe the formal Scripture principle as the Reformed starting-point? What is meant here by 'absolute submission to God's Word'? How is this Word related to the Word of the sinner's justification?

According to Alexander Schweizer, in *Die Glaubenslehre der evangelisch-reformierten Kirche* ('*The Doctrine of the Evangelical Reformed Church*'), vol. I, 1844, we have to look for a material principle in the Reformed Church as well. 'The fundamental aim of the Reformed Church is to eliminate all idolatry of the

[8] p. 70.

creature or pagan obscuration of the knowledge of God, by returning to pure original Christianity. Hence the most basic dogma, or material principle, as it is called, is that posited in biblical Christianity, the principle of sole and absolute dependence on God, a kind of religious determinism produced in the interests of an unrestricted praise of God.'[9] Schweizer thus sets against the Lutherans' anthropological material principle, that not works but faith alone saves, a Reformed theological one, namely the principle of absolute dependence on God.[10] In explanation of this he says: 'Obviously the points of doctrine emphasised in Reformed Symbolics and Polemics have the common aim of affirming without qualification the almighty glory of God: (1) Christ's divinity is sharply distinguished from His creatureliness. (2) The action of Divine grace is independent of and unconditioned by the will of the creature, hence, strict predestination. (3) The efficacy of grace in the sacrament is independent of the creaturely elements and simply signified and sealed by these.'[11] No one would deny that Schweizer, too, observed something that is true. But we cannot fail to notice in the view of this theologian, that he looks at the confessions through the spectacles of the greatest theologian of the nineteenth century, Friedrich Schleiermacher,[12] and reads the latter's theology into Reformed doctrine. Schweizer's personal philosophical approach emerges in his interpretation of 'sole and absolute dependence on God' according to Schleiermacher 'a feeling'—as a theological principle.

M. Schneckenburger in *Vergleichende Darstellung des lutherischen und reformierten Lehrbegriffs* ('*Lutheran and Reformed Views of Doctrine Compared*'), Part II, 1855, followed even more closely in Schleiermacher's footsteps by looking for the distinction between the Lutheran and Reformed views of doctrine in 'the difference in their religious dispositions'.[13] 'The Lutheran approach is mainly theoretical and contemplative: in the contemplation of the perfection of Christ, which he knows is given to him in a real mystical union, the subject has what he needs, life and complete fulfilment. . . . The subject behaves recep-

[9] p. 40. [10] p. 42. [11] p. 22.

[12] Friedrich Daniel Ernst Schleiermacher, 1768-1834. See Karl Barth, *From Rousseau to Ritschl*, London 1959, ch. VIII. [13] PT II, p. 280.

tively. The Reformed approach is mainly practical: it is essential to be active, and complete fulfilment is found only in giving active expression to the salvation received by faith in Christ. For the regenerate subject action is not just an almost negligible consequence of believing but its very essence.'[14] Schneckenburger also calls it a 'difference in mental and reflective attitude'. 'With his contemplative mental approach [the Lutheran] directs his attention upwards to the Divine radiance which shines into his life in justification, and is unconcerned about its necessary translation into action.' 'The Reformed Christian looks horizontally towards the End, the blessedness to which his life brings him ever nearer.' 'For him the ideal is not really certain until it has been expressed empirically in deliberate action.'[15] Hence, according to Schneckenburger, we could 'describe the Lutheran approach as feminine, the Reformed as masculine. . . . Certainly a womanly character will appear more attractive and at home in the Lutheran type of piety than in the very precise Reformed type, where true womanliness is easily lost amid inflexible principles.'[16] We cannot but be reminded here of Schleiermacher's *Weihnachtsfeier*,[17] with its hymn in praise of feminine receptivity. Schneckenburger is a warning example that theology is always in danger of reading its own views into the doctrine of the Reformation.

The extent of Schleiermacher's influence is seen in the fact that even a Reformed theologian like E. F. K. Müller (in his *Symbolik*, 1896), in some measure agrees with the view of Schneckenburger. He speaks, however, not of religious dispositions but of 'a characteristic difference in the evangelical assurance of salvation'[18] in the two confessions. 'The difference between a partial immediacy and a total ordering of life is paralleled not merely in the dogmatic systems, but even in the history and whole attitude to life of the two Churches. The assurance of salvation (in Reformed Protestantism) is not content, as in Lutheranism, with an immediate, naive, emotional reliance on the Word, but strives rather for a total

[14] PT I, pp. 164f. [5] PT I, pp. 285-7. [16] PT I, p. 163.

[17] *Werke*. PT I, pp. 461ff. Eng. trans. *Christmas Eve: A dialogue on the celebration of Christmas*, tr. W. Hastie, Edinburgh 1890.

[18] E. F. K. Müller, *Symbolik*, p. 391.

development: hence the appeal to the absolute grace which stands behind the Word, and, linked with this, a reaching forward to manifest this grace in a life of action. . . . These two concerns of the moral and spiritual life, which conflict only in appearance, are held together by an active surrender to the glory of God, elevated to the highest degree of assurance of salvation.'[19] In his attempt to understand the two confessions Müller, like Schweizer and Schneckenburger, keeps to the theological path taken by Schleiermacher. Under the influence of the Erlangen School,[20] he deviates from this path slightly only in finding the key to an understanding not in a difference in religious disposition, but in the assurance of man's salvation, expressed in the one way or the other. In the last resort he keeps to the anthropocentric approach and the question is: Is this in order? Does Müller in this way do justice to the Reformers and their successors? That is not to suggest that we should instead seek for some other principle as the distinguishing feature. The Reformers were concerned neither with an objective principle nor with a subjective disposition, even one in the form of the assurance of salvation, but with something quite different.

3. Our Task

That brings us to our task, namely, to find out for ourselves what Lutherans and Reformed have known and communicated as the Gospel. Since the 1920's the message of the Reformers has become available to us in a new way. At that time a penetrating and fruitful study of Luther began. A new interest in Calvin also emerged.[21] Reformed theologians like Karl Barth engaged in the study of Luther's theology, and Lutheran theologians like Karl Holl and others, shared in the rediscovery of Calvin. There was a mutual giving and receiving just as the Lutheran and Reformed theologies had themselves once originated in such mutual exchange. In view of the inter-relatedness

[19] *Op. cit.*, pp. 392f.

[20] Erlangen School; J. Chr. K. von Hofmann (1810-77), G. Thomasius (1802-75), Fr. H. R. Frank (1827-94). See R. S. Franks, *A History of the Doctrine of the Work of Christ*, London and New York 1918, vol. II, pp. 297-328.

[21] Cf. W. Niesel, *Die Theologie Calvins*, 2nd edn. Munich 1957, Eng. trans. *The Theology of Calvin*, tr. H. Knight. London 1956.

of the two traditions, we shall not present each of them separately. At some risk that neither will appear in as clear a light as it would in a separate presentation, we shall follow a different course from that adopted in Parts I and II, and present Lutherans and Reformed discussing together the different points of doctrine. We shall listen to what the two confessions have to say about particular questions and try to learn why they think that, for the sake of the Gospel, they must speak as they do.

Considerable difficulties, of course, at once arise.

(*a*) No attempt has ever been made to establish a single Reformed Church, still less a Calvinist one. Calvin himself never regarded those who accepted the Augsburg Confession as members of a different Church. Indeed, as a testimony to the Church's unity, he himself signed the *Confessio Augustana*, with the reservation, of course, that he interpreted it in the same sense as its author.[22] He had little taste for the controversy with the protagonists of Luther's theology. Calvin's successor Beza, too, was most ecumenically minded. It was Lutheranism which finally isolated itself from the other Churches by the Formula of Concord.

(*b*) Since there was never any design of forming a united Reformed Church no Reformed counterpart to the Book of Concord exists either. On the Reformed side we find no universally recognised symbolic book. The collections of confessional documents cannot of course be so regarded. There is not even a single confessional document recognised by all Reformed Churches. On the contrary there are a great number of such documents varying in content to some extent. We need only recall the confessions influenced by Zwingli and those influenced by Calvin, to mention but two groups. The Churches in various places stated their position in the form of a Confession, when and wherever they were compelled to do so. Many confessions were adopted by Synods, others are more private in character. The overall picture is thus very varied. But even in the case of Lutheranism, we must not overlook the striking

[22] J. Calvin, *Opera quae supersunt omnia*, VOLS. I-LIX, edd. G. Baum *et al.*, Brunswick and Berlin 1863-1900 (Corpus Reformatorum VOLS. XXIX-LXXXVII), henceforth cited as *Opera*, VOL. XVI, p. 430 (letter of 8 April 1557).

fact that the Formula of Concord is not universally recognised.

(*c*) Although the field under consideration is easier to survey in Lutheranism we can interpret Lutheran doctrine correctly only when we view it in its historical development and in its various representatives. This applies still more to Reformed doctrine. To forget this is to run the risk of treating everything as on the same level, and of becoming unhelpful and tedious.

(*d*) Our task, however, is not to provide a history of dogma of the kind bequeathed to us in so impressive a form by H. E. Weber. Certainly we must ask about the official doctrine of the two confessions. We must therefore keep to the confessional documents which are authoritative for us. Since the Heidelberg Catechism in particular is authoritative for the Reformed Churches in Germany, we shall refer to those confessions of faith which are close to it in substance. We cannot in either case leave out of account the writings of the men who alone made the production of these confessions possible. Nor can we ignore later theological work even if it has not yet found expression in statements of faith. Consistently to maintain a firm hold here, to distinguish between essentials and non-essentials, and to avoid the danger of stirring all these testimonies into a mixture to suit one's own tastes, is a task easy to criticise but difficult to fulfil.

(*e*) It is especially difficult to find the right starting-point for this discussion between the two branches of Protestantism. Should we begin with the doctrine of the Lord's Supper, which is still the main point at issue today? But to do so would be to run the risk of finding ourselves in the well-worn tracks again, and indeed of somewhat oversimplifying the differences between the two partners. We do not share the opinion, however, of some denominationalists who think that Luther was in fact wrong when he declared his complete agreement with Zwingli right up to the very edge of the deep division about the Lord's Supper. Even so, there are many differences to be noted on both sides, even when they do not have divisive force.

(*f*) Finally, a difficulty of presentation. It is impossible for us to ignore the position which we ourselves occupy. There is no neutral position above the two Reformation parties. We shall try to ensure that both sides are allowed to speak frankly, but we do not claim an impartiality which is quite impossible here. This does not mean we wish to insist on a Reformed position. Definitely not! For it is surely characteristic of our Churches to describe themselves as 'Reformed in accordance with God's Word'. That makes it plain that it is not a question of our holding unalterable positions but rather of being ready to quit every position when God's Word calls us. Only in this freedom, which loosens all bonds, can we give the voice of our fathers a hearing in the following pages: but, in this freedom, this voice must be allowed to make its contribution to the discussions with Lutheran theology.

CHAPTER I

UNION WITH CHRIST

1. The Basic Confession of the Reformed Churches

The basic affirmation of the faith of the Reformed Churches is expressed in Q. 1 of the Heidelberg Catechism: 'That I, with body and soul, both in life and in death, am not my own, but belong to my faithful Saviour Jesus Christ.'[1] Jesus Christ once did something which has brought even me today under His authority. He is not simply a figure in the remote past, but the most living presence. As Lord of Lords, He exercises His gracious rule over those who are His. We are subject to Him and His saving power. Reformed theology starts its thinking from Easter and the Ascension and sees the Cross of Christ in their light.

It must however be said further that our salvation is wholly and completely outside us (*extra nos*) in Christ. We shall have more to say about that when we come to the doctrine of justification. Yet this Lord in whom our salvation is enclosed is very near to us. 'As long as Christ remains outside of us, and we are separated from him, all that he has suffered and done for the salvation of the human race remains useless and of no value for us.'[2] The reason is that the blessings of salvation are not ordinary gifts of God but lie enclosed in Christ.[3] 'Therefore,' says the Genevan Reformer, 'to share with us what he has received from the Father, he had to become ours and to dwell within us. For this reason, he is called "our Head" (Eph.

[1] The Reformed catechisms are quoted throughout in the version given in T. F. Torrance, *The School of Faith. The Catechisms of the Reformed Church*, London 1959.

[2] Calvin, *Institutio Christianae Religionis*, henceforth cited as *Inst.*, III.1.1. The English edition used in the present work is the new translation made by Ford Lewis Battles in collaboration with other scholars under the editorship of John T. McNeill, published in 1961 as VOLS. XX and XXI of The Library of Christian Classics (edited by John Baillie, J. T. McNeill and Henry P. Van Dusen). Volume and page reference in brackets are to this edn. Here VOL. I, p. 537.

[3] *Ibid.* (VOL. I, p. 537).

4.15), and "the first-born among many brethren" (Rom. 8.29). We also, in turn, are said to be "engrafted into him" (Rom. 11.17) and to "put on Christ" (Gal. 3.27); for, as I have said, all that he possesses is nothing to us until we grow into one body with him.'[4] This insight is expressed in Q. 20 of the Heidelberg Catechism which says that only those are saved by Christ 'who through true faith are incorporated into Him and receive all His benefits'.

According to Reformed doctrine then, the answer to the question how salvation (justification, sanctification, and eternal life) is brought to men is that not only the preparation for salvation but also its actual communication to men, depends wholly on Jesus Christ. 'When speaking of the free mercies of God, I invariably begin with Christ, and rightly so, for until He becomes ours we must necessarily be completely devoid of all the gifts of grace which are wholly enclosed in Him.'[5]

Thus for both Calvin and the Heidelberg Catechism, 'that joining together of Head and members, that indwelling of Christ in our hearts—in short, that mystical union' is fundamental. 'We do not, therefore, contemplate him outside ourselves from afar in order that his righteousness may be imputed to us but because we put on Christ and are engrafted into his body—in short, because he deigns to make us one with him. For this reason, we glory that we have fellowship of righteousness with him.'[6] Calvin never tires of emphasising this, especially in his sacramental doctrine. God's gift to us is Christ Himself. What we receive is not gifts or powers, important as these are, but God Himself in the form of His Son.[7] The result of this event is that believers 'are not merely united with Him but one with Him, and indeed in such a unity that in it, in a sense, there is a certain shadowing forth of that most single unity, in which the Divine Persons are a single entity among themselves'.[8]

[4] *Ibid.*

[5] Calvin, *Opera*, VOL. IX, p. 88 (Second Defence in answer to Westphal, 1556). *Tracts and Treatises*, ed. T. F. Torrance, Edinburgh 1959, VOL. II, p. 302.

[6] *Inst.*, III.11.10 (VOL. I, p. 737).

[7] *Inst.*, III.2.24 (VOL. I, p. 570).

[8] 'Nec uniti tantum cum ipso, sed et Unum, et quidem unitate tali, in qua quodammodo adumbratio aliqua est simplicissimae istius unitatis, qua personae divinae inter se unum sunt.' H. Witsius, Dutch theologian 1636-1708, quoted by H. Heppe, *Die Dogmatik der ev.-reform. Kirche*, 1861, p. 376, Eng. trans. *Reformed Dogmatics*, tr. G. T. Thomson, London 1950, p. 512.

This union with Christ does not, of course, mean a *mixture of substance* with Him.[9] Calvin does go so far as to speak, on the basis of Eph. 5.30, of a 'sacred wedlock' between Christ and us 'through which we are made flesh of his flesh and bone of his bone, and thus one with him'.[10] But he vigorously rejects that 'gross mingling of Christ with believers' (*crassa mixtura Christi cum fidelibus*) taught by Andreas Osiander.[11] Such a mixture of substance would mean that 'God—transfusing himself into us, as it were—makes us part of Himself'.[12] What is really involved is the miracle 'that although Christ is in Heaven and we are on the earth, we are, nevertheless, "flesh of His flesh" and "bone of His bone" '.[13]

Peter von Mastricht (*d.* 1706) describes this union as follows: It is (1) 'real, not imaginary or in intention only' (*realis, non imaginaria tantum aut intentionalis*), i.e. not just an agreement of the feelings and will; 'nor merely accidental' (*nec accidentalis tantum*), i.e. not merely as between one friend and another; 'but in its own way substantial' (*sed suo modo substantialis*), i.e. a union between one person and another in the way we saw that the Persons of the Trinity are bound to each other; but even so not a 'mixture of substances' (*substantialis mixtio*), as if man were no longer sinful man and Christ no longer remained what He in His uniqueness is.

It is (2) 'total' (*totalis*) 'in so far as the whole Christian is united to the whole Christ, united in body and soul, with Christ's natures, the human and the divine'. We recall our starting-point, the words of the first question of the Heidelberg Catechism, 'with body and soul'. What is meant therefore is not merely a communion of souls or a community of religious feeling (Schleiermacher). It is not just a union with Christ's Divinity but with His whole Person, in which divinity and humanity are united. The Reformed doctrine of the Lord's Supper is here already in principle decided from the outset. For Reformed preaching it is fundamental that union is with the whole God-man and not merely with one aspect of His

[9] Calvin, *Inst.*, III.11.5 (VOL. I, p. 730).
[10] *Inst.*, III.1.3 (VOL. I, p. 541).
[11] *Inst.*, III.11.10 (VOL. I, p. 737).
[12] *Inst.*, III.11.5 (VOL. I, p. 731).
[13] Heidelberg Catechism, Q. 76 (Torrance, *School of Faith*, p. 83).

being. That being so, this cannot be any less the case in the Lord's Supper.

Union with Christ is (3) 'indissoluble and eternal' (*indissolubilis et aeterna*), not transient merely, in no sense a merely historical link even though it appears in the form of such a link.

It is (4) therefore 'spiritual' (*spiritualis*). This does not mean that it is an 'immaterial' union (we saw that it is *totalis*) or merely 'spiritual' in the sense that we acquire the spirit of Christ. Rather is it '*spiritualis*' because it is 'wrought by the One Spirit who is in Christ and Christians (Rom. 8.11), in Christ of course as the Head, but in Christians as the members'.[14] This is a basic doctrine of Calvin which we shall meet again, especially in the doctrine of the sacraments: 'The Holy Spirit is the bond by which Christ effectually unites us to himself.'[15] It was also taken into the Heidelberg Catechism.[16] This doctrine means that if there is to be any contemporaneity, any encounter, any union between the Son of God and us sinners, then God Himself must act as Creator. As great a miracle is involved here as the miracle of the Incarnation of God's Son. The miracle of Christmas must be followed by the miracle of Pentecost if the former is to reach its goal in us. Hence this union is called a *unio mystica*, because its realisation lies wholly beyond our possibilities and capacities. Just as the Son of God did His saving work *for* us, so today the Holy Spirit completes His work *in* us so as to make the act of salvation fruitful for us and to bind us together with Christ. The work of the Triune God for fallen man thus comes to fruition. Calvin's basic reason for rejecting Andreas Osiander is that the latter does not observe 'the bond of this unity' which we have with Christ.[17] According to Osiander, there results an identity between Christ and us which is altogether excluded if Christ is to be and remain for us what He is. We become 'indirectly identical' with Him (Karl Barth). He remains Himself and I remain myself. He is wholly and completely the Giver and I am the one who receives. 'I am,' as the Heidelberg Catechism says, 'His own.'

This *unio mystica* must be clearly distinguished from the

[14] Heppe, *Reformed Dogmatics*, p. 512.
[15] *Inst.*, III.1.1 (VOL. I, p. 538).
[16] E.g. Q. 53, 76, 79, 80 (Torrance, *School of Faith*, pp. 78, 83ff).
[17] *Inst.*, III.11.5 (VOL. I, p. 730).

mystical union with the Divine, described by the mystics. According to them, man is released from the material world, stripped of all opposition to God, and so finally reaches and loses himself in the Supreme Being. The mystic passes through various stages of being, in order to arrive at the supreme stage. He loses himself in order to merge into the supreme good (*summum bonum*). The mystical union spoken of by Reformed theologians and confessions on the basis of the New Testament, is something quite different. The relationship here is not between created being and Divine being but between the sinner and the Redeemer. It is not a doctrine of being (ontology) but a doctrine of salvation (soteriology). Since man does not merely stand on a level of being below God, but is His creature and, moreover, a creature who runs away from his Creator, the possibility of his submerging or losing himself in God just does not arise. Man may submerge himself in some sort of divinity but not in God the Lord, to whom we belong. If this is ignored, as was the case sometimes in pietism and romanticism (Schleiermacher), the doctrine of the *unio mystica* seriously endangers the whole of theology. Jesus Christ's place as the Mediator between God and man is assailed and indeed, becomes superfluous: and an immediacy of man to Christ is claimed in forgetfulness of the fact that man is and remains a sinner. Theology is changed into mysticism.

How little the doctrine of the *unio mystica* has in common with mysticism is finally clear from the fact that, here especially, a man like Calvin keeps strictly to the eschatological boundary. 'Not only,' he says, 'does Christ cleave to us by an indivisible bond of fellowship, but, with a wonderful communion, day by day, he grows more and more into one body with us until he becomes completely one with us.'[18] This does not mean that, by a continuous process, we attain perfect union in this life. 'If you are united with our Lord Jesus Christ in this world,' he writes in a letter, 'and are a member of His body, for He took our flesh so as to be utterly our brother, and if you live obediently to His Gospel, which directs us to seek our salvation wholly in Him, then you will attain the life promised to those who believe, because you look for Him to awaken us all to-

[18] *Inst.*, III.2.24 (VOL. I, pp. 570f).

gether in His glory.'[19] Only then shall we 'be made conformable to the glorious body of Christ'.[20] Beyond the union enjoyed with Christ here, stands the consummation at the Last Day. Our union now is with the Christ whom we know will come again and manifest the true life of His own. But He is already our Lord and we already belong to Him here and now. Calvin goes on to describe this union, on which the impartation to us of all Christ's gracious gifts rests, in the following contexts: man's regeneration (including penitence), justification, prayer, election. Obviously, these do not form a temporal sequence of acts, since election is dealt with last. Rather they are gracious gifts which have been given to us along with our calling and ingrafting into Christ. Later theologians likewise deal consecutively with the doctrines of calling, conversion, faith, justification, and sanctification. The Heidelberg Catechism, too, develops all its questions and answers about the whole of the Christian faith on the basis of Q. 1, with its affirmation of our union with Christ. Even apart from this catechism, which is quite alone in giving a Christocentric basis to its whole teaching, the others too, by arranging their material in the way just indicated, show that everything said about the appropriation of the salvation won for us by Christ, also has its starting-point in Christ Himself. Above, in Him—but, in a miraculous way, that means not 'far from us' (*procul a nobis*)—is the source from which all blessings flow down to us. What later was sought and increasingly found in pietism by religious people only in special experiences, has, according to Reformed doctrines, been promised and given by Christ to the sinner from the very beginning: namely, full communion with Christ by the Holy Spirit.[21]

2. Luther's Doctrine of Union with Christ and its Modification in Lutheranism

We now turn to the Lutheran teaching about union with Christ. In Luther himself we find statements quite similar to those in Calvin and the Heidelberg Catechism. It is probable

[19] Calvin, *Opera*, vol. xii, p. 715 (Letter 1031, 13 June, year unknown).
[20] Heidelberg Catechism, Q. 57 (Torrance, *School of Faith*, p. 79).
[21] Westminster Larger Catechism, 1648, Q. 66; Shorter Catechism, 1648, Q. 30f (Torrance, *School of Faith*, pp. 197, 266f).

that Calvin learned from Luther here. We read in Luther's *Liberty of a Christian Man* (1520) that faith 'unites the soul to Christ as the bride to the bridegroom. From this marriage it follows, as St Paul says, that Christ and the soul become one body: so that what each possesses, good things as well as bad, becomes the common property of them both. What Christ has is the property of the believing soul, what the soul has becomes Christ's. Since Christ has all blessings and salvation, these become the soul's. Now the joyful exchange and conflict begins; for since Christ is God and man, one who has never sinned, one whose righteousness is invincible, eternal and almighty, when such a one makes His own the sins of the believing soul—by the wedding ring, i.e. by faith—and deals with them, as if he himself had committed them, then these sins must be swallowed up and drowned in Him.'[22] Even earlier, in the 1519 *Commentary on Galatians*, Luther spoke frequently of union with Christ: 'You are righteous . . . because by faith in Christ you have put on Christ.' 'To put on Christ means to put on righteousness, truth, all grace and the fulfilment of the whole Law.'[23] We may also cite the Small Catechism's explanation of the second article of the Creed, where it is stated that Jesus Christ did His atoning work for me 'in order that I may be (wholly) His own'.[24] The earlier Lutheran theologians adopted Luther's doctrine of union with Christ. H. E. Weber mentions, among others, Bugenhagen, Brenz, and the Frankish Confessions.[25] Andreas Osiander fully accepted the concern underlying it, but

[22] Luther, *Werke. Kritische Gesamtausgabe*, ed. J. C. F. Knaake, Weimar 1883ff, henceforth cited as W.A., VOL. VII, pp. 25f. Also in *Primary Works*, edd. Wace and Buchheim, pp. 264f; and *Reformation Writings*, tr. B. L. Woolf, VOL. I, p. 363.

[23] 'Justus es . . . quia in Christum credens Christum induisti.' 'Christum . . . induere est iustitiam veritatem omnemque gratiam totiusque legis plenitudinem induere.' W.A., VOL. II, pp. 529f, as quoted by E. Hirsch, *Die Theologie des Andreas Osiander*, Göttingen 1919, p. 57. Cf. also the passage quoted by H. I. Iwand in *Glaubensgerechtigkeit nach Luthers Lehre*, Theologische Existenz heute, No. 75, Munich 1941, p. 64, from the 1535 *Commentary on Galatians* (W.A., VOL. XL, I, p. 285): 'Verum recte docenda est fides, quod per eam sic conglutineris Christo, ut ex te et ipso fiat quasi una persona' (Faith therefore must be purely taught: namely that by faith thou art so entirely and nearly joined unto Christ that he and thou are made as it were one person) (trans. from Luther, *Commentary on Galatians*, ed. P. S. Watson, London 1953).

[24] *Concordia*, p. 161; Kidd, *Documents*, p. 212; Luther, *Primary Works*, edd. Wace and Buchheim, p. 10.

[25] H. E. Weber, *Reformation, Orthodoxie und Rationalismus*, PT I, *Von der Reformation zur Orthodoxie*, VOL. I, Gütersloh 1937, p. 48.

changed it into a doctrine of man's deification. We have seen earlier how his views were rejected by Calvin.

In comparing the teaching of the two confessions, Osiander's views must be left out of account. But the question then arises, at what point does a difference in doctrine emerge? In the original form of the doctrine, there is no difference at all. That should be of great importance for the relationship between the two confessions. If we look closer, and ask what union with Christ implies for the individual, perhaps we shall notice a difference between the two sides. But this we must defer until later.

If we concentrate on the heart of the doctrine, we notice that the Formula of Concord already prepared the way for a strange inversion of the doctrine found in Luther and his associates. 'For although in the elect, who are justified by Christ and reconciled with God, God the Father, Son, and Holy Ghost, who is the eternal and essential righteousness, dwells by faith (for all Christians are temples of God the Father, Son, and Holy Ghost, who also impels them to do right), yet this indwelling of God is not the righteousness of faith of which St Paul treats and which he calls *iustitiam Dei*, that is, the righteousness of God, for the sake of which we are declared righteous before God; *but it follows the preceding righteousness of faith*, which is nothing else than the forgiveness of sins. . . .'[26] That is obviously formulated so as to exclude the peculiar doctrine of Osiander, who said that by union with Christ, we share His eternal Divine righteousness and in this way become righteous. But the defence adopted against this view has destroyed the Formula's own position, since it speaks of a faith arising in man which is not an encounter with Christ. This encounter only comes after faith. The fact that we receive everything that Christ has gained for us, only in Him, has been forgotten. Later theologians deal with faith, justification, calling, illumination, regeneration and conversion, the mystic union, renewal,[27] in the section 'On the grace of appropriation through the Holy Spirit' (*De gratia spiritus sancti applicatrice*). Quenstedt

[26] Formula of Concord (1580), Thorough Decl. IV (*Concordia*, p. 254).

[27] 'Fides, iustificatio, vocatio, illuminatio, regeneratio, et conversio, unio mystica renovatio.' H. Schmid, *Die Dogmatik der evangelisch-lutherischen Kirche*, Erlangen 1843, pp. 305f.

says of this sequence: 'Regeneration, justification, union, and renewal are simultaneous and coincide more exactly than a mathematical point, so that they cannot be separated or divided from each other. To our minds, justification and regeneration appear to precede the mystical union. For only when a man receives faith at his regeneration and has been justified by faith *does he begin to be mystically united with God*.'[28] Quenstedt has retained part of Luther's basic insight when he says these acts are still simultaneous. But the psychologising which follows is curious. It surely turns the *unio mystica* into the uncertain terminus of a sequence of acts. This terminus is practically superfluous since man already has justification by faith, which is the decisive thing. It seems as if, in order to come to terms with pietism, it was thought desirable to accept the *unio mystica* as the supreme form of individual piety. However that may be, certainly the basic fact of the *unio cum Christo* has become simply one act alongside others, indeed, to our mode of perception, belongs to the final stage of our Christian development. Objections were raised to this perversion of Luther's doctrine of the *unio*. D. Hollaz, for example, returned to the original meaning of the doctrine.[29] And what the theologians obscured, the hymn-writers expressed with pristine clarity. Philip Nicolai sang of the believers' union with Christ, in the chorale 'How lovely shines the Morning Star',[30] and so, too, Martin Schalling in the hymn 'With all my heart, I love thee Lord'.[31]

What then can we say about the difference between the Heidelberg and Westminster Catechisms[32] on the one hand and the Formula of Concord on the other, between the Reformed theologians and the Lutherans?

First, we would again stress that the Reformers themselves

[28] 'Regeneratio, iustificatio, unio et renovatio tempore simul sunt et quovis puncto mathematico arctiores adeo, ut divelli et sequestrari nequeant, cohaerent. Secundum nostrum tamen concipiendi modum ordine prior est iustificatio et regeneratio unione illa mystica. Quando enim in regeneratione homo fide donatur et per fidem iustificatus est, tum demum incipit mystice cum Deo uniri.' Schmid, *op. cit.*, p. 364. [29] *Ibid.*

[30] Philipp Nicolai (*d.* 1608), Lutheran hymn-writer. For English versions of this hymn see Catherine Winkworth, *Christian Singers of Germany*, London 1869, pp. 159ff and *Oxford Book of Carols* No. 104. Also cf. John Julian's *Dictionary of Hymnology*, London 1898, 1907, pp. 805ff.

[31] Martin Schalling (*d.* 1608), a favourite pupil of Melanchthon. Cf. Julian, *Dictionary of Hymnology*, p. 1004.

[32] Cf. also Second Helvetic Confession, 1566, ch. xv (Schaff, III.266ff).

agreed in giving a Christocentric answer to the question how we appropriate salvation. It was truly said at the Barmen Confessional Synod that 'the difference between authentic Reformation theology and the Orthodox theology which appeared later, is much greater than was for a long time realised. As pupils of the Reformers, our task is to resume our conversation at the point where it was broken off in the sixteenth century, rather than to choose the eighteenth-century starting-point.'[33]

Secondly, we must say that the basic insight of the Reformers, namely, that Christ comes to meet us in His Word and that we receive salvation in Him, has been more faithfully kept in Reformed theology than in Lutheran orthodoxy, from the Formula of Concord onwards. In its controversy with Osiander, Lutheranism did not confine itself to combating his error, but allowed the truth of the Gospel itself to be obscured.

Thirdly, it is clear that the doctrine of justification did not dominate Reformed theology as it did the Lutheran. In the Reformed view, the doctrine of the sinner's justification is a witness to Christ. The same appears to have been the case with Luther. But it was certainly not without Luther's influence that in Lutheranism this witness gradually became a doctrine, isolated from Christ, about the relation between God and man. But, that 'no flesh should glory', we must remember that not every Reformed theologian gave a strictly Christocentric answer to the question how salvation is received. Even in modern times the doctrine of justification has been emphasised by many disciples of H. F. Kohlbrügge[34] in a manner quite alien to Reformed tradition.

The Barmen Declaration once again testified plainly that Jesus Christ is the One Word of God that concerns us and that He is God's declaration of the forgiveness of all our sins. We do not receive this forgiveness before we meet Him nor apart from Him. When Christ Himself turns to us, then we receive what He has won for us.

[33] *Bekenntnissynode der deutschen evangelischen Kirche*, Barmen 1934, *Vorträge und Entschliessungen*, ed. Karl Immer, pp. 14f.

[34] H. F. Kohlbrügge (1803-75) founder of the Dutch Reformed congregation at Elberfeld in Prussia. He was a convert to the Reformed faith from Lutheranism. See H. Calaminus in *New Schaff-Herzog*, VOL. VI, pp. 369f. Also G. C. Berkouwer, *The Triumph of Grace in the Theology of Karl Barth*, London 1956, pp. 46f.

CHAPTER 2

JUSTIFICATION AND SANCTIFICATION[1]

1. The Reformed View

Reformed doctrine regards justification and sanctification as simultaneous gifts arising from union with Christ. According to Q. 1 of the Heidelberg Catechism, with which we began, the only comfort in life and in death is 'that I, with body and soul, . . . am not my own but belong to my faithful Saviour, Jesus Christ'. The communion which Christ gives us is here described in such a way as to be equivalent to the faithful Saviour's sovereignty over the individual. 'Union with Christ' necessarily implies that my whole life is claimed by Him. He has taken us out of the Devil's hands into His own. We therefore belong to Him, or, in biblical language, we are holy. Later on, the catechism gives a very full answer to the question, 'How are you righteous before God?'[2] But here already at the very beginning, where a comprehensive confession of what the fact of Christ means for us is called for, it is stated: I am sanctified by Him. This is an important feature of Reformed doctrine, or, more accurately, of the Calvinist theology, with which the Heidelberg Catechism is impregnated.

Calvin taught that the two supreme gifts we receive by

[1] Cf. Barth, *Church Dogmatics*, vol. iv, 1, pp. 514-642; 2, pp. 499-613.

[2] Q. 60. It is given in full here, since most Lutherans are unfamiliar with it, or, at any rate, so far as their attitude to the Reformed Church is concerned, ignore the fact that whereas this Reformed Catechism states the *articulus stantis vel cadentis ecclesie* clearly and fully, Luther's Small Catechism does not give it special mention. 'How are you righteous before God? Answer: Only through true faith in Jesus Christ; wherefore although my conscience already accuses me that I have grievously sinned against all the commandments of God, and have not kept any one of them, and that I am still ever prone to all evil, yet God, without any merit of my own, out of sheer grace, grants and imputes to me the perfect satisfaction, righteousness and holiness of Christ, as if I had never committed a single sin, and had myself accomplished all the obedience which Christ has fulfilled for me, if only I receive such a benefit with a believing heart' (Torrance, *School of Faith*, p. 79). Cf. Schaff, iii.326f, German and English.

union with Christ are the forgiveness of sins and sanctification, or, as he says in his major work, justification and regeneration.[3] But the distinctive thing in this teaching is that he first of all lays the foundation, by speaking of our union with Christ, next he deals with the gift of sanctification, and only then develops his doctrine of justification. Not all Reformed theologians proceed in this way. As a rule they deal first with justification and then with sanctification, as do most of the confessional documents. But even in them there is a special emphasis on the doctrine of sanctification, which in Calvin is further strengthened by the systematic arrangement.

This distinctive treatment of the doctrine of man's appropriation of the salvation won by Christ makes two things clear.

(*a*) The doctrine of justification does not give us a view of God's general relationship to man. It bears witness rather to God's present action towards us through Christ. It refers to the fact that God comes to meet me in Christ, and, in Him, restores the relationship to God which we have broken. This meeting, God's new relationship to us, means that we are wholly claimed by Him. When Christ turns to us we exchange masters and are henceforth ruled by His Spirit.[4] There can be no thought of our being able to continue in the condition in which we actually find ourselves. As, without Christ, we spend our lives running away from God, so, by Christ, we are turned towards Him. But this event is not simply a turning around but a dying and rising again with Christ. The meeting with Christ affects us as radically as that. Calvin rightly speaks here therefore of a rebirth. But since this is worked out in our existence and manner of life, he can also call it sanctification. If the term rebirth (*regeneratio*) indicates the radical nature of the change in our whole existence, the term sanctification (*sanctificatio*) reminds us that we are henceforth called to obey Christ every moment of our lives. There is then no longer any part of our life that is withdrawn from the gracious sovereignty of Christ. That is the first thing, which Calvin firmly secures by placing first the doctrine of sanctification, and which the Heidelberg Catechism makes plain from the outset, by means of its first

[3] *Inst.*, III.11.1 (VOL. I, p. 725).
[4] Calvin, *Opera*, VOL. LV, p. 403 (Comment on Jas. 2.14).

question. What we receive from God is not certain abilities or truths but simply the one gift, Jesus Christ Himself. But that means all preoccupation with ourselves, with our sins and their obliteration, is excluded. The primary, basic fact is that we belong not to ourselves but to the Lord (*nostri non sumus, sed domini*).[5] Christ stands before us as our eternal King 'who governs us by His Word and Spirit'.[6] 'Therefore, if anyone is in Christ, he is a new creation, the old has passed away, behold, the new has come' (2 Cor. 5.17).

(*b*) That brings us to the second reason for the emphasis on and the priority given to the doctrine of sanctification. When Christ honours us with this union, the question 'what ought we to do?' has in principle already been answered. The Heidelberg Catechism asks: 'But does not this teaching'—namely, the basic Reformation doctrine of justification by faith alone—'make people careless and profane?' and it answers: 'No, for it is impossible that those who are ingrafted into Christ through faith should not bring forth fruits of thankfulness.'[7] By referring to our sanctification at the very outset, Calvin and the Heidelberg Catechism remove all grounds for the objection made by Roman theologians who 'charge us with abolishing good works and with seducing men from the pursuit of them, when we say that men are not justified by works and do not merit salvation by them'.[8] 'For,' says Calvin, 'when this topic is rightly understood' (i.e. regeneration or sanctification) 'it will better appear how man is justified by faith alone and simple pardon; nevertheless actual holiness of life, so to speak, is not separated from free imputation of righteousness.'[9] 'That is to say, that the two propositions are quite consistent—viz. that we are not without good works, and yet that we are accounted righteous without works.'[10] Calvin thus develops the main principles of Christian ethics within the framework of his major dogmatic work, even

[5] Cf. *Inst.*, III.7.1 (VOL. I, pp. 689f).
[6] Heidelberg Catechism, Q. 31 (Torrance, *School of Faith*, p. 74).
[7] *Op. cit.*, Q. 64. [8] *Inst.*, III.16.1 (VOL. I, p. 797).
[9] *Inst.*, III.3.1 (VOL. I, p. 593).
[10] *Ibid.* These words are found in the French edition. See H. Beveridge's translation of the *Institutes*, Edinburgh 1845. Cf. *Inst.*, III.16.1. 'Thus it is clear how true it is that we are justified not without works yet not through works, since in our sharing in Christ, which justifies us, sanctification is just as much included as righteousness' (VOL. I, p. 798).

before he has dealt in detail with the doctrine of justification. So too, Question 1 of the Heidelberg Catechism already contains an ethics in embryo when it says that Jesus Christ by His Holy Spirit makes me willing and ready in heart 'henceforth to live unto Him'. This arrangement of the material is possible because what is said about the appropriation of salvation is centred on Christ, and indeed because the whole concern is to bear witness to Christ's approach to us. Calvin gives the Roman theologians no opportunity to substantiate their familiar objections to the Reformers' doctrine of grace, for long before the Reformation catchword, for which they are waiting, has even been mentioned, they are presented with a Christian ethic which rules out their objection to the Reformers' *sola fide*. They are shown by our practice that we have no occasion to borrow from them in the matter of good works. Where Christ approaches man, the question about ethics has already in principle been answered.

But many have objected because Calvin speaks of two gifts being imparted to us and, moreover, gives precedence to one over the other. In recent times, H. E. Weber concludes: 'Thus Calvin the pioneer of orthodoxy further develops the ambiguity already evident in Melanchthon.'[11] This criticism misses the central point of Calvin's theology, the fact that the doctrines of sanctification and justification are for him simply the unfolding of the fact of Christ in its application to us. In support of this Calvin appeals to 1 Cor. 1.30: 'Christ Jesus, whom God made our wisdom, our righteousness and sanctification and redemption.' 'Therefore Christ justifies no one whom he does not at the same time sanctify. These benefits are joined together by an everlasting and indissoluble bond.'[12] 'As Christ cannot be torn into parts, so these two which we perceive in him together and conjointly (*simul et coniunctim in ipso*) are inseparable, namely, righteousness and sanctification.'[13] Righteousness and sanctification are a reality in Jesus Christ and in Him constitute a unity.[14] 'Since, therefore, it is solely by expending himself that the Lord gives us these benefits to enjoy, he

[11] H. E. Weber, *Reformation, Orthodoxie und Rationalismus*, PT. I, VOL. I, p. 227.
[12] *Inst.*, III.16.1 (VOL. I, p. 798). [13] *Inst.*, III.11.6 (VOL. I, p. 732).
[14] *Inst.*, III.16.1 (VOL. I, p. 732).

bestows both of them at the same time, the one never without the other.'[15] This is because they are in fact not two, but a single gift, Jesus Christ Himself. Anyone wishing to separate either of these gifts received in Him from the other, sanctification from justification perhaps, would not be speaking of the authentic Christ for us. When Calvin, in the course of his theological presentation, placed one doctrine before the other, he did not mean that the one act of God towards us precedes the other, either in time or in importance. In Christ both gifts are received simultaneously and together (*simul et coniunctim*).

Having said that, we must also remember the other truth: that justification and sanctification are to be carefully distinguished.[16] This does not happen if our thinking begins, not with Christ, but with one or other of the two gifts received in Him. One gift is then swallowed up by the other and the special character of each is obscured. To link justification directly with sanctification, as Andreas Osiander did, robs the doctrine of justification of its unconditionally comforting character. If God were only to justify us in view of a new life previously begun in us, we should never be certain of salvation but would constantly have to ask whether the new life begun in us really qualified for God's verdict of justification. 'But God does not receive us into favour because He sees that we are changed to a better mind, as though conversion were the cause of pardon; but He embraces us according to His free mercy.'[17] There is only one sufficient reason for God's verdict of justification, our union with Christ. He alone is also the guarantor of our sanctification. 'By His Holy Spirit' He makes us 'willing and ready in heart henceforth to live unto Him.'[18] In Him, and only in Him, justification and sanctification are one. Calvin avoided over-speculation about this problem, for that would have meant leaving out of account the living and present Christ.

2. The Lutheran View

Turning now to the Lutheran version of the doctrine, we recall that, in Luther's exposition of the second article of the Creed,

[15] *Ibid.*
[16] *Inst.*, III.16.1, 11.6 (VOL. I, pp. 798, 732).
[17] Calvin, *Opera*, VOL. XXXIX, p. 120 (Comment. on Jer. 36.7).
[18] Heidelberg Catechism, Q. 1 (Torrance, *School of Faith*, p. 69).

Christ's atoning work changed our life in order that we might 'be (wholly) His own and live under Him in His Kingdom, and serve Him in everlasting righteousness, innocence, and blessedness'.[19] We called attention to the importance which Luther attached to the idea echoed here of our union with Christ. But what Luther said in his Small Catechism, about the alteration of our life by Christ's work, had little influence on the other Lutheran confessional documents. To test the whole of Lutheran theology by this insight of Luther would need a separate enquiry, but, in face of the total picture this theology presents, E. F. K. Müller was surely right in saying that 'it would never have occurred to a Lutheran to arrange the chapters of Book III (of the *Institutio*), dealing with the appropriation of salvation, in the way that Calvin does'.[20]

In the Augsburg Confession, Art. III, dealing with God's Son and His work, is followed by Art. IV, on justification. In opposition to Rome's 'righteousness of works', the Reformation movement singled out this doctrine as the article by which the Church stands or falls (*articulus stantis vel cadentis ecclesiae*): 'Also they teach that we cannot obtain forgiveness of sins and righteousness before God by our own merit, work, or satisfaction, but that we receive forgiveness of sins and become righteous before God by grace for Christ's sake through faith, when we believe that Christ suffered for us and that, for His sake, sin is forgiven and righteousness and eternal life given to us. For God counts and imputes this faith as righteousness before Him, as Saint Paul says to the Romans in chapters 3 and 4.'[21] This faith embraces the forgiveness of sins; it is a living personal relationship to God. In the *Loci* of 1521, Melanchthon says that by grace (*χάρις*) Scripture always means favour, God's gracious thoughts towards us, which we grasp by faith.[22] The Romans, on the contrary, empty faith of meaning and teach

[19] Small Catechism (*Concordia*, p. 161; Schaff. III,79).

[20] Müller, *Symbolik*, p. 474.

[21] 'Item docent, quod homines non possint iustificari coram Deo propriis viribus, meritis aut operibus, sed gratis iustificentur propter Christum per fidem, cum credunt se in gratiam recipi et peccata remitti propter Christum qui sua morte pro nostris peccatis satisfecit. Hanc fidem imputat Deus pro iustitia coram ipso, Rom. 3 et 4' (Kidd, *Documents*, p. 263; Schaff, III.10; *Concordia*, pp. 12f).

[22] Melanchthon, *Loci Communes*, 'de gratia' (P. Melanchthon, *Opera quae supersunt omnia*, VOLS. I-XXVIII, edd. C. G. Bretschneider and H. E. Bindseil, Brunswick

men to 'bargain with God on the basis of works and merits'.[23] 'But God cannot be treated with, God cannot be known, sought or understood except in and through the Word . . . and from this alone it should be evident that we become just before God only by faith, because, if justification occurs only through the Word, and the Word is grasped only by faith, it follows that faith justifies.'[24]

In the Lutheran doctrine too, this event results in man's rebirth. For we have to remember that 'because in repentance, i.e. in the terrors experienced therein', this same justifying faith 'comforts and encourages hearts, it regenerates us and brings the Holy Ghost, that then we may be able to fulfil God's Law, namely to love God, truly to fear God, truly to be confident that God hears prayer, and to obey God in all afflictions: it mortifies concupiscence, etc.'[25] 'This same strong consolation is a new birth and a new life.'[26] So, too, Luther: 'Where there is forgiveness of sins, there too is life and blessedness.' But when the soul 'has the Word, it needs nothing besides, the Word has everything: food, joy, peace, light, knowledge, righteousness, truth, wisdom, liberty and abundance of all good things'.[27] And it was Luther in particular who constantly stressed that *iustificare* meant that man is really made righteous.[28]

Lutheran doctrine then, seems to see the matter in much the same way as Calvin and his followers. E. F. K. Müller con-

1854 (Corpus Reformatorum VOLS. I-XXVIII), henceforth cited as *Opera*, VOL. XXI, p. 158. See Eng. trans. by C. L. Hill, *The Loci Communes of Philip Melanchthon*, Boston 1944, pp. 169f, henceforth cited as Hill).

[23] Melanchthon, *Apologia Confessio Augustanae*, henceforth cited as *Ap. C.*, Art. IV (II). (*Opera*, VOL. XXVII, p. 438 (Latin), VOL. XXVIII, p. 68 (German); *Concordia*, p. 37, col. 1.)

[24] 'At cum Deo non potest agi, Deus non potest apprehendi nisi per verbum. Ideo iustificatio fit per verbum. . . . Et vel hinc argumentum sumi potest, quod fides iustificet, quia si tantum fit iustificatio per verbum et verbum tantum fide apprehenditur, sequitur, quod fides iustificet.' *Ap. C.*, Art. IV (II) (*Opera*, VOL. XXVII, p. 439 (Latin), VOL. XXVIII, p. 79 (German); *Concordia*, p. 37, col. 2).

[25] 'Quia in poenitentia, hoc est in terroribus, consolatur et erigit corda, regenerat nos et affert Spiritus Sanctum, ut deinde legem Dei facere possimus, videlicet diligere Deum, vere timere Deum, vere statuere, quod Deus exaudiat, obedire Deo in omnibus afflictionibus, mortificat concupiscentiam etc.' *Opera*, VOL. XXVII, p. 435, VOL. XXVIII, p. 65f; *Concordia*, p. 37, col. 1). Cf. Augsburg Confession, XX (*Concordia*, p. 15, col. 3; Kidd, *Documents*, p. 269; Schaff, III.24f).

[26] 'Illa consolatio est nova et spiritualis vita.' *Ap. C.* (*Opera*, VOL. XXVII, p. 439, VOL. XXVIII, p. 70; *Concordia*, p. 37, col. 1).

[27] *The Liberty of a Christian Man*, 1520. W.A., VOL. VII, p. 22; also in *Primary Works*, edd. Wace and Buchheim, p. 258.

[28] References in K. Holl, *Gesammelte Aufsätze*, Tübingen 1923, VOL. I, p. 127.

cedes this when he says that, so far as this claim made upon man is concerned, 'all the necessary elements for it can be pointed out in detail, in Luther especially'.[29] Recently H. E. Weber has convincingly demonstrated that according to the earliest Lutheran teaching: 'Justification means "to become good and just". It is therefore the rebirth that we need.'[30] It is also to be taken as pointing to the 'ethical renewal'.[31] 'We may describe the Catholic accusation, that God's claim is ignored, as a crude and clearly mistaken parody of Evangelical doctrine.'[32] Weber documents his thesis primarily from the writings of Melanchthon, including the *Apology*. He shows that this theologian, like Calvin, stressed the simultaneity (*simul*) of the gift of the Spirit and justification,[33] and that he can occasionally even describe obedience as the goal of justification.[34]

All this must be conceded. But we must also make the following observations:

(1) Even Melanchthon did not keep strictly to Luther's insight that justification and sanctification are imparted to us by the Christ who is present in His Word. On the other hand, Osiander's anxiety to defend Luther's Christocentric approach led him to pervert this into a false mysticism. Unfortunately, the Formula of Concord, in its protest against Osiander, did not return to Luther's teaching that we receive everything in Christ alone.

(2) The experience produced by faith in the revealed Word is essentially an individual faith in the forgiveness of sins. Luther's question: 'How can I find a gracious God?' remained central to Lutheranism. Interest is centred on the individual, his sin and the forgiveness he experiences. Faith rests on the declaration of justification. We need only recall the many Lutheran hymns which have this theme. E. F. K. Müller rightly points out that a large section in any good Lutheran hymnbook is devoted to hymns of the Cross and consolation.[35]

(3) The works of the justified man are often spoken of as fruits which faith necessarily produces. 'Also they teach that this faith is bound to bring forth good fruits and that it is

[29] Müller, *Symbolik*, p. 313.
[30] H. E. Weber, *Reformation, Orthodoxie und Rationalismus*, PT I, VOL. I, p. 80.
[31] *Ibid.* [32] *Op. cit.*, p. 82. [33] *Op. cit.*, p. 81.
[34] *Op. cit.*, p. 87. [35] Müller, *Symbolik*, p. 308f.

necessary to do good works commanded by God, because of God's will.'[36] The Formula of Concord uses similar language: Good works follow from true faith 'as fruits of a good tree'.[37] They are also called 'fruits of the Spirit . . . which the Spirit of God . . . works through the regenerate . . . as though they knew of no command'.[38] Good works are certainly fruits of the Holy Spirit, but, if we speak of them only in this way, we may easily forget that the Spirit is given through the Word, which, because it is Christ the Lord Himself who encounters us in it, is always at one and the same time, both a declaration of forgiveness and a claim to the whole of our life.

In Lutheranism, the question about the true basis of human conduct is more important than the fact that Christ claims us for His Kingdom 'that we may order our whole life, in thought, word and work, that Thy name may not be blasphemed on our account, but be honoured and praised'.[39] Our life not only has a basis but a goal, too, and every day we need a summons to move towards this goal.

(4) Finally, the Lutheran doctrine of the justified sinner's life and works is so influenced by the controversy with Roman theology that these works are scarcely ever mentioned without the additional qualification that they are in no sense meritorious in God's sight. That is obviously true, since all our knowledge begins with the fact that it is in Christ that God accepts sinners and gives them all things. But just because this is true, the way Lutheranism states it sounds rather grudging. It fails to make it clear that despite the sin which still hampers him, the justified sinner can in some measure live to the glory of God.

It was therefore, a welcome sign when, at Barmen in 1934, Lutherans, too, joined in declaring: 'As Jesus Christ is God's declaration of the forgiveness of all our sins, so in the same way and with the same seriousness He is God's mighty claim upon our whole life. Through Him we obtain joyful deliverance from the godless bondage of this world, for the free, grateful service

[36] 'Item docent, quod fides illa debeat bonos fructos parere, et quod oporteat bona opera mandata a Deo facere propter voluntatem Dei.' Augsburg Confession VI (Kidd, *Documents*, p. 263; Schaff, III.11; *Concordia*, p. 13, col. 1).

[37] Formula of Concord (Schaff, III.122; *Concordia*, p. 221, col. 2).

[38] Formula of Concord (Schaff, III.133; *Concordia*, p. 223, col. 2).

[39] Heidelberg Catechism, Q. 122. Cf. Westminister Larger Catechism, Q. 190 (Torrance, *School of Faith*, pp. 94, 231).

of His creatures.'[40] That makes it quite clear that more is involved than comfort for the soul. It is a matter of Christ Himself and of the fact that sinners accepted by Him can, under Him, really live to His glory.

[40] Barmen Thesis., No. 2.

CHAPTER 3

FAITH AND REPENTANCE

So far we have asked about the gracious gift which man receives from God on the basis of Christ's reconciliation. Calvin and the Heidelberg Catechism answer, as we saw, that the gift is Christ Himself. For Luther too, the gift is union with the living Christ. But the interest of Lutheranism is focused on the sinner's justification by the word of grace addressed to him. Reformed doctrine does not concentrate so exclusively on this article of faith, because it knows that justification is given to us in Christ and in Him alone. Its concern is to stress that the Saviour is our Lord. The emphasis is thus differently placed on the two sides. The same thing inevitably happens when we come to ask how man responds to God's gracious gift. We now turn to this question. From the objective we turn to look at the subjective, at the recipient of the divine gift of salvation, and here too we shall find the same differences emerging.

1. The Reformed View: Repentance as the Fruit of Faith

We saw that in Reformed teaching, union with Christ is effected by the Holy Spirit. He is the bond that unites us with Christ. This union takes place as the Holy Spirit produces faith in us. He enlightens us so that we may believe the Gospel.[1] Faith is the 'principal work' of the Spirit.[2] Faith is 'a firm and certain knowledge of God's benevolence toward us, founded upon the truth of the freely given promise in Christ, both revealed to our minds and sealed upon our hearts through the Holy Spirit'.[3] This faith can therefore also be called 'confidence'.[4] 'But this faith,' the Second Helvetic Confession

[1] *Inst.*, III.14 (VOL. 14, p. 541). [2] *Ibid.*
[3] *Inst.*, III.2.7 (VOL. I, p. 551). [4] *Inst.*, III.2.15 (VOL. I, p. 561).

emphasises, 'is God's gift alone, which God of His free grace grants to His elect according to His Will, whenever, to whomsoever and in whatsoever measure He may will, doing so indeed through the Holy Spirit by means of the preaching of the Gospel and believing prayer.'[5] That implies that, alone, faith can do nothing.[6] We do not please God on account of the worthiness of our faith.[7] Faith is an empty vessel,[8] or, as the Belgic Confession says, 'an instrument with which we embrace Christ' and 'which keeps us in communion with Him in all His benefits'.

Calvin says: 'Our immediate transition, however, will be from faith to repentance . . . repentance not only constantly follows faith, but is also born of faith. For since pardon and forgiveness are offered through the preaching of the Gospel, in order that the sinner, freed from the tyranny of Satan, the yoke of sin, and the miserable bondage of vices, may cross over into the Kingdom of God, surely no one can embrace the grace of the gospel without betaking himself from the errors of his past life into the right way, and applying his whole effort to the practice of repentance.'[10] Calvin rightly points out that the summons to repentance issued by John the Baptist and Jesus rests upon grace and the promise of salvation. It is as if they said: Since the Kingdom of Heaven is at hand, therefore repent! The prophecy of Isaiah 40 which was thereby fulfilled also begins with a message of comfort and joy. Calvin does not mean that there is any interval of time between the birth of faith and the emergence of repentance, but 'that a man cannot apply himself seriously to repentance without knowing himself to belong to God. But no one is truly persuaded that he belongs to God unless he has first recognised God's grace.'[11]

Repentance can of course be regarded as including man's entire conversion to God. Faith is then a part of repentance.

[5] 'Haec autem fides, merum est Dei donum, quod solus Deus ex gratia sua electis suis secundum mensuram, et quando, cui et quantum ipse vult, donat, et quidem per Spiritum Sanctum mediante praedicatione evangelii et oratione fideli.' Second Helvetic Confession, ch. XVI (Schaff, III.268), probably so formulated under the influence of the Augsburg Confession, ch. V.

[6] Scots Confession, 1560, ch. XII (Schaff, III.450f).

[7] Heidelberg Catechism, Q. 61 (Torrance, *School of Faith,* p. 80).

[8] *Inst.*, III.11.10 (VOL. I, p. 737).

[9] Belgic Confession, Art XXII (Schaff, III.407f); cf. Scots Confession, Art. III (Schaff, III.440f).

[10] *Inst.*, III.3.1 (VOL. I, p. 592f).

[11] *Inst.*, III.3.2 (VOL. I, p. 594).

But strictly speaking repentance is different from faith and should be kept distinct from it. 'Even though they cannot be separated, they ought to be distinguished. As faith is not without hope, yet faith and hope are different things, so repentance and faith, although they are held together by a permanent bond, require to be joined rather than confused.'[12]

Repentance is then defined as 'the true turning on our life to God, a turning that arises from a pure and earnest fear of him; and it consists in the mortification of our flesh and of the old man, and in the vivification of the Spirit'.[13] The Second Helvetic Confession gives a similar definition: 'By repentance we mean (1) that change of mind produced in the sinner by the Word of the Gospel and by the Holy Spirit and received by true faith, whereby the sinner at once recognises his innate corruption and all his sins branded as such by God's Word, and (2) is heartily sorry for them, and not only laments and confesses them sincerely and with shame before God, but also (3) condemns them with horror, and (4) earnestly seeks amendment, striving continually for that innocence and virtue in which he tries to live a holy life all the rest of his days.'[14]

These last words bring us to another feature of Reformed doctrine, but before we look at this, let us sum up what has already been said.

(*a*) Faith precedes repentance in significance though not in temporal sequence. But repentance does not follow from faith, i.e. it is not a movement originating in faith, regarded as a human response to the heard Word of God. 'We declare emphatically that this repentance is a pure divine gift, not a work of our own strength.'[15]

(*b*) Faith is not to be identified with repentance. When we consider the entire action in which God takes possession of man, then of course faith too is a part of it. But because God's Word reaches us as gift and claim, repentance in the strict sense must be distinguished from faith.

[12] *Inst.*, III.3.5 (VOL. I, p. 597). Cf. Westminster Larger Catechism, Q. 77 (Torrance, *School of Faith*, p. 200).

[13] *Inst.*, III.3.5 (VOL. I, p. 597). Cf. Heidelberg Catechism, Q. 88 (Torrance, *School of Faith*, p. 87).

[14] Second Helvetic Confession, ch. XIV (Schaff, III.262, cf. I.406).

[15] 'Diserte vero dicimus hanc poenitentiam mere esse Dei donum et non virium nostrarum opus.' Second Helvetic Confession, ch. XIV (*ibid.*).

(*c*) Repentance is (and this is point 4 which we met above, at the end of the definition from the Second Helvetic Confession) not merely sorrow for past sins but a sincere resolve to do better and a continual striving for purity.[16] Calvin stressed this last point especially. 'When they understand vivification as the happiness that the mind receives after its perturbation and fear have been quieted, I do not agree. It means, rather, the desire to live in a holy and devoted manner, a desire arising from rebirth; as if it were said that man dies to himself that he may begin to live to God.'[17]

The Heidelberg Catechism gives a similar explanation when dealing with penitence in Q. 90: 'What is the resurrection of the new man? Answer: Heartfelt joy in God through Christ, and a passionate love to live according to the will of God in all good works.' Thus the catechism too emphasises that the man to whom genuine repentance is given, does not stand still, but in his own behaviour imitates the turnabout executed by the prodigal son in the parable when he resolved to go to his father. That is not a man's own arbitrary decision but, as we saw, a divine gift. That is why the first question of the Heidelberg Catechism says that Christ 'by His Holy Spirit . . . makes me willing and ready in heart henceforth to live unto Him'. Reformed theology emphasised this aspect of repentance not in order to urge man to a false high-handed striving for sanctity, but rather to save him from neglecting to use this gift and so from succumbing by a perverse quietism and falling a victim to the world and the Devil. Hence the appearance of ethics within the context of this theology. This theology sees man's life as a movement starting from a decisive break and moving towards a goal. This goal is eschatological. The Heidelberg Catechism asks: 'Can those who are converted to God keep these commandments perfectly?' Answer: 'No, for even the holiest of all, while in this life, have only a small beginning of this obedience. Nevertheless they begin to live with earnest purpose not only according to some but according to all God's commandments.' The following reason is then given for the preaching of God's commandments: 'that we may continually

[16] Cf. Westminster Larger Catechism, Q. 76 (Torrance, *School of Faith*, p. 199).
[17] *Inst.*, *III*.3.3 (VOL. I, p. 595).

apply ourselves and ask God for the grace of His Holy Spirit, that we may be more and more renewed in the image of God, until we attain the goal of full perfection after this life'.[18] This movement of human life was described by Calvin as a discipleship of Christ, under the headings: self-denial, bearing the Cross, meditation on the future life.[19] It is no accident that Psalm 84 ('How lovely is Thy dwelling place', 'We travel on as pilgrims')[20] is sung so fervently in Reformed Churches, or that it was a Reformed hymn-writer, F. A. Lampe, who wrote 'My Life is but a pilgrimage',[21] and G. Tersteegen 'Come children, let us go!'[22] The view of repentance outlined above is one of the roots of the much-discussed activism of Reformed Protestantism.

(*d*) Finally, the life of repentance is worship. Good works are 'those only which are done from true faith, according to the law of God, for His glory'.[23] The assignment of this goal to human life means not that we have to bow down to some tyrant, but rather 'that with our whole life we may show ourselves thankful to God for His goodness and that He may be glorified through us'.[24] Even our eternal salvation is described as the praise of God.[25] Then, at the consummation, man finally reaches the goal for which he has been destined from the beginning: 'to praise and glorify' God.[26] The very fact that we are called 'Christians' reminds us that we have been taken into the threefold ministry of Christ: 'in order that I also may confess His name, may present myself a living sacrifice to Him, and may with a free conscience fight against sin and the Devil in this life, and hereafter, in eternity, rule with Him over all creatures'.[27] Much nonsense has been written about the 'Glory of God' (*gloria Dei*) in Reformed Protestantism. The

[18] Heidelberg Catechism, Q. 114f (Torrance, *School of Faith*, pp. 92f).

[19] 'De abnegatione nostri: de crucis tolerantia; de meditatione futurae vitae.' *Inst.*, III.7-9 (VOL. I, pp. 689-719).

[20] 'Wir wallen in der Pilgerschaft.'

[21] 'Mein Leben ist ein Pilgrimstand.' Friedrich Adolf Lampe (1683-1729) a German Reformed pastor and theologian. See E. F. K. Müller in *New Schaff-Herzog*, VOL. VI, p. 405.

[22] 'Kommt, Kinder, lasst uns gehen.' Gerhard Tersteegen (1697-1769), the German Reformed mystic and hymn-writer. See Julian, *Dictionary of Hymnology*, pp. 1142-5.

[23] Heidelberg Catechism, Q. 91 (Torrance, *School of Faith*, p. 87).

[24] *Op. cit.*, Q. 86.

[25] *Op. cit.*, Q. 58.

[26] *Op. cit.*, Q. 6.

[27] *Op. cit.*, Q. 32.

glory of God is not some principle which we have to defend. By pointing to the glory of God, we are declaring that the whole life of the Christian can echo with the praise of God, indeed that his entire life may *be* such a praise of God and His Anointed One, because of the great things He has done. What is little will certainly then appear as little. Man does not occupy the centre of the stage, neither the old man in his sinful need, nor the new man with his pious acts. Any possibility of man gazing admiringly at himself in the mirror is excluded. The objectivity requisite here consists in the praise of God.

'*Worship, glory, thanks and praise be to our God in His sanctuary. To the God who lays burdens upon us but carries us with our burdens and meets us with His grace! Are not praise and glory due to Him who is the King of glory? to the God of perfect blessedness?*'[28]

We said earlier that the goal of Christian life is an eschatological one. What we have just said does not cancel that out. Our praise here is imperfect. Again and again we bring dishonour on our Lord. We continually forget the first commandment. Therefore, part of the worship of God which Reformed theology teaches is Calvin's sigh: 'O Lord, how long?' (*Quousque Domine?*).[29] But 'in all afflictions and persecutions' we may 'with uplifted head', 'wait for the Judge from Heaven'.[30] Here in this expectation of the returning Christ, it becomes clear once again that the *gloria Dei* which applies to our life bears no resemblance to the worship of a tyrant by those subject to him. The Lord whom we begin to glorify here on earth, and whom one day we shall praise for ever, is the Saviour 'who shall take me with all His chosen ones to Himself into heavenly joy and glory'.[31]

2. The Lutheran View: Faith as the Completion of True Repentance

Implicitly we have already brought out the contrast with Lutheran theology. E. F. K. Müller writes of Luther's view: 'The sequence is always repentance and faith, never faith and

[28] Ps. 68.10 in M. Jorissen's metrical version.
[29] Calvin, *Opera*, VOL. XXI, pp. 41, 161. Cf. Beza's *Life of Calvin*, Eng. trans. in *Tracts and Treatises*, VOL. I, p. cxxi.
[30] Heidelberg Catechism, Q. 52 (Torrance, *School of Faith*, p. 78).
[31] *Ibid.*

repentance. Even when Luther stresses the constant need for repentance he hardly ever advances beyond the basic scheme, in which *poenitentia* means the knowledge of sin, which is followed by the knowledge of grace, and in which moreover the movement of life, which is the real centre of interest for the Lutheran spirit, seems to be settled and strictly speaking can only be repeated over and over again.'[32] Müller himself says that this scheme is 'hardly ever' transcended. But it does sometimes happen; e.g. in the treatise 'On the Babylonian Captivity of the Church', Luther wrote: 'A contrite heart is a great matter indeed and can only proceed from an earnest faith in the divine promises and threats—a faith which, contemplating the unshakeable truth of God, makes the conscience to tremble, terrifies and bruises it, and when it is thus contrite, raises it again, consoles and preserves it. Thus the truth of the threatening is the cause of contrition and the truth of the promise is the cause of consolation when it is believed. . . . Therefore, faith above all things ought to be taught and called forth; when faith is produced, contrition and consolation will follow of their own accord by an inevitable consequence.'[33] But this is an example of the second case envisaged by Müller, of the lifelong repentance of the Christian, to which R. Seeberg has referred, and not of the initial repentance of the hitherto unconverted man. For the latter the truth is that 'Christ and grace begin their work only when sin has been acknowledged'.[34] Thus Luther in his major commentary on Galatians: 'Now when a man is humbled by the Law and brought to the knowledge of himself, then followeth true repentance (for true repentance beginneth at the fear and judgment of God).'[35] Melanchthon's teaching

[32] Müller, *Symbolik*, p. 314.

[33] 'Magna res est cor contritum, nec nisi ardentis in promissionem et comminationem divinam fidei, quae veritatem Dei immobilem intuita, tremefacit, exterret et sic conterit conscientiam, rursus exaltat et solatur servatque contritam, ut veritas comminationis sit causa contritionis, veritas promissionis sit solacii, si credatur. . . . Proinde fides ante omnia docenda et provocanda est, fide autem obtenta contritio et consolatio inevitabili sequela sua sponte venient.' W.A., VOL. VI, p. 545; see *Primary Works*, edd. Wace and Buchheim, pp. 368f.

[34] R. Seeberg, *Lehrbuch der Dogmengeschichte*, VOL. IV, Leipzig 1920, p. 258. Eng. trans. *Textbook of the History of Doctrines*, trans. C. E. Hay, Grand Rapids 1952, VOL. II, p. 248.

[35] 'Humiliato autem homine per legem et redacto in sui cognitionem, tum vere constitutus est poenitens, vera enim poenitentia incipit a timore et iudicio Dei.' W.A., VOL. XL, I, p. 231; *Commentary on Galatians*, ed. P. S. Watson, p. 136.

in the *Apology* is quite general: 'We say that the parts of repentance are contrition and faith.'[36] 'But as the Confutation condemns us for having assigned these two parts to repentance we must show that not we, but Scripture expresses these as the chief parts in repentance or conversion. For Christ says, Matt. 11.28: "Come unto Me, all ye that labour and are heavy laden and I will give you rest." Here there are two members. The "labour" and the "burden" signify the contrition, anxiety and terrors of sin and death. "To come to Christ" is to believe that sins are remitted for Christ's sake; when we believe, our hearts are quickened by the Holy Ghost, through the Word of Christ. Here, therefore, there are these two chief parts, contrition and faith.'[37] According to this view man has a relationship to God apart from Christ. Before man grasps Christ in faith he can know how he stands with God because of another word of the same God to him. In the Lutheran view, this shattering of human existence and the sorrow it causes are in the strict sense man's repentance or conversion. In faith this comes to completion. Here again Luther's controversy with Roman theology still exercises a baleful influence. The term 'contrition' was adopted from the sacrament of penance and only prevented the discarding of the idea that mere contrition and, even less, attrition (imperfect contrition) are not enough, and that faith must be added if there is to be real conversion. Instead, criticism ought to have gone further, as it did occasionally in Luther, and showed that knowledge of sin and therefore penitence too, exist only in the encounter with Him who was crucified for us.

According to traditional doctrine then, a distinction has to be made between a repentance which saves because faith is joined to it, and a repentance which is fruitless because faith is not added. 'This faith shows the distinction between the contrition of Judas and Peter, of Saul and David. The contrition of Judas or Saul is of no avail, for the reason that to this there is not added this faith, which apprehends the remission of sins, bestowed as a gift for Christ's sake. Accordingly, the contrition of David or Peter avails, because to it there is added faith,

[36] *Ap. C.*, Art. XII (V) (*Opera*, VOL. XXVII, p. 537, VOL. XXVIII, p. 161; *Concordia*, p. 78, col. 2).

[37] *Ap. C.*, Art XII (V) (*Opera*, VOL. XXVII, p. 543, VOL. XXVIII, p. 169; *Concordia*, p. 81, col. 1).

which apprehends the remission of sins granted for Christ's sake.'[38] Calvin does not recognise a repentance like that of Saul and Judas as real repentance at all. Acknowledging the gravity of their sin, these men were only afraid of God's wrath and 'that very thought overwhelmed them'. 'Therefore their repentance was nothing but a sort of entryway of Hell, which they had already entered in this life.'[39] This is of a piece with Calvin's conviction, already noted, that faith cannot be placed second to repentance. The Christological basis of the doctrine of the appropriation of salvation becomes obscured when repentance is treated in the way it is in the *Apology*. There is no repentance apart from the knowledge of God's goodness in Christ. In the case of David and Peter it was not that something extra, i.e. faith, was added to what Saul and Judas experienced, but rather that there was a completely different attitude.

But as we have already said, there is, according to Lutheran doctrine, not only an initial repentance but also a *lifelong repentance*. We must now see what this means. In his first Thesis of 1517, Luther declared: 'When our Lord and Master Jesus Christ said: "Do penance, etc." He wished the whole life of the believer to be a repentance.'[40] 'It signifies that the old Adam in us should by daily contrition and repentance, be drowned and die with all sins and evil lusts, and, again, a new man daily come forth and arise, who shall live before God in righteousness and purity forever.'[41] This repentance required of a Christian throughout life is seen primarily as a negative movement, a renunciation of sin, a putting to death (*mortificatio*) of the old Adam. There is also a reference to the making alive (*vivificatio*) linked with this but it is not the main interest. The inner man, says Luther, finds 'in his own flesh a contrary will . . . which faith cannot and will not endure but strives with cheerfulness and zeal to keep it down and restrain it'.[42] In the

[38] *Ap. C.*, Art. XII (V) (*Opera*, VOL. XXVII, p. 542, VOL. XXVIII, p. 168; *Concordia*, p. 80, col. 2). [39] *Inst.*, III.3.4 (VOL. I, p. 596).

[40] 'Dominus et magister noster Jesus Christus dicendo: Poenitentiam agite etc. omnem vitam fidelium poenitentiam esse voluit.' W.A., VOL. I, p. 233. (Kidd, *Documents*, p. 21; *Primary Writings*, edd. Wace and Buchheim, p. 414; Bettenson, *Documents*, pp. 260f.)

[41] Luther, Small Catechism (Schaff, III.86f; *Concordia*, p. 162).

[42] *The Liberty of a Christian Man*, 1520 (*Primary Works*, edd. Wace and Buchheim, pp. 272f).

Smalcald Articles we read: 'And in Christians this repentance continues until death, because, through the entire life it contends with sin remaining in the flesh, as Paul, Rom. 8.14-25, shows that he 'wars with the law in his members, etc.'; and that, not by his own powers, but by the gift of the Holy Ghost that follows the remission of sins. This gift daily cleanses and sweeps out the remaining sins, and works so as to render man truly pure and holy.'[43] It is significant that the Formula of Concord quoted these words, with the comment: 'These words say nothing whatsoever of our will, or that even in regenerate men it works anything of itself, but ascribe it to the gift of the Holy Ghost . . . and our own powers are entirely excluded therefrom.'[44] Once again the Roman controversy determines the line of thought. Occasionally, there is a reference to the positive ordering of the Christian life, but even then opposition to the idea of merit is linked with it. 'And this promise (2 Tim. 4.8) saints should know, not that they may labour for their own profit, for they ought to labour for the glory of God.'[45] The picture presented here is just the same as that which emerged in the previous chapter on justification and sanctification. E. F. K. Müller's verdict is: 'A vigorous, positive, edifying and militant activity is . . . absent.' 'Personal faith thus dwindled into an orthodoxy which clung above all to the correct formula "*sola fide*", and was inclined to be suspicious of any unusual signs of ethical concern or personal independence.'[46]

[43] Luther, Smalcald Articles, 1536 (so named after 1553). *Concordia*, p. 145, col. 2.

[44] Formula of Concord, Thor. Decl. II, *Concordia*, p. 245, col. I.

[45] 'Hanc promissionem scire sanctos oportet, non ut propter suum commodum laborent, debent enim laborare propter gloriam Dei.' *Ap. C.*, Art. III (*Opera*, VOL. XXVII, p. 511, (Latin), cf. German text VOL. XXVIII, p. 128; *Concordia*, p. 67, col. I).

[46] E. F. K. Müller, *Symbolik*, pp. 315, 317.

CHAPTER 4

GOSPEL AND LAW[1]

1. The Lutheran Doctrine of God's Proper Work and God's Strange Work

The Lutheran doctrine of repentance and faith just outlined rests on a characteristically Lutheran view of the relation between Law and Gospel. As a rule, it is asserted that there are two Words of God to man: the Law and the Gospel, and that these reach man in that order. In his *Loci*, Melanchthon, for example, says: 'Altogether the Scripture has two parts, the Law and the Gospel. The Law points to sin, the Gospel to grace. The Law shows the disease, the Gospel the remedy. In Paul's words, the Law ministers death, the Gospel ministers life and peace. The Law is the strength of sin, the Gospel is the power of salvation to everyone who believes.'[2] 'Just as the Law commands what is right and reveals sins, so the Gospel is the promise of God's grace or mercy, and is therefore the forgiveness of sins and the witness of God's love to us, so that our hearts, assured of God's love by this witness, believe all guilt to be forgiven them, and, thus uplifted, love, praise, and delight in God.'[3]

[1] See further: Karl Barth, 'Evangelium und Gesetz', *Theol. Ex. h.* No. 32, 1935 (Eng. trans. *Gospel and Law*, Scottish Journal of Theology Occ. Papers No. 8, 1959, pp. 3-27); Edmund Schlink, 'Gesetz und Evangelium', *Theol. Ex. h.* No. 53, 1937; Hermann Diem, 'Luthers Predigt in den zwei Reichen', *Theol. Ex. h.* N.S. No. 6, 1947; Alec Vidler, *Christ's Strange Work*, London 1944; Schrey, Walz, Whitehouse, *The Biblical Doctrine of Justice and Law*, London 1955.

[2] 'Duae in universum scripturae partes sunt, lex et evangelium. Lex peccatum ostendit, evangelium gratiam. Lex morbum indicat, evangelium remedium. Lex mortis ministra est, ut Pauli verbis utamur, evangelium vitae ac pacis. Lex virtus peccati est, evangelium virtus salutis omni credenti.' Melanchthon, *Loci Communes*, '*de evangelio*' (*Opera*, VOL. XXI, p. 139; cf. Hill, p. 144).

[3] 'Sicut lex est, qua recta mandantur, qua peccatum ostenditur, ita evangelium est promissio gratiae seu misericordiae Dei adeoque condonatio peccati et testimonium benevolentiae Dei erga nos, quo testimonio certi animi nostri de benevolentia Dei credant sibi condonatam omnem culpam et erecti ament, laudent Deum, exhilarentur et exultent in Deo.' *Op. cit.*, '*Quid evangelium*' (*Opera*, VOL. XXI, p. 140; cf. Hill, p. 145).

In the *Apology*, too, we read: 'All Scripture ought to be distributed into these two principal topics, the Law and the promises'[4]; and the Formula of Concord says: 'We believe, teach and confess that the Law is properly a divine doctrine, which teaches what is right and pleasing to God, and reproves everything that is sin and contrary to God's will . . . But the Gospel is properly such a doctrine as teaches what man who has not observed the Law, and therefore is condemned by it, is to believe, namely that Christ has expiated and made satisfaction for all sins, and has obtained and acquired for him, without any merit of his, forgiveness of sins, righteousness that avails before God, and eternal life.'[5] Luther himself had already summed them up briefly: 'The Law teaches what your duty is and what you lack, Christ gives you what you should do and have.'[6] A modern Lutheran could therefore say that different modes of God's action are manifested in Law and Gospel, and that a higher synthesis of wrath and grace, of Law and Gospel has not been revealed to us.

The Law was given by God to expose man's sin and to shake the sinner to the foundations. 'The chief office or force of the Law is that it reveal original sin with all its fruits, and show man how very low his nature has fallen, and has become utterly corrupted: as the Law must tell man that he has no God nor regards God, and worships other gods, a matter which before and without the Law he would not have believed.'[7] The *Apology* says briefly: 'The Law is the word which reproves and condemns sins.'[8] But since by original sin man has corrupted his whole nature, his whole being, the Law is not simply directed against sin itself, both original and actual sin, but against man as a whole. Man's 'nature or person is accused or condemned by God's Law'.[9] The Law's condemnation terrifies man and he experiences God's wrath. It is continually stressed that the

[4] 'Universa scriptura in hos duos locos praecipuos distribui debet: in legem et promissiones.' *Ap. C.*, Art. IV (II) (*Opera*, VOL. XXVII, p. 429, VOL. XXVIII, p. 58; *Concordia*, p. 32, col. 2).

[5] Formula of Concord, Epitome V, 1 and 4 (Schaff, III.126f; *Concordia*, p. 222).

[6] 'Lex docet, quid debeas et quo careas; Christus dat quid facias et habeas.' W.A., VOL. II, p. 500.

[7] Smalcald Articles, III, ii (*Concordia*, p. 142).

[8] 'Lex est verbum quod arguit et condemnat peccata.' *Ap. C.*, Art. XII (*Opera*, VOL. XXVII, p. 545, VOL. XXVIII, p. 171; *Concordia*, p. 81, col. 2). Cf. *Ap. C.*, Art. III: 'But the Law always accuses us' (*Concordia*, p. 42, col. 1).

[9] Formula of Concord, Thor. Decl. I, 1, (*Concordia*, p. 236, col. 2).

sinner in this way has a foretaste of the despair of Hell. 'This, then, is the thunderbolt of God by which He strikes in a heap both manifest sinners and false saints, and suffers no one to be in the right, but drives them all together to terror and despair.'[10] The purpose of this function of the Law is man's condemnation: 'But whenever the Law alone, without the Gospel being added, exercises this its office there is death and hell, and man must despair, like Saul and Judas.'[11]

The Gospel, as we saw, has the opposite effect. The Formula of Concord declares: 'that the Gospel is not a preaching of repentance or reproof but properly nothing else than a preaching of consolation, and a joyful message which does not reprove or terrify, but comforts consciences against the terrors of the Law, points alone to the merits of Christ, and raises them up again by the lovely preaching of the grace and favour of God, obtained through Christ's merit'.[12] The Gospel is simply the message of Christ: 'Christ is the pledge of all these promises: therefore all the promises of Scripture must be referred to Him, who was manifested obscurely at first but then ever more clearly.'[13]

It follows from this statement by Melanchthon that *Law and Gospel do not coincide with Old Testament and New Testament respectively*: 'For Scripture has not transmitted the Gospel in such a way that thou mayest only regard as Gospel what Matthew, Mark, Luke, and John wrote, and as Law, only the books of Moses. On the contrary, the plan of the Gospel is spread through the whole: the promises are scattered throughout all the books of the Old and New Testaments. And again, laws are found scattered throughout all the books of the Old and New Testaments.'[14] Indeed we must notice that it is especially in the

[10] Smalcald Articles, III, iii (*Concordia*, p. 142).
[11] *Loc. cit.* (*Concordia*, p. 143, col. 1).
[12] Epitome v, vi (*Concordia*, p. 222; Schaff, III.128).
[13] 'Illarum promissionum omnium pignus est Christus, quare in eum referendae sunt omnes scripturae promissiones, qui obscure primum, postea subinde clarius revelata est.' Melanchthon, *Loci Communes*, '*Quid evangelium*' (*Opera*, VOL. XXI, p. 140; cf. Hill, pp. 145f).
[14] 'Neque vero ita legem et evangelium tradidit scriptura, ut evangelium id modo putes, quod scripserunt Matthaeus, Marcus, Lucas et Joannes, Mosi libros nihil nisi legem. Sed sparsa est evangelii ratio, sparsae sunt promissiones in omnes libros veteris ac novi testamenti. Rursum leges etiam sparsae sunt in omnia tum veteris tum novi testamenti volumina.' *Op. cit.*, '*De evangelio*' (*Opera*, VOL. XXI, p. 139; cf. Hill, p. 144).

New Testament books that 'Christ takes the Law into His hands and explains it spiritually, Matt. 5.21ff; Rom. 7.14. And thus the wrath of God is revealed from Heaven against all sinners (Rom. 1.18), how great it is; by this means they are directed to the Law and then first learn from it to know aright their sins.'[15] It must even be said of Christ's passion and death that it is 'an earnest and terrible proclamation and declaration of God's wrath, whereby men are first led into the Law aright . . . so that they first know aright how great things God in His Law requires of us'.[16] 'Yet as long as all this [i.e. Christ's passion and death] proclaims God's wrath and terrifies man, it is still not properly the preaching of the Gospel . . . and therefore a foreign work of Christ, by which He arrives at His proper office, that is, to preach grace'.[17] Thus even Christ employs the Law to terrify sinners. He uses this Word of God first, before the other Word, the Word of comfort, and in so doing performs a strange work which is not the work He primarily came to do. He begins in the role of Moses. He must do this first of all before the good news can help man. It can hardly be more plainly stated than is done here in the Formula of Concord—and this passage reproduces Luther's own view[18]—that two Words of God must come to man in a fixed sequence if he is to be saved.

Law and Gospel have always been joined, and must always be preached together. Yet they must be carefully distinguished. Only so can the Divine action of salvation for the sinner be successful. 'From the beginning of the world these two proclamations have been ever and ever inculcated alongside each other in the Church of God, with a proper distinction. . . . These two doctrines, we believe and confess, should ever and ever be diligently inculcated in the Church of God, although with the proper distinction of which we have heard, in order that through the preaching of the Law and its threats in the ministry of the New Testament the hearts of impenitent men may be terrified, and brought to a knowledge of their sins and to repentance; but not in such a way that they lose heart and despair in this process, but that . . . they may *flee to Christ*.'

[15] Formula of Concord, Epitone v, vii (*Concordia*, p. 222; Schaff, III.129).
[16] *Ibid.* [17] *Op. cit.*, v, viii. [18] *Bekenntnisschriften* (*Luth.*), p. 956, n. 1.

[E.T. has 'be comforted by the preaching of the holy Gospel concerning Christ'.][19]

In both cases God is at work: in the one case He does a strange work (*opus alienum*), in the other, His proper work (*opus proprium*). Christ Himself as we have seen, does the same. Nor does the Holy Spirit act differently: He must 'not only comfort but also through the office of the Law reprove the world of sin, John 16.8, and thus must do, as the prophet says, Isa. 28.21, *opus alienum ut faciat opus proprium*, that is He must do the work of another (which is to reprove) in order that He may (afterwards) do His own work which is to comfort and preach of grace'.[20] This distinction between proper and strange work goes back to Luther himself who used it constantly.

The Law has a *different significance for those who are justified and regenerated by God's Spirit*. We heard earlier that 'those regenerated by faith have impulses agreeing with God's Law'.[21] They 'accordingly begin to become friendly to the Law and to do the works of the Law'.[22] 'We, therefore, profess that it is necessary that the Law be begun in us, and that it be observed continually more and more. And at the same time we comprehend both spiritual movements and external good works (the good heart within and works without).'[23] But this obligation to keep the Law is strictly a fruit of life in the Holy Spirit and therefore in faith. 'But when man is born anew by the Spirit of God and liberated from the Law, that is, freed from this driver, and is led by the Spirit of Christ, he lives according to the immutable will of God comprised in the Law, and so far as he is born anew, does everything from a free, cheerful spirit; and these are called not properly works of the Law, but works and fruits of the Spirit.'[24] For the justified man in whom God's Spirit is at work, the Law is really superfluous. 'If the believing and elect children of God were completely renewed in this life by the indwelling Spirit, they would need no Law and hence no one

[19] Formula of Concord, Thor. Decl. v, 23f (*Concordia*, p. 261, col. 1).

[20] *Ibid.* (*Concordia*, p. 260, col. 1).

[21] *Ap. C.*, Art. III (*Opera*, VOL. XXVII, p. 455; *Concordia*, p. 46, col. 2).

[22] *Ap. C.*, Art. XII (V) (*Opera*, VOL. XXVIII, p. 177, VOL. XXVII, p. 551; *Concordia*, p. 85, col. 1).

[23] *Ap. C.*, Art. III (*Opera*, VOL. XXVIII, p. 82, cf. Latin version VOL. XXVII, p. 449; *Concordia*, p. 42, col. 2).

[24] Formula of Concord, Thor. Decl. VI (*Concordia*, p. 263, col. 1).

to drive them either, but they would do of themselves, and altogether voluntarily, without any instruction, admonition, urging or driving of the Law, what they are in duty bound to do according to God's will, just as the sun, moon, and all the constellations of Heaven have their regular course of themselves, unobstructed, without admonition, urging, driving, force, or compulsion, according to the order of God which God once appointed for them, yea, just as the holy angels render an entirely voluntary obedience.'[25] In this view the Law is still in some sense the 'driver', even for the believer, because there is still sin in him. He should really have no need of the Law at all.

The significance of the Law for the believer who, because he is not yet at the goal, still needs exhortation, is described in the Formula of Concord under the heading 'Of the Third Use of the Law'.[26] According to this official document, 'the Law was given to men for three reasons: first, that thereby outward discipline might be maintained against wild, disobedient men (*usus politicus*); secondly, that men thereby may be led to the knowledge of their sins (*usus paedagogicus*); thirdly, that after they are regenerate and the flesh notwithstanding cleaves to them, they might on this account have a fixed rule according to which they are to regulate and direct their whole life (*usus normativus*)'.[27] Luther had already taught the first two uses of the Law in the Smalcaldic Articles.[28] As his attitude in the Antinomian controversy shows, he did not mean thereby to exclude the normative meaning of the Law for believers. It is of importance in the interpretation of Luther that in the Small Catechism he expounded the ten commandments in this way. The Formula of Concord quotes, in support of this third use of the Law, Psalms I and 119: 'Blessed is the man whose delight is in the Law of the Lord, and in His Law doth he meditate day and night.' It goes on: 'For the Law is a mirror in which the will of God and what pleases Him are exactly portrayed, and which should (therefore) be constantly held up to the believers and be diligently urged upon them without ceasing.'[29]

[25] *Loc. cit.* (*Concordia*, p. 262, col. 1).
[26] Epitome VI (*Concordia*, p. 223; Schaff, III.130).
[27] *Loc. cit.* (*Concordia*, p. 223, *Status controversiae*; Schaff, III.130f).
[28] *Bekenntnisschriften* (*Luth.*), pp. 435f; Smalcald Articles, III, ii (*Concordia*, p. 142).
[29] Formula of Concord, Thor, Decl. VI (*Concordia*, p. 262, col. 1).

It is significant that the Formula of Concord reverts at once from this view of the Law to the second use. In none of his actions here is the regenerate man yet perfect, but stained with sins. Therefore for him too the Law performs the office for which in Lutheran doctrine it really exists: it judges and punishes him. 'Therefore, as often as believers stumble, they are reproved by the Holy Spirit from the Law, and by the same Spirit are raised up and comforted again with the preaching of the Holy Gospel.'[30] 'For the old Adam, as an intractable, refractory ass, is still a part of them, which must be coerced to the obedience of Christ, not only by the teaching, admonition, force, and threatening of the Law, but also often times by the club of punishments and troubles, until the body of sin is entirely put off.'[31] Schlink is perfectly correct when he says that, according to Lutheran doctrine, the way leads from Law to Gospel and thence by way of regeneration and new obedience back again to the Law and to the revelation of God's wrath.[32] In the Lutheran view the formula 'Law and Gospel' can in this sense be reversed to read 'Gospel and Law'. But no decisive importance is attached to such a primacy of Gospel over Law.[33]

From this Lutheran doctrine the doctrine of repentance and faith and of justification and sanctification necessarily follows, as we have indicated above.

2. The Reformed View: Christ the Starting-point for the Interpretation of the Law

Reformed theology recognises the contrast between Law and Gospel, in a similar way to Lutheranism. We read in the Second Helvetic Confession: 'The Gospel is indeed opposed to the Law. For the Law works wrath and pronounces a curse, whereas the Gospel preaches grace and blessing.'[34] But in an

[30] *Loc. cit.* (*Concordia*, pp. 262f). [31] *Loc. cit.* (*Concordia*, p. 263, col. 2).

[32] Edmund Schlink, *Theologie der lutherischen Bekenntnisschriften*, Munich 1948, pp. 177f.

[33] H. Diem rightly says: 'Of much greater importance is the fact that there can never be any preaching of the Law at all, unless it is made quite clear that this preaching presupposes that the Law in question was given by the same God who reveals His grace in the Gospel.' ('Luthers Predigt in den zwei Reichen', *Theologische Existenz heute*, new series, No. 6, Munich 1947, p. 19).

[34] Second Helvetic Confession, XIII: 'Evangelium quidem opponitur legi. Nam lex iram operatur et maledictionem annunciat, evangelium vero gratiam et benedictionem praedicat' (Schaff, III.260).

exposition of 2 Cor. 3 a little later it adds: 'For "letter" in contrast to "Spirit" while referring of course to everything external, especially to that doctrine of the Law *which in the absence of the Spirit and faith in the hearts of those who do not have a living faith*, works wrath and awakens sin. Hence the Apostle also calls it a ministration of death.'[35] And therefore: 'We know that the Scriptures of the Law, when interpreted by the Gospel, are useful to the Church and therefore the reading of the Law is not to be abolished from the Church. For even though the face of Moses was covered by a veil, the Apostle states emphatically that *this veil has been removed and destroyed by Christ*.'[36] This Confession therefore begins its doctrine of the Law in an altogether positive way: 'We teach that God's Law shows us God's will, what He wills and does not will us to do, what is good and just and what is evil and unjust. We therefore confess the Law to be good and holy.'[37] The Second Helvetic Confession also recognises what the Formula of Concord calls the second use of the Law, but the important thing for it is that the Law has been fulfilled by Christ, that the veil has been removed by Him, and a true understanding of the Law made possible. It sees the Law within the context of the Church and not in abstraction from the gift of the Spirit and faith.

Calvin made it quite clear that this is the only proper way to speak of the Law, i.e. not of Law in the abstract. As an exegete, he observed correctly that Paul did sometimes speak of Law in the abstract (*nuda lex*) but only when he was dealing with false teachers who said righteousness could be achieved by works of the Law, whereas in fact 'the Law was otherwise graced with the covenant of free adoption'.[38] The Law is embedded in God's grace and faithfulness to His people. 'God certainly

[35] 'Nam Litera quae opponitur spiritui, significat quidem omnem rem externam, sed maxime doctrinam legis, sine spiritu et fide in animis non viva fide credentium, operantem iram et excitantem peccatum. Quo nomine et ministerium mortis ab Apostolo nuncupatur.' *Loc. cit.* (Schaff, III.261).

[36] 'Scimus scripturam legis si exponatur per evangelium, ecclesiae utilem, et idcirco eius lectionem non exterminandam esse ex ecclesia. Licet enim velo obtectus fuerit Mosis vultus, Apostolus tamen perhibet, velum per Christum tolli atque aboleri.' *Op. cit.*, XII (Schaff, III.260).

[37] 'Docemus, Lege Dei exponi nobis voluntatem Dei, quid a nobis fieri velit aut nolit, quid bonum et iustum, quidve malum sit et iniustum. Bonam igitur et sanctam confitemur esse Legem.' *Loc. cit.* (Schaff, III.259).

[38] *Inst.*, II.7.2 (VOL. I, p. 351).

requires each one of us to devote himself to Him, to renounce all self-will, to be subject to Him and quietly to let Him lead us, but before He requires that, He gives us Himself.'[39] Here is no hard opposition between God and man, no compulsion and no bondage. 'That must surely soften our hearts, were they harder than stone. For who are we, that our Lord should condescend so far as to enter into a covenant with us and to assure us He wishes to be our Father and Saviour? . . . That must strike home to us so as to make us at once surrender ourselves wholly to Him, because He attracts and invites us to do so by His own example.'[40]

The Mosaic Law in particular rests on the covenant made by God with Abraham. 'Moses was not made a lawgiver to wipe out the blessing promised to the race of Abraham. Rather, we see him repeatedly reminding the Jews of that freely given covenant made with their fathers of which they were the heirs. It was as if he were sent to renew it.'[41] This is Calvin's attitude to the entire Old Testament Law: 'I understand by the word "law" not only the Ten Commandments, which set forth a godly and righteous rule of living, but the form of religion handed down by God through Moses.'[42] A mistaken legalistic interpretation of the Law (as if we could undertake to carry out its requirements) is excluded by the ceremonies attached to it. Those rites were all 'given by God to undergird the commandments, in order to help and further faith'.[43] They show us the way on which we can travel in accordance with God's will in holiness and righteousness, for the sacrifices and ceremonies of the Old Testament point to the One who fulfils the Law, namely to Christ.[44] The Gospel of Christ is 'foreshadowed by the sacrifices and other ceremonies of the Law'.[45] 'Whatever the Law teaches, whatever it commands, whatever it promises, has always a reference to Christ as its main object.'[46] 'Hence no one can rightly understand it who does not continually aim at this mark.'[47] The Law was given therefore 'not to restrain the

[39] Calvin, *Opera*, VOL. XXVIII, p. 513 (Sermon on Deut. 29.9-18).
[40] *Ibid.* [41] *Inst.*, II.7.1 (VOL. I, p. 348). [42] *Ibid.*
[43] *Opera*, VOL. XLVIII, p. 305 (Comment on Acts 13.39).
[44] *Opera*, VOL. XLIX, p. 59 (Comment on Rom. 3.21).
[45] Heidelberg Catechism, Q. 19 (Torrance, *School of Faith*, p. 72).
[46] *Opera*, VOL. XLIX, p. 196 (Comment on Rom. 10.4). [47] *Ibid.*

folk of the Old Covenant under itself, but to foster hope of salvation in Christ until his coming.'[48] Here is *the heart of the Reformed doctrine of the Law*, here, too, is where it differs from the Lutheran doctrine as it is usually presented. 'Without Christ the Law is valueless.'[49] That applies to the ceremonial Law: 'The whole cultus of the law, taken literally and not as shadows and figures corresponding to the truth, will be utterly ridiculous,' is Calvin's vigorous conclusion.[50] 'The force and effect of all ceremonies did depend upon Him.'[51] The same applies to the so-called moral Law. Calvin, who stated plainly that the Law is 'enclosed' in the covenant of grace, can go on to say, in thoroughly Pauline and Lutheran fashion, that the commandments are meant to drive us to Christ.[52] But the Law based on the covenant of grace not only has this pedagogic purpose, but above all a positive directing one: 'The third and principal use [sc. of the law] . . . finds its place among believers in whose hearts the Spirit of God already lives and reigns.'[53] It 'points out the goal toward which throughout life we are to strive'.[54] In our existing condition, we continually need not only instruction but also exhortation.[55] If we allow the Law to perform this service we shall always see it as related most intimately to the promised and given Mediator.[56]

Because in the Reformed view the Law must be understood from Christ as the centre, the emphasis is on the so-called third use of the Law, which is really not the third but the principal use (*praecipuus*).[57] It is true that in the Heidelberg Catechism as in Lutheranism there is then, at this point, a return to the pedagogic use. 'Why then, does God have the Ten Commandments proclaimed to us so strictly if no one can keep them in this life? Answer: First, that all our life long, we may learn more and more to know our sinful nature and so more eagerly to seek forgiveness of sins and righteousness in Christ.'[58] But

[48] *Inst.*, II.7 (VOL. I, p. 348, chapter heading).
[49] *Opera*, VOL. XLVII, p. 124 (Comment on John 5.38).
[50] *Inst.*, II.7.1 (VOL. I, p. 349).
[51] *Opera*, VOL. XLVIII, p. 305 (Comment on Acts 13.29); *Inst.*, III.2.32 (VOL. I, pp. 579f). [52] *Inst.*, II.7.8 (VOL. I, pp. 356f). [53] *Inst.*, II.7.12 (VOL. I, p. 360).
[54] *Inst.*, II.7.13 (VOL. I, p. 362). Cf. Geneva Catechism, Q.229: 'it shows us the mark at which we ought to aim' (Torrance, *School of Faith*, p. 39).
[55] *Inst.*, II.7.12 (VOL. I, pp. 360f).
[55] *Inst.*, II.7.12 (VOL. I, pp. 360f). [56] *Ibid.* [57] *Ibid.*
[58] Heidelberg Catechism, Q. 115 (Torrance, *School of Faith*, p. 93).

characteristically the catechism is not content with that but goes on: 'Secondly, that we may continually apply ourselves and ask God for the grace of the Holy Spirit, that we may more and more be renewed in the image of God, until we attain the goal of full perfection after this life.'[59] Thus by the guidance of the Law as a lamp to our feet, there takes place a 'beginning of obedience', which though 'small', is such that those 'who are converted to God' 'begin to live with earnest purpose not only according to some but according to all of God's Commandments'.[60]

We can sum up the Reformed doctrine of the Law by saying that we are allowed to 'praise' God with our imperfect obedience. What is accomplished by justified sinners is not simply nothing. Because we belong to Christ our works have some value. 'For the Lord then,' says Calvin, 'freely bestows all things upon us so as to add to the full measure of his kindness this gift also; that not rejecting our imperfect obedience, but rather supplying what is lacking to complete it, he causes us to receive the benefit of the promises of the law, as if we had fulfilled their condition.'[61] If we enjoy union with Christ, not only we ourselves but even our works too, are just in God's sight.[62] This doctrine of the *justification of works* (which was developed in the Reformed Church) is of the greatest consequence for ethics. It makes it clear that the man who belongs to Christ need not be the prey of continual remorse. On the contrary he can go about his daily work confidently and joyfully.

Calvin, therefore, condemns it as a mistake ever to contrast Law and Gospel in the way that we contrast 'the merit of works with the free imputation of righteousness'.[63] When Paul from time to time contrasts the righteousness of the Law and that of the gospel, 'the gospel did not so supplant the entire law as to bring forward a different way of salvation. Rather it confirmed and satisfied whatever the law had promised, and gave substance to the shadows.'[64] The Gospel is 'the clear manifestation of the mystery of Christ'. In the broadest sense it includes

[59] *Ibid.* [60] *Op. cit.*, Q. 114.
[61] *Inst.*, II.7.4 (VOL. I, p. 352). Cf. Scots Confession, Art. XV (Schaff, III.456f).
[62] *Inst.*, III.17.10 (VOL. I, p. 813).
[63] *Inst.*, II.9.4 (VOL. I, p. 426). [64] *Ibid.* (VOL. I, p. 427).

'all those testimonies which God formerly gave to the fathers, of His mercy and paternal favour, but is more eminently applicable to the promulgation of the grace exhibited in Christ'.[65]

In view of Christ's appearance, we can say that for us the *Law has been abrogated.* This means: (1) *our liberation from the curse* of the Law. Because Christ took on Himself the whole curse, we are liberated from it.[66] For believers the Law is not the same as it was for them when they were without faith in Christ. It no longer condemns and destroys them. Melanchthon had earlier taught the same in his *Loci.*[67] But Calvin adds typically: 'not that the law no longer enjoins believers to do what is right'.[68] (2) Christians are *no longer under the compulsion* of the Law, only rendering obedience because compelled by the Law, 'but that freed from the Law's yoke they willingly obey God's will'.[69] Like children we can firmly trust 'that our services will be approved by our most merciful Father, however small, rude and imperfect these may be'[70] Here, too, Calvin agrees with Melanchthon, who speaks, however, not of a beginning of obedience, accepted by God, but, quoting 2 Cor. 3.17, 'Where the Spirit of the Lord is, there is freedom', of the gift of the Holy Spirit, who causes God's Law to take effect in us.[71] Calvin on the other hand, keeps here to the pedagogic function of the written Law. (3) We are *freed from any obligation to observe the external requirements of the ceremonial and juridical law.* If we were to observe them we should only be using the Old Testament shadows once again to obscure the light which has been given us in Christ.[72] But our exemption from these ceremonies is such 'that we still have their truth and substance in Jesus Christ, in whom they have their fulfilment'.[73] By abolishing the observance of these ceremonies Christ 'has by his death sealed their force and effect'.[74] We find no such statements in

[65] *Inst.*, II.9.2 (VOL. I, p. 424). Cf. Second Helvetic Confession, XIII (Schaff, III.260ff). [66] *Inst.*, II.7.14f (VOL. I, pp. 362f).

[67] Melanchthon, *Loci Communes*, 'De humanis legibus' (*Opera*, VOL. XXI, p. 136; cf. Hill, p. 139). [68] *Inst.*, II.7.14 (VOL. I, p. 362).

[69] *Inst.*, III.19.4 (VOL. I, p. 836). [70] *Inst.*, III.19.5 (VOL. I, p. 837).

[71] Melanchthon, *Loci communes*, *De humanis legibus* (*Opera*, VOL. XXI, p. 137; Hill, p. 140). [72] *Inst.*, II.7.16 (VOL. I, pp. 364f).

[73] 'Ut nobis illarum veritas et substantia in Jesu Christi maneat in quo suum complementum habent.' Belgic Confession, 1561, Art. XXV (Schaff, III.412f). Cf. French Confession, 1559, Art. XXIII (Schaff, III.372f).

[74] *Inst.*, II.7.16 (VOL. I, p. 365).

Melanchthon about the substance of the ceremonies. On this third point Calvin's agreement with his friend is only apparent. For in his view the accounts of the Old Testament ceremonies still preach Christ to us today. It was no accident that a later theologian like H. F. Kohlbrügge commented on the book of Leviticus: 'the sacrifices of the Old Testament are still of supreme value for us as shadows and types of the only sacrifice valid in God's sight, the sacrifice of Christ which took place on the Cross'. 'For the sacrifices belong to the New Testament, to the covenant of grace, as types and parables.'[75] The same also applies to the civil regulations of the Mosaic Law: 'Surely every nation is left free to make such laws as it foresees to be profitable for itself. Yet these must be in conformity to that perpetual rule of love, so that they indeed vary in form but have the same purpose.'[76]

The Second Commandment, *prohibiting the worship of images*, is not part of the ceremonial law which has been abrogated. The Reformed Churches numbered and learned the Commandments as they are numbered in the Bible, in contrast to the traditional Roman method going back to Augustine, and used by Luther,[77] and followed the ancient Church practice[78] of permitting the use neither of pictures nor crucifixes in worship. Pictures were not allowed even for instructional purposes. 'For we must not be wiser than God who will not have His people instructed by means of dumb idols but by the living proclamation of His Word.'[79] Calvin shows how necessary this

[75] H. F. Kohlbrügge, *Schriftauslegung*, Elberfeld 1911, VOL. XIV, p. 1.

[76] *Inst.*, IV.20.15 (VOL. II, p. 1503). Cf. Westminster Confession, 1647, XIX, 4 (Schaff, III.641).

[77] Deleting the second Commandment and dividing the tenth into two. Fortunately there have always been Lutherans who have urged a return to the biblical version of the Decalogue. Heinrich Vogel, in his Dogmatics, *Gott in Christo* (Berlin 1951, p. 967), has followed the text of Scripture, regarding the second Commandment 'as a separate command, not one which is covered by the first'. Cf. *Inst.*, II.8.12 (VOL. I, p. 378 and n. 16).

[78] Cf. Second Helvetic Confession, Art. IV: 'We likewise endorse the action of blessed Bishop Epiphanius [*d.* 403] who once, on entering the Church porch, tore down and removed a curtain bearing an image depicting Christ or one of the saints, for he knew it to be contrary to the authority of Scripture for a human image to be displayed in the Church of Christ. He also prohibited the hanging of such curtains in the Church of Christ in future therefore, as being contrary to our faith' (*In epist. Hieronymi*, ep. 51, 9; *Corpus Scriptorum Ecclesiasticorum Latinorum*, VOL. LIV, p. 411, 1.9). Latin text in Schaff, III.242.

[79] Heidelberg Catechism, Q. 98 (Torrance, *School of Faith*, p. 89).

Second Commandment is for us, emphasised as it is in Scripture by a special promise and warning, by pointing out that 'man's nature, so to speak, is a perpetual factory of idols'.[80] We are inclined to worship God under the guise of images and pictures we ourselves have constructed. The Second Commandment recalls us from this false path back to God's revelation and the means by which it is proclaimed, the oral preaching of the Word and the visible sacramental signs.[81]

The Reformed Churches therefore do *not teach any abolition of the Law itself*. For it is rightly regarded as enclosed in the covenant of grace and therefore understood from Christ as the centre. When Christ is seen behind the Law, its curse and compulsion fall away, the ceremonial and civil regulations need no longer be observed, but the helpful directions of the Law still apply to us foolish men.[82] When the New Testament informs us that the Law worketh wrath and slays men, 'we neither dishonour the Law, nor detract at all from its excellence'.[83] For the Law was given us by God for saving purposes. If anything different results the fault is in man who perverts it.[84]

[80] *Inst.*, I.11.8 (VOL. I, p. 108).

[81] We should be wary of the argument that nowadays people are immune to the danger of idolatry, at least in so far as this refers to objects of pictorial art. If that were so, the crucifix would not have the importance it certainly does have for many Protestants, for whom an act of worship is unthinkable without one. How many ministers glance at the crucifix when they turn to face the altar during a Lutheran service! On the subject of idolatry see Karl Barth, 'Predigt uber 2. Mose 20, 4-6', *Theologische Existenz heute* No. 22, and in 'Fürchte Dich nicht!', *Sermons 1934-48*, Munich 1949, pp. 84-93; Otto Weber, *Jahwe der Gott und Jahwe der Götze*, Neukirchen 1933; 'Das Moderamen des Reformierten Bundes zum 2. Gebot', in *Reformierte Kirchenzeitung*, 1953, pp. 75f.

[82] Cf. *Inst.*, II.7.14 (VOL. I, pp. 362f).

[83] *Inst.*, II.7.7 (VOL. I, p. 356).

[84] *Opera*, VOL. XXXIX, p. 42 (Comment on Jer. 32-40).

CHAPTER 5

THE DOCTRINE OF HOLY SCRIPTURE[1]

THE account just given of the relation of Gospel and Law makes it clear that the doctrine of Scripture is not quite the same on the two sides. What exactly is the position here?

1. The Lutheran View

In the Lutheran view there is a criterion by which Scripture can be tested. For Luther's view, the Prefaces to the New Testament are very instructive. He regards the New Testament as 'a good tidings and cry, published by the Apostles in all the world, concerning a true David who fought and conquered sin, death, and the Devil' and 'without their deserving it, redeemed' all the captives.[2] We saw earlier that, according to the original Lutheran view, the Gospel is a 'joyful message'. This understanding was preserved right down to the Formula of Concord. Luther warns us not to turn the New Testament into a book of rules for living, not to turn Christ into a second Moses. Even when we know the Gospel story as told by the Evangelists we still do not yet know the Gospel. On the contrary we only know this when '*the voice*' comes and says to the individual reader personally that Christ, with His life, teaching, works, death, resurrection and all He is and has, belongs to him.[3] For Luther's attitude to Holy Scripture, it is of great significance that, on the basis of this insight, he arrived

[1] Barth, *Church Dogmatics*, VOL. I, 2, ch. 3 (Holy Scripture); B. A. Gerrish, 'Biblical Authority and the Continental Reformation', in *Scottish Journal of Theology*, X (1957); J. K. S. Reid, *The Authority of Scripture*, 1957; A. Richardson and W. Schweitzer, *Biblical Authority for Today*, London 1951; P. S. Watson, *Let God Be God*, London 1947.

[2] Luther, *Sämtliche Werke*, 2nd edn., ed. E. I. Enders, Erlangen 1862-84, Vol. 63, p. 109, henceforth cited as E.A. Vol. numbers in Arabic figures refer to German, and in Roman figures to Latin works. Cf. *Reformation Writings*, ed. Woolf, VOL. II, pp. 279f.

[3] E.A., Vol. 63, p. 109.

at a varied assessment of the individual books of the New Testament. 'As a result of all this, you can now properly assess all the books, and tell which are the best.'[4] In his view these are: John's Gospel, 1 John, the Pauline epistles, and 1 Peter. These present Christ and everything it is necessary and saving to know. 'St James' Letter is a right strawy letter compared with these; for there is surely nothing evangelical in it at all.'[5] The proper touchstone for every book is whether or not it sets forth Christ. 'What does not teach Christ is not apostolic, even if St Peter and St Paul teach it. Again, what preaches Christ is apostolic, even if it is Judas or Annas or Pilate or Herod that does it.'[6] As a result of this conviction Hebrews, Jude, and the Apocalypse, as well as James, were pushed into the background. The *Apology* says much the same though a little more cautiously: The article 'Of Justification' 'is of especial service for the clear correct understanding of the entire Holy Scriptures, and alone shows the way to the unspeakable treasure and right knowledge of Christ, and alone opens the door to the entire Bible'.[7] For this reason the Roman Church's interpretation of Scripture was rejected: 'For in the doctrine of our adversaries we condemn this, that in such passages of Scripture, understood either in a philosophical or a Jewish manner, they abolish the righteousness of faith and exclude Christ as Mediator.'[8] Anyone who thinks he finds in Scripture a philosophy or moral law, misreads it. Scripture is in fact a witness to Christ.

According to Luther, *God's own voice calls to us* from Holy Scripture, announcing the forgiveness of sins. Anything which disagrees with this call, is no concern of ours. But if God's living Word addresses us from the words of the Bible, how was it possible for Luther to answer his opponents: 'If our opponents claim Scripture for themselves against Christ, let us claim Christ against Scripture.'[9] How can we have Christ apart from Scripture, and then, with His help, test the individual books of the Bible to see whether they set forth Christ or not? Luther

[4] *Op. cit.*, p. 114. [5] *Op. cit.*, p. 115. [6] *Op. cit.*, p. 157.

[7] *Ap. C.*, Art. IV (II) (*Opera*, VOL. XXVIII, p. 57 (German); *Concordia*, p. 32, col. 2).

[8] *Ap. C.*, Art. III (*Opera*, VOL. XXVII, p. 512 (Latin); *Concordia*, p. 68, col. 2).

[9] 'Quod si adversarii scripturam urserint contra Christum, urgemus Christum contra Scripturam.' *Disputationen Dr. M. Luthers in den Jahren 1535-1545*, ed. P. G. Drews, Göttingen 1895-6, p. 12.

would have replied that in any given case we must learn by faith whether Christ speaks to us in a particular book of the Bible or not.[10] But does not this bring us close to subjectivism? Does this not make every minister into a little pope? Luther himself saw this difficulty quite clearly. Two days before he died he wrote on a scrap of paper: 'No one can understand Virgil in the Bucolics and Georgics unless he has been a shepherd and farmer for five years. No one understands Cicero's letters unless he has been engaged for twenty years in the affairs of some great state. No one should think he has sufficiently grasped the meaning of the Scriptures unless he has governed Churches for a century with the prophets. For mighty is the miracle (1) of John the Baptist, (2) of Christ, (3) of the Apostles. Do not then attempt this Divine Aeneid, rather bow down and humbly worship their footprints. We are beggars, that's certain!'[11] More dubious even than Luther's procedure in making Christ a criterion for the books of the Bible, is the statement of the *Apology* that the doctrine of justification alone opens the door into the whole Bible. Has not a doctrinal principle already taken the place of the livingly experienced Word as the touchstone for the biblical books? This comes very close, at the least, to making a principle into the Judge of Holy Scripture.

2. The Reformed View: Scripture as Witness to Christ

How does the Reformed view of Scripture compare with that? In the Second Helvetic Confession we read: 'We believe and confess that the Canonical Scriptures of the holy Prophets and Apostles of both Testaments are the one true Word of God and have sufficient authority, in and of themselves, independently of men: God Himself spoke to the Fathers, Prophets, and Apostles and through Holy Scripture still *speaks* to us too.'[12] Similarly Calvin says: 'Holy Scripture is like a dead impotent thing to us until we have learned that God speaks and makes

[10] Cf. Karl Holl, *Luther, Tübingen* 1923, p. 576f.

[11] 'Virgilium in Buccolicis et Georgicis nemo potest intelligere nisi fuerit quinque annis pastor et agricola. Ciceronem in epistolis nemo intelligit, nisi 20 annis sit versatus in re publica aliqua insigni. Scripturas sacras sciat se nemo gustasse satis, nisi centum annis cum Prophetis ecclesias gubernarit. Quare ingens est miraculum 1. Joh. Baptistae, 2. Christi, 3. Apostolorum. Hanc tu ne divinam Aeneida tenta, sed vestigia pronus adora. Wir sind Bettler: hoc est verum.' E.A., vol. xvii, 60, pp. 1ff.

[12] Second Helvetic Confession, Art. 1 (Schaff, iii.236).

His will known to us there.'[13] He read the Bible 'as if there the living words of God were heard'.[14] But what does he mean by 'the living words of God'? Calvin says: 'If through the Spirit it [the written word] is really branded upon hearts, if it shows forth Christ, it is the word of life "converting souls".'[15] Therefore: 'We must read Scripture expecting to find Christ there. Anyone who departs from this aim may labour and study all his life and never arrive at the knowledge of the truth. Or can we be wise without the wisdom of God?'[16] 'In a word, we must learn from Scripture to put our trust in God and to walk in the fear of Him, and, since Jesus Christ is the goal of the Law, to strive for nothing else but to know Him.'[17] The Old and New Testaments are not just words; with these words they proclaim the One Word of God, through whom God makes Himself known—Jesus Christ.

Of course the words of the Bible are not the Word of God in the sense that the divine truth has passed directly into the words of Holy Scripture, as one particular theory of inspiration implies. Alongside the Incarnation of the Word in Jesus Christ there is no second incarnation. Calvin often compares the written Word with a mirror, therefore: 'Instead of having the actual thing we have to be satisfied with the Word.'[18] Similarly he calls the written word an 'instrument' of the Holy Spirit.[19] Or he speaks of Christ as the soul of the Law. Separated from Christ the Law is like a dead letter. Christ alone gives it life.[20] That applies to the whole Bible. Therefore the substance with which the Bible is concerned is not identical with the words.[21]

Nor can it be divorced from these words. If it is, the words say nothing but are simply dead. The one Word of God and the words of Holy Scripture are inseparable; because it pleased God to reveal Himself in Jesus Christ, and the Bible announces this revelation. Just as God once condescended to meet us in our flesh in His Son, so in Scripture He again adapts Himself

[13] *Opera*, VOL. LIV, p. 285 (Sermons on 2 Tim. and Titus).
[14] *Inst.*, 1.7.1 (VOL. I, p. 74). [15] *Inst.*, 1.9.3 (VOL. I, p. 95).
[16] *Opera*, VOL. XLVIII, p. 125 (Comment on John 5.39).
[17] *Opera*, VOL. IX, p. 825 (Préface des anciennes Bibles genevoises).
[18] *Opera*, VOL. L, p. 63 (Comment on 2 Cor. 5.7).
[19] *Inst.*, 1.9.3 (VOL. I, p. 96).
[20] *Opera*, VOL. XL, p. 395 (Comment on Ezek. 16.61).
[21] *Opera*, VOL. L, p. 45 (Comment on 2 Cor. 4.3).

to our comprehension and speaks to us in a way we can hear. He speaks to us as a nurse speaks to her children.[22]

We cannot understand this language by our own powers. We shall only hear the Scriptures rightly when God Himself 'reveals his majesty' in them.[23] This is the work of the Holy Spirit.[24] The Holy Spirit who employed the prophets and Apostles as His instruments and still makes use of their testimony today must, in accordance with Isa. 54.13, still work in us today if the written Word is to become for us God's Word.[25] It is in this living, comprehensive sense, which actually includes us who live today, that we must speak of the inspiration of Scripture. 'For as God alone is a fit witness of himself in his Word, so also the Word will not find acceptance in men's hearts before it is sealed by the inward testimony of the Spirit.'[26] By His Spirit the Lord brings to life for us the prophetic–apostolic witness to Himself, and the Spirit proves Himself to be the Third Person of the Trinity by speaking only of that which the biblical writers speak, namely of God's revelation in history in Jesus Christ.

Reformed theology, just like Lutheran, knows that it is God's Word which addresses us from the Bible and produces faith and that this Word is Christ Himself. But this address does not become an experience within our control on the basis of which we can read through the Bible and test whether it 'sets forth Christ'. Calvin read the whole Bible expecting to find Christ there. In doing so he did not adhere rigidly to the letter of Scripture but used all the means then available to pursue a critical exegesis. But he was sure that it was no fault of Scripture if it remained obscure to the reader at any point. For 'we are completely and utterly incapable of understanding Scripture. We must first receive from God the intelligence for this, and God gives us this when we turn to Him, by His Spirit.'[27] The Holy Spirit is the true Interpreter of Scripture,[28] and not we ourselves on the basis of some experience of Christ, or of

[22] *Opera*, VOL. XXVI, p. 387 (Sermons on Deut. 2-9).
[23] *Inst.*, I.813 (VOL. I, p. 92).
[24] Westminster Confession, I, 5 (Schaff, III.602f).
[25] *Inst.*, I.7.5 (VOL. I, p. 80).
[26] *Inst.*, I.7.4 (VOL. I, p. 79). [27] *Opera*, VOL. IX, p. 825.
[28] *Opera*, VOL. VI, p. 270 (*Responsio contra Pighium*, 1543).

justification, or still less of any theological principle regarded as the touchstone for our judgment. In this expectation of the help of the Spirit, Calvin sought Christ in the books of the Bible. He wrote commentaries on almost all of them. The explanation of the fact that he commented on all the New Testament books except the Apocalypse, may be that this last was a closed book to him. But he did not make that a reason for passing an adverse judgment on it. On the contrary he says of the whole Bible: 'But above human judgment we affirm with utter certainty (just as if we were gazing upon the majesty of God himself) that it has flowed to us from the very mouth of God by the ministry of men.'[29] We heard how Luther, on his deathbed, spoke of the study of Scripture. Those words written on that scrap of paper, words born of a deep humility towards Holy Scripture—did they not amount to a recantation of the much too ebullient utterances made in the 1520's and 1530's? Is not this Luther at one with Calvin?

In the recent past, the Bible was once again acknowledged, by the German Confessing Church, to be a witness to Christ. The Free Reformed Synod declared in January 1934: 'The Word spoken by God once and for all is heard by the Church, through the free grace of the Holy Spirit, in the twofold but united and mutually complementary witness of the Old and New Testaments, i.e. in the witness of Moses and the prophets to the coming Jesus Christ, and in the witness of the Evangelists and Apostles to the Jesus Christ who has come.'[30] A few months later representations of both confessions declared more briefly and plainly: 'Jesus Christ, as He is attested to us in Holy Scripture, is the One Word of God, which we have to hear and which we have to trust and obey in life and in death.'[31] Here it is stated plainly that the Bible is not a book filled with religious truths or moral laws, nor a collection of pious writings,

[29] 'Supra humanum iudicium certo certius constituimus (non secus acsi ipsius Dei numen illic intueremur) hominum ministerio ab ipsissimo Dei ore ad nos fluxisse.' *Inst.*, I.7.5 (VOL. I, p. 80).

[30] *Erklärung uber das rechte Verständnis der reformatorischen Bekenntnisse in der deutschen evangelischen Kirche der Gegenwart*, 4 January 1934, Section II, 2 (Niesel, *Bekenntnisschriften und Kirchenordnungen*, pp. 328ff). This 'First Barmen Declaration' was the work of Karl Barth, who introduced the discussion of it at the meeting of the Free Reformed Synod on 3 January 1934. It was adopted by the Synod on the following day as 'a testimony to the truth of Holy Scripture'.

[31] Barmen Declaration (May 1934), Thesis No. I.

but a witness to Jesus Christ, to God's Word, who exists outside of us but who comes to us. The Protestant 'Scripture-principle' was thus cleansed of all obscurities and distortions. In the Church of the Gospel it is not a question of an infallible book, a 'paper pope', but of Christ clothed in the words of His witnesses, the apostles and prophets, of the Christ who by His Spirit proves Himself a living Lord who still uses the words of His messengers to announce His presence today, where and when He wills. At Barmen thc false positions of Protestant orthodoxy and liberalism were broken through, and the true approach to the Bible found. The Churches knew themselves henceforth to be 'under the Word'.

CHAPTER 6

THE DOCTRINE OF PREDESTINATION[1]

1. The Position of Luther and Calvin

It is a common and stubbornly persisting error to regard the doctrine of predestination as a peculiarity of the Reformed faith. It is true that it plays an important part in that faith. Indeed, in the Arminian controversy at the beginning of the seventeenth century, it was, in many circles in the Reformed Churches, the point where the ways divided. The Synod of Dort (1618-19) devoted five canons to the condemnation of the Arminians,[2] or the Remonstrants, as they called themselves.[3] In Canon 1, it affirmed a strict doctrine of predestination. Whatever our attitude to this, we should remember that Luther too upheld a rugged doctrine of predestination, especially in the *De servo arbitrio* written against Erasmus in 1525, and that he never departed from this view. 'I regard no book as so much my own as the "Bondage of the will" and the "Catechism".'[4]

According to Luther, predestination means the 'dreadful hidden will of God, who, according to His own counsel, ordains such persons as He wills to receive and partake of the mercy preached and offered'.[5] Predestination is the way the salvation in Christ is applied to those chosen for it by God.

In view of the importance that Luther attached to his book against Erasmus, we could even say that he stressed the doctrine of predestination far more than Calvin did. We shall look in

[1] Cf. Karl Barth, *Church Dogmatics*, vol. ii, 2, pp. 3-506; F. W. Camfield, *Reformation Old and New*, London 1947, Ch. iv, 'God's Election of Grace'.

[2] Jacobus Arminius, 1560-1609, of Leyden.

[3] After the Remonstrance of 1610.

[4] Luther, Letter to Capito (9 July 1537) (W.A., *Briefwechsel* vol. viii, p. 99). Cf. R. Seeberg, *Die Lehre Luthers*, Leipzig 1933, pp. 188-91.

[5] 'Occulta illa et metuenda voluntas Dei, ordinantis suo consilio, quos et quales praedictae et oblatae misericordiae capaces et participes esse velit' (W.A., vol. xviii, p. 684; also in *Bondage of the Will*, trans. J. L. Packer and O. R. Johnston, London 1957, p. 169).

vain in Calvin for as harsh a form of the doctrine and such extreme expressions of it as we find in Luther's *De servo arbitrio*.[6] The original *Institutio* of 1536 contains no special section on this doctrine, which is treated there only in the context of what is said about the Church. Predestination is treated as a separate theme for the first time in the Geneva Catechism of 1537, and in the expanded later editions of the *Institutio*, and even here not at the beginning, as we might have expected, but in the section dealing with the doctrine of the appropriation of salvation. In the definitive 1559 edition of the *Institutio*, it comes almost at the end of this section. The Second Geneva Catechism did not devote a special section to this theme. For Calvin therefore, the doctrine of predestination is not fundamental in the sense that all other doctrines are deduced from it. It was nevertheless sufficiently important for him to defend in a work which refutes the Roman version of it.[7] Even here he stresses its positive evangelical meaning: 'This great subject is not, as many imagine, a mere thorny and noisy disputation, nor a speculation which wearies the minds of men without any profit; but a solid discussion eminently adapted to the service of the godly because it builds us up soundly in the faith . . . and lifts us up into an admiration of the unbounded goodness of God towards us, for our salvation is then sure to us when we find the cause of it in the breast of God. Thus when we lay hold of life in Christ, made manifest to our faith, the same faith being still our leader and guide, our sight is permitted to penetrate much further, and to see from what source that life proceeded.'[8] Our knowledge of the true life in Christ is linked with the knowledge that God's love prepared this life for us 'freely and of His mere grace without any respect of men', as the Second Helvetic Confession says.[9]

[6] For Luther's teaching see H. Vogel, 'Praedestinatio gemina', in *Theologische Aufsätze, Karl Barth zum 50. Geburtstage*, Munich 1936.

[7] *De aeterna Dei praedestinatione*, 1552 (*Opera*, VOL. VIII, pp. 257ff).

[8] 'Non esse, ut quibusdam falso videtur argutam hanc vel spinosam speculationem, quae absque fructa ingenia fatiget: sed disputationem solidam et ad pietatis usum maxime accommodari: nempe: quae ad fidem probe aedificet . . . et in admirationem extollat immensae erga nos Dei bonitatis. . . . Tunc enim demum nobis certa est nostra salus, quum in Dei pectore causam reperimus. Sic enim vitam in Christo manifestam fide apprehendimus ut eadam fide duce procul intueri liceat, ex quo fonte vita prodierit.' *Opera*, VOL. VIII, p. 260. See H. Cole, *Calvin's Calvinism*, London 1927, p. 29.

[9] Second Helvetic Confession, Art. X: 'libere et mera sua gratia, nullo hominum respectu' (Schaff, III.252).

2. Double Predestination as Taught by the Reformers

The Reformers regard predestination as twofold. The authoritative Chapter 21 of Calvin's *Institutio*, Book III, is entitled 'Eternal Election', or 'God's Predestination of some to Salvation and of Others to Destruction'. The famous definition in section 5 of this chapter reads: 'We call predestination God's eternal decree, by which he determined with himself what he willed to become of each man. For all are not created in equal condition; rather, eternal life is fore-ordained for some, eternal damnation for others. Therefore, as any man has been created to one or the other of these ends, we speak of him as predestined to life or to death.'[10] In Luther's *De servo arbitrio* we read: 'God would be ludicrous if He could not and did not do all things, or if anything were done without Him. But if the foreknowledge and omnipotence of God are conceded, it naturally follows by irrefutable logic that we were not made by ourselves, nor live by ourselves but only through His omnipotence. Seeing that He foreknew that we should be what we are, and now makes us such, and moves and governs us as such, how, pray, can it be pretended that it is open to us to become something other than that which He foreknew and is now bringing about?' 'Doubtless it gives the greatest possible offence to common sense or natural reason, that God, who is proclaimed as being full of mercy and goodness, and so on, should of His own mere will abandon, harden and damn men.'[11] Luther thus ascribes to God 'the will and power of hardening, showing mercy and doing all things',[12] as Calvin did later.

[10] 'Praedestinationem vocamus aeternum Dei decretum, quo apud se constitutum habuit, quid de uno quoque homine fieri vellet. Non enim pari conditione creantur omnes: sed aliis vita aeterna, aliis damnatio aeterna praeordinatur. Itaque prout in alterutrum finem quisque conditus sit, ita vel ad vitam vel ad mortem praedestinatum dicimus.' *Inst.*, III.21.5 (VOL. II, p. 926).

[11] 'Aeque ridiculus fuerit [Deus], si non omnia possit et faciat aut aliquid sine ipso fiat. Concessa autem praescientia et omnipotentia, sequitur naturaliter irrefragibili consequentia: Nos per nos ipsos non esse factos, nec vivere, nec agere quicquam, sed per illius omnipotentiam. Cum autem tales nos ille ante praescierit futuros talesque nunc faciat, moveat et gubernet, quid potest fingi quaeso, quod in nobis liberum sit aliter et aliter fieri, quam ille praescierit aut nunc agat?' (W.A., VOL. XVIII, p. 718; *Bondage of the Will*, tr. Packer and Johnston, pp. 216f). 'Scilicet hoc offendit quam maxime sensum illum communem . . . quod Deus mera voluntate sua homines deserat, induret, damnet' (W.A., VOL. XVIII, p. 719; *Bondage of the Will*, p. 217).

[12] W.A., VOL. XVIII, p. 707; *Bondage of the Will*, p. 200.

It is a Reformed confession which states that, in this Divine transaction, the scales are not evenly weighted but the balance tipped in favour of man's election to salvation. 'Election is the immutable purpose of God, whereby before the foundations of the world were laid He elected from the whole human race, that had fallen from its primeval integrity into sin and destruction by its own fault, according to the most free good pleasure of His will, out of pure grace, a fixed number of men neither better nor worthier than others, but prostrate with the others in a common wretchedness, to salvation in Christ . . . for a proof of His mercy and for the praise of the riches of His glorious grace.'[13]

Within Lutheranism the departure from Luther's teaching on this subject has been written into the Formula of Concord. This distinguishes between God's foreknowledge (*praescientia*) both of good and evil, and His predestination: 'The predestination or eternal election of God, however, extends only over the godly beloved children of God, being a cause of their salvation which He also provides, as well as disposes what belongs thereto.'[14] The saying in Matt. 22.14, 'Many are called but few are chosen', is to be interpreted as follows: 'that they either do not at all hear God's Word, but wilfully despise it, stop their ears and harden their hearts, and in this manner foreclose the ordinary way to the Holy Ghost, so that He cannot perform His work in them.'[15] We recall Luther's statement: 'God would be ludicrous if He could not and did not do all things, or if anything were done without Him.' Luther's doctrine of predestination in the *De servo arbitrio* cannot be improved in the way attempted by the Formula of Concord. On the contrary, the latter destroys, in favour of man's freedom of choice, the testimony which the doctrine of predestination is meant to offer to God's freedom and power.

[13] 'Est autem electio immutabile Dei propositum, quo ante iacta mundi fundamenta e universo genere humano, ex primaeva integritate in peccatum et exilium sua culpa prolapso, secundum liberrimum voluntatis suae beneplacitum, ex mera gratia, certam quorundam hominum multitudinem, aliis nec meliorum nec digniorum, sed in communi miseria cum aliis iacentium, ad salutem elegit in Christo . . . ad demonstrationem suae misericordiae et laudem divitiarum gloriosae suae gratiae.' Synod of Dort, Can. I, 7 (Schaff, III.553, cf. III.582; Heppe, *Reformed Dogmatics*, p. 163).

[14] Formula of Concord, Epitome, XI, iv (Schaff, III.166; *Concordia*, p. 230).

[15] Epitome, XI, xii (Schaff, III.168f; *Concordia*, p. 230).

3. Christ and Predestination

Luther says at the end of the *De servo arbitrio*: 'If we believe that Christ redeemed men by His blood, we are forced to confess that all of man was lost; otherwise, we make Christ either wholly superfluous, or else the redeemer of the least valuable part of man only; which is blasphemy and sacrilege.'[16] It is clear from this that Christ is the basis of his thinking. So he warns the reader: 'We may not debate the secret will of Divine Majesty, . . . but let man occupy himself with God Incarnate, that is, with Jesus crucified, in whom, as Paul says, are all the treasures of wisdom and knowledge, though hidden; for by Him man has abundant instruction both in what he should and in what he should not know.'[17] On the words 'Many are called but few are chosen' Luther later commented: 'Set forth and climb up into Heaven, and make reckoning with yourself what must be the heart of God towards us men, seeing the Son of God did all that for our sakes, and seeing He did it of the will and commandment of the Father. Is it not so that your reason will constrain you, so that you have to say: Since God has thus given His only begotten Son for our sakes, He can never intend evil towards men, He never wills that they should perish, seeing that He asks and uses the very highest means to help them to life.'[18] The Formula of Concord similarly says: 'This predestination of God is not to be investigated in the secret counsel of God but to be sought in the Word of God, where it is also revealed.'[19] It adds: 'But the Word of God leads us to Christ who is the Book of Life. . . .'[20] And the 'Thorough Declaration' has this splendid sentence: 'Accordingly this eternal election of God is to be considered in Christ, and not outside of or without Christ.'[21]

Calvin too taught that we know our election in Christ.

[16] W.A., VOL. XVIII, p. 786; *Bondage of the Will*, tr. Packer and Johnston, p. 318.

[17] 'De secreta illa voluntate maiestatis non esse disputandum. . . . Occupet vero sese cum Deo incarnatu seu cum Iesu crucifixo, in quo sunt omnes thesauri sapientiae et scientiae, sed absconditi; per hunc enim abunde habet, quod scire et non scire debeat' (W.A., VOL. XVIII, p. 689; *Bondage of the Will*, pp. 175f).

[18] W.A., VOL. LII, p. 140, Sermon on Matt. 20.1-16. Cf. Barth, *Church Dogmatics*, VOL. LII, 2, p. 61.

[19] Epitome, XI, v (Schaff, III.166; *Concordia*, p. 230).

[20] Epitome, XI, vi (Schaff, III.166; *Concordia*, p. 230).

[21] Thor. Decl. XI (*Concordia*, p. 291, col. 2).

'Accordingly, those whom God has adopted as his sons are said to have been chosen not in themselves but in his Christ (Eph. 1.4); for unless he could love them in him, he could not honour them with the inheritance of his Kingdom if they had not previously become partakers of him. But if we have been chosen in *him*, we shall not find assurance of our election in ourselves; and not even in God the Father, if we conceive him as severed from his Son. Christ, then, is the mirror wherein we must, and without self-deception may, contemplate our own election. For since it is into his body the Father has destined those to be ingrafted whom he has willed from eternity to be his own, that he may hold as sons all whom he acknowledges to be among his members, we have a sufficiently clear and firm testimony that we have been inscribed in the book of life [cf. Rev. 21.27] if we are in communion with Christ.'[22] We do not need to comb the heights with our thoughts, in a vain attempt to fathom God's plan. 'But see! God Himself condescends to us, and shows us the reason for it in His Son, as if to say: Here I am! Look at Me! and know that I have adopted you as My children!'[23] In the Divine Word addressed to us in Christ our election not only can be known but becomes absolutely certain, because in Jesus Christ, we are also confronted with its basis and cause. 'Our Lord Jesus Christ is the foundation both of the promise of salvation and of our gracious election, which took place before the creation of the world.'[24] With a reference to Jesus' words: 'I know whom I have chosen' (John 13.18) Calvin states unambiguously in the final edition of his *Institutio*: 'Christ makes himself the Author of election.'[25] When God's Word comes to us, when Christ Himself draws near to us in it, we are confronted by *the basis* both of *the reality* of our election and *our knowledge of it*. The Second Helvetic Confession too says quite plainly: 'We condemn those who, when they ask whether they have been elect from eternity and what God decreed for them then, ignore Christ. We must hear and believe the preaching of the Gospel and be firmly assured: if thou dost believe and

[22] *Inst.*, III.24.5 (VOL. II, p. 970).

[23] *Opera*, VOL. VIII, p. 114: 'Mais voilà Dieu qui s'abaisse à nous; il nous montre dequoy en son Fils; comme s'il disoit: Me voicy: contemplez-moy, et cognoissez comment je vous ay adoptez pour mes enfants' (*Congrégation sur l'élection éternelle*, 1551).

[24] *Ibid.*

[25] *Inst.*, III.22.7 (VOL. II. p, 941).

thou art in Christ, thou art elect.'[26] Our election, too, is given in and with our union with Christ.

4. A Double Will of God?

Luther's doctrine of predestination is much cruder than Calvin's. We noted the passage in the *De servo arbitrio* where Luther speaks of two different wills in God, the 'hidden will' and the 'revealed will': 'Nor is it for us to ask why He does so, but to stand in awe of God, who can do, and wills to do, such things.'[27] Calvin does not accept the idea of a twofold will in God: 'Moreover, since he is the eternal wisdom of the Father, his unchangeable truth, his firm counsel, we ought not to be afraid of what he tells us in his Word varying in the slightest from that will of the Father which we seek. Rather he faithfully reveals to us that will as it was from the beginning and ever shall be.'[28] Otherwise God's perfect revelation in Jesus Christ would be called in question. As Calvin sees it, this is the danger of Luther's position. Yet even for Calvin God's will is not simply embodied in Christ. 'We see here that God begins with Himself when He condescends to choose us: but He will have us begin with Christ.'[29] Calvin therefore teaches (following Augustine): 'Those who come to Christ were before sons of God in His divine heart, while they were in themselves still His enemies; and because they were pre-ordained unto eternal life, they were therefore given unto Christ.'[30] Similarly the Second Helvetic Confession says: 'God freely and of pure grace predestined and elected from all eternity . . . the saints whom He wills to save in Christ.'[31] The difference from Luther comes out in the fact that in all these passages the one divine will is regarded as really revealed in Christ.

The Formula of Concord strongly condemns the doctrine of a double will in God which we found in Luther, though it avoids referring to the Reformer by name: 'However, that "many are called and few chosen" is not owing to the fact that

[26] Second Helvetic Confession, Art. x (Schaff, III.252, cf. I.401).
[27] W.A., vol. xviii, p. 690; *Bondage of the Will*, tr. Packer and Johnston, p. 176.
[28] *Inst.*, III.24.5 (vol. II, p. 971).
[29] *Opera*, vol. viii, p. 319 (Cole, *Calvin's Calvinism*, p. 133).
[30] *Op cit.*, p. 292 (Cole, *Calvin's Calvinism*, p. 84).
[31] Second Helvetic Confession, Art. x (Schaff, III.252; cf. I.401).

the call of God which is made through the Word had the meaning as though God said: Outwardly through the Word, I indeed call to My Kingdom all of you to whom I give My word; however, in My heart I do not mean this with respect to all, but only with respect to a few; for it is My will that the greatest part of those whom I call through the Word shall not be enlightened nor converted, but be and remain damned, although through the Word, in the call, I declare Myself to them otherwise. *Hoc enim esset Deo contradictorias voluntates affingere*; that is: For this would be to assign contradictory wills to God. That is, in this way it would be taught that God, who surely is Eternal Truth, would be contrary to Himself, whereas on the contrary God punishes also in men this wickedness when a person declares himself to one purpose and thinks and means another in his heart.'[32] A double will in God is thus rejected, but the basis of election in Christ not stated unambiguously. Even for the Formula of Concord there is in God a divine plan of election which is so to speak above Christ: 'In this His counsel, purpose and ordination God has prepared salvation not only in general, but has in grace considered and chosen to salvation each and every person of the elect who are to be saved through Christ.'[33]

In Calvin too we find a divine plan above Christ. Only occasionally in Calvin does the essential truth shine forth that we have in Christ not just the basis of our knowledge of election but also its basis in reality. But in Calvin, unlike the Formula of Concord, predestination is always double predestination. His explanation of Matt. 22.14 is: 'There is the general call, by which God invites all equally to himself through the outward preaching of the word—even those to whom he holds it out as a savour of death, and as the occasion for severer condemnation. The other kind of call is special, which he deigns for the most part to give to the believers alone, while by the inward illumination of the Spirit he causes the preached Word to dwell in their hearts.'[34]

[32] Thor. Decl. XI (*Concordia*, p. 289, col. 2).

[33] *Loc. cit.* (*Concordia*, p. 288, col. 1).

[34] 'Est enim universalis vocatio, qua per externam verbi praedicationem omnes pariter ad se invitat Deus. . . . Est altera specialis qua utplurimum solos fideles dignatur: dum interiori sui Spiritus illuminatione efficit ut verbum praedicatum eorum cordibus insideat.' *Inst.*, III.24.8 (VOL. II, p. 974).

5. The Teaching of Lutheran and Reformed Orthodoxy

Lutheran orthodoxy, adopting from the Formula of Concord the distinction between God's foreknowledge (*praescientia Dei*) and His fore-ordination (*praedestinatio*), developed the doctrine as follows: Because God foresees (*praevisio*) the response of individual men to His universal plan of salvation (*voluntas universalis sive antecedens*), this plan becomes His special will as applied to each individual case (*voluntas specialis sive consequens*). This however does not mean that two wills are attributed to God, but only that there is a difference because the special will of God (*voluntas specialis sive consequens*) includes those who either respond or do not respond to God's general will (*voluntas universalis sive antecedens*). Included in election as the action of God's will, is Christ's saving work. The Divine will is not absolute (*absoluta*) therefore but relative (*ordinata*), resting as it does on Christ as Mediator, and conditional (*conditionata*) since the faith produced by the Holy Spirit is part of the event. It is obvious that an attempt is here made to give predestination a Christocentric basis. But there are serious objections to the form this attempt takes. To combat the absolute decree of the Reformed theologians, Lutheran orthodoxy openly adopted the Jesuit doctrine of God's *scientia media*, according to which God's decision is governed by the human decisions which He foresees. This endangers the fundamental concern of the Reformers. The doctrine of predestination becomes instead a doctrine of man's election of God.

The Reformed Churches adhered to their doctrine of an 'unchangeable decree of God' (*immutabile Dei propositum*),[35] God's 'absolute decree', and thus pointed to the absolute freedom of God. Whatever else may be thought of this view, at least it banished the danger of Pelagianism which appeared in Lutheranism.

6. The Function of the Doctrine of Predestination

In Luther the doctrine of predestination safeguards the truth that man's will is in bondage. The converse of this is the full assurance of salvation: 'But now that God has taken my salva-

[35] 'Immutabile Dei propositum.' Synod of Dort, Can. I, 7 (Schaff, III.553, cf. III.582; Heppe, *Reformed Dogmatics*, p. 163).

tion out of the control of my own will and put it under the control of His, and promised to save me, not according to my working or running, but according to His own grace and mercy, I have the comfortable certainty that He is faithful and will not lie to me, and that He is also great and powerful so that no devils or opposition can break Him or pluck me from Him.'[36] The Formula of Concord takes a similar view: 'Accordingly the Holy Spirit teaches us this doctrine for no other reason than to direct us thereby to the revealed Word of God, which we are to receive with faith, to strengthen our faith and fully assure us of our salvation.'[37]

In Calvin the doctrine of predestination is the ultimate expression of the evangelical doctrine of grace. It magnifies God's glory and brings us a real humility.[38] It makes assurance of salvation really sure: 'The elect can indeed waver and even fall: yet they are not crushed, because the Lord stretches forth His hand to help.'[39]

In neither denomination was attention kept strictly focused on Jesus Christ, 'the One Word of God, which we must hear and which we must trust and obey in life and in death'.[40] Efforts were made to do this, but strangely enough both sides allowed their attention to be diverted from Jesus Christ, as God's Word to us, especially in the case of Luther with his intolerable speculation about two wills in God. But, as we have seen, Lutheranism's departure from Luther's doctrine offered no solution but instead merely produced new dangers. In our own days, Karl Barth, by taking up the Christocentric approaches in both traditions while radically rejecting the solutions they offered, has tried to interpret the doctrine of election in a thoroughly Christocentric way. According to him, Jesus Christ is 'the electing God'[41] and 'the elect man'.[42] In the revealed God (*deus revelatus*) we meet the electing God and to believe in Him is to be elect. Jesus Christ is therefore not only the basis of our knowledge of election but also, as Eph. 1.4 says,

[36] W.A., VOL. XVIII, p. 783; *Bondage of the Will*, tr. Packer and Johnston, p. 314.
[37] Thor. Decl. XI (*Concordia*, pp. 287f).
[38] *Inst.*, III.21.1 (VOL. II, p. 921).
[39] Calvin, *Institutio*, 1536 (*Opera selecta*, edd. P. Barth and W. Niesel, Munich 1926-52, VOL. I, p. 87).
[40] Barmen Thesis No. 1.
[41] Barth, *Church Dogmatics*, VOL. II, 2, p. 103.
[42] *Op. cit.*, p. 116.

the basis of its reality. The traditional positions of both confessions have thus been challenged and theology at a decisive point warned against all speculations and directed to its real task, namely to be a theology of revelation.

CHAPTER 7

THE DOCTRINE OF THE CHURCH[1]

THE doctrine of predestination brings us to the problem of the Church. Interpreted Christocentrically, predestination clearly concerns not simply God and the individual but God and the individual within the Church of God. Thus the Heidelberg Catechism declares its faith that the Son of God 'gathers . . . for Himself . . . unto everlasting life, a chosen community', and 'that I am, and forever shall remain, a living member of the same'.[2]

1. The Lutheran View: The Invisible Church and the Visible Church and the Relation Between them

Luther distinguishes between *an inward* and *an outward Church* or Christendom, as he preferred to call it: 'Christendom means, as we confess in our Creed, an assembly on earth of all who believe in Christ. . . . Therefore the essence, life, and nature of Christendom is not a bodily assembly but an assembly of hearts in one faith.'[3] The unity of Christendom rests upon Christ.[4] 'The first, which is the natural, fundamental, essential and genuine Christendom, we call a spiritual inward Christendom. The other, which is made and external, we call a bodily outward Christendom; not that we divorce them from each other, but just in the same way that when thinking of a man's soul I call him a spiritual man, and when thinking of his body a bodily man, or just as the Apostle speaks of an inward man and an outward man.'[5] In this outward Church there are hypocrites. These must be tolerated because only God knows

[1] See further: Karl Barth, *The Living Congregation of the Living Lord Jesus Christ* (in Amsterdam Series, *Man's Disorder and God's Design,* London 1948, VOL. I, pp. 67-76; *The Nature of the Church*, ed. R. N. Flew, London 1952.

[2] Q. 54 (Torrance, *School of Faith*, p. 78).

[3] W.A., VOL. VI, pp. 292f.

[4] *Op. cit.*, p. 295.

[5] *Op. cit.*, pp. 296f.

who they are: 'The Church is twofold, in number and significance, in appearance and truth, in name and in substance. . . . Moreover those who only pretend to be religious, and are therefore hypocrites, of whom there are many in the community of Christians, in the company of believers, we tolerate only so long as they do not teach anything contrary to the confession of sound doctrine.'[6] This outward Church exists in various places, it is 'bodily and visible'. But the Church in which we believe according to the Creed, is 'neither bodily nor visible' but 'a community or congregation of saints in faith, though no one sees who is holy or faithful'.[7] The true Church—it is clear from this—is not an idea of the Church, existing somewhere beyond the phenomenal world, but is here on earth, only we are unable to determine its boundaries because none of us can recognise with certainty the faith of others.

Nevertheless there are *signs* by which we can tell for certain that in any one place, in the outward Church therefore, the inward spiritual Church is also present. 'The external signs by which we can tell where this same Church is present in the world are baptism, sacrament and Gospel, and not Rome or any other place. For where there is baptism and Gospel, no one should doubt that there are also saints there, even if they are only children in the cradle.'[8] For where the Word is proclaimed God will not have it fruitless, but gives His Holy Spirit and a spiritual society arises. According to Luther, it is above all the preaching of the Word which is to be for us a sure sign of the presence of the true Church. 'The Gospel comes before the bread of the Supper and Baptism as the only quite certain and supreme characteristic mark of the Church . . . in short

the whole life and substance of the Church lies in God's Word. I am not speaking of the written Gospel but of the Gospel preached orally.'[9] The outward Church has the task of proclaiming this Word. Sinners, even hypocrites, must be tolerated in the Church, but, as we have heard, not those who propagate false doctrine. Even in the outward Church there can be no toleration of those who preach falsehood, as the Romans and enthusiasts were then doing. There are, of course, not two

[6] W.A., VOL. XLIII, pp. 428f. [7] W.A., VOL. VI, p. 300f.
[8] *Op. cit.*, p. 301. [9] W.A., VOL. VII, p. 721.

Churches, a visible one and an invisible one, standing independently side by side. What binds them together is the living Word, Christ Himself. Where something different is preached this bond is snapped and the outward Church is in mortal danger. Where this Word is preached, the Church can be perceived, but is at the same time invisible, since the Word must be accepted by faith. Because the Word is preached in the visible Church, it is within it that faith arises, and so, to receive salvation, one must belong to this visible Church.

So far as *the Church's order* is concerned Luther teaches that all Christians are priests. 'For all who believe that Christ is their priest in Heaven in the presence of God, and who lay upon Him and pour out through Him their prayer, praise, need and very selves—see! all these are His true priests wherever they may be. . . . It [faith] alone is the true priestly office and it lets no one at all be anything else; therefore all Christians are priests, whether young or old, master or servant, wife or maiden, educated or ignorant.'[10] Nevertheless not every member of the Church may perform the ministry of preaching, but only those whom the Church thinks specially equipped and has therefore called to do so. In 1523 Luther wrote a fine tract on this subject: 'Why a Christian congregation or Church has the right and power to decide all doctrine and to call, induct, and depose teachers, the reasons and cause shown from Scripture.'[11] It remains true: 'All Christians are priests, but not all are ministers, for in addition to being a Christian and a priest, a minister must also have an office and be entrusted with a parish.'[12]

The Lutheran confessions retained the essence of this teaching. The famous definition in the Augsburg Confession runs: 'The Church is the congregation of saints [the assembly of all believers] in which the Gospel is rightly taught [purely preached] and the Sacraments are rightly administered [according to the Gospel].'[13] The detailed definition of the Church given in the adjoining articles is all-important because it is

[10] W.A., VOL. VI, p. 370. [11] W.A., VOL. XI, pp. 408ff.
[12] W.A., VOL. XXXI, pp. 1, 211.
[13] Augsburg Confession, VII: 'Est autem ecclesia congregatio sanctorum in qua evangelium pure docetur et recte administrantur sacramenta' (Schaff, III.11; Kidd, *Documents*, p. 264; *Concordia*, p. 13).

through the means of grace, Word and Sacrament, that faith arises.[14] There is no need for the believer to be held back by the fact that 'many hypocrites and evil persons' are also to be met with where the Word is rightly preached and the sacraments administered in accordance with their institution, for the means of grace are still efficacious even so.[15] 'The Church properly' (*ecclesia proprie dicta*)[16] is therefore not the Church in which the Word and sacraments are administered, but rather the 'congregation of saints and true believers'[17] or the 'fellowship of faith and of the Holy Ghost in hearts'.[18] 'And this Church alone is called "the body of Christ" because Christ renews, sanctifies, and governs her by His Spirit.'[19] But this Church is found *in the visible Church to the extent that this latter performs its task*; only 'those in whom Christ does not act are not the members of Christ'.[20] To rule out any misunderstanding it is stated pointedly: 'We are speaking not of an imaginary Church which is to be found nowhere; but we say and know certainly that this Church, wherein saints live, is and abides truly upon earth; namely that some of God's children are here and there in all the world, in various kingdoms, islands, lands and cities, from the rising of the sun to its setting. . . . And we add the same Church has these outward marks: the ministry or Gospel and the Sacrament. And this Church is properly "the pillar of the truth" as Paul says.'[21] This does not mean that the Church has only to preach the Gospel and administer the Sacraments, and for the rest to let things take their course. According to the Smalcaldic Articles 'manifest and obstinate sinners' are to be excluded from 'the Sacrament and other communion of the Church' by the use of the lesser excommunication.[22]

[14] *Op. cit.*, v (Schaff, III.10; Kidd, *Documents*, p. 263; *Concordia*, p. 13).

[15] *Op. cit.*, VIII (Schaff, III.12; Kidd, *Documents*, p. 264; *Concordia*, p. 13).

[16] 'Ecclesia proprie (dicta).' *Ibid.* [17] *Ibid.*

[18] *Ap. C.*, Art. VII and VIII (*Opera*, VOL. XXVII, p. 525; cf. VOL. XXVIII, p. 143; *Concordia*, p. 71, col. 1). [9] *Ibid.*

[20] *Loc. cit.* (*Opera*, VOL. XXVII, p. 525, VOL. XXVIII, p. 144; *Concordia*, p. 71, col. 2).

[21] 'Neque vero somniamus nos Platonicam civitatem . . . sed dicimus existere hanc ecclesiam, vidilicet vere credentes ac iustos sparsos per totum orbem. Et addimus notas: puram doctrinam evangelii et sacramenta. Et haec ecclesia proprie est columna veritatis.' *Ap. C.*, Art. VII and VIII (*Opera*, VOL. XXVII, p. 527, VOL. XXVIII, p. 148; *Concordia*, p. 73, col. 1).

[22] Smalcald Articles, III, ix (*Bekenntnisschriften* (*Luth.*), p. 457, 1; *Concordia*, p. 147). Cf. Preface to the Formula of Concord (*Bekenntnisschriften* (*Luth.*), p. 756).

According to the Augsburg Confession the ministry of preaching was instituted by God so that the Gospel might always be preached and the sacraments administered.[23] Appealing to 1 Pet. 2.9, Melanchthon, in his tract *De potestate Papae*, says that priesthood belongs to the whole Church, and the latter has therefore 'the right to choose and ordain ministers',[24] and, in view of the Apostle's words in Eph. 4.8, he says: 'He includes pastors and teachers among the essential gifts imparted to the Church, and adds that these are given for the purpose of upbuilding the body of Christ.'[25] For the sake of order individuals are called to the ministry instituted by God and as a rule only these may preach in the Church.[26] But 'in emergencies even a layman can absolve and become a minister and pastor to others'.[27]

2. The Reformed View: the Church as the Mother of Believers and the Body of Christ

Calvin's doctrine of the Church is similar to Luther's but especially to Melanchthon's, as we have gathered it from the Augsburg Confession and the *Apology*. But it also has features which are characteristic of the Genevan Reformer. He begins Book IV of the *Institutio* with a chapter headed: 'The True Church with which as Mother of all the Godly we must keep unity'.[28] He certainly has in view here the organised Church in which we live, but knows too—and we shall hear more of this—that this Church is not simply identical with the true Church. The Church is our mother because God placed the treasure of the Gospel within her so that the preaching of the gospel might flourish.[29] God 'instituted "pastors and teachers" (Eph. 4.11) through whose lips he might teach his own; he furnished them with authority; finally, he omitted nothing that might make for holy agreement of faith and for right order.

[23] Augsburg Confession, v (Schaff, III.10; Kidd, *Documents*, p. 263; *Concordia*, p. 13).

[24] Melanchthon, *Tract. de pot. pap.*, 69 (*Opera*, VOL. III, pp. 283f).

[25] *Op. cit.*, 67 (*Opera*, VOL. III, p. 283).

[26] Augsburg Confession, XIV (Schaff, III.15f; Kidd, *Documents*, p. 265; *Concordia*, p. 14).

[27] 'In casu necessitatis absolvit etiam laicus et fit minister ac pastor alterius.' Melanchthon, *Tract. de pot. pap.*, 67 (*Opera*, VOL. III, p. 283).

[28] *Inst.*, IV.1 (VOL. II, p. 1011). Thus Luther too, in the Large Catechism, Creed, Art. III: 'the mother that begets and bears every Christian through the Word of God' (*Concordia*, p. 194, col. 2).

[29] *Inst.*, IV.1.1 (VOL. II, p. 1012).

First of all, he instituted sacraments, which we who have experienced them feel to be highly useful aids to foster and strengthen faith.'[30] That sounds very like Article VII of the Augsburg Confession. Only in this sense are we to interpret Calvin's words about the Church as a divinely established order. He means by this, that God wills to have it so, in order that He may teach us by human means.[31] God Himself is not bound to this medium of conversation, to this order, but He has bound us to it.[32] Therefore there is no salvation outside the Church, because God wills to let Himself be found only where His Word is proclaimed.[33] When God binds us to this order of teaching and hearing, He humbles us, because by so doing He directs us to men. At the same time He also shows His mercy, because it means that we can bear His Word without perishing.[34]

But the Church is not only like a mother to the faithful. When by her ministry the Word of God comes to us, 'the renewal of the saints is accomplished; thus the body of Christ is built up; thus "we grow up in every way into him who is the Head" and grow together among ourselves'.[35] The Church therefore is not an inflexible institution superior to believers, but *a living organism, a communion of mutual service*.[36] Christ does not hand over the gifts of His Spirit, which equip us for the service of others, to one individual. Each receives from Him, according to I Cor. 12, a special gift, enabling him to help to edify and influence the whole Church.[37] By thus directing all the members to mutual service, the dominance of the Church by individuals which destroys the Church is excluded and Christ's own rule in the Church confirmed. This does not mean there is no superiority and subordination in the Church. It does mean that the brotherly solidarity and mutual help of the individual members must be maintained, if Christ is to be acknowledged as the One Head of the One Body which has many members. In the Reformed, Presbyterian view this biblical truth is fundamental for understanding the Church

[30] *Ibid.* [31] *Inst.*, IV.I.5 (VOL. II, p. 1017). [32] *Ibid.*
[33] *Inst.*, IV.I.4 (VOL. II, p. 1016). [34] *Inst.*, IV.I.5 and I.I (VOL. II, p. 1018, 1012).
[35] *Inst.*, IV.3.2 (VOL. II, p. 1055). [36] *Inst.*, IV.I.3 (VOL. II, pp. 1014f).
[37] *Opera*, VOL. XLIX, p. 238 (Comment on I Cor. 12.4), VOL. LI, p. 192 (Comment on Eph. 4.7); Heidelberg Catechism, Q. 55 (Torrance, *School of Faith*, p. 78).

and its order. In Lutheranism the concept of the body of Christ does not play this role so far as the form of the Church is concerned. There in theory the universal priesthood is taught, but in practice an authoritative position is given to ministers and bishops. In the Reformed view there is *no equal endowment of all* which then for the sake of government makes a choice of individuals necessary. Rather there is from the beginning *a diversity of gifts to all*, which they are to use together in the service of the exalted Lord.

Calvin also referred to the Church as '*the multitude of the elect*'.[38] This reference is intended to increase our confidence that 'our salvation rests upon sure and firm supports, so that, even if the whole fabric of the world were overthrown, the Church could neither totter nor fall. . . . It stands by God's election.'[39] It also brings out the truth that the Lord alone "knows who are his".[40] It is in this context that Calvin speaks of the invisible Church[41]; but he immediately stresses our obligation to maintain communion with the visible Church. Anyone separating from her disowns God and Christ,[42] who wills that she should be and remain our mother. But—and the concept of invisibility brings this out—only God can tell who really belongs to the Church. But we too are allowed the possibility of recognising the Church in so far as it is necessary for us to do so.[43] This is necessary, since we are not given over completely to the Church in which we live, but committed to her only to the extent that she is really the Church. The ecclesiastical communion in which we stand is the Church when she is claimed by Holy Scripture.[44] 'The Church is seen where Christ appears and where His Word is heard.'[45] Where the Head is, there, too, is the body. Thus Calvin, like the Augsburg Confession, names Word and Sacrament as the marks of the Church.[46] For Christ's promise, 'Where two or three are gathered in my name there am I in the midst of them' (Matt. 18.20), cannot fail us.[47]

[38] *Inst.*, IV.I.2 (VOL. II, p. 1014).
[39] *Inst.*, IV.I.3 (VOL. II, p. 1015).
[40] *Inst.*, IV.I.2 (VOL. II, p. 1013).
[41] *Inst.*, IV.I.7 (VOL. II, p. 1021).
[42] *Inst.*, IV.I.10 (VOL. II, p. 1024).
[43] *Inst.*, IV.I.8 (VOL. II, p. 1023).
[44] *Opera*, VOL. XLI, p. 482 (Sermon on Dan. 8).
[45] *Opera*, VOL. VII, p. 31 (*Tracts and Treatises*, VOL. I, p. 103).
[46] *Inst.*, IV.I.8 (VOL. II, p. 1023).
[47] *Inst.*, IV.I.9 (VOL. II, p. 1023).

This comforting truth does not absolve us from the *task of discipline* in the Church, from watchfulness over the life of her members, not for the sake of some ideal perfection, but for the sake of Christ. When He judges and yet rebellion against Him is tolerated without rebuke, the Church is in mortal danger. 'As the saving doctrine of Christ is the soul of the Church, so does discipline serve as its sinews, through which the members of the body hold together, each in its own place.'[48] For this reason many of the confessions rank the exercise of discipline alongside preaching and the administration of the sacraments as a third mark by which the true Church on earth can be recognised.[49] To prevent contempt for the Divine Word, ministers and elders must watch over the individual members of the Church and apply the Word to each of them with particular exhortation.[50] This is to be done and the Church thus maintained in Christ, by regular *visiting*. Church discipline therefore is an altogether positive task. Only those who refuse to listen to a personal appeal and persist in despising Christ in word and deed must in the last resort be excluded from the Church.[51] Otherwise the Lord's name is dishonoured and the Church by 'silence and connivance' makes herself an accomplice in 'such horrible sins'.[52] At the same time, such an act of discipline is a final clear appeal to those concerned to repent, and equally a warning to others not to fall away from the Lord.[53]

We saw earlier that Calvin's view of *the ordering of the Church* rests on the fact that the Church is *the body of Christ with many members and gifts*. He certainly teaches that the ministries of pastors, doctors, presbyters, and deacons are essential for the proper upbuilding of the Church[54]; but this is not because he wishes to establish a rigid system of ministries, but simply to indicate the ministerial functions which must be exercised in every congregation. A' Lasco reckoned only three such permanent functions, because he included the preachers with the

[48] *Inst.*, IV.12.1 (VOL. II, p. 1230).

[49] Belgic Confession, Art. XXIX (Schaff, III.419f); Scots Confession, Art. XVIII (Schaff, III.460ff); Emden Catechism, 1554, the work of John à Lasco, Q. 51.

[50] *Inst.*, IV.12.2 (VOL. II, p. 1230).

[51] *Inst.*, IV.12.5 (VOL. II, pp. 1232ff); Heidelberg Catechism, Q. 85 (Torrance, *School of Faith*, p. 86).

[52] Heidelberg Catechism, Q. 99.

[53] *Inst.*, IV.12.5 (VOL. II, p. 1233); Westminster Confession, XXX, 3 (Schaff, III.668).

[54] *Inst.*, IV.3.4 and 8f (VOL. II, pp. 1056f, 1060ff).

presbyters. We have here not a scheme, but gifts and tasks given by the exalted Lord, and just as the Lord Himself acts here by His Spirit, so He also in special times gives special gifts for extraordinary ministrations.[55] In every ministry He Himself acts in His Church. Hence the various ministries 'in all the variety of ministry and gifts each holds its promise and authority directly from the Church's Lord'.[56] The congregation has to take this into account in the choice of its minister. This choice is, moreover, simply the recognition of the choice already made by the Lord Himself by His distribution of His gracious gifts. In its own choice the congregation puts forward the one who has been equipped by the Lord Himself for a particular ministry.[57] Therefore such a choice is made by prayer for 'the Spirit of counsel and discretion'.[58] The choice of ministers is not the prerogative of any individual but of the whole congregation,[59] just as Reformed teaching utterly *rejects all 'one man' systems*, because this conflicts with the nature of the Church as Christ's body: 'The earthly counterpart to the government of local congregations by the Heavenly Lord, is not the rule of one congregation over the rest nor that of an episcopal ministry set over other offices, but the ministry which local congregations owe each other and seek to render each other by Synods composed of their appointed delegates.'[60] Using the gifts of grace available to them, our Reformed fathers sought to build up such a community of mutual service under the sole Headship of Christ, firmly knit together by mutual obligations, as a community Church which was able to withstand the storms of the Counter-Reformation.

3. The Reformed Emphasis Compared with the Lutheran

Luther and Lutheran confessions made it quite clear that what matters in the Church is the living presence of Christ in His Word. In the dispute with Rome they were almost content simply to insist on this fact. All other aspects of the Church's

[55] *Inst.*, IV.3.4 (VOL. II, pp. 1056f).
[56] Düsseldorf Thesis No. 13 (Niesel, *Bekenntnisschriften und Kirchenordnungen*, p. 328).
[57] *Inst.*, IV.3.11 and 15 (VOL. II, pp. 1062f, 1065f).
[58] *Inst.*, IV.3.12 (VOL. II, p. 1064).
[59] *Opera*, VOL. XLVIII, p. 120 (Comment on Acts 6.3).
[60] Düsseldorf Thesis No. 14.

life are unimportant provided only that this all-important spring of life is flowing: 'And to the true unity of the Church it is enough to agree concerning the doctrine of the Gospel and the administrations of the Sacraments (in accordance with God's Word). Nor is it necessary that human traditions, that is, rites or ceremonies, instituted by men, should be everywhere alike.'[61] To this definition of the Church's nature the Augsburg Confession simply adds the comment that the Church's primary function remains effective despite the presence of hypocrites: the Sacraments are 'effectual (by reason of the institution and commandment of Christ) notwithstanding they be administered by evil men'.[62] Wherever the Word is preached, the sinner can find the declaration of forgiveness. Therefore care must be taken to see that there are always preachers available. In the doctrine of the Church that is the dominant concern on the Lutheran side. This definition of the Reformers' view of the Church in opposition to that of Rome did not do justice to the fact that preaching has the Church as its goal and that where Christ is present in His Word a living congregation arises.[63] Luther himself had seen something more of this truth: 'I believe that there is upon earth a little holy group and congregation of pure saints, under one head, even Christ, called together by the Holy Ghost in one faith, one mind and understanding, with manifold gifts, yet agreeing in Love, without sects or schisms. I am also a part and member of the same, a sharer and joint owner of all the goods it possesses, brought to it and incorporated into it by the Holy Ghost by having heard and continuing to hear the Word of God, which is the beginning of entering it. . . . Thus, until the last day, the Holy Ghost abides with the holy congregation or Christendom, by means of which He fetches us to Christ and which He employs to teach and preach

[61] Augsburg Confession, VII: 'Et ad veram unitatem ecclesiae satis est consentire de doctrina evangelii et de administratione sacramentorum. Nec necesse est ubique similes esse traditiones humanas seu ritus aut ceremonias ab hominibus institutas' (Schaff, III.12; Kidd, *Documents*, p. 264; *Concordia*, p. 13).

[62] Augsburg Confession, VIII: 'Sacramenta et verbum propter ordinationem et mandatum Christi sunt efficacia, etiamsi per malos exhibeantur' (*ibid.*).

[63] During the Church Conflict in Germany, constant reference was rightly made to the fact that in Art. VII, 'On the Church', the Augsburg Confession speaks not only of the pure preaching of the Gospel and the right administration of the sacraments but also of the 'assembly of the faithful' ('Versammlung der Glaübigen') where these actions take place and which is, for this reason, the Church.

to us the Word, whereby He works and promotes sanctification, causing it [His community] daily to grow and become strong in the faith and its fruits which He produces.'[64] Luther also had views about the proper ordering of the Church, but he lacked the will and strength to carry out reforms in this direction. In his preface to the 'German Mass' he writes: 'Those who really want to be Christians and to confess the Gospel in deed and word, would have to enrol by name and assemble themselves apart in some house to pray, to read, to baptise, receive the sacrament and to do similar Christian works. For in such a regime, it would be possible to discover and punish and correct and exclude those who do not behave as Christians, and to excommunicate them according to Christ's rule in Matt. 18. Here too, a common collection of alms could be enjoined on Christians, to be given voluntarily and distributed to the poor, following Paul's example in 2 Cor. 9. Here there need not be much singing or elaborate. Here, baptism and the sacrament could be administered in a brief and simple manner, and everything directed to the Word and prayer and love.[65] . . . In short, if one had people and individuals who really wanted to be Christians, the rules and forms could soon be drawn up. But I cannot and will not order or establish such a community or congregation yet, for I do not yet have the people and individuals to do this, nor, so far as I can see, are there many pressing for this.'[66] It went no further than isolated comments of this kind. There was never any development of this tendency in Lutheranism. Luther himself, of course, did not approve of the regional Church government which began to be established at that time, with the intolerable claim of the princes to the right to interfere in spiritual matters,[67] but he did not lead any opposition to this momentous distortion of the Church's true form.

Lutheranism's interest in personal salvation, and its one-sided pre-occupation with the doctrine of justification, ob-

[64] Large Catechism, II, Creed, Art. III (*Concordia*, p. 195, col. 2; *Primary Works*, edd. Wace and Buchheim, p. 104).

[65] If only present-day Lutherans were genuinely Lutheran in their liturgical experiments and willing to base their work on this principle instead of going back to the Roman Mass! On this subject see the fine book by R. Hupfeld, *Liturgische Irrwege und Wege*, Gladbeck 1952.

[66] W.A., VOL. XIX, p. 75 (see *Reformation Writings*, ed. B. L. Woolf, VOL. II, pp. 320f).

[67] Cf. Karl Holl, *Luther*, Tübingen 1923, pp. 375ff.

scured the fact that the Christian message is primarily concerned not with salvation of the individual man, nor, of course, even with the salvation of many men, but with the Saviour Himself and with the gracious rule He establishes among men, and therefore with His Church and its individual members. We have to notice two points: that the Word is addressed to the individual, but, at the same time, it also joins him to the body of Christ.[68] It is not enough to know where the true Church is to be found and to know that there is the place where I can become sure of justification through the preached Word. Theology has rather to consider the service Christ has entrusted to His Church and how He wishes to see His company formed and held together under His Sceptre, so as to be able to carry out its ministry in the world to the glory of Christ.

Reformed theology treated with great breadth the doctrine of the Church as a living organically articulated community, without losing sight of the individual, and with no thought of establishing principles for an authoritarian Church but offering guidance rather for the assembly of God's people to the praise of God's glory, in a world which though lost has been placed under God's promise. The Reformed Church orders bear testimony to this concern, as do the various formularies for public worship in which, no longer tied to the framework of the Roman Mass, the preaching of the Word, accompanied by Sacrament, prayer, hymn-singing, and thank-offering are properly given the central place.[69] Calvin spent his whole life serving this true gathering of God's people in many places,[70] and created the necessary conditions to ensure that the tumults

[68] Heidelberg Catechism, Q. 20 (Torrance, *School of Faith*, p. 72).

[69] Cf. W. Niesel, 'The order of public worship in the Reformed Churches', in *Scottish Journal of Theology*, 1948, pp. 381f; W. Niesel, 'Wie verhielten sich die Reformatoren zur biblischen Lehre vom Gottesdienst?' in *Evangelische Theologie*, XVI, pp. 534ff; M. Albertz, *Kirchenbuch Ordnungen für die Versammlungen der nach Gottes Wort reformierten Gemeinden*, Munich 1941. C. E. B. Cranfield, 'Divine and human action. The biblical concept of worship', in *Interpretation*, XII (October 1958), pp. 387-98.

[70] Notice the words spoken on his death-bed about the early days of the Reformation in Geneva—words so characteristic of Calvin and of the Reformed outlook: 'When I first came to this Church there was practically nothing here. There was preaching but that was all. . . . There was no talk of any reformation and everything was in disorder' (*Opera*, VOL. IX, p. 891, *Discours d'adieu*, 1564). The papacy had been driven out 'but matters were not yet brought to a settled state' (*Opera*, VOL. XXXI, p. 26, Comment on Psalms, Preface).

of the Counter-Reformation could not suppress again what had so recently been born of God's Word and Spirit. In the Reformed countries, the Jesuits found not just preaching stations, but witnessing and active congregations with well-ordered ministries and firmly bound together as their Synods showed.[71] In these synods all the congregations were represented by delegates, and they discussed as brothers subject to the Word, urgent questions of common concern, or matters which could not be settled by individual congregations. Preaching stations would have vanished the moment the local ruler gave his support to Rome. The confessing congregations persisted even without government protection, indeed even against hostile governments, as in France, Holland, and the Lower Rhine. That was no accident, since the Lord promised His presence not to individuals but to the congregation gathered together in His name. To this He gave the assurance that even the gates of Hell would not prevail against it.

In our own days, the Evangelical Church in Germany in 1633, found itself in a position where its very existence was threatened by the State. This led, first on the Reformed side, to a self-examination which bore fruit in the Düsseldorf Theses: 'The providence of God has brought us to an hour when we must ask ourselves again: *What is an evangelical Church?*'[72] At Barmen a year later, representatives of both confessions gave the answer: 'The Christian Church is the community of brethren in which Jesus Christ acts presently as Lord in Word and Sacrament by the Holy Spirit. In the midst of the sinful world it has, as the Church of forgiven sinners, to witness by its faith and obedience, its message and its order, that it is His alone, that it lives and desires to live only by His consolation and by His orders, in expectation of His Coming.'[73]

[71] Cf. Elberfeld Theses, 1933, No. 6: 'The special responsibility of the Synod is the oversight of the ministry in virtue of which the local Church (congregation) lives in the one Evangelical Church.' The unofficial group of professors, pastors, elders and deacons which, in May 1933, produced 'A Theological Statement on the form of the Church' (i.e. Düsseldorf Theses) met again in June 1933 at Elberfeld and drew up 'Requirements for the form of the Church', a series of eighteen Theses known as the Elberfeld Theses. See K. D. Schmidt, *Die Bekenntnisse und grundsätzlichen Äusserungen zur Kirchenfrage des Jahres 1933*, Göttingen 1934, pp. 158-60; also Niesel, *Bekenntnisschriften und Kirchenordnungen*, p. 326, n. 5.

[72] Niesel, *Bekenntnisschriften und Kirchenordnungen*, p. 327.

[73] Barmen Thesis No. 3.

This thesis expresses the common faith of the Reformers that *Christ's presence* in Word and Sacrament is the absolute basis of the Church. But it states equally plainly that the Church, under the preaching of Christ, is a '*community of brethren*', *the form of which is by no means unimportant*, but is meant to show that the Church belongs to Jesus Christ. Thus the direct right to interfere in spiritual affairs (*ius in sacra*), which the civil authorities had claimed, was at last challenged. 'We reject the false doctrine that the Church is permitted to form its message or its order according to its own preferences or according to prevailing philosophical or political convictions.' But the Church is not even its own master, determining its own message and order. It lives utterly and completely in service as a community of brethren, All forms of domination are completely excluded from it. 'The various ministries in the Church do not establish any lordship of some over others but only the exercise of that service which is entrusted to and required of the whole Church.'[74] There cannot be a Church of ministers or of bishops but only a Church of congregations subject to the Word. It should not prove difficult for Lutherans and Reformed on the basis of the joint statements made at Barmen about the Church, also to reach agreement about other questions of Church life and order. Nor does this mean that everything must look the same on both sides. We are summoned not to any fixed Church system but to the obedience of faith. But that certainly means we must re-examine forms and customs of our Church life in the light of the insights newly given to us, and be willing to quit the customary paths when the Word points us to a new way.

[74] Barmen Thesis No. 4.

CHAPTER 8

THE DOCTRINE OF THE SACRAMENTS

THE Church is recognisable as a unique society in this world, above all by the Sacraments. That is why these are also mentioned in the Barmen thesis dealing with the Church. What do the two confessions teach about the Sacraments?

1. Word and Sign

In Art. XIII of the Augsburg Confession we read: 'Of the use of the Sacraments they teach that the Sacraments were ordained, not only to be marks of profession among men, but rather to be *signs and testimonies of the will of God toward us*, instituted to awaken and confirm faith in those who use them.'[1] Sacraments are 'signs of grace'.[2] They are not primarily signs by which men accomplish something. That was stressed in opposition to Zwingli's teaching that, by means of the sacrament, believers are enabled to visualise Christ's death on the Cross and to confess their faith. The view that the sacraments are so entirely in man's control that through them man can obtain something from God, was even more vigorously rejected. 'Theologians are rightly accustomed to distinguish between a sacrament and a sacrifice. . . . A sacrament is a ceremony or outward sign or work in which God presents to us that which the promise annexed to the ceremony offers. . . . A sacrifice, on the contrary, is a ceremony or work which we render God

[1] Augsburg Confession, XIII: 'De usu sacramentorum docent, quod sacramenta instituta sint non modo ut sint notae professionis inter homines, sed magis ut sint signa et testimonia Dei erga nos ad excitandam et confirmandam fidem in his, qui utuntur, proposita' (Schaff, III.15; Kidd, *Documents*, p. 265; *Concordia*, pp. 13f).

[2] *Ap. C.*, Art. XXIV (*Opera*, VOL. XXVII, p. 621, VOL. XXVIII, p. 284; *Concordia*, p. 123, col. 1).

S

in order to afford Him honour.'[3] Thus it is stressed, against the Romans, that there is only *one* expiatory sacrifice, Christ's sacrifice on the Cross.

The following distinction is customary: 'In a Sacrament there are two things, a sign and the Word.'[4] It continues: 'The ceremony (outward sign) is, as it were, a picture or seal, as Paul (Rom. 4.11) calls it, of the Word, making known the promise.'[5] This picture of the Word 'signifies the same thing as the Word'.[6] Augustine was therefore right when he called it 'a visible Word' (*verbum visibile*).[7] *The main thing in the Sacrament is the Word*: 'Therefore we always teach that the Sacraments and all external things which God ordains and institutes should not be regarded according to the coarse, external mark, as we regard the shell of a nut, but as the Word of God is included therein.'[8] Even in reference to the Lord's Supper Luther emphasised: 'It is not the eating and drinking, indeed, that does them, but the words which stand there, namely, "Given, and shed for you, for the remission of sins." Which words are, beside the bodily eating and drinking, as the chief thing in the Sacrament.'[9]

But although everything depends on the Word, according to Luther the sacramental elements acquire a significance which makes them more than signs and seals. Not by chance does Luther so often quote Augustine's dictum: 'Let the Word be added to the element and it will become a sacrament.'[10] Luther comments: 'The Word must make a sacrament of the element, else it remains a mere element. . . . It is true, indeed, that if you take away the Word or regard it without words, you have nothing but mere bread and wine. But if the words remain with them, as they shall and must, then in virtue of the

[3] *Ap. C.*, Art. XXIV (*Opera*, VOL. XXVII, p. 611, VOL. XXVIII, p. 271; *Concordia*, p. 117, col. 2).

[4] *Ap. C.*, Art. XXIV (*Opera*, VOL. XXVII, p. 621, VOL. XXVIII, p. 285; *Concordia*, p. 123, col. 1).

[5] *Ibid.* cf. *Opera*, VOL. XXVII, p. 206.

[6] *Ap. C.*, Art. XIII (*Opera*, VOL. XXVII, p. 570, VOL. XXVIII, p. 206; *Concordia* p. 95, col. 1).

[7] *Ibid.*

[8] Luther, Large Catechism, IV (*Concordia*, p. 206, col. 1; *Primary Writings*, edd. Wace and Buchheim, p. 132).

[9] Small Catechism, VI (Schaff, III.91f; *Concordia*, pp. 163f).

[10] 'Accedit verbum ad elementum et fit sacramentum.' Augustine, *In Ioann.*, 80, 3 (Migne, P.L., VOL. XXXV; trans in Nicene and Post-Nicene Fathers, VOL. VII, p. 344).

same, it is truly the body and blood of Christ. For as the lips of Christ say and speak, so it is, as He can never lie or deceive.'[11] 'The sacrament is, then, a holy and divine matter and sign,'[12] and Baptism 'not only natural water but a divine, heavenly, holy and blessed water'.[13] This does not mean that *the element* is changed by the Word, but that it has indeed been given a new dimension, it has become *a means of grace*.

The Heidelberg Catechism asks: 'What are the Sacraments?' and answers: 'The Sacraments are visible, holy signs and seals, ordained by God in order that He, by their use, may the more fully declare and seal to us the promise of the Gospel.'[14] 'The Holy Spirit teaches in the Gospel and establishes by the Holy Sacraments.'[15] Calvin declares: The sacrament is 'an outward sign by which the Lord seals on our consciences the promises of his good will toward us in order to sustain the weakness of our faith; and we in turn attest our piety toward him', or, 'a testimony of divine grace toward us, confirmed by an outward sign, with mutual attestation of our piety toward Him'.[16] Calvin thus includes in his definition both the objective and subjective significance of the sacrament. There is complete agreement with the Augsburg Confession. Both Calvin and the Heidelberg Catechism follow Melanchthon's confessional document. How far the agreement extends can be seen from the fact that the Geneva Catechism at first mentions only the objective aspect of the sacrament.[17] Only much later does it ask: 'Do these two Sacraments not serve any other end? Answer: Yes, they do. They are also signs and marks of our profession. That is to say, by them we declare that we are the people of God and make confession of our Christianity.'[18]

[11] Large Catechism, v (*Concordia*, p. 210, col. 2; *Primary Writings*, edd. Wace and Buchheim, pp. 144f).

[12] Large Catechism, IV (*Concordia*, p. 206, col. 1; *Primary Writings*, edd. Wace and Buchheim, p. 132).

[13] *Ibid.* Cf. Small Catechism, IV, iii (Schaff, III.86; *Concordia*, p. 162, col. 2).

[14] Q. 66. Cf. Westminster Catechism, Q. 162 (Torrance, *School of Faith*, pp. 80, 224).

[15] Q. 67.

[16] 'Externum esse symbolum, quo benevolentia erga nos suae promissiones conscientiis nostris Dominus obsignat ad sustinendam fidei nostrae imbecillitatem: et nos vicissim pietatem erga eum nostram . . . testamur.' 'Divinae in nos gratiae testimonium externo signo confirmatum, cum mutua nostrae erga ipsum pietatis testificatione.' *Inst.*, IV.14.1 (VOL. II, p. 1277).

[17] Q. 310ff (Torrance, *School of Faith*, p. 54). Cf. Second Helvetic Confession, XIX (Schaff, III.285).

[18] Q. 362 (Torrance, *School of Faith*, p. 63).

The Reformed Churches also adopted the traditional teaching that the sacrament consists of Word and Sign.[19] Calvin says: 'Because we are of flesh, they are shown us under things of flesh, to instruct us according to our dull capacity, and to lead us by the hand as tutors lead children.'[20]

So too the Word is regarded as the main thing: 'Faith rests upon the Word of God as a foundation; but when the sacraments are added, it rests *more firmly upon them as upon columns*.'[21] In opposition to the Roman practice of reciting the words of institution inaudibly, as the means of consecrating the elements, it was stressed: 'When we hear the sacramental word mentioned, let us understand the promise proclaimed in a clear voice by the minister, to lead the people by the hand wherever the sign tends and directs us.'[22] Calvin took endless trouble to make it clear to the Protestant opponents of the Lutheran sacramental teaching, especially to the Zwinglians, that God instituted the external signs for our benefit.[23] But to avoid misunderstanding he also clearly stated: 'I assign this particular ministry to the sacraments . . . not that I suppose there is some secret force or other perpetually seated in them by which they are able to promote or confirm faith by themselves.'[24] On both sides it must be noticed that 'nothing is given to them which should not be given, and conversely nothing taken away which belongs to them'.[25] That is a statement to which every Lutheran could subscribe.

2. The Content of a Sacrament

If the Sacraments are signs and seals what is it they signify and seal? What is the *res* or *materia sacramenti*?

The answer given by the Formula of Concord is: 'That such merits and benefits of Christ shall be presented, offered and distributed to us through His Word and Sacraments.'[26] Luther's teaching earlier was the same: 'We further believe that in this Christian Church we have forgiveness of sin which is wrought

[19] E.g. *Inst.*, IV.14.4 (VOL. II, p. 1279).
[20] *Inst.*, IV.14.6 (VOL. II, p. 1281).
[21] *Ibid.* (VOL. II, p. 1281).
[22] *Inst.*, IV.14.4 (VOL. II, pp. 1279f).
[23] *Inst.*, IV.14.5-13 (VOL. II, pp. 1280ff).
[24] *Inst.*, IV.14.9 (VOL. II, p. 1284).
[25] *Inst.*, IV.14.17 (VOL. II, p. 1293).
[26] Thor. Decl. XI (*Concordia*, p. 288, col. 1, 2).

through the holy sacraments and absolution.'[27] Melanchthon therefore calls sacraments '*signs of the remission of sins*'. 'For they offer the remission of sins.'[28] The justification of the sinner, which is the basic Lutheran doctrine, is conveyed to men by the sacraments. In the doctrine of the Lord's Supper it is of course emphasised strongly that the content of the sacrament does not consist in the fruits which we receive from it, but in the body and blood of Christ. But Christ's body and blood are the pledges of the forgiveness of sins.

On the Reformed side it is stated characteristically: *The substance of the sacraments is Christ.*[29] Calvin again stresses that we cannot receive Christ's gracious gifts unless we receive Christ Himself as our own: 'Therefore let it be regarded as a settled principle that the sacraments have the same office as the Word of God: to offer and set forth Christ to us, and in him the treasures of heavenly grace.'[30] 'As much, then, as you will profit through the sacraments in the partaking of Christ, so much profit will you receive from them.'[31] The confessions also teach this: 'The main thing offered by God in all sacraments and expected by believers in every age [others speak of it as the substance and matter of the sacrament] is Christ as Saviour, that only sacrifice, that Lamb of God slain from the foundation of the world, that Rock from which all who went before us drank . . . by whom they are washed from all their sins and nourished by the true body and blood of Christ unto everlasting life.'[32] It must also be noticed that the whole Christ is meant, not merely His Spirit for example; indeed His human form comes to have special importance for us: 'sacraments . . . even though they direct our faith to the whole Christ and not to a half-Christ . . . teach that the matter both of righteousness and of salvation resides in his flesh; not that as mere man he justifies or quickens by himself, but because it pleased God to reveal in the Mediator what was hidden and incomprehensible

[27] Large Catechism, II (*Concordia*, p. 195, col. 2; *Primary Writings*, edd. Wace and Buchheim, p. 104).

[28] *Ap. C.*, XII (*Opera*, VOL. XXVII, p. 542, VOL. XXVIII, p. 169; *Concordia*, p. 81, col. 1).

[29] French Confession, XXXIV (Schaff, III.379); Belgic Confession, XXXIII (Schaff, III.424).

[30] *Inst.*, IV.14.17 (VOL. II, p. 1292).

[31] *Inst.*, IV.14.15 (VOL. II, p. 1291).

[32] Second Helvetic Confession, XIX (Schaff, III.286).

in himself.'[33] The Geneva Catechism at once guards against a possible misunderstanding. The sacraments are instruments in the hands of the Heavenly Lord, they are not the Lord Himself: 'We are not to be taken up with the earthly sign so as to seek our salvation in it, nor are we to imagine that it has a peculiar power enclosed within it. On the contrary, we are to employ the sign as a help, to lead us directly to the Lord Jesus, that we may find in Him our salvation and all our well-being.'[34] For Reformed doctrine this emphatic reference to Christ is essential. The sacraments perform a service but only this service. They *are not the source of salvation, but simply guide us to that source*. 'Are both these then, the Word and the sacraments, designed to direct our faith to the sacrifice of Jesus Christ on the Cross as the only ground of our salvation?' 'Yes indeed,' answers the Heidelberg Catechism.[35] The Crucified Himself as the only sacrificial Lamb is the source of life, and as the Risen One He is present whenever His Church celebrates the Sacrament.

3. The Sacraments and Faith

As we saw at the beginning, according to the Lutheran doctrine the sacraments are given 'to awaken and confirm faith'. 'Wherefore we must so use the Sacraments that faith be added to believe the promises which are offered and set forth through the sacraments.'[36] The contrary Roman doctrine that the faith of the recipient is not essential, and 'that the sacraments confer grace *ex opere operato*, without a good disposition on the part of the one using them, provided he do not place a hindrance in the way' is therefore rejected.[37] 'The promise is useless unless it is received by faith. But the sacraments are the signs and seals of the promises. Therefore, in the use of the sacraments faith ought to be added.'[38] Strictly speaking we should say that the Holy Ghost produces faith. But the Holy

[33] *Inst.*, III.11.9 (VOL. I, p. 736).

[34] Geneva Catechism, Q. 318 (Torrance, *School of Faith*, p. 55; Calvin, *Theological Treatises*, ed. and tr. J. K. S. Reid, London 1954, p. 132).

[35] Heidelberg Catechism, Q. 67 (Torrance, *School of Faith*, pp. 80f).

[36] 'Ad excitandam et confirmandam fidem.' 'Itaque utendum est sacramentis ita, ut fides accedat, quae credat promissionibus, quae per sacramenta exhibentur et ostenduntur.' Augsburg Confession, XIII (Schaff, III.15; Kidd, *Documents*, p. 265; *Concordia*, p. 14).

[37] *Ap. C.*, Art. XIII (*Opera*, VOL. XXVII, p. 542, VOL. XXVIII, p. 169; *Concordia*, p. 95, col. 2.

[38] *Ibid.*

Ghost who creates faith acts on men by the means of the Word and sacraments.[39] Luther stressed this strongly in his conflict with the enthusiasts, whom he regarded as at one with the Papacy because they made themselves judges of the testimony of Scripture on the basis of a claim to possess the Spirit. 'Therefore we ought and must constantly maintain this point that God does not wish to deal with us otherwise than through the spoken Word and the sacraments. It is the Devil himself whatsoever is extolled as Spirit without the Word and sacraments.'[40]

On the Reformed side, too, the sacraments are directed towards faith. They do not create faith. But not even the Lutheran Confessions assert that, if we notice what they actually say. They relate faith strictly to the promise. But according to Reformed doctrine, *the sacraments confirm faith.* The Holy Spirit who produces faith by the preaching of the Gospel 'confirms it by the use of the holy Sacraments'.[41] 'What! Does a visible and natural sign have this power to assure the conscience?' asks the Geneva Catechism. Answer: 'No, not of itself, but in so far as it is ordained of God to this end.' 'But it is surely the proper office of the Holy Spirit to seal the promises of God in our hearts,' says the catechism. 'How can you attribute this to the sacraments?' Answer: 'There is a great difference between the one and the other. The Spirit of God in very truth is the only One who can touch and move our hearts, enlighten our minds, and assure our consciences; so that all this ought to be judged as His own Work, that praise may be ascribed to Him alone. Nevertheless, the Lord Himself *makes use of the sacraments as inferior instruments* according as it seems good to Him, without in any way detracting from the power of His Spirit.'

'You think then, that the efficiency of the sacraments does not consist in the outward element but proceeds entirely from the Spirit of God?' 'Yes, for the Lord is pleased to work by these instruments which He has instituted: without detracting from His own power.'[42] Calvin also expresses a similar view

[39] *Ap. C.*, Art. XXIV (*Opera*, VOL. XXVII, p. 621, VOL. XXVIII, p. 285; *Concordia*, p. 123, col. 1).

[40] Smalcald Articles, III, vii (*Concordia*, p. 147, col. 2).

[41] Heidelberg Catechism, Q. 65 (Torrance, *School of Faith*, p. 80); *Inst.*, IV.14.7.

[42] Geneva Catechism, Q. 311-13 (Torrance, *School of Faith*, p. 54; *Calvin's Theological Treatises*, ed. J. K. S. Reid, p. 131; French text in Niesel, *Bekenntnisschriften und Kirchenordnungen*, p. 35.

in his *Institutio*: 'Therefore I make such a division between Spirit and sacraments that the power to act rests with the former, and the ministry alone is left to the latter—a ministry empty and trifling, apart from the action of the Spirit, but charged with great effect when the Spirit works within and manifests his power.'[43]

On the Reformed side, then, a clear distinction is made not only between the gift given in the sacrament and the elements, but also between the governing function of the Spirit and the ministerial function of the sacraments. Conflict between the two confessions was therefore unnecessary, for the Augsburg Confession also teaches: 'For through the Word and Sacraments as through instruments the Holy Ghost is given, who works faith *where and when it pleases God*.'[44] The confessional writings composed by Luther himself, the two Catechisms and the Smalcaldic Articles, certainly appear to point in a different direction and to assume a co-operation between Spirit and sacramental signs during the administration. In opposition to the danger of binding God's Spirit to the signs the Consensus of Zürich (1549) explicitly affirmed God's freedom: 'Grace is so little bound to the performance of the sacraments that their fruits are sometimes received after the performance.' 'Therefore the benefit we receive from sacraments ought by no means to be bound to the time of their administration, as if God's grace adhered to the visible sign at the very moment when it is offered.'[45] And 'Believers partake of Christ even before and after the use of the sacraments.'[46] *The freedom of the Spirit and His Sovereignty even over the means* He uses to deal with us 'where and when He will' must be safeguarded if God's Divinity is not to be endangered. This sovereignty of God's Spirit was attested on the Lutheran side not only in the Augsburg Confession but more recently at Barmen when Lutherans joined with Reformed to confess together: 'The Christian Church is the community of brethren in which Jesus Christ acts presently *as Lord*

[43] *Inst.*, IV.14.9 (VOL. II, p. 1284).

[44] Augsburg Confession, V: 'Nam per verbum et sacramenta tamquam per intrumenta donatur Spiritus Sanctus, qui fidem efficit, ubi et quando visum est Deo in his, qui audiunt evangelium' (Schaff, III.10; Kidd, *Documents*, p. 263; *Concordia*, p. 13).

[45] *Consensus Tigurinus*, 1549, Art. XX (Kidd, *Documents*, p. 655; cf. Schaff, I.471ff).

[46] *Op. cit.*, Art. XIX.

in Word and sacrament through the Holy Spirit.'[47] It is at least possible that the foundation pillars for a bridge of understanding between the two confessions in a matter which has given rise to so much conflict have already been established.

[47] Barmen Thesis No. 4.

CHAPTER 9

BAPTISM AND THE LORD'S SUPPER[1]

Now let us look briefly at the doctrine of Baptism, and then turn to the different view of the Lord's Supper on the two sides.

1. The Lutheran Doctrine of Baptism

We have already referred to Luther's words in the Small Catechism about the water used in baptism: 'But with the word of God it is a baptism, that is, a gracious water of life and a washing of regeneration in the Holy Ghost.'[2] The water of baptism by God's word and command 'sanctified so that it is nothing else than a *Divine Water*.'[3] 'Therefore it is not only natural water but a Divine, Heavenly, Holy and Blessed water, and in whatever other terms we can praise it—all on account of the Word.'[4] To understand this it is important to notice the two negative statements Luther makes in the Smalcaldic Articles: 'And for this reason we do not hold with Thomas and the preaching friars [or Dominicans] who forget the Word and say that God has imparted to the water a spiritual power, which through the water washes away sin. Nor do we agree with Scotus and the discalced friars [Minorites or Franciscans], who teach that, by the assistance of the divine will, baptism washes away sins, and that this ablution occurs only through

[1] See further: Karl Barth, 'Die kirchliche Lehre von der Taufe', *Theol. Ex. h.*, N.S. No. 4, 1947 (trans. E. A. Payne, *The Teaching of the Church regarding Baptism*, London 1948); Oscar Cullmann, *Die Tauflehre des Neuen Testaments*, Zürich 1948 (trans. J. K. S. Reid, *Baptism in the New Testament*, London 1950); Joachim Jeremias, *Die Kindertaufe in der ersten vier Jahrh.*, 1958 (Eng. trans. *Infant Baptism in the first four centuries*, London 1961); Wilhelm Niesel, 'Intercommunion in the German Evangelical Church', in *Intercommunion*, edd. D. Baillie and J. Marsh, London 1952, pp. 281ff.

[2] Small Catechism, IV (Schaff, III.86; *Concordia*, p. 162, col. 2).

[3] Large Catechism, IV (*Concordia*, p. 205, col. 2).

[4] *Loc. cit.* (*Concordia*, p. 206, col. 1).

the will of God, and by no means through the Word or water.'[5] Luther rejects the view that the washing away of sins is effected by the consecrated water, and the opposite view that it is not done through the water at all, but only by the Divine command. For Luther, the truth lies in between: the cleansing takes place through the water, so long as the Word is present. 'Word and water are never to be separated in the Sacrament,' says a modern interpreter.[6] 'It becomes beneficial to you if you have yourself baptised with the thought that this is according to God's command and ordinance, and besides, in God's name, in order that *you* may receive *in the water* the promised salvation.'[7] But a few lines further on Luther says that baptism is 'a treasure *comprehended in the Word*, and offered to us and received by faith'.[8] What does he really mean?

In the Lutheran view baptism is 'necessary and effectual to salvation'.[9] The German text of the Augsburg Confession simply says 'that it is necessary', but this 'necessary' must be taken in the sense of the Latin text. Baptism 'works forgiveness of sins, delivers from death and the devil, and gives eternal salvation'.[10] Indeed it brings 'the entire Christ and the Holy Ghost with His gifts'.[11] Baptism is not, however, an absolute necessity as it is in Roman teaching, but binding on all men because Christ wills to use it as an instrument (*necessitas medii*), and for this reason instituted it (*necessitas praecepti*). Hence the rule of the Lutheran Church that in virtue of the universal priesthood every Christian can *in emergency* baptise. But when no one is available, it is not to be thought that the person who would otherwise have received baptism is lost. Only the spurning of baptism incurs divine judgment.

While complete forgiveness is given in baptism, man's renewal or regeneration is a continuing event in the person baptised. For baptism 'signifies that the old Adam in us should, by daily contrition and repentance, be drowned and die with all sins and evil lusts, and again, a new man daily come forth and arise,

[5] Smalcald Articles, III, v (*Concordia*, p. 146).
[6] E. Schlink, *Theologie der lutherischen Bekenntnisschriften*, Munich 1948, p. 208.
[7] Large Catechism, IV (*Concordia*, p. 207, col. 1). [8] *Ibid.*
[9] *Ap. C.*, IX: 'necessarius et efficax ad salutem'; Germ. text: 'dass sie nötig sei' (*Opera*, VOL. XXVII, p. 533, VOL. XXVIII, p. 156; *Concordia*, p. 76, col. 2).
[10] Small Catechism, IV, ii (Schaff, III.85; *Concordia*, p. 162).
[11] Large Catechism, IV (*Concordia*, p. 207, col. 2).

who shall live before God in righteousness and purity forever'.[12]

As we saw, baptism is directed to *faith*. Of course 'my faith does not make baptism but receives it'.[13] It is in the strict sense the *acceptance of the gift of salvation*. This acceptance is part of baptism. Luther therefore assumes faith even in baptised infants: 'We bring the child in the conviction and hope that it believes, and we pray that God may grant it faith; but we do not baptise it upon that, but solely upon the command of God. Why so? Because we know that God does not lie. I and my neighbour and, in short, all men, may err and deceive, but the Word of God cannot err.'[14]

2. The Reformed Doctrine of Baptism

In Reformed doctrine, too, baptism means 'to have the forgiveness of sins from God, through grace, for the sake of Christ's blood, which He has shed for us in His sacrifice on the Cross, and also to be renewed by the Holy Ghost, and sanctified to be a member of Christ, so that we may more and more die unto sin, and lead a life blessed by God and without blame'.[15] The Geneva Catechism seeks further clarification and asks how this grace is applied to us in baptism: Answer: 'In it we are clothed with Jesus Christ, and receive His Spirit, provided that we do not make ourselves unworthy of the promises given to us in it.'[16] The French Confession begins Article 35 with the words: 'Baptism is given as a pledge of our adoption for by it we are grafted into the body of Christ.'[17] We have already pointed out in the previous chapter this Christocentric approach to the sacraments. Not only in the Lord's Supper but in baptism too it is *principally a matter of Christ* Himself. God gives us nothing less than union with His Son. Christ is 'the proper object of baptism'.[18] Baptism assures us 'that we are . . . so united to Christ himself that we become sharers in all his blessings'.[19]

This is not accomplished by the outward washing, of course. 'For the blood of Jesus Christ alone and the Holy Spirit cleanse

[12] Small Catechism, IV, iv (Schaff, III.86f; *Concordia*, p. 162).
[13] Large Catechism, IV (*Concordia*, p. 208, col. 1).
[14] Large Catechism, IV (*Concordia*, p. 208, col. 2).
[15] Heidelberg Catechism, Q. 70 (Torrance, *School of Faith*, p. 81).
[16] Geneva Catechism, Q. 331 (Torrance, *School of Faith*, p. 58).
[17] Scots Confession, XXI; Westminster Confession, XXVIII, I (Schaff, III.661f).
[18] Calvin, *Inst.*, IV.15.6 (VOL. II, p. 1308). [19] *Ibid* (VOL. II, p. 1307).

us from all sin,' as the Heidelberg Catechism stresses.[20] It continues characteristically: 'Why then does the Holy Spirit call baptism the washing of regeneration and the washing away of sins?' Answer: 'God speaks thus not without great cause: namely, not only to teach us thereby that just as the impurity of the body is taken away by water, so our sins also are taken away by the blood and Spirit of Christ; but much more than by this divine pledge and true sign He may assure us that we are as *really washed from our sins* spiritually as *our bodies are washed with water physically*.'[21] Reformed teaching distinguishes clearly, therefore, between sign and seal on the one hand and what is signified, the substance of baptism, on the other. *But the two are not separated.* What God offers in His Word and what the external sign of water is intended to seal to us, also takes place: 'He does not feed our eyes with a mere appearance only, but leads us to the present reality and effectively performs what it symbolises.'[22]

Baptism becomes effective by the power of the Holy Spirit in faith.[23] This action of the Spirit which establishes the bridge between Christ and the candidate for baptism, is not of course tied to the moment of administration. 'For to those baptised in infancy God gives regeneration in childhood, youth, and sometimes even for the first time in old age. Thus the benefit of baptism extends to the whole course of life, because the promise it contains is constantly at work.'[24] In baptism the promise of incorporation into Christ's body is confirmed by the sign. We can trust this promise and know that God fulfils it and, by His Spirit, awakens faith in the baptised person in His own appointed time.[25]

On the ground of this promise rooted in God's gracious covenant, our Reformed fathers also practised infant baptism. 'For since they as well as their elders belong to God's covenant and His community, and both redemption from sin in the blood of Christ and the Holy Spirit who works faith are promised to them no less than to adults, they are also by baptism, as a sign of the Covenant, to be incorporated into the Christian Church,

[20] Heidelberg Catechism, Q. 72 (Torrance, *School of Faith*, p. 82).
[21] Q. 73. [22] *Inst.*, IV.15.14 (VOL. II, p. 1314).
[23] French Confession, XXXVIII (Schaff, III.381; Kidd, *Documents*, p. 672).
[24] *Consensus Tigurinus*, XX (Kidd, *Documents*, p. 655).
[25] Westminster Confession, XXVIII, 6 (Schaff, III.663).

and distinguished from the children of unbelievers, as was done in the Old Testament through circumcision, in place of which baptism is ordained in the New Testament.'[26] Even circumcision was a sacrament of repentance (Deut. 10.16, 30.6; Jer. 4.4) and of faith (Rom. 4.11f). 'And yet God has not excluded little children from it.'[27] To refuse to baptise children would be to put them in an inferior position to the children of the Israelites. Children may be baptised 'as a sign and testimony that they are heirs of God's blessing promised to the seed of the faithful, that when they come of age they are to acknowledge the truth of their baptism, in order to derive benefit from it'.[28] Calvin refused to be led astray by the objection raised by the Baptists: 'that accordingly all are baptised into future repentance and faith'. His defence is that 'though these have not yet been formed in them [i.e. children] the seed of both lies hidden within them by the secret working of the Spirit'.[29] By this doctrine, borrowed from Luther, he wished to emphasise that our faith is pure receptivity, a work of the Holy Spirit, who however—and here is an important correction of Luther, though in accord with Article V of the Augsburg Confession—is not bound spatially or temporally to the administration of water baptism. We shall understand the reason for this correction better when we come to consider the difference between the two denominations in the doctrine of the Lord's Supper.

Because Christ instituted baptism the Reformed Churches, too, acknowledge its necessity. It is not an absolute necessity,[30] but one which rests on Christ's command (*necessitas praecepti*). Divine judgment is only incurred therefore by those who spurn baptism. The Reformed Churches, for this reason, rejected emergency baptism, which the Lutherans adopted from Rome. Only the preacher called by the congregation is authorised to baptise and no one else, least of all the midwife.[31] All superstition and difficult practical problems were thereby eliminated. From this decision it is also clear that the biblical truth of the

[26] Heidelberg Catechism, Q. 74 (Torrance, *School of Faith*, p. 82).
[27] Geneva Catechism, Q. 334 (Torrance, *School of Faith*, p. 58).
[28] *Op. cit.*, Q. 339. [29] *Inst.*, IV.16.20 (VOL. II, p. 1343).
[30] Westminster Confession, XXVIII, 5 (Schaff, III.663).
[31] Second Helvetic Confession, XX (Schaff, III.290f); Scots Confession, XXII (Schaff, III.471f).

priesthood of all believers was not interpreted as the basic principle for the ordering of the Church's ministry, as in Lutheranism. Individual members of the Church are endowed by God with differing gifts and therefore have differing tasks.

We start with an account of the Reformed doctrine of the Lord's Supper, omitting Zwingli's view, since this plays no part in the Reformed Churches today. For Zwingli the Lord's Supper was a purely subjective act of believers. They already have everything, they have Christ in faith, when they come to the Supper. By celebrating the sacrament they remember Christ's death, thank God for it, and confess their faith to the world.[32] We have seen that Calvin rejected this view of the sacrament which regards it merely as a human act.

3. The Reformed Doctrine of the Lord's Supper

According to the Reformed view the Lord's Supper is essentially God's action towards us, and here too everything depends on the divine promise. 'What would the whole assembly of believers achieve by consuming a little bread and wine, unless *that voice from Heaven* proclaimed aloud that Christ's flesh is the spiritual food and His blood the true drink?'[33] Yet, because of our frailty, God not only approaches us by His Word in our ears, but our other senses too, by the elements of bread and wine, so that we have no excuse for not attending to Him.[34] Bread and wine are signs of the spiritual reality of the Lord's Supper, which proclaims the Word to us, and, at the same time, tokens and pledges which make the spiritual reality 'as certain for us as if we had seen it with our own eyes.'[35]

What is this *spiritual reality*, proclaimed to us by the Word and sealed by the signs? When we are commanded to take Christ's body this means He really becomes ours. Because the promise tells us this we can be certain that what is promised is imparted to us, 'as if Christ here present were himself set before our eyes and touched by our hands'.[36] The symbols bread and wine are just as trustworthy as the Word of promise. God does not

[32] Cf. my article in *Theologische Blätter*, 1932, pp. 12ff.
[33] *Opera*, VOL. IX, pp. 21f (*Defensio doctrinae de sacramentis*, 1555).
[34] *Opera*, VOL. XLVI, p. 679 (Sermons on the Harmony of the Gospels).
[35] *Inst.*, IV.17.1 (VOL. II, p. 1361). [36] *Inst.*, IV.17.3 (VOL. II, p. 1362).

deceive us by them.[37] Calvin therefore plainly asserts: 'I say, therefore, that in the mystery of the Supper, Christ is truly shown to us through the symbols of bread and wine, his very body and blood.'[38] The symbols are not the substance itself but the means by which the Lord acts effectively in us.[39] The 'matter or substance' of the Supper is '*Christ with his death and resurrection*' or 'his very body and blood, in which he has fulfilled all obedience to obtain righteousness for us'.[40] That is to say Christ 'not only died and rose again for us once, but also truly feeds and nourishes us with His flesh and blood, so that we may be one with Him and share His life'.[41] The gift of the Supper is not Christ's Spirit. 'There is certainly a spiritual eating of Christ's body, but not in such a way that we imagine the food is changed into Spirit, but in such a way that the Lord's body and blood are maintained in their nature and property, and are imparted to us spiritually.' 'By spiritual food we do not mean some sort of imaginary food, but the body of the Lord given for us.'[42] Nor is the gift of the Supper Christ's divine nature or His human nature as such, but rather the bodily form in which He was given over to death and rose again for us. It is not the imparting of some material to us but the gift of union with the Mediator. In the Supper we receive Christ's true body and blood so 'that we may grow into one body with him'.[43] We are thus 'united more and more to His blessed body by the Holy Spirit' so 'that although He is in Heaven and we on the earth, we are nevertheless flesh of His flesh and bone of His bone'.[44]

From union with Christ we receive everything else: justification, sanctification, eternal life. 'Those benefits would not come to us unless Christ first made himself ours.'[45] *There is no effect* (effectus) *of the Supper apart from the substance of the Supper*, no salvation apart from union with the God-man Jesus Christ.[46]

[37] *Inst.*, IV.17.10 (VOL. II, p. 1371). [38] *Inst.*, IV.17.11 (VOL. II, p. 1372).
[39] *Opera*, VOL. IX, pp. 17f (*Defensio doctrinae de sacramentis*).
[40] *Inst.*, IV.17.11 (VOL. II, p. 1372).
[41] French Confession, XXXVI (Schaff, III.380; Kidd, *Documents*, p. 671). Cf. Westminster Shorter Catechism, Q. 96 (Torrance, *School of Faith*, p. 276).
[42] Second Helvetic Confession, XXI (Schaff, III.291).
[43] *Inst.*, IV.17.11 (VOL. II, p. 1372).
[44] Heidelberg Catechism, Q. 76 (Torrance, *School of Faith*, p. 83).
[45] *Inst.*, IV.17.11 (VOL. II, p. 1372).
[46] *Opera*, VOL. IX, p. 88 (*Secunda defensio contra Westphalum*, 1556).

To the question how it is possible for us to partake of Christ in the Supper, Calvin answers: 'The bond of this connexion is therefore the Spirit of Christ, with whom we are joined in unity and who is like a channel through which all that Christ himself is and has is conveyed to us.'[47] We have to speak of a 'spiritual eating' in the Supper because in it we partake of Christ's body and blood '*by the Holy Spirit*'.[48] This answer amounts to the assertion of an absolute Divine miracle.[49] The Holy Spirit is spoken of here 'not because we put imagination and fancy in the place of fact and truth, but because the greatness of this mystery exceeds the measure of our senses and the ordinary course of nature.'[50] The Third Person of the Trinity Himself creates the bond between Christ and us, and to this end employs preaching and the sacramental signs. Because Christ's body and blood are not lifeless things[51] there can be no talk of a static gift of Christ in the Supper but only of a *living gift* by the power of the Lord Himself, by His Spirit.[52]

Signs and substance must therefore be clearly distinguished in the Supper. If not, the heavenly glory of Christ is attacked and we are in danger of idolising the elements.[53] At the same time Christ's true manhood is called in question when His body and blood are in any sense tied to the elements,[54] for then we should have to say that they can be simultaneously present in different places, and in that case what possible meaning could be given to the phrase 'body of Christ'? Calvin saw a great danger threatening the Lutherans here and vigorously defended '*the truth of the human nature* on which our salvation rests'.[55] If

[47] 'Vinculum ergo istius coniunctionis est Spiritus Christi, cuius nexu copulamur: et quidam veluti canalis, per quem quicquid Christus ipse et est et habet, ad nos derivatur.' *Inst.*, IV.17.12 (VOL. II, p. 1373).

[48] Second Helvetic Confession, XXI (Schaff, III.293).

[49] *Inst.*, IV.17.24 (VOL. II, p. 1390).

[50] French Confession, XXXVI (Schaff, III.380; Kidd, *Documents*, p. 672).

[51] *Inst.*, IV.17.33 (VOL. II, p. 1406).

[52] On the Lutheran side, it is stated that the Holy Spirit has nothing to do with the Lord's Supper as such, His part being simply to create faith in those who receive it efficaciously. This astonishing assertion (we need only recall John 6), compels us to ask what is meant here by 'Holy Spirit'. The Third Person of the Divine Trinity? or some kind of 'spirit' as contrasted with 'matter'?

[53] 'Praesertim ut Spiritui Sancto Christoque suam gloriam vindicaris, ne quidquam ad ministros vel elementa transferatur.' Calvin to Bucer. *Opera*, VOL. XIII, p. 439.

[54] The Lutheran 'in, with and under' is expressly rejected by the Westminster Confession, XXIX, 7 (Schaff, III.666).

[55] *Opera*, VOL. IX, p. 208.

T

the flesh of Christ is transformed into spirit, the Mediator's solidarity with us is at an end.[56]

Failure to distinguish properly between signs and substance also results in the strange assertion of a false immediacy between the substance of the Supper and those who partake of it. 'But the manner of our *partaking* of the same is *not by the mouth* but *by the Spirit through faith*.'[57] If, in contrast to this, it is asserted, for example, that there is a mutual interplay (however formulated) between signs and substance, then even the wicked receive Christ's body in the Supper. But this is impossible, for with Christ there is always His life-giving Spirit.[58] This does not mean that the Supper's efficacy depends on its human recipients. It is the Lord's will that the bread should be Christ's body for all.[59] Calvin even says 'that the flesh and blood of Christ are no less truly given to the unworthy as to God's elect believers'.[60] But the obduracy of the unworthy prevents God's gifts from entering into them[61]; and they 'become guilty of the body and blood of the Lord to their own damnation'.[62] In other words, Christ passes them by and withholds from them His Spirit, who ingrafts the elect into His body. This preserves the objectivity of what is given in the Supper but distinguishes it from the objectivity of a thing.[63] It is the objectivity of Christ the Lord, of the freedom and sovereignty of the Lord who freely gives Himself by the power of His Spirit in Word and signs.

The faith awakened in us by the Holy Spirit is not simply the eating of Christ's body. Calvin stresses that against Zwingli and his supporters.[64] By the Spirit we are not merely exhorted to have faith in Christ but led to real union with Him. The Holy Spirit creates in us the faith which relates us to Christ but He also gives faith its fulfilment.[65] Of itself our faith is always an empty vessel, but the Spirit who creates and strengthens it by

[56] *Inst* , IV.17.24 (VOL. II, p. 1391).
[57] Belgic Confession, XXXV (Schaff, III.430).
[58] *Inst.*, IV.17.33 (VOL. II, pp. 1405f).
[59] *Opera*, VOL. XVI, p. 678 (Letter of October 1557).
[60] *Inst.*, IV.17.33 (VOL. II, p. 1407). [61] *Opera*, VOL. XVI, p. 678.
[62] Westminster Confession, XXIX, 8 (Schaff, III.667).
[63] 'Surely Christ is too unworthily torn apart if his body, lifeless and powerless, is prostituted to unbelievers.' *Inst.*, IV.17.33 (VOL. II, p. 1406).
[64] *Inst.*, IV.17.5 (VOL. II, p. 1365). [65] *Ibid.* (p. 1364).

Word and elements, in doing so, also gives it its content, i.e. Jesus Christ. This gift applies to the whole man. We become Christ's possession, body and soul.[66]

4. The Lutheran Doctrine of the Lord's Supper Compared with the Reformed Doctrine

It is difficult to describe the Lutheran view of the Supper and to compare it with the Reformed since there is no uniform Lutheran doctrine, not even in the Lutheran confessions. The Augsburg Confession and *Apology* contain Melanchthon's doctrine, the Catechism gives Luther's own view, and the Formula of Concord shows the position finally reached after much doctrinal controversy.[67]

For Luther, in the Supper we have *Christ's body and blood in, with, and under the bread and wine*.[68] 'It is the true body and blood of our Lord Jesus Christ, under the bread and wine, given unto us Christians to eat and to drink, as it was instituted by Christ Himself.'[69] That this is so is due, of course, solely to the word of institution. 'It is the Word (I say) which makes and distinguishes this Sacrament so that it is not mere bread and wine, but is, and is called, the body and blood of Christ.'[70] 'It is true, indeed, that if you take away the Word, or regard it without the words, you have nothing but mere bread and wine. But if the words remain with them, as they shall and must, then, in virtue of the same, it is truly the body and blood of Christ.'[71] Bread and wine have no symbolic or productive power in themselves. The use of them and the service they perform in the Supper depends wholly and exclusively on Christ's command to employ them. His Word alone ensures that the communicants do not receive mere bread and wine: 'You have here His body and blood by virtue of these words which are added to the bread and wine.'[72] By the words of Christ the Supper is not just a gracious food—we recall the phrase 'a gracious water of life' in Luther's doctrine of baptism—but 'the true body and

[66] *Inst.*, IV.17.12 (VOL. II, p 1373).

[67] H. Gollwitzer has brought out these differences very clearly in his book, *Coena domini*, Munich 1937.

[68] W.A., VOL. XXVI, p. 447.

[69] Small Catechism, v (Schaff, III.90; *Concordia*, p. 163, col. 2, vi).

[70] Large Catechism, v (*Concordia*, p. 210, col. 2).

[71] *Ibid.*

[72] *Loc. cit.* (*Concordia*, p. 211, col. 1).

blood of our Lord Jesus Christ'.[73] Christ's body and blood are therefore the treasure of the Supper for us because through them we obtain the forgiveness of sins.[74] Hence 'Christ's body can never be an unfruitful, vain thing, that effects or profits nothing'.[75] 'For this reason we go the the Sacrament because there we receive such a treasure by and in which we obtain forgiveness of sins. . . . For on this account He bids me eat and drink, that it may be my own and may benefit me, as a sure pledge and token, yea, the very same treasure that is appointed for me against my sins, death, and every calamity.'[76] In the Supper the communicant receives what Christ has pledged against sin and death, namely, Christ's body and blood, and therefore the certainty that he enjoys the forgiveness of sins.

The substance of the Supper, Christ's body and blood, are offered to all who eat the bread and wine: 'Therefore, just as the Ten Commandments, the Lord's Prayer, and the Creed retain their nature and worth, although you never keep, pray, or believe them, so also does this venerable Sacrament remain undisturbed, so that nothing is detracted or taken from it, even though we employ and dispense it unworthily.'[77] Man's attitude to the Supper can in no way affect the gift offered in it. This emphasis on the objectivity of the Sacrament necessarily implies that it is eaten by the wicked (*manducatio impiorum*). If the gift of the Supper is tied to the bread and wine then it is *eaten with the mouth* and received even by the wicked. Hence the lapidary words in the Smalcaldic Articles: 'Of the Sacrament of the Altar we hold that bread and wine in the Supper are the true body and blood of Christ, and are given and received not only by the godly, but also by wicked Christians.'[78] Of course: 'Christ's body eaten physically without Spirit or faith' is 'poison and death'.[79] But it is still the case that 'Whoever takes this bread takes Christ's body. Whoever eats this bread, eats Christ's body; whoever chews this bread with teeth and tongue chews Christ's body with teeth and tongue. Yet it remains utterly true that no one sees, takes, eats or chews Christ's body

[73] *Loc. cit.* (*Concordia*, p. 210, col. 2). [74] *Loc. cit.* (*Concordia*, p. 211, col. 2).
[75] *Ibid.* [76] *Ibid.*
[77] *Loc. cit.* (*Concordia*, p. 210, col. 1).
[78] Smalcald Articles, III, vi (*Concordia*, p. 146).
[79] W.A., VOL. XXVI, pp. 292f.

in the way that other food is visibly seen and eaten. For what is done to the bread is rightly and truly applied to Christ's body because of the sacramental union.'[80]

To receive the Sacrament rightly, of course, *faith* is necessary. 'The treasure, indeed, is opened and placed at everyone's door, yea, upon his table, but it is necessary that you should also claim it and confidently view it as the words suggest to you.'[81] The reason for this is the purpose of the Supper, made known by Christ. 'Because He offers and promises forgiveness of sin, it cannot be received otherwise than by faith.'[82] 'For since this treasure is entirely presented in the words, it cannot be apprehended and appropriated in any other way than with the heart. For such a gift and eternal treasure cannot be seized with the fist. . . . But this is done by the faith of the heart which discerns this treasure and desires it.'[83]

For Luther this treasure is equivalent to the word of the Gospel which is also heard everywhere in Scripture.[84] For the forgiveness of sins won for us on the Cross 'cannot come to us in any other way than through the Word'.[85] If Luther had said no more than that, an agreement with the Calvinistic Protestants would not have been difficult. It is all the more astonishing that he was not content to stop there, since the Reformation viewpoint is here expressed quite plainly. But Luther also taught and, as the years passed, increasingly stressed, in opposition to Zwingli, that in the Supper, in virtue of the Words, the communicants were offered, *in the elements, Christ's body and blood as a pledge of forgiveness of sins.* In the previous chapter on the Sacraments, we saw how, in Luther's view, the elements take on a new dimension as a result of the words of institution and become the bearers of the sacramental grace. Because of the sacramental union it is 'now no longer merely oven-baked bread, but flesh-bread or body-bread, that is to say, it has become one sacramental substance and one thing with Christ's body'.[86]

How did Luther envisage this presence of Christ's body and blood in the elements? Here again it would not have been difficult for Luther and Calvin to reach agreement, if Luther

[80] *Op. cit.*, p. 442. [81] Large Catechism, v (*Concordia*, p. 212, col. 1). [82] *Ibid.* [83] *Ibid.* [84] *Loc. cit.* (*Concordia*, p. 211, col. 2). [85] *Ibid.* [86] W.A., VOL. XXVI, p. 445.

had remembered his own warning to Zwingli: 'We must not ask how it happens that Christ's body is in the Supper but simply believe God's Word.'[87] For Calvin, in particular, readily acknowledged the great mystery involved here.[88] But in the first place, as we have just heard, Luther laid great stress on the union of Christ's body and blood with the elements, a union which implies an eating with the mouth (*manducatio oralis*) and an eating by the wicked (*manducatio impiorum*). In the second place, in his controversy with Zwingli, he did try, in spite of his own warning, to explain how we are to envisage the presence of Christ's body and blood. Luther's objection to Zwingli was that Christ's body does not stay in one particular place, like a bird in a nest.[89] God's right hand where Christ is, means in fact God's Almighty rule. Christ's body shares this glory, and therefore God's omnipresence too.[90] Where God works and rules, Christ too is present bodily: but He does not wish to allow us to find Him everywhere, but only where His Word points us. 'He is everywhere, but He does not want you to seek Him everywhere; but if you seek Him where His Word is, you will surely find Him. . . . He is present there with the Word, but not in the same way as here in the Sacrament, where He binds His body and blood with the Word, to be received by us bodily in the bread and wine.'[91] Christ provides the interpretation: 'Because I will to attach Myself to My Word so as to make it unnecessary for you to seek Me everywhere as the fanatics do, here I am! It would be beyond you and you are too small to grasp Me even here, without My Word.'[92] It has, therefore, been argued that Luther did not teach a simple ubiquity of Christ's body but a 'multivolent presence', resting on the will of God expressed in the words of institution. According to Luther, this presence of Christ's body and blood is possible, because in his view there are three ways in which something can be present in one place.

1. *Localiter* or *circumscriptive*, just as wine is in the chalice and as Christ 'walked bodily on earth'.[93]

[87] W.A., VOL. XXVI, p. 297; VOL. XXIII, p. 145.
[88] *Inst.*, IV.17.7 (VOL. II, p. 1367).
[89] W.A., VOL. XXIII, p. 159. [90] *Op. cit.*, p. 145.
[91] W.A., VOL. XIX, p. 492; Seeberg, *Die Lehre Luthers*, p. 470.
[92] W.A., VOL. XXIII, p. 153. [93] W.A., VOL. XXVI, p. 335.

2. *Diffinitive*, just as an angel or devil can be in a whole house or even in just one room or in a box, or as a sound can be heard even in the most varied places. 'In this mode, Christ's corpse came out of the sealed tomb and passed through closed doors to the disciples.'[94]

3. '*Repletive*, that is, when something is at one and the same time wholly and completely in all places and occupies all places, and yet is not bounded or confined by the extent of any place where it may be. This manner pertains to God alone.'[95] This mode of presence is Christ's also, 'because He is with God one person'. 'For since Christ is one person with God, you must place this nature of Christ as far *outside the creatures* as God is outside them, and again as deep and near *in all creatures* as God is in them.'[96] When we put alongside these statements Luther's confession: 'But how it happens we know not. It is beyond nature and reason even of the angels in Heaven, known and understood only by God,'[97] we must ask once more whether Calvin's answer is not the right one here: 'The bond of unity is the Spirit of Christ.'[98] Does not Luther's proposed solution, to think of Christ's body and blood as bound to the elements '*repletive*', endanger Christ's true humanity? This fear is warranted since Luther asserts that Christ's body is itself present 'in all creatures', 'in stone, fire, and water',[99] and also in the elements of the Supper, even had Christ never spoken the words of institution, simply because God's right hand is everywhere and Christ's body is there.[100] Luther's ideas here border on pantheism and raise seriously the question whether the Incarnation of God's Son has any meaning at all? This question is all the more insistent because, according to Luther, Christ's body was also omnipresent during His earthly life.[101] For the sake of its witness to the true humanity of the Mediator, Reformed doctrine could not accept Luther's view of the mode of the presence of the body and blood in the Supper, but had to enter its protest at this point.

The Formula of Concord formally adopted Luther's view of the threefold mode of the presence of Christ's body and de-

[94] *Op. cit.*, p. 328. [95] *Op. cit.*, p. 329. [96] *Op. cit.*, p. 336. [97] *Ibid.*
[98] See above, p. 273. [99] W.A., VOL. XIX, p. 492.
[100] W.A., VOL. XXIII, p. 145. [101] *Op. cit.*, p. 147.

clared that in the Supper when Christ's body and blood are consumed 'this participation occurs with the mouth, while the mode is spiritual'.[102] As it stressed, this does not refer to 'the spiritual communion, when, through faith, true believers are in the Spirit incorporated into Christ the Lord, and become true spiritual members of His body', but to 'the spiritual, supernatural, heavenly mode, according to which Christ is present in the Holy Supper, working not only consolation and life in the believing but also condemnation in the unbelieving'.[103] On the other hand 'piratical thoughts of the gross carnal presence' of the body of Christ must be rejected.

In the Augsburg Confession Melanchthon does not speak of any such supernatural presence of Christ's body and blood in the elements: 'Of the Supper of the Lord they teach that the Body and Blood of Christ are truly present, and are distributed to those who eat in the Supper of the Lord.'[104] (The German text adds 'under the form of bread and wine'.) Since it was required at the discussions in which he took part, Calvin subscribed to the Augsburg Confession, but, of course, always emphasised: 'in the same sense as its author'.[105] The latter made it clear that for him there was no question of the presence of the substances: 'We speak of the presence of the *living Christ*.'[106] 'The *corporalis praesentia* (bodily presence) of Christ is affirmed by Melanchthon without being emphasised.'[107] In later years Melanchthon taught: 'The Lord's Supper is in no sense an empty charade: this eating is truly a sign and pledge that the Son of God, our Lord Jesus Christ, is in those who eat.'[108] That could have been written by Calvin. According to Melanchthon, Christ is present *in the whole action of the Supper*, not just in the bread and wine. Melanchthon says: 'with the bread' (*cum pane*) and not 'in the bread' (*in pane*). Christ's presence in the Supper includes the elements, but in what manner is not stated. It happens 'together with and concurrently with' the action of the Supper. To that extent

[102] Thorough Decl., VII (*Concordia*, p. 273, col. 2). [103] *Ibid.*

[104] 'De coena domini docent, quod corpus et sanguis Christi vere adsint et distribuantur vescentibus in coena domini et improbant secus docentes.' Augsburg Confession, x (Schaff, III.13; Kidd, *Documents*, p. 264. German text adds 'unter der Gestalt des Brots und Weins' after 'adsint'). [105] See above, p. 178.

[106] *Ap. C.*, x (*Concordia*, p. 77, col. 1). [107] Gollwitzer, *Coena domini*, p. 68.

[108] Melanchthon, *Opera*, VOL. VIII, p. 941; Gollwitzer, *Coena domini*, p. 66.

Melanchthon's doctrine has something in common with Luther's and differs from Calvin's, for whom 'concurrently with' refers not to time but strictly to a concurrence of the Holy Spirit. Moreover Melanchthon affirms that Christ's body is present in virtue of the ubiquity of Christ's whole person: 'In other words, we say that Christ's body does not of necessity have to be in one place only. We say therefore that it can be in different places concurrently, whether this happens in some spatial manner or in some other mysterious way, by which all places are at the same time present *to the person of Christ as one point*.'[109] The last phrase called for further discussion since it asserts that everything is present to the person of Christ. For the reasons already given, Calvin rejected a ubiquity of Christ's body, however formulated. He recalled with approval the Scholastic distinction: 'Although the whole Christ is everywhere, still the whole of that which is in him is not everywhere.'[110] In a memorandum to the Council of Stadt-Wesel about the foreign Reformed congregation there, Melanchthon outlined the necessary attitude to the Reformed theologians as follows: 'Luther accepted the strangers from Strassburg and Augsburg because they confessed that Christ is substantially and effectively present in the action (*usu*). All other explanations are excluded. It is essential to acknowledge plainly that the Lord's Supper is not merely a sign of the Covenant or of human fellowship, without reference to the presence and action of the Son of God. . . . We do not say, as Osiander did: This bread is God. Nor do we say that the bread is changed, but we say with Paul, who is referring strictly to the reception (*de ipsa sumptione*), the bread is the communion of Christ's body. By this [reception], Christ imparts His body to the communicants and testifies that they are members of His body, in whom He wills truly to work, since He is the Head who accomplishes everything in His members. But I avoid any discussion in the course of which a host of difficult questions may be raised by many people.'[111]

With a similar ecumenical attitude, the Confessional Synod of the Evangelical Church of the Old Prussian Union, meeting

[109] Melanchthon, *Opera*, VOL. II, p. 222.

[110] 'Quamvis totus Christus ubique est, non tamen totum quod in eo est, ubique esse.' *Inst.*, IV.17.30 (VOL. II, p. 1403).

[111] Quoted by Gollwitzer, *Coena domini*, p. 95.

at Halle (Saale) in 1937 during the German Church Struggle, affirmed: 'Our Lord and Saviour Jesus Christ, who for our sakes came in the flesh, offered Himself for us once and for all on the Cross, and rose again bodily from the dead, is *Himself the gracious gift* in the Supper He instituted in His Church.'[112] That makes it quite plain that in the Lord's Supper it is not a question of any kind of substance, nor merely of Christ's body and blood, but, as Melanchthon and Calvin affirmed, of the living Christ Himself. A clear and significant clarification of the testimony of our Reformation fathers was thereby effected. The conclusion drawn from this was no less important. 'The differences still existing between us in the doctrine of the Holy Supper concern the mode and form in which the Lord gives Himself in the Supper. They do not touch the fact that the gift in the Supper is the Lord Himself.'[113] Membership of one or other of the Reformation Churches therefore constitutes no ground for exclusion from celebrations of the Supper; nor do common celebrations by members of the two confessions conflict with the administration of the Sacrament in accordance with Scripture.[114] The Synod did not deny that differences still exist on both sides about the manner of Christ's presence, but —and this was the great achievement—it declared that this was of secondary importance compared with the common confession of the Lord's presence. None of the positions which may be held on this question, can, if we remember the presence of the Lord Himself, be so important as to divide Christ's congregations from each other. Lutherans and Reformed could not in future ignore this breach which was then made in the fixed front line between the two Churches, especially as the original Reformation truth, that it is Christ who is present, once more shone clearly here.

Meanwhile we have since been led to take a further significant step forward. A commission of theologians from the Lutheran, Reformed, and Union Churches, appointed by the Council of the Evangelical Church in Germany, after many years' labour, produced together Eight Theses about 'the essen-

[112] See Niesel, in *Intercommunion*, edd. Baillie and Marsh, pp. 282ff.
[113] *Ibid.*
[114] W. Niesel, *Um Verkündigung und Ordnung der Kirche*, Bielefeld 1949, p. 37.

tial content of the biblical doctrine of the Supper', and published them on 2 November 1957. The very important fourth thesis reads: 'The words spoken by our Lord Jesus Christ, in offering to us the bread and the cup, tell us what He Himself gives in this Supper to all who come to it. He, the crucified and risen Lord, permits Himself in His body delivered to death for all and in His blood shed for all, to be taken by us through His promised Word with the bread and wine, and thereby associates us, by the power of the Holy Spirit, with the victory of His Kingdom so that, by faith in His promise, we have forgiveness of sins, life and salvation.'[115] The Commission explained, of course, that 'what this result means for the questions of intecommunion and reunion, needs further theological study'.[116] But proof has been given that theologians of the different Reformation Churches can today bear common testimony on the basis of Scripture about the meaning of the Lord's Supper.

[115] See *Zur Lehre vom Heiligen Abendmahl*, Munich 1958 (Report of the German Evangelical Church's discussions on the Lord's Supper, 1947-57). Also J. C. McLelland, 'Reformed and Lutheran Relations', in *Reformed and Presbyterian World*, xxvi 2 (June 1960), pp. 60f.

[116] *Zur Lehre vom Heiligen Abendmahl.*

CHAPTER 10

CHRISTOLOGY[1]

SINCE our purpose is to draw out the doctrinal differences between the two Churches, we must now glance at their Christology. We are not suggesting that we shall discover here the deepest level of these differences. There is a logic-chopping denominationalism which insists that all our differences are due to a difference in Christology. We saw earlier that Luther himself did not look for ultimate principles, supposed to underly the whole conflict between the two confessions. It would, indeed, be a sure sign of decadence, if we were to regard the Christian faith as a doctrinal system resting on one particular principle.

The disagreement about Christology emerged, of course, in the doctrine of the Lord's Supper.

1. THE LUTHERAN EMPHASIS

According to the Formula of Concord, what is at stake in Christology is the supreme consolation of Christians, 'which they have in the afore-cited promise concerning the presence and dwelling with them of their Head, King and High Priest, who has promised them that not only His mere divinity would be with them, which to us poor sinners is as a consuming fire to dry stubble, but that He, He, the man who has spoken with them, who has tried all tribulations in His assumed human nature, and who can therefore have sympathy with us, as with men and His brethren—He will be with us in all our troubles also according to the nature according to which He is our brother and we are flesh of His flesh'.[2] The very same concern led a man like Calvin to reject the Lutheran doctrine of Christ's

[1] See further: Karl Barth, *Church Dogmatics*, VOL. I, 2, pp. 1-202 (The Incarnation of the Word); *Essays in Christology for Karl Barth*, ed. T. H. L. Parker, London 1956; A. B. Bruce, *The Humiliation of Christ*, 5th edn., Edinburgh 1905.

[2] Form. Conc. Thor. Decl., VIII (*Concordia*, p. 283, col. 1).

person. It is necessary then to examine closely what the Formula of Concord teaches about Christ.

In the Epitome we read: 'As the two natures are united personally, i.e. in one person, we believe, teach and confess that this union is not such a copulation and connexion that neither nature has anything in common with the other personally, i.e. because of the personal union, as when two boards are glued together, where neither gives anything to the other or takes anything from the other. But here is the highest communion, which God truly has with the assumed man . . . as the ancient teachers of the Church explained this union and communion of the natures by the illustration of iron glowing with fire, and also by the union of body and soul in man.'[3] On the basis of the personal union (*unio personalis*) of the divine and human nature it was further asserted—and this is the real Christological interest—that Christ's human nature shared the majesty of the divine nature, since in Christ dwells all the fullness of the Godhead bodily.[4] 'Thus there is and remains in Christ only one divine omnipotence, power, majesty, and glory, which is peculiar to the divine nature alone; but it shines, manifests, and exercises itself fully, yet voluntarily, in, with and through the assumed, exalted nature in Christ; just as in glowing iron there are not two kinds of power to shine and burn . . . but the power to shine and to burn is a property of the fire; but since the fire is united with the iron, it manifests and exercises this its power to shine and to burn in, with, and through the glowing iron, so that thence and from this union also the glowing iron has the power to shine and to burn, without conversion of the essence and of the natural properties of fire and iron.'[5] *This permeation of Christ's human nature by the majesty of the divine nature* means above all 'that also according to His assumed human nature and with the same, He can be, and also is, present where He will'.[6]

That was Luther's teaching too. We have already spoken of this in discussing the doctrine of the Supper. The conjunction of the two natures in Christ's person means for Luther that Christ's humanity is 'wholly and completely *elevated into God*

[3] Epitome, VIII, Aff. V (Schaff, III.149f; *Concordia*, p. 226).
[4] Thor. Decl. VIII (*Concordia*, p. 280, col. 2).
[5] *Ibid.* [6] *Loc. cit.* (*Concordia*, p. 282, col. 1).

above all creatures'.[7] It has not been changed by the *unio personalis*. 'In essence it cannot be God, but because it reaches and cleaves and exists high above all creatures to the essential God, so it must at least be God personally and must therefore also be wherever God is.'[8]

This majesty has belonged to Christ's human nature not only from the Ascension onwards, but ever since the Incarnation. Therefore even the body inhabited by Christ on earth was ubiquitous.[9] As R. Seeberg notes, Luther attached very little importance to the transformation of Christ's body at the Resurrection: 'He did not become a different person when He was transformed, but as before so afterwards He was present everywhere.'[10] The Formula of Concord teaches the same.[11]

This view of the communication of the properties of each nature to the other (*communicatio idiomatum*)[12] in the person of the God-man, raises not only the serious question whether the revelation of God in the flesh is not thus endangered, but also the related question how then the life of Jesus as recorded in the Gospels is to be understood. The Formula of Concord, in the light of its Christological assumptions, seeks to explain the earthly life of the God-man in the following terms: 'This majesty He always had according to the personal union, and yet He *abstained* from it in the state of His humiliation, and on this account truly increased in all wisdom and favour with God and men; therefore He exercised this majesty, *not always*, but

[7] W.A., VOL. XXVI, p. 340. [8] *Op. cit.*, p. 341. [9] W.A., VOL. XXIII, p. 147.

[10] *Ibid.* Cf. Seeberg, *Die Lehre Luthers*, p. 470, n. 1.

[11] Thor. Decl. VIII (*Concordia*, p. 276, col. 1).

[12] A distinction was made between the three genera of the *communicatio idiomatum*. 'The first two genera refer only to the mode of speech and in this sense were accepted by Reformed theologians as well. The *genus idiomaticum* [cf. Thor. Decl. VIII, *Concordia*, p. 278, col. 1] is illustrated by Rom. 1.3: the Son of God was born. The *idioma* of one nature is applied to the whole person of the God-man. The *genus apotelesmaticum* [cf. Thor. Decl., VIII, *Concordia*, p. 279, col. 1] *quod ad rationes officii Christi attinet*, is illustrated by 1 Tim. 2.5: the man Christ Jesus who gave himself as a ransom.' 'In consequence of the teleological union of the two natures for the work of redemption' there is 'attributed to one nature a redemptive action which it could not perform of itself but only in virtue of the *unio hypostatica*'. 'What is chiefly in view is the third genus, the so-called *genus majestaticum*. According to this, in the unity of the person of Christ the properties of the divine nature are added to the human nature.' 'Conversely a kind of *genus tapeinoticum* was proposed, though only within certain limits [Thor. Decl. VIII, *Concordia*, p. 278, col. 2]. It is incorrect to say . . . that the expressions "God suffered", "God died", are only *praedicationes verbales* . . . i.e. mere words and that it is not so in fact.' E. F. K. Müller, *Symbolik*, pp. 354f. Cf. McNeill and Battles, VOL. 1, p. 483, n. 4.

when it pleased Him, until after His resurrection He entirely laid aside the form of a servant, but not the (human) nature, and was *established in the full use*, manifestation, and declaration of the divine majesty, . . . so that now not only as God, but also as man He knows all things, can do all things, is present with all creatures, and has everything under His feet and in His hands.'[13] This means that the God-man always shared the divine majesty, even on His human side, but during His earthly life He divested Himself of it until after the Resurrection, when, laying aside the servant form, He made full use of it. But during the time of His earthly life, Christ's humanity was so controlled by the divine person that even then, when the Son of God wished, the divine majesty shone through the human nature.

On the basis of these statements later Lutheran theologians developed *a doctrine of the two states of Christ*, the state of humiliation (*status exinanitionis*) and the state of glory (*status exaltationis*). We have just heard how, according to the Formula of Concord, Jesus Christ in the state of humiliation showed Himself to be man by abstention (*κενώσις*) from the use of the divine properties. That accords with the view of Martin Chemnitz (*d.* 1586) and of the Giessen school later.[14] But another view is expressed even in the Formula of Concord. In the Thorough Declaration we read: 'This was *concealed* and withheld at the time of the humiliation.'[15] This concealment (*κρύψις*) of the divine properties in which Christ's human nature shared, was taught by Johann Brentz (*d.* 1570) and by the Tübingen school later.[16] In the *Solida Decisio* (1624), the Saxon theologians[17] decisively rejected the view of the Tübingen school, on the ground that it made Christ's sufferings unreal. So it was not only Reformed theologians who regarded this form of Christology as a 'departure from the Chalcedonian Christology' and therefore rejected it, but careful Lutherans did so too.

[13] Epitome, VIII, xi (Schaff, III.152; *Concordia*, p. 227).

[14] On Martin Chemnitz (1522-86) see J. Kunze in *New Schaff-Herzog*, VOL. III, pp. 24f. On the Giessen School see VOL. III, pp. 57f.

[15] Thor. Decl. VIII (*Concordia*, p. 280, col. 2).

[16] On Johann Brenz (1499-1570) see G. Bossert in *New Schaff-Herzog*, VOL. II, pp. 260f. On the Tübingen School see VOL. III, pp. 57f.

[17] The Saxon theologians were led by Matthias Höe von Höenegg, court preacher at Dresden.

Unlike the sixteenth- and seventeenth-century theologians, the Kenotic school[18] which arose within Lutheranism in the last century, regarded not the God-man but the pre-Incarnate Word (λόγος ἄσαρκος) as the subject of the humiliation, and thus jeopardised the truth that in revelation we encounter the *Logos*, God Himself and God alone. It amounted to a complete denial of God's revelation.

2. The Reformed Emphasis Contrasted with the Lutheran

We remarked earlier that Calvin too stressed that it is in the man Jesus that God encounters us. He was in full agreement with the Lutherans here. 'If our Lord Jesus Christ had not assumed a human body or had even kept His divinity separate from it, where would all the blessings be which we have today? But because he was God and man in one, and the two natures are united, see, we can therefore come boldly to Him and regard Him as our brother, quite certain that He regards and acknowledges each one of us as a member of His body.'[19] For this reason Calvin vigorously opposed Scholasticism: 'Hence all knowledge of God without Christ is a vast abyss which immediately swallows up all our thoughts. . . . Common is the axiom of the schools that God is the object of faith. Thus of hidden majesty, Christ being overlooked, they largely and refinedly speculate, but with what success? They entangle themselves in astounding dotages, so that there is no end to their errors.'[20] He therefore rejects firmly the heretical doctrine of Nestorius (*d.* 451) of a 'double Christ'.[21]

But Calvin rejected just as vigorously the error of Eutyches (*d.* after 454) as also the novelties of the Lutheran Christology which showed a similar tendency. In our concern to engage strictly in a theology of revelation we must take care 'lest, while meaning to show the unity of the person we destroy either nature'.[22] The one person of Christ so consists of two natures that each nevertheless retains unimpaired its own distinctive

[18] Gottfried Thomasius, *Christi Person und Werk*, Erlangen 1856-62. Cf. A. B. Bruce, *The Humiliation of Christ*, 5th edn. Edinburgh 1905, pp. 138-44.

[19] *Opera*, VOL. XLVI, p. 110 (Sermons on the Harmony of the Gospels).

[20] *Opera*, VOL. LV, p. 226 (Comment on 1 Pet. 1.21).

[21] *Inst.*, II.14.4 (VOL. I, p. 486).

[22] *Ibid.* (VOL. I, p. 487).

character.'[23] Otherwise we should find ourselves teaching the existence of 'some sort of intermediate being which was neither God nor man'.[24] Christ's solidarity with us would be challenged and our salvation imperilled.[25] But any confusion of the divinity and humanity of Christ would endanger the true divinity of the Mediator[26] and obscure the truth that in Him God Himself meets us.

Christ is 'God *manifest* in the flesh'.[27] To proclaim that is the task of Christology. Calvin opposes any naturalistic, materialistic conception of the Incarnation. The *Logos* 'chose for himself the virgin's womb as a *temple* in which to *dwell*'.[28] Calvin saw this freedom and superiority of the *Logos* in relation to the human existence of Jesus Christ, threatened from two sides: by the Lutheran *communicatio idiomatum* (the communication of the properties of the divine nature to the human nature), and by the Christological views of the Baptists. He gave both the same answer: when we say the Son of God came down to this world we do not mean that 'divinity left heaven to hide itself in the prison house of the body, but because even though it filled all things, still in Christ's very humanity it dwelt bodily, that is, by nature, and in a certain ineffable way'.[29]

This critical marginal note later came to be known, very misleadingly, as the *Extra Calvinisticum*. Karl Barth has pointed out that this was not Calvin's own invention. The Genevan Reformer simply used a statement endorsed by all previous tradition against a strange and newly constructed Christology.[30] Above all, its use was never intended to divert men from the Mediator to a divinity outside the Incarnate Word. The truth was quite the opposite. But against Luther and Menno Simons[31] (*d.* 1559) it had to be emphasised that, for our sakes, the divinity remains what it was in Christ. It does not disappear into Christ's human existence.[32]

[23] *Inst.*, IV.17.30 (VOL. II, p. 1402).
[24] *Ibid.*
[25] *Inst.*, IV.17.29 (VOL. II, pp. 1399f).
[26] *Inst.*, II.14.7 (VOL. I, pp. 490f).
[27] *Opera*, VOL. XLVI, p. 170 *et passim.*
[28] *Inst.*, II.14.1 (VOL. I, p. 482).
[29] *Inst.*, IV.17.30; II.13.4 (VOL. II, pp. 1402f; VOL. I, p. 481).
[30] *Church Dogmatics*, VOL. I, 2, pp. 168f.
[31] Menno Simons (*b.* in Holland 1492, *d.* in Germany 1559) one of the most influential leaders of the Anabaptist group known as the Mennonites. See S. Cramer and J. Horsch in *New Schaff-Herzog*, VOL. X, pp. 423-9.
[32] Cf. Heidelberg Catechism, Q. 48 (Torrance, *School of Faith*, p. 77).

Reformed theology, too, developed a doctrine of Christ's *two states*. In the conflicts between the schools in Lutheranism, it was unable to side with either party, because it did not teach the *genus majestaticum*, and therefore did not share the underlying premise of the whole controversy. The humiliation of Jesus Christ—the Godman is regarded as the subject not the pre-Incarnate *Logos*—is not simply His being made man but His taking the form of a servant and therefore His assumption of sinful flesh. 'The state of Christ's humiliation was that lowly condition in which He . . . took upon Himself the form of a servant.'[33] The great nineteenth-century Reformed preacher H. F. Kohlbrügge impressed this doctrine on his hearers with forceful words: 'So then, the Word emptied Himself and took the form of a servant. He went about here on earth entangled in flesh and blood, just as we are. Holy, because He was the Word . . . yet He came into the world to go about in the person of a sinner. . . . He remained the Word, yet never was there any as sinful, as needy, as powerless before the Law as He; for the Lord laid all our sins upon Him.'[34] So strongly did Kohlbrügge emphasise God's condescension to our human sphere that he regarded Jesus' birth of a virgin as part of the Son's servant form. It was not a sign of His glory, but of the shame He took upon Himself.[35] Reformed theology also regarded the descent into Hell (*descensus ad inferos*) as part of Christ's humiliation. This is taken to mean 'His unspeakable anguish, pains, and terrors which He suffered in His soul on the Cross and before'.[36] Whereas the old theologians regarded Christ's exaltation as divided into three acts, Resurrection, Ascension, and Session at God's right hand, H. F. Kohlbrügge pioneered a deepening of our thoughts here and sought to go beyond this artificial succession of humiliation and exaltation: 'For even in the dust and bloody sweat, even in contending with death, He showed His divine majesty, the majesty of His love and grace to us lost sinners.'[37] Even in the humiliation Christ already shows His majesty.

[33] 'Humiliationis Christi status erat humilis illa conditio, qua . . . formam servi in se suscepit.' Westminster Larger Catechism, Q. 46 (Torrance, *School of Faith*, p. 193).

[34] *Im Anfang war das Wort*, Elberfeld 1877, p. 75.

[35] *Betrachtung über das erste Kapitel des Evangeliums nach Matthaus*, Elberfeld 1844, pp. 128f.

[36] Heidelberg Catechism, Q. 44 (Torrance, *School of Faith*, p. 76).

[37] *Passion-Predigten*, Elberfeld 1889, VOL. I, p. 53. Cf. *Zacharias und Elisabeth*, Elberfeld 1877, p. 65.

It can at least be suggested that Kohlbrügge, the Reformed Lutheran, may have opened up the way to a possible agreement between the two confessions on the question of Christology. Or is Karl Barth right when he says: 'that perhaps there can be no amicable compromise in Evangelical theology as regards the order of merit between these two views. Perhaps if it is to be Evangelical theology at all . . . there always has to be a static and a dynamic, an ontic and a noetic principle, not in nice equilibrium, but calling to each other and questioning each other. That is, there must be Lutherans and Reformed, not in the shadow of a unitary theology, but as a twofold theological school—for the sake of the truth about the reality of Jesus Christ, which does not admit of being grasped or conceived by any unitary theology.'[38]

[38] *Church Dogmatics*, VOL. I, 2, p. 171.

CHAPTER II

THE SOVEREIGNTY OF GOD[1]

We might have ended this survey of the two confessions with the chapter on Christology, but since the doctrine of the two Kingdoms has been under discussion recently we must glance briefly at this question too.

1. The Lutheran Doctrine of Spiritual and Earthly Government

Luther's well-known statement in his treatise on 'Secular Authority' runs: 'Therefore has God established the two Kingdoms, the spiritual which makes Christians and pious people by the Holy Spirit under Christ, and the earthly one which checks non-Christians and wicked people so that they must maintain peace and be still whether they like it or not.'[2] 'Therefore these two Kingdoms must be carefully separated and both allowed their place. The one to produce piety; the other to create external peace and prevent evil deeds. Neither is sufficient in the world without the other. For without Christ's spiritual Kingdom no one can be pious in God's sight by means of worldly government. . . . For where worldly government and law alone rules, there is bound to be much hypocrisy. . . . But where spiritual government alone rules a land and its people, wickedness knows no restraint.'[3] Luther's doctrine in this matter was conditioned by his conflict with opponents on the right and on the left: with Rome and its theory of the two swords entrusted to the Pope's keeping, the spiritual sword and the worldly sword; and with the Enthusiasts who likewise

[1] See further: Karl Barth, *Rechtfertigung und Recht*, Theol. Studien, No. 1, 1938 (trans. G. Ronald Howe, *Church and State*, London 1939); Karl Barth, *Christengemeinde und Bürgergemeinde*, Munich 1946 (trans. in *Against the Stream*, ed. R. Gregor Smith, London 1954, pp. 15-50); Dietrich Bonhoeffer, *Ethik*, Munich 1949 (Eng. trans. 1955).

[2] W.A., vol. xi, p. 251. [3] *Op. cit.*, p. 252.

wanted to subordinate public life to the Christian Church. In view of this conflict it is easy to see why Luther insisted above all that the two governments should be carefully separated. The statements made in the Lutheran confessions for the most part point in the same direction. 'Therefore the power of the Church and the civil power must not be confounded',[4] as the Romans have done who 'have cooked together the Kingdom of Christ which is spiritual and the Kingdom of the World and external discipline'.[5]

When so much depends on making a true distinction here, we must be quite clear about the two things to be distinguished. It is important therefore to realise that *spiritual government* is not identical with the organised Church, nor *worldly government* with the State. It is in no sense merely a matter of two different spheres, but essentially of two *different modes of God's government.*

'Christ establishes His spiritual Kingdom in man's heart by the preaching of the Word and by His Spirit, causing faith, eternal righteousness and eternal life to begin in them.'[6] To the extent, but only to the extent, that the Church and its ministers let themselves be employed for that end, are they pioneers of the spiritual Kingdom to which 'all true believers in Christ' belong.[7] But as baptised Christians the statesmen Luther had to deal with were also destined for this spiritual Kingdom and therefore summoned to its assistance. Hence 'we must let them be priests and bishops and regard their office as one which also belongs to and is useful to the Christian Church'.[8] There is a difference here only 'of function or work not of status'.[9] Thus the principal task of the Church is to establish Christ's spiritual Kingdom by preaching and sacraments. That does not mean that a politician cannot serve this Kingdom directly: 'When David or a prince preaches or says we must fear God and obey His Word, he is not a lord of that same Word, but a servant and an obedient man and is not

[4] Augsburg Confession, XXVIII (*Concordia* p. 23, col. 1; Schaff, III.61; Kidd, *Documents*, p. 283).

[5] *Ap. C.*, XVI (*Opera*, VOL. XXVII, p. 581, VOL. XXVIII, p. 224; *Concordia*, p. 101, col. 1).

[6] *Loc. cit.* (*Opera*, VOL. XXVII, p. 581, VOL. XXVIII, p. 223; *Concordia*, p. 100, col. 2).

[7] W.A., VOL. XI, p. 249. [8] W.A., VOL. VI, p. 408. [9] *Ibid.*

meddling in spiritual or Divine matters.'[10] But the politician may not enforce religion for the State's own selfish ends. That would be to make himself master of God's Word and to misuse it. Only as humble service can he do anything at all for Christ's Kingdom. But this he can do.

On the other hand, the earthly Kingdom is not simply the State with its executive power. It embraces all the following functions: 'the government of the country and its people, the judgment and settlement of disputes in accordance with the Imperial and other laws, the punishment of evildoers by the sword and other means with all severity, the declaration and waging of war, buying and selling, the holding and protection of houses, farms and other property, the taking of required oaths in law courts, and the contracting of marriages'.[11] In other words, earthly government means the whole life of society and its employment in the service of God and not simply the State authority, even though it is primarily the latter's duty to secure earthly government. The earthly Kingdom is a complex structure embracing many different responsibilities in which all share, and which even a Christian, however little he himself may need a compulsory rule of law, cannot ignore for his neighbour's sake.[12] Earthly government can be divided at least into 'administration', i.e. State (*politia*), and 'family life' (*Ehestand*) or '*oeconomia*'. This Latin word shows that more is meant than 'family life', and later theologians used the word '*Nährstand*' (productive employment). Just as a politician can share the task of the Christian Church, provided he does so as a genuine servant, so, conversely, the Church can concern itself with the life of society, provided its aim in doing so is not to rule but to serve. 'When therefore a preacher, in the exercise of his office, says to Kings and princes and to all the world: Thank and praise God and keep His Commandments, he is not thereby meddling in worldly government but serving and obeying the supreme government.'[13] Luther him-

[10] W.A., VOL. LI, p. 240, quoted from Steck, 'Die beiden Reiche' in *Die Stimme der Gemeinde*, III (1951), No. 6.

[11] *Ap. C.*, XVI (*Opera*, VOL. XXVII, p. 581, VOL. XXVIII, p. 223; *Concordia*, p. 100 col. 2).

[12] W.A., VOL. XI, p. 253; Augsburg Confession, XVI (Schaff, III.16; *Concordia*, p. 14; Kidd, *Documents*, p. 266).

[13] W.A., VOL. LI, p. 240.

self exercised such a ministry in a far-reaching manner. There was scarcely a single public question of his day about which he did not declare his position, in his speeches and writings.

It follows from all this that the spiritual Kingdom and the earthly Kingdom are not opposed as good and evil, Christian and un-Christian. Nor is it the case that neither has anything to do with the other. If the spiritual Kingdom rests on God's plan of redemption, everything belonging to earthly government rests on the Divine ordinance.[14] *Both Kingdoms have their basis in God's will.* Only the task and aims are different and this is why they must be kept distinct. The aim of Christ's spiritual Kingdom is to order men's relationship to God for eternal life, the aim of the earthly Kingdom is to order human relationships in this life so that 'un-Christian and wicked people' may not carry out their evil plans unchecked but must 'keep the peace outwardly'.[15] As we saw, this does not prevent Christians to whom God has entrusted the one task from accepting the other also, nor vice versa, so long as this is done only with the intention to serve.

The belief in *the autonomy of State and economics*, i.e. of the total life of society, ought in fact never to have arisen.[16] The less so, since it was clearly stated in reference to the worldly Kingdom, that the Christian 'should in such duties practice Christian love and genuine good works each according to his calling'.[17] There can therefore be no question of an unconditional duty to obey the earthly government. It is the duty of Christians 'to obey their own magistrates and laws, save only when commanded to sin, for then they ought to obey God rather than men'.[18] But this hint, which emphasises a responsible Christian co-operation in the life of society in accordance with the commandment

[14] W.A., VOL. XI, p. 251; Augsburg Confession, XVI (Schaff, III.16f; *Concordia*, p. 14; Kidd, *Documents*, p. 266). [15] W.A., VOL. XI, p. 250f.

[16] Luther's 'doctrine of the three estates' has been blamed for this. In fact, Luther does not speak only of spiritual and earthly government. Alongside *politia* and *oeconomia*, the two areas in which earthly government is exercised, he sets a third, that of the organised Church. The existence of these three spheres side by side easily led to the view that each of them, including the State, was autonomous, even where people were ready to regard them as resting upon the divine will.

[17] Augsburg Confession, XVI (Schaff, III.16; *Concordia*, p. 14; Kidd, *Documents*, p. 266).

[18] *Ibid.* Cf. W. A. Schulze, 'Reformation und Widerstandsrecht', in *Evangelische Theologie*, VIII, pp. 372ff.

to love, was not followed out. When in opposition to a mistaken monastic ethic, Luther insisted that every service in a worldly calling is a service of God, he gave fresh impulse to the false idea of an autonomous ethics of vocation. In conflict with Roman Catholic moral teaching, moreover, great emphasis was laid on the fact that civil works of righteousness are not meritorious in God's sight. Hence a modern Lutheran writer on ethics rightly says on the question of the autonomy of the world: 'The Gospel has not completed its task if it concerns itself solely with the sinner's justification or with religious attitudes and relegates to eschatology the biblical demand for sanctification. No! The Christian faith must influence human life in every aspect.'[19] One Lutheran who realised something of this truth, and therefore struggled against the Church's retreat from the world into a false spirituality, was Christoph Blumhardt (*d.* 1919). The biblical truth surely shines forth once more when this Suabian theologian says: 'Christianity is not a religion like any other religion, aiming above all things to make us happy. Christ came rather to establish God's Kingdom here on this earth, so that God's Will should be done on earth, then, of course, that we too should be happy.'[20] 'We have simply become accustomed to thinking of God as up there in the sky. We do not realise that God must mean something in all our concerns, and so we dismiss the thought. But God is in fact waiting for us to begin, waiting for us to prepare the way for Him. . . . These volunteers of God must be everything they are from Him. They must be merchants, farmers, husbands, wives, and children, of the kind He wants, then they will be blessed. . . . God does not yet rule among us men. . . . Other causes rule among us and we expect the dear God to bless them. But it is God who must rule, and other causes must take second place. The whole of our life must be employed with one end in view: to put God and His glory before all else.'[21] Christoph Blumhardt had learned both from the work done by his father Johann Christoph Blumhardt (*d.* 1880)—who summed up his experience in the truth: 'Jesus is Victor'—and from the miraculous power God had also given to him too, that through

[19] N. H. Söe, *Christliche Ethik*, 2nd edn. Munich 1957, p. 163.
[20] *Vom Reiche Gottes*, 3rd edn. Berlin 1925, p. 33. [21] *Op. cit.*, p. 36.

Jesus Christ, God wills to rule everything here on earth now and to bring His saving rule to completion in spite of all opposition. He knew that under Christ's rule, we not merely receive comfort but are claimed in every area of our life.

2. The Same Doctrine, Developed Further by the Reformed Churches

It will come as a surprise to many to read Calvin's words on this subject: 'Let us first consider that there is a twofold government in man: one aspect is spiritual, whereby the conscience is instructed in piety and in reverencing God; the second is political, whereby man is educated for the duties of humanity and citizenship that must be maintained among men. . . . These two, as we have divided them, must always be examined separately; and while one is being considered, we must call away and turn aside the mind from thinking about the other. There are in man, so to speak, two worlds, over which different kings and different laws have authority.'[22] These words, which first appeared in the 1536 *Institutio* but remained unaltered through all the later editions including the final one, show clearly how faithful a student of Luther Calvin was. But if that were the whole story further enquiry into the Reformed teaching on this point would be unnecessary. In complete agreement with Luther, Calvin regards the Word of God as the 'royal sceptre' of the Divine Kingdom,[23] and therefore defines the nature of the Kingdom as the forgiveness of sins.[24] But later he added: 'God reigns where men, both by denial of themselves and by contempt of the world and of earthly life, pledge themselves to his righteousness in order to aspire to a heavenly life. Thus there are two parts to this kingdom: first, that God by the power of his Spirit correct all the desires of the flesh which by squadrons war against him; second, that he shape all our thoughts in *obedience* to his rule.'[25] This addition by Calvin to the ideas he adopted from Luther's doctrine is not

[22] *Inst.*, III.19.15; cf. IV.20.1 (VOL. I, p. 847; VOL. II, pp. 1485f). That is liable to be misunderstood. Calvin later described the relationship between the two kingdoms differently (see below, p. 298). His meaning here can only be that Christ, by His Word of grace, governs His own directly, whereas He exercises earthly government indirectly, by the agency of the earthly rulers.

[23] *Inst.*, III.20.42; cf. I.6.3 (VOL. II, p. 905; VOL. I, p. 73).

[24] *Inst.*, III.3.19 (VOL. I, pp. 613f).

[25] *Inst.*, III.20.42 (VOL. II, pp. 905f).

surprising. We have seen that Calvin knows of no declaration of forgiveness which is not inseparably bound up with the divine claim to the whole of our life. When speaking of God's Kingdom he strongly emphasises that God wills to *govern* those whom He pardons by His Word. The Word and Spirit of Christ the eternal King are shown to be at work because by them 'He governs us . . . and defends and maintains us in the redemption obtained for us'.[26] According to the Geneva Catechism the Kingdom of God means 'that He leads His own and governs them by His Spirit, and on the other hand, casts down and confounds the reprobate who refuse to subject themselves to His rule, and so makes it clear that there is no power which can resist His power.'[27]

God's sovereignty also means, therefore, God's engagement in human history. The Geneva Catechism calls for intercession that God 'may cause His truth to shine more and more, and manifest His justice so that Satan and the powers of darkness may be put to confusion and all iniquity be destroyed and abolished', and, it adds, 'we pray that it [God's Kingdom] may continually increase and advance until at last it comes to its perfection in the day of judgment'.[28] This movement also dominates the exposition of the second petition of the Lord's Prayer in the Heidelberg Catechism.[29] When we hear words like this we cannot but think of Blumhardt. The Kingdom of God does not consist only of spirituality. It embraces men both soul and body, and all their concerns, as pardoned sinners who are called as members of Christ to thankful *service*: and God's Kingdom is constantly invading our time here on earth. Therefore Christians must live with a *responsibility* for God's Kingdom.[30] According to Calvin their business is to act in such a way that Christ's Kingdom may find unlimited expression, not only in the ministry of the Word but also in claiming public life.[31] We should be attacking Christ's throne, he says, if we did not first recognise that the Lord rules His Church by His Word, and secondly did not do all in our power to see to it that

[26] Heidelberg Catechism, Q. 31 (Torrance, *School of Faith*, p. 74).
[27] Geneva Catechism, Q. 268 (Torrance, *School of Faith*, p. 47).
[28] *Op. cit.*, Q. 269f. [29] Heidelberg Catechism, Q. 123.
[30] 'Nobis praecipi studium quotidiani progressus.' Calvin, *Inst.*, III.20.42 (VOL. II, p. 905). [31] *Opera*, VOL. XXVII, p. 466 (Sermons on Deut. 10-21).

the positions of earthly authority ordained by God for the welfare of mankind are occupied by God-fearing men.[32] Even when they are not, neutrality is ruled out. Either we are concerned that God should be honoured in public life, or we are helping 'to have Him excluded from our midst'.[33] This certainly does not mean that a pagan government has no genuine authority,[34] but it does mean that we must do all in our power to obtain good politicians, judges, and officials. Because those who occupy places of authority are God's ministers and officers,[35] obedience is due to them, but not unconditionally. The limits to obedience indicated here are the same as in the Augsburg Confession.[36] But, according to Calvin, only those who occupy official places of government are competent to take measures against a government which is abusing its power.[37] Calvin was anxious that no injury be done to civil authority as such, and therefore to the authority behind it of Him who has instituted all earthly authority. 'We must esteem highly all earthly governments because they are an image of the Kingdom of our Lord Jesus Christ.'[38]

In the person of Jesus Christ the eternal King, the spiritual Kingdom and the earthly Kingdom are ultimately joined together. Reformed theology says this more clearly than the Lutheran. By His Son God rules His Church, but to His sceptre He has also subjected the nations.[39] The purpose of Christ's Ascension was 'that He might show Himself there as Head of His Christian Church, through whom the Father governs all things'.[40] The two Kingdoms are 'inseparably joined' but must not be 'confused'.[41]

Therefore Christians—ministers not excluded[42] have a joint responsibility for worldly government, as we have seen, and *holders of government office have a responsibility to God.* In their

[32] *Op. cit.*, p. 467. [33] *Ibid.*
[34] *Opera*, VOL. LIV, p. 557 (Sermons on 2 Tim. and Titus).
[35] *Inst.*, Preface (VOL. I, p. 12).
[36] Augsburg Confession, XVI (Schaff, III.16; *Concordia*, p. 14; Kidd, *Documents*, p. 266).
[37] 'Pro officio intercedere' (Fr. 'de s'opposer et resister'). *Inst.*, IV.20.31 (VOL. II, pp. 1518f). [38] *Opera*, VOL. LIII, p. 132 (Sermons on I Tim.).
[39] *Inst.*, II.15.5 (VOL. I, pp. 500f).
[40] Heidelberg Catechism, Q. 50 (Torrance, *School of Faith*, p. 77).
[41] Geneva Church Order, 1561 (Niesel, *Bekenntnisschriften und Kirchenordnungen*, p. 63). [42] *Opera*, VOL. XLIII, p. 79 (Comment on Amos 5.10).

position they have to keep God's law which is the eternal rule of righteousness for all nations,[43] and must acknowledge 'that they are to appear before the Lord Jesus Christ to give account of their official actions'.[44] Therefore 'they ought to realise that they must continually be occupied with God's Word and need the help of the Holy Spirit, so as to rule the nations with all the greater moderation, give honour to God and obey His Laws . . . and to pray God's help for all this'.[45] They have a twofold reason for doing so: 'their office exceeds their own strength, and so they will never achieve success unless God gives them His Holy Spirit'.[46] Because the earthly authority receives its office from the Lord, whose primary concern is to extend His spiritual Kingdom over men, it also has a *joint responsibility* for this. God tells us this in the first table of His Law. This means that the earthly authority has a duty to uphold the preaching of the Gospel, and to support the Church which has been entrusted with this preaching.[47] If it does not do so it will have to take the consequences: for 'he is deceived who looks for lasting prosperity in his kingdom when it is not ruled by God's sceptre, that is, his Holy Word; for the heavenly oracle that proclaims that "where prophecy fails the people are scattered" (Prov. 29.18) cannot lie.'[48] Such action does not trespass on Christ's spiritual Kingdom. So long as rulers keep within their limits they can do much for the spiritual Kingdom of Him who is also their Lord. The Lord Himself of course performs the all-important thing 'through the spiritual sword of His Word, when this is preached by the ministers'.[49]

The relationship between the State and the Church which has to summon men to the spiritual Kingdom has been excellently stated recently by the Synod of the Reformed Church in the Netherlands: 'State and Church both serve God's plan, but not in the same way. The Church preaches God's salvation.

[43] *Inst.*, IV.20.15 (VOL. II, p. 1503).
[44] *Opera*, VOL. LIII, p. 139 (Sermons on 1 Tim.)
[45] *Opera*, VOL. XXIX, p. 553 (Sermons on Deut. 32-34).
[46] *Opera*, VOL. XXVII, p. 468 (Sermons on Deut. 10-21).
[47] *Inst.*, IV.20.3 and 5 (VOL. II, pp. 1488, 1490); *Opera*, VOL. XXXVII, p. 211 (Comment on Isa. 49.23); Scots Confession, XXIV; Belgic Confession, XXXVI; Westminster Confession, XXIII, 3 (Schaff, III 474f, 432f, 653f).
[48] *Inst.*, Preface (VOL. I, p. 12).
[49] Calvin to Lord Somerset, *Opera*, VOL. XIII, p. 72.

The State orders man's outward life in the direction of this salvation. To do this it pays attention to the Church's proclamation, but acts with its own direct responsibility to God. The same revelation of God is the light on the Church's pathway as it is on that of the State but of course in such a way that their jurisdictions remain distinct, and the Church does not dominate the State nor the State the Church.'[50]

Those final words could have been uttered by Luther. But could the Lutherans not accept this in its entirety, and the co-ordination and differentiation of the two modes of God's rule as stated here? At any rate Lutherans and Reformed declared together at the Barmen Confessional Synod that God's Kingdom also rules over the State, that both governors and governed have a responsibility within it, and that the Church has a task to perform in relation to it. 'It holds up before the world God's Kingdom, God's commandment and righteousness, and so the responsibility of rulers and ruled alike.'[51] How could it be otherwise since it is the people of the King of Kings?

From our discussion of the different questions at issue between Lutherans and Reformed, it will have become clear that it is impossible to sum up the main difference here in a single formula. Both are agreed on the basic Reformation doctrines. This unity becomes evident at many points, even in the doctrine of the Lord's Supper. In the Barmen Theological Declaration both Lutherans and Reformed confessed the message of the Reformation. The differences which remain should be approached on the basis of the Word which God at that time 'put into the mouth' of representatives of both confessions, and be tested by reference to that Word.[52] Perhaps these differences cannot be completely overcome, perhaps it will still be the case that we have further serious questions to put to each other: but, after all that we have learned in each other's company, the brotherly union cannot again be broken wherever it is a matter of Christ, of the Holy Scriptures as the witness to Him, and of His presence by His Word in the strength of the Holy Spirit in faith.

[50] *Lebendiges Bekenntnis*, Ref. Kirche No. 1, Neukirchen 1951.
[51] Barmen Thesis No. 5.
[52] Cf. too, the Theses on Baptism drawn up by a joint Commission of Lutheran and Reformed theologians from Europe, Faith and Order Publications No. 27, Geneva 1959, pp. 42f.

PART B. ANGLO-SAXON CHURCHES OF THE REFORMATION

OUR detailed review of the doctrinal difference between the Lutheran and Reformed Churches should not blind us to the existence of other large and important Churches which emerged in the context of the Reformation. The Ecumenical Movement has brought us on the Continent nearer to them and has to some extent helped to correct the mistaken approach to them which has traditionally been ours.

The difference which arose in the sixteenth century about the doctrine of the Lord's Supper is by no means the only one which conditions the relationships between different Churches throughout the world today. What creates difficulties for us here on the Continent plays only a very small part in Churches where this particular dispute was not settled in the way it was in Germany and neighbouring countries. The problem of intercommunion does, of course, arise in the Ecumenical Movement and a very difficult problem it is, but the difficulties there are quite different from those over which Christians in Central Europe rack their brains. Above all, there are other serious problems and barriers of quite a different kind which tower up between the Churches. And quite different answers are offered to us which promise real help. We shall want to hear at least the most important of these.

CHAPTER 12

THE ANGLICAN CHURCH

FIRST to claim our attention is the Anglican Church (the Reformed Church of England as by Law established). This is not simply the established Church of England. On the contrary, we meet here a world-wide communion of Churches of similar character. All the Churches included in it, the Church of Ireland, the Church in Wales, the Episcopal Church in Scotland, the Protestant Episcopal Church in the U.S.A., the Anglican Church in Japan, the Anglican Church in China, and the Anglican Churches in those countries overseas which were once or still are closely bound to Great Britain, regard the Established Church of England as their Mother Church. So far as organisation is concerned these Churches are only loosely connected together by a meeting of their bishops every ten years at the Lambeth Conference, so named after the Palace of Lambeth in London where the meetings are held. This conference of bishops is a voluntary assembly under the presidency of the Archbishop of Canterbury and has no legislative authority. It must not therefore be mistaken for a synod. It is not even the equivalent of the general assemblies of the other world-wide communions at which Churches are represented by appointed delegates and not simply by leading ministers without special authorisation. The findings of these Lambeth Conferences are nevertheless of very great importance for the constituent Churches.

1. The Doctrinal Basis

It is not easy to describe the particular character of this Church's message. The Anglican Church has, of course, a confession of Faith, the Thirty-Nine Articles, which were adopted in 1563, and represent a revision of the Forty-Two Articles drawn up by Archbishop Cranmer in 1552; but these

Articles do not have the significance which a confessional document has in the Lutheran Church.[1] We must remember 'that the Articles themselves constantly appeal to *Scripture* as the pre-eminent guide in matters of faith'.[2] In regarding a confessional document as a pointer to Holy Scripture the Anglican Church closely approximates to the Reformed Churches.[3] The question asked at ordinations is significant: 'Are you persuaded that the Holy Scriptures contain sufficiently all doctrine required of necessity for eternal salvation through faith in Jesus Christ? And are you determined out of the said Scriptures to instruct the people committed to your charge, and to teach nothing (as required of necessity to eternal salvation) but that which you shall be persuaded may be concluded and proved by the Scripture?'[4] In view of the supreme importance of ordination vows in the life of the Church's ministry, the following statement of the Anglican position on the question of the relation between Scripture and Tradition, must be accepted as accurate: 'The view of the Anglican Church is clear. Scripture is the final court of appeal in matters of faith. . . . The Church finds her sphere of authority only in interpreting and teaching the faith contained in Scripture.'[5] Those theologians are therefore correct when they say there, rather anxiously, that the rejection of the 'Supremacy of Scripture' over all tradition

[1] Lutheran influence can be traced in the contents. Cranmer made use of the Thirteen Articles agreed on in 1538 by English and German Lutheran divines, and largely based on the Augsburg Confession. The Thirty-Nine Articles were also influenced by the Württemberg Confession of 1551, composed by Johann Brenz. See Schaff, I.612f, 627ff.

[2] G. K. A. Bell, *A Brief Sketch of the Church of England*, London 1929, henceforth cited as *Brief Sketch*, p. 76. Art XX: 'Ecclesiae non licet quicquam instituere, quod verbo Dei scripto adversetur.' The Church is 'divinorum librorum testis et conservatrix, attamen ut . . . praeter illos nihil credendum de necessitate salutis debet obtrudere' (cf. Schaff, III.500).

[3] The Eucharistic doctrine in Arts. XXVIII and XXIX is also Reformed in emphasis. Significant, too, is the fact that Art. XXIX, which rejects the Lutheran *manducatio oralis*, was struck out by Queen Elizabeth, but reinstated shortly afterwards. Anglican divines also attended the Synod of Dort (1618-19), an indication of how closely the Anglican Church in those days felt itself to be linked with the other Churches which had been reformed in the sixteenth century. See Schaff, I.512f.

[4] *Book of Common Prayer*, Form and Manner of the Ordering of Priests, Q. 2 (*Corpus Confessionum*, ed. C. Fabricius, Berlin 1931ff, PT XVII, p. 331). Cf. Art. VI.

[5] Bishop Gore, as quoted in *The Fulness of Christ*, London 1950, p. 88. The Lambeth Appeal, 1920, described as the first essential for a united Church: 'The Holy Scriptures, as the record of God's revelation of Himself to man, and as being the rule and ultimate standard of faith' (G. K. A. Bell, *Documents bearing on the Problem of Christian Unity*, 1st Series, London 1924, p. 3).

would split the Anglican Church.[6] By its submission to the message of salvation contained in the Bible, this Church shows that its rightful place is among the Churches who in the sixteenth century allowed themselves to be reformed on the basis of Scripture and led back to obedience to the Gospel—the authentic apostolic tradition.

2. Prayer Book and Sacraments

To an unusual extent, the Anglican Church is a praying Church. Every member has in his hands the Book of Common Prayer, composed in 1549 and adopted in its present form in England in 1662, containing the orders of service for daily morning and evening prayer, and for all other Church rites and ceremonies, together with a lectionary providing for a systematic reading of the whole Bible through during the year. Printed with it, is the entire Psalter for regular reading, as well as the Thirty-Nine Articles. The 1920 Lambeth Conference described the Prayer Book as 'the Anglican standard of doctrine and practice'.[7] The Thirty-Nine Articles can only be understood therefore in the setting of the Prayer Book. Shortly after the composition of the Prayer Book, many Roman customs such as the rules governing oral confession, exorcism, and the sign of the cross were, on the advice of Calvin and other Reformed theologians, expunged from it, though the last-mentioned was reintroduced in 1604 as a ceremony to be used immediately after baptism. It was stated in a rubric that kneeling at the reception of communion did not imply adoration 'for that were idolatry to be abhorred by all true Christians'.[8]

It therefore follows that in Anglican worship 'there is officially no altar, but only a table, which must not be embellished with any sort of picture, crucifix or candles'.[9] But, in fact, the situation in many churches is very different, because of the Tractarian movement. There we find 'much colour, much music, much beauty of all kinds, with a crucifix and lights on the altar, the rood over the chancel, pictures of saints in the windows or on the walls, vestments, an elaborate ceremonial, a

[6] *The Fulness of Christ*, p. 87. [7] Bell, *Brief Sketch*, p. 65.

[8] *Book of Common Prayer*, Order of the Administration of the Lord's Supper or Holy Communion, concluding rubric (*Corpus Confessionum*, ed. Fabricius, PT XVII, p. 194). [9] E. F. K. Müller, *Symbolik*, p. 430.

choral Eucharist, daily celebrations, and with emphasis on sacramental teaching'.[10]

Meanwhile, a further notable step has been taken. In 1906 a revision of the Prayer Book was initiated, the final result of which was, however, rejected by the British Parliament in 1927 and 1928. The underlying reason for the rejection was the fact that the Revised Book permitted the elements not consumed at the Communion Service to be reserved in a special place in the church for distribution to sick members on the days following.[11] But in 1929 the Convocations of Canterbury and York—periodical assemblies of bishops and other ministers, divided into Upper and Lower Houses—contrary to the decision of Parliament, authorised the bishops to follow the altered Prayer Book of 1928 at their discretion.[12] Since then the reservation of the consecrated eucharistic elements has been permitted. This regulation applies of course only to the Church of England and not to the other Anglican Churches. The exposition and adoration of the consecrated bread remains prohibited in England as before.

It must be noted that in all the Anglican Churches the Lord's Supper is regarded as an eating and drinking of the body and blood of Jesus Christ.[13] But what is meant is that Christ is to be spiritual food for the communicant.[14] Only believers receive Him therefore.[15] Article XXIX specifically denies that the wicked partake of Him (*manducatio impiorum*). The formula used in administering the sacrament (and retained in the 1928 Prayer Book) accordingly reads: 'The body of our Lord Jesus Christ which was given for thee, preserve thy body and soul unto everlasting life. Take and eat this in remembrance that Christ died for thee, and feed on Him *in thy heart by faith* with thanksgiving.'[16] These words express a view of the Lord's Supper closely related to that of the Reformed Churches.

[10] Bell, *Brief Sketch*, p. 68.

[11] *Book of Common Prayer with the Additions and Deviations proposed in 1928*, Alternative Order of Holy Communion, rubric after the Blessing; Alternative Order for the Communion of the Sick, rubric 1 and 3 (*Corpus Confessionum*, ed. Fabricius, PT XVII, pp. 287f, 207).

[12] Bell, *Brief Sketch*, p. 64.

[13] *Book of Common Prayer*, Communion Service, Prayer of Humble Access; Catechism (*Corpus Confessionum*, ed. Fabricius, 17, pp. 188, 249).

[14] Communion Service, Exhortation 1 (*op. cit.*, p. 180).

[15] Catechism (*op. cit.*, p. 249).

[16] Communion Service, at the delivery of the bread (*op. cit.*, p. 190).

But it is not easy to reconcile with this, the fact that at the end of the prayer of consecration, while uttering the appropriate words of institution, the priest must lay his hand upon the bread he has broken and then on the cup,[17] and according to the 1928 Book, must even say in this prayer of consecration: 'With Thy Holy and Life-giving Spirit vouchsafe to bless and sanctify both us and these Thy gifts of Bread and Wine, that they may be unto us the Body and Blood of Thy Son, our Saviour Jesus Christ.'[18] Taken in conjunction with the permission to reserve the consecrated elements for the communion of the sick, this can surely only mean that it has now become permissible in the Church of England to believe that during the Supper a change takes place in the elements. Of course, the 1928 Book still retains the old formula alongside the new, when it says, in the note appended to the alternative order of the Communion to which reference was made above, 'the natural Body and Blood of our Saviour Christ are in Heaven and not here, it being against the truth of Christ's natural Body to be at one time in more places than one'.[19] Thoroughly evangelical are the directives that now as before, there are to be no private masses, that the priest may only celebrate the Lord's Supper if in his judgment 'there be a convenient number to communicate with the priest',[20] and, above all, that he must offer the communicants the cup as well as the bread.[21]

The original view of *Baptism*, still in force in the Anglican Church today, is the same as that of the Reformed Churches. Baptism is not simply a declaration of faith, but a sign of regeneration and incorporation into Christ's body. It is of course a departure from the Reformed view when the priest after the baptism declares: 'This child is regenerate,' and the difference is magnified when the new 1928 order of baptism is used. This puts a surprising emphasis on the significance of the baptismal water, by requiring the prayer: 'Sanctify this water to the mystical washing away of sin,'[22] and so encouraging the

[17] Communion Service, Prayer of Consecration, rubric (*op. cit.*, p. 189).

[18] 1928 Alternative Communion Service (*op. cit.*, p. 204).

[19] 1662 Communion Service, final rubric (*op. cit.*, p. 194). Cf. the same view in the Reformed Churches (above, p. 273).

[20] Communion Service, rubric (*op. cit.*, p. 192).

[21] Art. XXX.

[22] Baptism Service (*Corpus Confessionum*, ed. Fabricius, PT XVII, p. 224).

view that the baptismal water does not have to fulfil its function by serving as a sign and seal in virtue of the words of institution together with the words of promise, but receives its efficacy as such through a prayer of consecration. But would not such a view conflict with the earlier traditions of the Anglican Church? Would it not moreover violate the freedom of the Gospel to which the apostolic tradition bears witness? The practice, resumed in the baptismal service on the basis of the 1604 Canons, whereby the priest immediately after baptism makes the sign of the cross on the child's head, is a ceremony without any efficacy and 'is no part of the substance of that Sacrament'.[23]

Important too, is the fact that, to the question *how many sacraments* Christ instituted, the Anglican Church gives the clear answer: '*Two only*.'[24] Other rites, such as Confirmation, to which great importance is attached, and which, 'as a pastoral link between the Bishop and the lay members of his flock',[25] is reserved to the Bishop 'or some other minister appointed by him',[26] and the ordination of priests, are not sacraments.

3. The Church and the Apostolic Ministry

We must now say something about the remarkable fact which we have already come up against several times; in the Anglican Church, different views exist side by side on fundamental questions of the Church's faith and order, each appealing to the Church's official documents. This has been described as the 'dialectical character' of the Anglican Church. It belongs, it is said, to its very nature to be able to contain within itself an Anglo-Catholic party and an Evangelical party and recently indeed even a third, a Modernist party, strongly influenced by modern science. It would be pointless to try to distill from

[23] Canons of 1604, can. 30. This continues: 'It is apparent in the Communion Book, that the infant baptised is, by virtue of baptism, before it is signed with the sign of the cross, received into the congregation of Christ's flock, as a perfect member thereof, and not by any power as ascribed unto the sign of the cross' (*Constitutions and Canons Ecclesiastical, 1604*, ed. J. V. Bullard, London 1934, p. 32; *Corpus Confessionum*, ed. Fabricius, PT XVII, p. 485).

[24] *Book of Common Prayer*, Catechism (*Corpus Confessionum*, ed. Fabricius, PT XVII, p. 248).

[25] Joint Report, *Relations between Anglican and Presbyterian Churches*, London 1957, p. 16.

[26] *Book of Common Prayer*, Order of Confirmation, rubric.

these an agreed 'Anglican' doctrine.[27] But this view is not unchallenged.

The co-existence mentioned is a relatively modern phenomenon and the tensions to which it gives rise cannot be underestimated. It is not just a question of 'two sides of the shield which are complementary to each other', but, at certain points, of contradictions which can only be endured in the hope that they will be overcome in the common search for truth.[28] There must, of course, in fact be some common views, in spite of all the differences, otherwise co-existence would be quite impossible. We shall now draw attention to these important common elements in the Anglican view of the Church and her work.[29]

It is repeatedly stated by Anglicans that in the sixteenth century in England no new Church was founded, but the existing Church of England was purified of papal corruptions. There is therefore a *continuity* between the Church of today and the pre-Reformation Church. The emergence of other Churches in England later, may have given rise to the idea that this continuity is to be regarded as a characteristic peculiar to the Anglican Church. But this is not the case. Both Luther, and above all Calvin, believed that by the Reformation the Church had been restored to its original character, and that this Church, not the Church of Rome, was the Catholic Church. The title 'reformed Church' which was used from the beginning even in circles mainly influenced by Luther, shows clearly that there was no intention of founding a new Church.[30] It is significant however, that the Anglican Church should stress the Church's continuity.

A second point arises in connexion with this The Augustinian distinction between the visible and the invisible Church, to which Luther had recourse, is never mentioned in the Anglican documents and therefore plays no great part in Anglican

[27] 'By paring away what is distinctive of each and concentrating on what is common to both.' L. Hodgson in *The Nature of the Church*, ed. R. N. Flew, p. 138.

[28] *The Fulness of Christ*, pp. 55f.

[29] No Anglican theologian, not even Hodgson, can go beyond these common elements if he wishes to say anything at all. It is a case of: 'Anglicans generally would accept . . . ,' or, 'the vast majority of Anglicans . . . ' or some such phrase.

[30] Formula of Concord, Thor. Decl., Comprehensive Summary (*Concordia*, p. 234, col. 2, 3).

theology. We recall the fact that the same is true even of Calvin. In agreement with the Reformation view of the extant Church as the mother of all believers, evangelically-minded Anglicans do not separate the visible Church and the invisible but affirm their unity,[31] while the Anglo-Catholics never develop any doctrine of the Church without acknowledging that there is much chaff among the wheat.[32] Both concern themselves with the Church present here on earth, and its work.

The Church is regarded as the *body of Christ*.[33] 'It is a Society founded and constituted by an invisible Head in whom resides all its vitality. . . . Christ is its life, its hope, the secret of that revival and restoration of which, because of the fallibility of its human element, it stands in permanent need.'[34] Such statements show that Anglicanism takes seriously the description of the Church as the body of Christ. Rome too uses this analogy, but does not see that the Church receives its character as Christ's body from its Head and constantly needs His awakening and renewal.

How faithfully Anglicanism keeps to the New Testament in its understanding of the Church, and rejects all liturgical isolation and self-preoccupation, is shown by its clear emphasis on the missionary *task of the Church*: 'Its mission is to proclaim to men God's saving purpose and the good news of forgiveness ready and waiting through the passion, death and resurrection of Jesus Christ, to call them to faith and repentance, to baptise them into the fellowship, to enlist them in His service and to keep them united to their Lord in the Spirit.'[35]

So important is this task that Jesus Christ did not simply leave it to each Christian, He appointed special ministers for it. For the fulfilment of the Church's mission in the world He founded '*the Apostolic ministry*'. This is continued by a special

[31] *The Nature of the Church*, ed. Flew, p. 134n.

[32] The difference between the two groups lies rather in the fact that Anglo-Catholics recognise only their own Church with its distinctive order, and other Churches possessing the same order, as the true Church (*ibid.*).

[33] T. F. Torrance has pointed out to me that Calvinist influence can be shown here.

[34] John A. F. Gregg in *The Universal Church in God's Design*, Amsterdam Assembly Series, VOL. I, p. 58. Cf. Hodgson, in *The Nature of the Church*, ed. Flew, p. 145: The Church 'must therefore continually turn in penitence to its Lord, that it may be cleansed from its blemishes. . . '.

[35] L. Hodgson, in *The Nature of the Church*, ed. Flew, p. 145.

commissioning, ordination, with the laying on of hands and the words: 'Take thou authority to preach the Word of God and to minister the holy Sacraments.'[36] This is quite similar to the appointment of men to the ministry of the Word and Sacraments in the Lutheran and Reformed Churches by ordination. During the service the ordinand receives a Bible and not the chalice and paten as oblates in the Roman Church do.

What then is the specifically Anglican view of the apostolic ministry? We are told that the office given by Christ to the Apostles was not a unique one limited to the Apostles, nor did it consist simply of the commission to preach the Gospel. It was rather the institution by Christ of a distinct official order of ministry: 'It was a ministry perpetuated through those whom the Apostles appointed to be their colleagues and successors, and it developed into the graded hierarchy of bishops, priests and deacons.'[37] In the strict sense the continuing ministry of the apostolate '*has been exercised throughout the history of Christendom* by means of the traditional *office of Bishop*',[38] for at their ordination bishops receive authority to ordain deacons and priests. The ministry of these latter is therefore derived from that of the bishops.

But it must also be noted that those ordained to the priesthood do not become priests in the strict sense. They do not receive the authority to offer to God the body and blood of Christ. The authority they receive is 'to preach the Word of God and to administer the holy Sacraments'. Nor do they receive from the bishops any kind of judicial authority over the faithful. Both bishops and priests answer the congregation's confession of sin by *declaring* forgiveness to it: 'Almighty God, our heavenly Father, who of His great mercy hath promised forgiveness of sins to all them that with hearty repentance and true faith turn to Him: Have mercy upon you: pardon and

[36] *Book of Common Prayer*, Ordering of Priests, at the delivery of the Bible to the ordinand (*Corpus Confessionum*, ed. Fabricius, PT XVII, p. 335).

[37] L. Hodgson, in *The Nature of the Church*, ed. Flew, p. 141. Above these, in the Church of England, are the two Archbishops, of Canterbury and of York. The former has the right, once reserved to the Pope, to grant certain dispensations in both provinces. He is moreover the chairman of the Lambeth Conferences which are held every ten years and attended by Anglican bishops from all parts of the world.

[38] Philip Usher, 'Anglikanische Theologie der Gegenwart', in *Ekklesia*, VOL. I, Gotha 1934, p. 111.

deliver you from all your sins. . . .'[39] Private confession is not obligatory. The hierarchical order should not therefore blind us to the evangelical character of the Anglican Church. The meaning of the office is wholly evangelical, and that is the important thing, for it is the priesthood exalted above the laity and the judicial function of bishops which makes the Roman Church what it is.

The Anglican Church has no explicit and binding doctrine of *episcopacy*. In the Preface to the ordination services it simply refers to the existence of the threefold ministry from apostolic times: 'It is evident unto all men diligently reading holy Scripture and ancient Authors, that from the Apostles' time there have been these Orders of Ministers in Christ's Church: Bishops, Priests, and Deacons.'[40] If, however, we add to this the words spoken at the consecration of a bishop: 'Receive the Holy Ghost for the office and work of a Bishop in the Church of God, now committed unto thee by the imposition of our hands,'[41] then we are bound to say that underlying all this there is the idea of apostolic succession in the episcopal office. There are, it is true, some Anglicans who protest against any stress being placed on such a continuity of office.[42] But even the Evangelicals in the Church of England hold 'firmly that episcopacy is the normal method for the transmission of ministerial authority'.[43] 'We can and must say that episcopacy and episcopal succession is the way in which the Church learnt under the Spirit's guidance to express and preserve the principle of a ministry which is one throughout the ages and one throughout all areas of the Church.'[44] On the other hand Anglo-Catholics hold 'episcopacy to be of the *esse* of the Church',[45] and do not regard as valid the ministries in Churches which

[39] *Book of Common Prayer*, Communion Service, Absolution after the General Confession (*Corpus Confessionum*, ed. Fabricius, PT XVII, p. 186).

[40] Ordination Service, Preface (*Corpus Confessionum*, ed. Fabricius, PT XVII, p. 321). It is also known as 'the historic episcopate', since the episcopal office has existed throughout the centuries from very early times.

[41] Form of Ordaining or Consecrating of an Archbishop or Bishop (*Corpus Confessionum*, ed. Fabricius, PT XVII, p. 342).

[42] Cf. the view quoted by L. Hodgson, *The Nature of the Church*, ed. Flew, p. 141n: 'Continuity must surely be primarily a matter of witness to the true faith and the Spirit's guidance and enabling.'

[43] Lambeth Conference, *Report*, 1948, PT II, p. 50.

[44] *The Fulness of Christ*, p. 66.

[45] Lambeth Conference, *Report*, 1948, PT II, p. 50.

lack the apostolic succession. Nevertheless we are assured that today there is 'no authoritative Anglican theologian who would categorically deny the spiritual efficacy of non-episcopal ministries'.[46] That is as much as we can gather about the episcopal office with apostolic succession. It is good to note that the basic concern here is not for a particular form of Church government but 'to secure to men the spiritual blessings entrusted to it [the Church] by its Lord, such blessings as the preaching of the Gospel which kindles faith, baptism ... absolution from post-baptismal sin, and communion'.[47]

We saw that Anglicanism wishes to take quite seriously the fact that as Christ's body the Church lives from its Head. On that assumption two questions must be put to the Anglicans concerning the doctrine of apostolic succession in the episcopal office. Ought not the Anglican Church to pay more attention to the hint which becomes audible within it that the Church's true continuity can only be given in the Word it proclaims, that is, in the *Head* who continually proclaims Himself anew? Ought not the Anglican Church to remember too that it is of the essence of the Church as the body of Christ, that Christ, the Head of the Church, distributes among the members of the Church different gifts for mutual service, and thus makes the Church a community of brothers, in which none is superior to the others, but only He the invisible Head stands above them all? It is plainly dangerous to extol the episcopal office of apostolic succession as a symbol of Church unity, in the way the Anglican Church does, for surely Rome can offer a much more impressive symbol of such unity?[48]

4. Concern for a United Church

Whatever criticisms may be levelled at the Anglican Church, in one respect it is ahead of many others, namely in its resolute will to unite the divided Churches. Many decisive impulses towards ecumenical action have come from the Anglican

[46] Philip Usher in *Ekklesia*, VOL. I, p. 111.

[47] L. Hodgson, in *The Nature of the Church*, ed. Flew, pp. 143f.

[48] See above, pp. 43, 45f. During the German Church Conflict we found by experience that an episcopal office became the point of entry for heresy and therefore a factor making for the disintegration of the Church. See on this K. Barth, *Theologische Existenz heute*, Munich 1933 (Eng. trans. by R. Birch Hoyle, London 1933).

Church, and its bishops have taken and continue to take a leading part in the movement which has resulted. As long ago as October 1910, a joint Committee of the General Convention of the Protestant Episcopal Church, held in Cincinnati, Ohio, U.S.A., presented a report proposing that all Christian communions throughout the world should come together 'for the consideration of questions touching Faith and Order'. This proposal was unanimously accepted by the Convention 'as the next step towards unity',[49] and led ultimately to the World Conference of Churches on Faith and Order at Lausanne in 1927.

In the 1920 Lambeth 'Appeal to all Christian people', Anglican bishops from all countries united in a call to unity and listed four points as essential for the reunion of the Churches:

'We believe that the visible unity of the Church will be found to involve the whole-hearted acceptance of:

'The Holy Scriptures as the record of God's revelation of Himself to man and as being the rule and ultimate standard of faith:

'And the Creed commonly called Nicene . . . and either it or the Apostles' Creed as the Baptismal Confession of belief:

'The divinely instituted sacraments of Baptism and the Holy Communion as expressing for all the corporate life of the whole fellowship in and with Christ:

'A ministry acknowledged by every part of the Church as possessing not only the inward call of the Spirit, but also the commission of Christ and the authority of the whole body.'[50]

Finally, the Lambeth Conference of 1948 went even further and in its encyclical letter made a statement which no other Church had so far ventured to make: 'Reunion of any part of your communion with other denominations in its own area must make the resulting Church no longer simply Anglican but something more comprehensive . . . a united Church, Catholic and Evangelical, but no longer, in the limiting sense of the word, Anglican.'[51]

[49] Bell, *Documents on Christian Unity*, Ser. 1, pp. 15f. See Rouse and Neill, *History of the Ecumenical Movement*, p. 407.

[50] Bell, *Documents on Christian Unity*, Ser. 1, p. 3.

[51] Lambeth Conference, *Report*, 1948, PT 1, p. 22.

At first the Anglican Church, obviously prompted by its concept of the ministry, pioneered relationships with those non-Roman Churches which acknowledge apostolic succession as the principle of their order. Then in 1947 the South Indian dioceses of the Anglican Churches of India, Burma, and Ceylon were united with Churches innocent of episcopal apostolic succession to form the Church of South India.[52] The Anglicans are now giving priority to the discussions with representatives of the Presbyterian Churches which had been begun much earlier.[53] We should not rightly understand the Anglican Church if we ignored this wide-ranging activity. Anglicanism has received something of the gift and will of the Lord Jesus Christ for His people 'that they may be one' (John 17.22).

But having unreservedly acknowledged that fact we must go on to record that Anglicanism cannot conceive of any unification of the Churches except on the basis of the apostolic succession in the episcopal ministry. The Lambeth Appeal is still careful to say: 'May we not reasonably claim that the episcopate is the one means of providing such a ministry? It is not that we call in question the spiritual reality of the ministries of those communions which do not possess the episcopate. . . . But we submit that considerations alike of history and of present experience justify the claim which we make on behalf of the episcopate.'[54]

But the Constitution of the United Church of South India shows that the union of the Anglican dioceses with the other Churches only came about because it was affirmed (1) that 'continuity with the historic episcopate will be effectively maintained', (2) that those chosen to be the first bishops would be consecrated by three bishops standing in the apostolic succession, and (3) that all future ministers would be episcopally ordained.[55] Reordination of those already holding ministerial office in the uniting bodies was only abandoned for pastoral

[52] Cf. *The Constitution of the Church of South India*, Madras 1952. The formation of a United Church of North India is imminent.

[53] See the Joint Reports, *Relations between Anglican and Presbyterian Churches*, 1957. Conversations between Anglicans and Methodists are also in progress. See *An Interim Statement*, London 1958.

[54] Bell, *Documents on Christian Unity*, Ser. 1, p. 3.

[55] *Constitution of the Church of South India*, VOL. II, p. 11.

reasons. But in time these men will die off and then there will be in this Church only episcopally ordained Presbyters and Deacons. The presence of non-episcopally ordained ministers in the Church of South India is still felt by Anglicans to be an 'anomaly', since the Churches of the Anglican communion 'allow no exception to the rule of an episcopally ordained ministry'.[56] By making apostolic succession in the episcopal office an indispensable condition for any union of Churches,[57] is not Anglicanism laying upon others a law which these others cannot rightly accept? This law must necessarily be felt to be a burden because Anglicanism cannot tell the others *what* it is it wishes to impose upon them. It is not only unable to state clearly and convincingly what it means by the episcopal office and apostolic succession,[58] but actually comprehends within its own borders completely divergent views about these things. This burden is made all the more oppressive for other Churches by the Anglican Church's insistence on this ministerial principle as the prerequisite for intercommunion with them.[59] But it, more than many, realises the great scandal caused by the inability of Christendom to sit down together at the Lord's table and because of this feels great sorrow.[60]

The Anglican Church rests its doctrine of the ministry upon Holy Scripture.[61] This decisive attitude binds it to the Reformed and Presbyterian Churches, who also derive their doctrine of the ministry from Scripture. Like them the Anglican Church realises that the whole life of the Church, including its order therefore, is claimed by God's Word.[62] This realisation is of the greatest importance for the unification of divided Christendom. Can unity still be impossible when men submit together to the Word of Scripture? But this encouraging knowledge must be used very differently than has been the case, for example, in the current conversations between Angli-

[56] *The Church of South India, United Report of the two Joint Committees of the Convocations* (of Canterbury and York), London 1955, p. 10.

[57] Lambeth Conference, *Report*, 1948, PT II, p. 50.

[58] It appears that most Anglicans now put less emphasis on the tactual succession (succession in consecration) and more on the succession in the see. But Evangelicals will naturally ask: Why then is there such a stress on the imposition of hands in ordination?

[59] Lambeth Conference, *Report*, 1948, PT II, p. 50.

[60] Cf. *Intercommunion*, edd. Baillie and Marsh, pp. 255ff.

[61] See above, p. 312.

[62] Cf. Barmen Thesis No. 3.

cans and Presbyterians. Surely both sides must ask far more stringently whether and how far their traditional orders can be retained at all, in face of the Words of Holy Scripture, which, in fact, means in face of the claim of the Church's Head?

CHAPTER 13

CONGREGATIONALISM

HAVING already dealt at length with the doctrine of the Reformed Churches, we do not need to speak here of the Reformed Churches that arose on Anglo-Saxon soil, where they are usually called Presbyterian Churches from their form of government.[1] Instead, we shall look briefly at a variant form of Reformed Christianity, namely, Congregationalism. This emerged in England, during the turn of the sixteenth to the seventeenth century, and spread from there to America especially and to the rest of the English-speaking world. This fact has been described as merely 'an accident of history'. 'Congregationalism', it is affirmed, 'derives from the fountain-head of Christianity itself and is part of the very life stream of the Gospel.'[2] The International Congregational Council, which met for the first time in London in 1891, embraces Churches with approximately two million members actively engaged in and supporting the work of Congregations.

1. The Concern of Congregationalism

We need only comment briefly on Congregationalists, since their concern is not to emphasise any special aspects of the Christian faith,[3] but simply to plead for a distinctive type of Church order. They were originally known as *Independents*. This admirably expresses their concern, namely, 'to stand

[1] The Reformed Church of Scotland calls itself simply the Church of Scotland, regarding itself primarily not as a special denomination, but rather as the Church of the country (just as the differently organised Church of England does in its part of the United Kingdom). In the U.S.A. there are, as well as the large Presbyterian Churches, two others of Dutch origin which also call themselves Reformed Churches, i.e. the Reformed Church in America, and the Christian Reformed Church.

[2] A. Peel and D. Horton, *International Congregationalism*, London 1949, p. 62.

[3] 'They have always claimed their place in the witness of the evangelical reformed Churches.' *Congregationalism in itself*, Statement, 1930; Peel and Horton, *International Congregationalism*, p. 114.

independent of, and irresponsible to, all authority, saving that only of the Supreme and divine Head of the Church, the Lord Jesus Christ'.[4] It is clear from this that in pleading for a particular Church order the Congregationalists are not concerned with something merely external, but with something which they regard as quite central, namely, with the *sole Headship of Christ* over His Church. They not only reject every form of State Church in favour of the Church's complete freedom from the State,[5] but also reject any form of Church government which might exercise control over the local congregations. They regard it as essential 'that these Churches, under the guidance of the Holy Scripture and in fellowship with one another, may determine—each for itself—their organisation, statements of belief, and forms of worship, may appoint and set apart their own ministers, and should co-operate in the work which Christ has committed to them for the furtherance of the Gospel throughout the world.'[6] That is to say, 'the Headship of Christ' finds concrete expression where His people are gathered together in one place under His Word and He Himself rules them by His Word and Spirit. The change of name from 'Independents' to 'Congregationalists' was in itself significant. They are not concerned with negations but with this wholly positive characteristic of the Church's nature. 'It is this emphasis on the particularity of the Church, much more than its emphasis on freedom, which is, perhaps, the greatest contribution of Congregationalism to the life of the whole Church.'[7]

To that extent, of course, as we shall see, the Baptists, too, are Congregationalists. Yet the Congregationalists differ from the Baptists in one very important respect in the doctrine of the Church. They take much more seriously than the Baptists do the fact that Christ is the Head of His Church who alone

[4] Declaration of the English Congregationalists, 1833, PT II, Art. IV (W. Walker, *The Creeds and Platforms of Congregationalism*, New York 1893, henceforth cited as *Creeds and Platforms*, p. 551; Schaff, III.733).

[5] Cf. *op. cit.*, Art. IX: 'They believe that the power of a christian Church is purely spiritual, and should in no way be corrupted by union with temporal or civil power' (Walker, *Creeds and Platforms*, p. 552; Schaff, III.734).

[6] Statement of Doctrine of the American Congregationalists, 1883, Art. X (Walker, *Creeds and Platforms*, p. 581).

[7] D. Jenkins, *Congregationalism, a Restatement*, London 1954, p. 44.

gathers His people. In this matter they share with other Reformed Churches the conviction that 'what constitutes a congregation as an independent Church is not the fact that it gathers together but the fact that it possesses the ordinance of Christ for His Church. That is to say, it is the marks of Christ which are *the marks of the Church* . . . wherever the Word is faithfully preached and the Sacraments administered according to Christ's appointment, there the Church is to be found.'[8] The words which follow seem to be addressed to the Baptists and their subjectivism: 'For what is a Church's ultimate *source of assurance* that it possesses Christ's Spirit? Is it that its members are good and kindly people and are diligent in the Lord's service? That should certainly be one of the marks of a Christian community but, for purposes of definition, it is a dubious and misleading criterion.'[9] The Word and the Sacraments alone constitute the Church, not the presence of a ministry—that is the demarcation line on the opposite side, occupied by the Anglicans—although the Congregationalists lay great stress on having in every congregation, besides the offices of the deacons, a 'learned' ministry[10] which liberates it from the 'excesses of spiritual anarchy' and by the preaching of the Word maintains the local congregation 'as a responsible part of the great Church'.[11]

In accord with this view of the nature of the Church, the Congregationalists adhere firmly to the *baptism* of the children of believing parents,[12] 'as a sign of cleansing from sin, of union to Christ, and of the impartation of the Holy Spirit',[13] and they celebrate the *Lord's Supper* 'as a symbol of His atoning death, a seal of its efficacy, and a means whereby He confirms and strengthens the spiritual union and communion of believers with Himself'.[14]

Congregationalists reject the use of *creeds* in public worship.

[8] *Op. cit.*, pp. 71f. [9] *Op. cit.*, p. 72.

[10] A 'learned' ministry. Cf. Roland H. Bainton, *Yale and the Ministry*, New York 1957.

[11] Jenkins, *Congregationalism*, p. 78f. Cf. Declaration of 1833, PT II, Art. XI (Walker, *Creeds and Platforms*, p. 552; Schaff, III.734).

[12] Declaration of 1833, PT I, Art. XVIII (Walker, *Creeds and Platforms*, p. 550; Schaff, III.732).

[13] Statement of Doctrine, 1883, Art. XI (Walker, *Creeds and Platforms*, p. 581).

[14] *Ibid.*

Nor do they require their members to subscribe to any such creed. This, however, is not because they reject the essential contents of these creeds, but because they respect the *authority of Holy Scripture* as the only source of doctrine. They maintain therefore 'that human traditions, fathers, and councils, canons and creeds, possess no authority over the faith and practice of Christians'.[15] But they do not rule out formal creeds altogether. They are ready, 'for general information', to draw up explicit statements of what they 'commonly' believe.[16]

The *freedom* to which Congregationalism calls Christians is therefore 'a founded freedom'.[17] This does not mean a freedom which springs from a vague experience of Christ and His Spirit, but one 'which arises from the experience of God in Christ as the Scriptures declare Him'.[18] Freedom is bound up with the concrete authority of Holy Scripture.[19] Here again it is manifest that the Congregationalists keep to the safe path of the Word and do not rely on personal experiences. But they believe they have seen deeper into the meaning of freedom than other denominations. They believe that 'if the Church is to remain an effective sphere for the operation of the freedom of God in His Spirit, that Church must always be mobile and supple, not so tied to secondary doctrinal and liturgical and institutional forms that it is never in a position to leave them all and follow Christ'.[20]

2. The Relationship between Local Congregations

We saw that Congregationalists, as their name suggests, wish to testify that the Church according to the New Testament is the local congregation where believers actually live together under the Word. Hence the guiding and government of all matters rests with each local congregation,[21] namely with the 'Church Meeting' to which every member belongs.[22] This meeting helps

[15] Declaration of 1833, PT II, Art. II (Walker, *Creeds and Platforms*, p. 551; Schaff, III.733).

[16] Declaration of 1833, Preliminary Notes, No. 5 (Walker, *Creeds and Platforms*, p. 548; Schaff, III.730).

[17] Jenkins, *Congregationalism*, p. 50.

[18] *Ibid.*

[19] Declaration of 1833, PT II, Art. III (Walker, *Creeds and Platforms*, p. 551; Schaff, III.733).

[20] Jenkins, *Congregationalism*, p. 68.

[21] See above, p. 320.

[22] *Congregationalism in Itself*, Statement 1930 (Peel and Horton, *International Congregationalism*, p. 114).

to clarify the various tasks of the ministers and deacons whom it elects.[23]

That itself suggests that the direct responsibility of each congregation to Christ its Lord cannot mean self-sufficiency.[24] Hence in many countries the congregations are organised into 'Unions'. The authority of these Unions is not 'legalistic, coercive or magisterial' but only spiritual or ministerial. In any kind of joint decision by congregations, just as in the Church Meeting in a local congregation, it can only be a question of seeking 'to find the will of Christ for His Church by prayer and discussion, and being led to a common mind should have the spiritual authority of the Church meeting'.[25] To prevent misunderstanding, it is emphasised 'this is a principle of unity and fellowship in the spirit, not a principle of individualism, will-worship, sectarianism or anarchy'.[26] Congregationalists believe that their 'essential contribution to the universal Church'[27] is precisely their answer to the question about the meaning of Church government and Church authority.

There can be no doubt that a genuine question is raised here. Are the Synods of the synodically organised Churches still synods in the original sense? Or is it not rather the case that they have developed on secular lines into parliaments with legislative authority? We need only recall the Huguenots' *Discipline ecclesiastique* of 1559, which begins: 'Firstly, no congregation can claim precedence or rule over any other', and place alongside it the penultimate Article 39: 'No congregation shall be free to do anything of great consequence involving the interests or detriment of other congregations, without the advice of the Provincial Synod.'[28] Synods originally were meetings for brotherly consultation, to which local congregations, through their representatives, brought problems they could not settle unaided, and sought advice, and, above all, discussed and clarified matters of more than local importance.[29]

[23] Declaration of 1833, PT II, Arts. V, VII (Walker, *Creeds and Platforms*, pp. 551f; Schaff, III.733). [24] See above, p. 320.

[25] *Congregationalism in Itself*, Statement, 1930 (Peel and Horton, *International Congregationalism*, p. 115). [26] *Ibid.*

[27] *Ibid.* [28] Niesel, *Bekenntnisschriften und Kirchenordnungen*, pp. 75, 79.

[29] Cf. Emden Church Order of 1571, *De provincialibus synodis*, Art. I and *Acta particularia* (Niesel, *Bekenntnisschriften und Kirchenordnungen*, pp. 285, 287ff); Herborn

But this did not prevent these synods from being able to claim authority under the Word for their decisions after such brotherly consultation. A really brotherly attitude can never be content merely with the counting of heads. At the time of the German Church conflict the Synods of the Confessing Church paid attention to this and benefited immeasurably as a result. But this understanding has since begun to disappear. All the more anxiously then do we wait to see how the *United Church of Christ* which, in June 1957, united the largest Congregationalist Union, the General Council of the Congregational Christian Churches in the U.S.A., with the Evangelical and Reformed Church, will organise the corporate life of its many congregations. By this union, the Congregationalists have shown by their deeds that they are concerned not with any abstract principle but with the Headship of Christ over His Church.

General Synod of 1586, *De conventibus*, Art. XXII (Niesel, *op. cit.*, p. 294); Church Order of Jülich and Berg, 1671, cc. 9 and 10 (Niesel, *op. cit.*, pp. 317f).

CHAPTER 14

THE BAPTISTS

1. The Baptists Distinguished from the Anabaptists of Reformation Times

Baptists form a large separate Church which originated in England and is now a world-wide communion. Since 1905 there has been in existence a Baptist World Alliance, whose affiliated Churches, just after the end of the Second World War, included a total membership of over 13 million. In addition there are also the Baptists of the Soviet Union who, in 1944, united with the Gospel Christians to form the most significant Christian body in Russia next to the Orthodox Church. They claim a membership of 4 million.[1] Unlike the Methodist movement, which we have still to consider, the Baptists arose during the first half of the seventeenth century in circles which had earlier separated from the established Church. The Baptist movement in Germany began only in 1834 in Hamburg through the work of Johann Gerhard Oncken[2] and is formed today into the 'Alliance of Evangelical Free Church Congregations'.

The Baptists are not to be confused therefore with the Anabaptists who appeared in the Reformation period, still less with the Mennonites, who came into existence later and still exist today. This distinction is important not merely historically but materially, since the Anabaptists of Reformation times differed in doctrine from the Churches of the Reformation much more than do the Baptists. In particular most of the Anabaptists of Reformation times asserted that the Holy Spirit operates directly on men, independently of the Word, and,

[1] H. W. Robinson, *The Life and Faith of the Baptists*, London 1946, henceforth cited as *Life and Faith*, p. 154.

[2] On Johann Gerhard Oncken (1800-84) see J. H. Cooke, *Johann Gerhard Oncken, His Life and Work*, London 1908.

since the age of the Spirit had begun, they rejected all secular authority and sought to establish their own community life.

Even today the Mennonites still refuse to swear on oath, or to perform any kind of service involving the use of weapons. Their founder Menno Simons (*d.* 1559) also taught a monophysite Christology.[3] None of this applies to the Baptists.

2. The Distinctive Baptist Witness

Like all who accept the sixteenth-century Reformation of the Church, the Baptists are concerned with the message of the Bible. They acknowledge 'the Divine Inspiration and Authority of the Holy Scripture as the supreme and sufficient rule of our faith and practice'.[4] Although, therefore, we find great prominence given by Baptists to the exegesis of Scripture, the recognition of the authority of the Bible does not mean that they regard themselves as tied to the words of Scripture as such. The Baptists realise that we are not subject to any paper pope. The Bible is absolutely authoritative because it reveals 'that our Lord and Saviour Jesus Christ, God manifest in the flesh, is the sole and absolute authority in all matters pertaining to faith and practice'.[5] The evangelical Scripture principle has been stated here clearly and unmistakably.

Important though that is, the distinctive Baptist view of Scripture still remains to be stated. The above sentences from the two documents were not quoted in full; the conclusion of them was left out. In the Statement it is: 'and *the right and duty of individual judgment in the interpretation of it*', and, in the Basis: 'and that each Church has liberty, under the guidance of the Holy Spirit, to interpret and administer His Laws'. For the Baptists what matters most is that the interpretation of Holy Scripture should be free, that is to say, not dictated by any human authority. This assertion is opposed not only to the claims of an authoritarian ecclesiastical teaching office, but also to the great importance attached by other Churches to

[3] See above, p. 289.

[4] Union Statement, 23 April 1888 (W. J. McGlothlin, *Baptist Confessions of Faith*, Philadelphia 1911, henceforth cited as *Baptist Confessions*, p. 292). Cf. *Glaubensbekenntnis des Bundes evangelischer freikirchlichen Gemeinden*, Nordhorn 1944.

[5] Basis of the Baptist Union of Great Britain and Ireland (H. W. Robinson, *Life and Faith*, p. 78). Cf. H. H. Straton, *Baptists, their Message and Mission*, Philadelphia 1941, p. 56.

confessions of faith. Not that the Baptists object to the content of such confessions, but for them it is necessary 'not only to believe the facts and doctrines of the Gospel, but to have undergone the spiritual change expressed or implied by them'.[6] They fear that the living truth may harden into formulae when men try to imprison it in a confession of faith, and that personal faith in this truth may be replaced by mere intellectual assent.[7] This certainly shows awareness of the danger of every kind of orthodoxy. But we are bound to ask whether this is the right way to avoid this danger.

In the last paragraph we encountered the watchword which is of supreme importance not only for the right interpretation of Scripture but also for the Baptist standpoint and teaching as a whole: *Freedom!* If we ask someone closely acquainted with a Baptist congregation what strikes him as being specially characteristic of it, he will tell us: its freedom in matters of faith and order. Even the writings of Baptist theologians are loud in praise of the fact that this communion stands for absolute freedom. 'Baptists have claimed freedom from the authority of any sacerdotal hierarchy, freedom from the State, freedom of conscience, freedom of private judgment. They have been, on the whole, consistently suspicious of creeds and verbal statements. . . . They have claimed the guidance of the living Spirit of Christ present within His Church, a guidance inspired, continued, and held in check by appeal to the Scriptures. . . . The final court of appeal has been neither to Church pronouncements, nor to history and tradition as such, but to the conscience of the Church inspired by the Spirit of God as a result of the study of the Bible. "The deepest impulse of Baptist life has been the upholding of the sole and exclusive authority of Jesus Christ against all possible encroachment" said Dr John Clifford at the Baptist World Congress of 1911.'[8] It is clear from these words that this freedom is one which is co-ordinated with the absolute authority of Jesus Christ. It exists because Jesus Christ has liberated men from the worst bondage of all, enslavement to evil. Hence 'only those who

[6] Union Statement, 1888 (McGlothlin, *Baptist Confessions*, p. 292).

[7] Cf. Robinson, *Life and Faith*, p. 80.

[8] E. A. Payne, *The Fellowship of Believers, Baptist Thought and Practice Yesterday and Today*, London 1944, p. 17.

know the liberty that is in Christ possess true freedom'.[9] Therefore the liberty proclaimed by the Baptists has nothing to do with licence. 'Recognising Jesus Christ's Headship alone, His will to him, the Baptist, is law.'[10]

The Baptists have unquestionably borne impressive and continued witness to this freedom in every area of life. We need only recall the leading part they played in the struggle for the abolition of the slave trade. It is good to note that despite the successes they achieved in this field a sober self-criticism is not lacking: 'Liberty within is a more difficult attainment than liberty without. Prejudices which we nurture within our own hearts are more subtle and dangerous than those whose folly and injustice we can see plainly when they belong to others.'[11] Genuine freedom, it is realised, is a gift for which we can only pray again and again.

This concept of freedom is safeguarded by the statement that 'the chief content' of man's fellowship with God is 'moral holiness, consecrated to the Holy God by moral character'.[12] Although after speaking of Christian liberty it is only a short step to go on to speak next of its roots in man's justification by God, the Baptists instead speak, in a way of their own, about 'personal regeneration'.[13] They do of course affirm 'justification by faith' but add immediately the explanation 'a faith that works by love and produces *holiness*'.[14] We must pay special attention to this if we are to understand the distinctive testimony of the Baptists. Their supreme concern is with man's *regeneration* and the Christian's daily *sanctification*.[15] By 'regeneration' they mean 'a profound transformation of the will and nature of the believer', by the Holy Spirit.[16] Man's response to regeneration is conversion. This does not necessarily mean 'a startling and dramatic experience'[17] but certainly a 'daily sanctification', a 'life in the Spirit'.[18] This emphasis on the sanctification of personal life is strongly reminiscent of Methodism, but the Methodist doctrine of Christian perfection is rejected. The

[9] Straton, *Baptists*, p. 93.
[10] Philip L. Jones, *A Restatement of Baptist Principles*, Philadelphia 1909, p. 82.
[11] Robinson, *Life and Faith*, p. 137.
[12] *Op. cit.*, p. 19.
[13] Straton, *Baptists*, p. 44.
[14] Union Statement, 1888 (McGlothlin, *Baptist Confessions*, p. 292).
[15] *Glaubensbekenntnis*, 1944, Art. v.
[16] *Ibid.*
[17] Robinson, *Life and Faith*, p. 76.
[18] *Glaubensbekenntnis*, 1944, Art. v.

transformation of the individual into 'the image of Christ' 'is not a single once and for all event but takes place in a continual growth by God's Spirit and under God's Word'.[19]

The belief in the fundamental importance of regeneration also underlies the *Baptist doctrine and practice of Baptism*. They express the conviction 'that the baptism instituted by Christ should be applied to those who have come to believe in the Lord Jesus and who, in obedience to Him, wish to profess their faith in the presence of many witnesses'.[20] The Western form of baptism is rejected and the candidate 'in accordance with the original Christian practice is plunged into a watery grave'.[21] But Baptists 'are far more concerned with the facts of conversion than with the mode of baptism'. Their 'endeavour is to be careful to admit to baptism only those who have had a definitive experience in their lives of God's grace through faith in Jesus Christ. Behind every Baptist there is the fact of personal regeneration.'[22] Infant baptism is therefore rejected. Baptism is thus not a means of grace for awakening faith, but 'God's gracious assurance' to one who is already a believer, that he has died with Christ and 'may walk in newness of life' with the Risen Lord.[23] What the believer already has through God's Word and Spirit, is confirmed for him in baptism, and in it he, for his part, pledges himself to the Lord and publicly confesses his faith in Him.[24] Instead of infant baptism the Baptists practice not simply adult baptism but believers' baptism.

They administer baptism, possibly under Greek Catholic influence,[25] by immersion, because they believe that only in this way can baptism symbolise the significance of Christ's death and resurrection in accordance with Rom. 6. It is because baptism does this, that it has become so important for the life and unity of the Baptist communion. It can even be said that immersion, carried out repeatedly in the presence of the congregation, takes the place among Baptists which the confessions of faith have in other Churches: 'The baptism of believers' has 'by its symbolism, constantly recalled men to the foundation of the Gospel in history, the death and resurrection

[19] *Ibid.* [20] *Op. cit.*, Art. VII. [21] *Ibid.*
[22] Straton, *Baptists*, p. 66. [23] *Glaubensbekenntnis*, 1944, Art. VII.
[24] *Ibid.* [25] *R.E.*, VOL. XXIII, p. 159.

of Jesus Christ. That act constantly repeated before the eyes of Baptists has taken the place of any formal creed, and helped to keep them an evangelical Church without any authoritative confession of faith.'[26] Whether this view is historically correct is a separate question altogether, but who would deny that baptism—just like the Lord's Supper—can also perform the positive service of keeping the Church's preaching faithful to the commission laid upon it? At the same time it must be recognised that the sacramental signs in themselves are not effective symbols but receive their meaning for us only by the preached Word which accompanies them.[27] If false apostles corrupt the content of the message, even the sacramental signs lose their illuminating power, and the faithful must confess their Lord with their lips by unmasking the false doctrine in well-directed words. That should be conceded by the Baptists.

Believers' baptism is 'the expression of the fundamental constitution of the Church. We become members of the living Body of Christ by being consciously and voluntarily baptised in the Spirit of Christ.'[28] Therefore the *Church* by its very nature —even if the actuality is far from being in accord with this—is '*the community of the regenerate*'.[29] Rejecting the Lutheran view, the Baptists emphasise that the Church 'is not already there where God's Word is preached and heard but only when men win through to new life and find themselves in the communion of God's children'.[30] Although this confession of faith is prefaced by the polemical statement 'that Christ is the invisible Head of His body the Church'[31] and that He makes 'all who receive the new life from God members of His body', the subjective emphasis comes out strongly even here in the doctrine of the Church. It can be said that the Church is 'a society of men and women drawn together by common convictions and needs'.[32] Even the significance of the Lord's Supper is some-

[26] Robinson, *Life and Faith*, p. 16.

[27] Even Robinson concludes the first of the two sentences quoted above with the significant words: 'which, as Paul argued, are represented in the act of believer's immersion and his rising from the waters of Baptism' (*op, cit.*, p. 16).

[28] *Op. cit.*, p. 73.

[29] *Op. cit.*, pp. 20f.

[30] *Glaubensbekenntnis*, 1944, Art. VI.

[31] Cf. also the Reply to the Lambeth Appeal: Jesus Christ is 'the sole and absolute authority' in the Church. Robinson, *Life and Faith*, p. 83.

[32] *Op. cit.*, p. 85.

times stated only with this emphasis: 'We avow our union with one another, while partaking of the symbol of the body of our Lord, broken for us, and of the blood shed for the remission of sins.'[33]

In the Baptist view the Church is manifested here on earth in the local congregation even if it be only two or three gathered in the name of Christ.[34] The local communities of believers do, however, find 'an extension and expression of their life in free association, first, with other Churches of their own faith and order, but also with other groups of Christians loyal to the central truths of the apostolic Gospel'.[35] Any assertion of the complete independence of local congregations, in the sense of isolation and self-sufficiency, is, we are assured, alien to the authentic Baptist view and is a modern aberration.[36] It is therefore stated in the 1944 Confession of the Baptists in Germany, that 'since in accordance with apostolic injunction the member has to adapt himself to the Body the individual has therefore to submit to the fellowship. *This rule also applies to the individual congregation as a member of the wider communion.*'[37]

The Baptists affirm the duty of every member 'to bear personal witness to the Gospel of Jesus Christ, and take part in the evangelisation of the world'.[38] They have also seen the important New Testament truth that the Holy Spirit gives different gifts for ministry in the Church,[39] and therefore the Risen Lord 'in addition to the co-operation of the individual members, appoints evangelists, pastors, teachers, elders, and deacons for special service to the Church'.[40] The exercise of each ministry, however, is dependent on the inward call anyone has received being recognised by the congregation by way of an outward call to some office. Subject to this condition, a pro-

[33] Union Statement 1888 (McGlothlin, *Baptist Confessions*, p. 292). Cf. *Glaubensbekenntnis*, 1944, but the latter gives priority to the belief 'that the Lord Jesus bequeathed the Supper to His Church in order that . . . it should remember the Crucified and have communion with Him'.

[34] Robinson, *Life and Faith*, p. 88.

[35] Payne, *The Fellowship of Believers*, p. 32. [36] *Ibid.*

[37] Philip L. Jones on the other hand still affirms: 'There is not among them even the authoritative council as among the Congregationalists, the Christian body of all their brethren most nearly akin to them in polity. Among Baptists the local Church is the final court of appeal.' *A Restatement of Baptist Principles*, Philadelphia 1909, p. 47. [38] Declaration of Principle (Robinson, *Life and Faith*, p. 78).

[39] *Op. cit.*, pp. 102ff. [40] *Glaubensbekenntnis*, 1944, Art. VI.

fessional ministry is regarded as permissible and has in fact become the general rule.[41]

The Baptists in Germany now have a kind of presbyterian and synodical form of government. The congregations are guided by elders chosen at a meeting of the whole congregation. Disciplinary decisions are of course made by the congregational meeting itself. Congregations are linked together in Unions and these in turn are represented in the Assembly of the Baptist Alliance in Germany, which has far-reaching power to admit and exclude congregations. The president of the Alliance, who is chosen by the Assembly, has above all the important task of 'keeping the list of ministers' from which alone congregations may choose their ministers. He also has 'to intervene promptly as peacemaker and adviser' in 'disputes in the congregations'.

Even in the country where the Baptist movement originated, the executive committee of a congregation often becomes in practice a kind of kirk session.[42] The local Churches have formed associations under the chairmanship of a president who is appointed for one year, and these associations in turn form the Baptist Union. Here too there is an accredited list of ministers,[43] to which congregations are limited in the choice of their minister. In other matters, of course, it is laid down 'that all larger groupings of Baptist Churches are for common action by representatives, not for the exercise of authoritative control'.[44]

Since the Baptists vigorously uphold the right of the local Church 'to be self-governing', it is even more to be expected that their conception of the Church also 'excludes any such relations with the State as may impair its liberty'.[45] The Baptists are the champions of the separation of Church and State.

From all that we have heard it is obviously the concern of the Baptists to emphasise the *subjective* aspect of our faith. This is made crystal clear in the new confession of faith of the German Baptists. Unlike the old confession, this no longer contains any

[41] Robinson, *Life and Faith*, pp. 104f. [42] *Op. cit.*, p. 88.

[43] Inclusion in this list is not automatically secured by a call to the ministry given by a local congregation. This call needs the confirmation of the local Union concerned. [44] Robinson, *Life and Faith*, p. 91.

[45] Reply to the Lambeth Appeal (Robinson, *op. cit.*, p.83).

reference to God's eternal election of men to salvation, but replaces it by a new Article 5 on regeneration and man's sanctification. In the matter of Church polity the other Reformation Churches could reach an understanding with the Baptists, and perhaps too in the question of a proper ordering of Baptism. But they could never agree that God's covenant with men depends on their consent. In the context of the Divine Covenant of grace, baptism is also valid for the children of believers, as 'the offer of a good conscience towards God' (1 Pet. 3.21). The essence of Baptism lies in this divine offer, and not in the candidate's personal enthusiasm or profession of faith, even though this must follow if the baptism is to be of any benefit to him. The Christian Church to which Baptism joins us is rooted in the sole action of God, and not in the regenerated person's experience of salvation nor in his desire for fellowship, though certainly the individual believers can and should be present with their faith and obedience and thus form 'the community of brothers',[46] the Christian Church. The call to be this comes from the Bible, the witness of the prophets and apostles, with such a claim that it is very misleading to extol the freedom of the reader and hearer at its expense.

The name which has become attached to the Baptists does not really explain what they are concerned to testify. The 'Believers' baptism' practised by them expresses this concern only in part. Their real concern is more comprehensive. We cannot escape the impression that they came to have this concern in reaction against the objectivism of the Anglican Church. But a return to subjectivism cannot heal that objectivism. Both must allow themselves to be questioned by God's Word, that is to say by Jesus Christ, in whom God Himself objectively *confronts us* but through whom we too are given the subjective freedom *to be ourselves* before God.

[46] Barmen Thesis No. 3.

CHAPTER 15

METHODISM

WE have now reached the point where we need to listen to what Methodism has to say to us. Originally a revivalist movement within the established Church of England in the middle years of the eighteenth century (the brothers John and Charles Wesley were converted in May 1738), Methodism today is a world-wide communion with 16 million members.[1] The movement's name was originally a nickname given to it because of 'the methodical character of its religious life'[2] but was then adopted by it. In 1739 John Wesley wrote his important tract on *The Character of a Methodist.*[3]

1. The Relation between Methodism and the Church of England

The Wesley brothers did not set out to propagate a new system of Christian doctrine nor did they fasten on one particular tenet in the doctrine of the Church of England, of which they were both ministers, and make it the central doctrine of a new Church. 'Whoever, therefore, imagines that a Methodist is a man of such an opinion is grossly ignorant of the whole affair.'[4] Nor was it Wesley's aim to introduce a new Church system or new forms of worship. He had no wish even to found a new religious society of his own alongside the established Church. All his life he firmly resisted any move to separate from the established Church. Methodism's concern is with the vital

[1] I. L. Holt, *The Methodists of the World*, New York 1950. Cf. Molland, *Christendom*, p. 271f.

[2] F. Loofs, 'Methodismus', in *R.E.*, VOL. XII, p. 755. Loofs cites the phrase 'method and industry in order to either learning or virtue' from *The main questions of the Holy Club* (*The Works of the Rev. John Wesley, A.M.*, 11th edn. with a life of the author by the Rev. John Beecham, D.D., and a general preface by the Rev. Thomas Jackson, London 1856, henceforth cited as Wesley, *Works*, VOL. I, p. 9).

[3] J. Wesley, *The Character of a Methodist* 1739, repr. London 1950 (*Corpus Confessionum*, ed. Fabricius, PT XX, pp. 709ff).

[4] *Op. cit.*, 1950 edn., p. 7 (*Corpus Confessionum*, PT XX, p. 709).

Christian experience of the Church's members. What this means we shall consider in a moment.

Methodism, therefore, with all evangelical Churches, believes 'the written Word of God to be the only and sufficient rule both of Christian faith and practice'.[5] John Wesley's sermons consist for the most part in a detailed scriptural proof of the truth of the particular text chosen as the basis for the sermon. Methodism retained most of the Anglican confession of faith. The Thirty-Nine Articles were reduced to twenty-five. Those omitted were the articles on the ancient creeds, the authority of the Church, the three offices (of bishop, priest, and deacon), excommunication, and several others including above all the one on predestination. Methodists also attach great importance to John Wesley's *Notes on the New Testament*, which is mainly a translation of J. A. Bengel's *Gnomon Novi Testamenti*, and, finally, to four small volumes of John Wesley's sermons, which appeared in print in the years 1746-60, and contain forty-four sermons. Adherence to these works of Wesley came to be required of candidates for the ministry. Nowadays, however, Methodists do not regard themselves as 'bound to accept all the details of Wesley's doctrine'.[6]

We must now indicate the basic tenets of Methodist doctrine and, to avoid misinterpretation, we shall keep closely to the account of Methodist teaching given by J. L. Nuelson.

2. Fundamentals of Methodist Teaching

'The universality of sin and of the corruption of human nature and the universality of Divine grace,' says Nuelson, 'constitutes one of the main features of the Methodist doctrine of redemption.'[7] We will not go into the concept of sin here, as this can only become clear in a later context. We simply recall here the fact that Wesley excluded from the Anglican confession of faith the article on predestination. This is all the more remarkable since that article refers only to the election to salvation and

[5] *Op. cit.*, 1950 edn., p. 7 (*Corpus Confessionum*, PT XX, p. 710).

[6] *Wesley-Predigten*, ed. J. W. Sommer, Bremen 1938, Preface, p. 10. Cf. *Wesley's Standard Sermons*, ed. E. H. Sugden, 4th edn. London 1956, VOL. I, pp. 17ff; VOL. II, pp. 331ff.

[7] J. L. Nuelson, *Die Lehre und die kirchengeschichtliche Bedeutung des Methodismus*, Zürich 1947, henceforth cited as *Lehre des Methodismus*, p. 9.

emphasises the comforting nature of the doctrine. As early as 1739 Wesley preached a sermon on 'Free Grace',[8] in which he opposed his friend Whitefield who held the Calvinist view. If this view is correct, says Wesley, 'then is all preaching vain'.[9] Above all, this doctrine of predestination 'has a manifest tendency to destroy holiness in general; for it wholly takes away those first motives to follow after it, so frequently proposed in Scripture, the hope of future reward and fear of punishment'.[10] So, too, 'it destroys the fruits of sanctification, for example, love to all men, even to the evil.[11] Finally it destroys comfort and joy in Christian living, because doubts can always arise about election.'[12] Indeed Wesley was convinced that this doctrine was calculated 'to overthrow the whole Christian Revelation',[13] since revelation would be reduced to an absurdity if everything were already determined by an eternal predestination. So the view was upheld that 'the salvation or damnation of each man depends on his own voluntary attitude to the influences of the Holy Spirit'.[14]

It is therefore characteristic of Methodist teaching to emphasise strongly man's voluntary response to 'God's gracious calling'. Attention is concentrated on what happens when a man hears this call and is influenced by it. Methodism does affirm, too, the sinner's justification by grace alone, but regards as more important still the regeneration given along with it, 'the great change which God works in the soul when He renews it in Christ Jesus according to the image of God, by which we become children of God'.[15] In this regeneration it is the subjective aspect which is stressed: '*Conversion* which refers to what man has to do, whereas regeneration is what God alone can do.'[16] This human response begins with the repentance to which God's grace summons the sinner. Repentance consists in 'acknowledging and confessing our sins with shame and sorrow, hating and forsaking them, and turning to God with all our heart'.[17] Repentance is thought of more as a turning away from sin, conversion as a turning towards God. The vital

[8] Sermon CXXVIII, on Rom. 8.32 (Wesley, *Works*, VOL. VII, pp. 356ff).
[9] Wesley, *Works*, VOL. VII, p. 359. [10] *Ibid.*
[11] *Op. cit.*, p. 360. [12] *Ibid.*
[13] *Op. cit.*, p. 362. [14] Nuelson, *Lehre des Methodismus*, p. 10.
[15] Nass, Large Catechism, 1868 (*Corpus Confessionum*, ed. Fabricius, PT XX, p. 638).
[16] *Ibid.* [17] *Op. cit.*, p. 637.

point is that all the emphasis is placed on this action by man in addition to his faith. 'The great change' which God works in a man has to be actively effected at the same time by the man himself. This change worked in man and worked out by man himself must be followed by the *assurance of salvation*. This refers not to the assurance which the sinner receives in the promise given in God's Word, but to a *special action of the Holy Spirit* in man, experienced by those who are already God's children. 'The testimony of the Spirit is an inward impression on the souls of believers, whereby the Spirit of God directly testifies to their Spirit, that they are children of God.'[18] The testimony of the Spirit is 'to be distinguished from what the Spirit does in regeneration. It is something added to this work, in order to convince the heart of its genuineness and reality. It is the positive seal which God imprints on His own, the pledge of the grace promised.'[19] According to Wesley, this does not mean an 'outward voice' employed by the Spirit nor a word from Scripture which He 'applies' to the heart, nor does it mean an 'inward voice', although none of these things are necessarily excluded. It means rather that 'He so works upon the soul by His immediate influence, and by a strong, though inexplicable operation, that the stormy wind and troubled waves subside, and there is a sweet calm: the heart resting as in the arms of Jesus, and the sinner being clearly satisfied that God is reconciled, that all his "iniquities are forgiven and his sins covered".'[20] This testimony of the Spirit is secured against all self-deception and false enthusiasm by the fruits which follow directly from it: 'Love, joy, peace, long-suffering, gentleness, goodness', without which 'the testimony itself cannot continue, for it is inevitably destroyed not only by the commission of any outward sin or the omission of known duty, but by giving way to any inward sin, in a word, by whatever grieves the Holy Spirit of God.'[21]

Already in those words we hear the doctrine which is most characteristic of Methodism, the doctrine of Christian *perfection*. We have heard how the assurance of salvation, given through

[18] Sermon XI, 'The Witness of the Spirit', Discourse II on Rom. 8.16 (*Works*, VOL. V, pp. 123f; *Standard Sermons*, VOL. II, p. 345). Cf. also Sermon X.

[19] Nuelson, *Lehre des Methodismus*, p. 13.

[20] Sermon XI (*Works*, VOL. V, p. 117; *Standard Sermons*, VOL. II, p. 345).

[21] *Works*, VOL. V, p. 116; *Standard Sermons*, VOL. II, p. 344.

the testimony of the Spirit, is destroyed not only by outward sins but even by sins of thought. If a Christian then is to remain in the proper Christian condition he must not sin at all. This position is already hinted at by Wesley's rejection of Article 15: 'Of Christ alone without sin'. This article declares: 'But all we the rest, although baptised, and born again in Christ, yet offend in many things; and if we say we have no sin, we deceive ourselves and the truth is not in us' (1 John 1.8). Wesley obviously took exception to this statement.

He asserted: 'A Christian is so far perfect, as not to commit sin,'[22] and, in support of this, he appeals to 1 John 5.18. The conflicting passage 1 John 1.8, he interprets as referring to the past, to the time when a man has not yet been cleansed by the blood of Christ. According to Wesley: 'my evil nature, the body of sin, is destroyed',[23] and therefore, 'deliverance from inward as well as from outward sin' has been given.[24] 'It remains, then, that Christians are saved in this world from all sin, from all unrighteousness; that they are now in such a sense perfect, as not to commit sin, and to be freed from evil thoughts and evil tempers.'[25] The character of a Methodist can be described thus: 'There is not a motion in his heart, but is according to His will. Every thought which arises points to Him, and is in obedience to the law of Christ.'[26] 'All the commandments of God he accordingly keeps, and that with all his might.'[27] Nuelson says therefore that 'the basic religious problem for Methodism' is 'How can I walk in holiness before God?'[28] He adds: 'Methodism does not teach an absolute or sinless perfection.'[29]

Nor does Wesley assert an absolute perfection. Christians are not free 'from ignorance, or mistake, or infirmities or temptations'.[30] 'How much soever any man has attained, or in how high a degree soever he is perfect, he hath still need "to

[22] Sermon XI, 'Christian Perfection', on Phil. 3.12 (*Works*, VOL. VI, p. 15; *Standard Sermons*, VOL. II, p. 169).

[23] *Works*, VOL. V, p. 16; *Standard Sermons*, VOL. II, p. 171. [24] *Ibid.*

[25] *Works*, VOL. V, p. 18; *Standard Sermons*, VOL. II, p. 173.

[26] *The Character of a Methodist*, 1950 edn., p. 12 (*Corpus Confessionum*, ed. Fabricius, PT XX, p. 715).

[27] *Op. cit.*, p. 13 (*Corpus Confessionum*, ed. Fabricius, PT XX, p. 716).

[28] Nuelson, *Lehre des Methodismus*, p. 14. [29] *Op. cit.*, p. 16.

[30] Sermon XL (*Works*, VOL. VI, p. 5).

grow in grace".'[31] But Wesley does say that the perfection which a man can obtain is sinless. For by sin he means 'outward sin . . . an actual, voluntary transgression of the law, of the revealed written law of God',[32] and says that genuine Christians are free from it, and even from sins of thought too. But we notice that in Wesley's view the regenerate Christian can lapse into sin again.[33] This is also the teaching of the catechisms.[34] In the German-English Catechism it is stated that the strength for our sanctification lies 'not in us but in Jesus Christ alone'.[35] We get the impression that Methodists nowadays are more cautious in their teaching on perfection. 'The view which is being increasingly accepted teaches a defeat of, and a complete victory over sinful wicked desires by the superior vital power of the Spirit.'[36] Indeed perfection can even be described as 'the ideal to be striven for, of a mature personality based on Christ and fully acquired in Him'.[37]

We are given no clear information about *the way to this perfection.*[38] According to Nuelson, various views are held. For the most part sanctification to perfection is thought of as a special act following justification both temporally and materially. 'By all the grace which is given at justification we cannot extirpate them (i.e. our enemies, both outward and inward sin),' says Wesley. 'Most sure we cannot, till it shall please our Lord to speak to our hearts again, to speak a second time, "Be clean".'[39]

After justification, which itself seems not to be simply equated with regeneration, there must be a 'second change' in man. In Nass's Larger Catechism, sanctification is defined as a special act of divine grace.[40] In a German edition, however, it says on the contrary that sanctification is 'the continued growth in grace'.[41] A different conception becomes evident here which presents sanctification to perfection as 'a process begun in justification

[31] *Ibid.*

[32] Sermon XIX, 'The great privilege of those that are born of God', on 1 John 3.9 (*Works*, VOL. V, p. 214; *Standard Sermons*, VOL. I, p. 304).

[33] *Works*, VOL. V, pp. 214ff; *Standard Sermons*, VOL. I, pp. 304ff.

[34] *Corpus Confessionum*, ed. Fabricius, PT XX, p. 638.

[35] *Op. cit.*, p. 662.

[36] Nuelson, *Lehre des Methodismus*, p. 16.

[37] *Op. cit.*, p. 32.

[38] *Op. cit.*, p. 16. See W. E. R. Sangster, *The Path to Perfection*, London 1943.

[39] Sermon, 'The Repentance of Believers', on Mark 1.15 (*Standard Sermons*, VOL. II, pp. 392f).

[40] *Corpus Confessionum*, ed. Fabricius, PT XX, p. 638.

[41] *Ibid.* (note).

and continuing to work gradually'.[42] But this doctrinal difference about the origin of sanctification does not matter greatly. In either case the concern is with the attainment of perfection.

Some have regarded this doctrine as scriptural.[43] But we can only do so if we accept Wesley's strained interpretation of 1 John 1.8, and follow the Methodist view of Rom. 7 as not referring to the Christian life.[44] But we readily agree that the Methodist doctrine raises a serious question for Reformation doctrine. The statement that man is at one and the same time just and sinful (*simul iustus et peccator*) can become a treacherous formula concealing the fact that God's Word is always at the same time His claim to the whole of our life. On the other hand, our question to the Methodists must be: Does the Methodist doctrine of salvation really reproduce the biblical message? It is not just a question of the interpretation of isolated passages, but of the whole Bible. We must ask: Is the Bible a book about the religious man? Who is it concerned with? The Holy God or holy men? We know of course that these are mutually related, but still we must not put the emphasis in the wrong place. The Bible is concerned with the righteousness and holiness of God, which have been revealed in Christ, and to Wesley's question: 'Surely the believer is holy *in himself*?' the right answer is still the one given by Count Nicholas von Zinzendorf, the founder of the Moravian Church (*Unitas fratrum*), 'No! No! *Only in Christ!* Not holy in himself.'[45] The Bible is concerned with God's Kingdom, and the goal of God's ways is 'that God may be all in all' (1 Cor. 15.28). Methodism may differ from pietism in that 'it seeks not just to save individual souls from destruction but tries to leaven the masses with the leaven of the Gospel',[46] but is chiefly concerned with a sanctified and perfect human life.

Contrary to the intention of its founder, the Methodist move-

[42] Nuelson, *Lehre des Methodismus*, p. 17.

[43] Loofs, in *R.E.*, VOL. XII, 799.

[44] Nuelson, *Lehre des Methodismus*, p. 16. Cf. the interpretation of Rom. 7 by a modern Methodist scholar, C. L. Mitton, 'Romans vii reconsidered', in *Expository Times*, LXV (1953-4), pp. 78-81, 99-103, 132-5, and the marginal note from the Reformed side by C. E. B. Cranfield, *op. cit.*, p. 221. Also Karl Barth, *Church Dogmatics*, VOL. IV, 1, pp. 581-91.

[45] See *The Journal of the Rev. John Wesley A.M.*, ed. Nehemiah Carnock, Standard edn. London 1909, VOL. II, pp. 488-90.

[46] Nuelson, *Lehre des Methodismus*, p. 28.

ment separated from the established Church in England and developed into a Church itself. Yet it has remained basically similar to it. In the Anglican Church holy order plays a leading role, in Methodism it is the holy man. That does not amount to a fundamental difference. Methodism found the Anglican Church with its order paralysed and lacking genuine life. Was the change which it set itself to bring about a reformation or just a reaction on the same level? The latter seems to us to have been the case. No one will deny that the Methodist message contains the clear notes of the Gospel and therefore influenced the Anglican Church in the spirit of the Reformation. We need only recall Wesley's forthright preaching of the sinner's justification. No one can evade the question which Methodism puts to us concerning our condition as Christians. But it was not a genuine answer to Anglicanism. Significantly enough it did not even wish to be such an answer. If it had, it would not have rested content with simply taking Question I of the Heidelberg Catechism into its proclamation, as it did in Nass's Shorter Catechism.[47] It would have seen that this Question I is not just one question among others but that it says everything. It affirms the gracious sovereignty of Jesus Christ over us. Of all men it is the man who desires salvation who needs to learn that this rests not with him but with Jesus Christ.

[47] Nass, Smaller Catechism (*Corpus Confessionum*, ed. Fabricius, PT XX, p. 653).

CHAPTER 16

THE SOCIETY OF FRIENDS (QUAKERS)

1. The Fountain of Truth and Knowledge

Quaker meetings differ from the services of all other Churches. Those who take part in them immerse themselves in silent meditation. If the Spirit does not prompt anyone to speak, meetings can end without this silence being broken ('silent meeting'). The silence is broken only when someone feels moved to share with the others what he himself has heard inwardly. The very form of their worship illustrates the difficulty of arriving at any firm outline of the Quaker message. For Quakers what matters is the repeated inner prompting of the Holy Spirit. To this extent they have something in common with the 'spiritualist' movements of the Middle Ages right down to the Quintinists (mistakenly known as Libertines) of Reformation times.[1] But the Society of Friends grew from the soil of the Reformation within the established Church in England. It came into existence as the result of the religious experiences of George Fox (1624-91) in the forties of the seventeenth century. This plain man, in his disappointment with conditions in the Church and his despair with himself, made the discovery that no human word could help him, not even the Word of Holy Scripture, but only a direct *revelation*. By such revelations he heard and recognised Christ and became sure of Him.

Quakers do not reject *the Bible*. This differentiates them from many of the 'spiritualists' of earlier ages. Indeed, present-day Quakers value Holy Scripture very highly. It represents the 'most important written expression of all religious experience'.

[1] Quintinists were the followers of a radical named Quintin, who was burned at Tournai in 1530. Cf. Calvin's *Contre la secte phantastique des Libertins* (*Opera*, VOL. VII, pp. 200ff).

But that means that religious experience, *faith* itself, *does not depend upon it.* Faith can benefit greatly from Scripture but it does not arise out of the Word of Scripture, and is not upheld by this Word. 'Yet *we may not call them the principal fountain of all truth and knowledge, nor yet the first adequate rule of faith and manners*; because the principal fountain of truth must be the truth itself; i.e. that whose certainty and authority depends not upon another.'[2] Scripture is 'only a declaration of the fountain and not the fountain itself'.[3] The 'fountain' itself is the Spirit, the 'saving and spiritual light' in man, as the Quakers often call it. But whatever expressions they may use to describe this divine power in man, they mean by it 'a spiritual, heavenly, and invisible principle, in which God, as Father, Son, and Spirit dwells'.[4]

The Quakers have recognised here something which is true. Scripture is no paper Pope. It is not a second incarnation of the Word, it is on the contrary a witness to the Incarnation of the Word in Jesus Christ. The Barmen Declaration rediscovered and reaffirmed this important truth about Scripture: 'Jesus Christ as He is attested to us in Holy Scripture is the One Word of God which we must hear.'[5] But the Quakers not only distinguish between Scripture and Revelation, they also dissolve their inseparable unity. As they see it, the Spirit's work is not to apply the testimony of the Lord's messengers, and to give it authority in men's hearts today. 'It is not said: "It shall teach you how to understand those things which are written" but "it shall teach you all things".'[6] It is emphasised repeatedly 'that Christians are always to be led inwardly and immediately by the Spirit of God dwelling in them.'[7] It is the Spirit who also shows men *truths not contained in Scripture* 'because there be many truths which, as they are applicable to particulars and individuals, and most needful to be known by them, are in nowise to be found in the Scripture'.[8] '*These divine inward revela-*

[2] Robert Barclay, *An Apology for the True Christian Divinity*, henceforth cited as *Apology*, p. 37 (page references here are to the 13th edn., Manchester 1869). On Robert Barclay see J. P. Wragge, *The Faith of Robert Barclay, An Essay on his life, and on the relevance of his thought for today*, London 1948. Also Lief Eeg-Olofsson, *The Conception of the Inner Light in Robert Barclay's Theology*, Lund 1955.

[3] Barclay, *Apology*, p. 35.

[4] *Op. cit.*, pp. 80f.

[5] Barmen Thesis No. 1.

[6] Barclay, *Apology*, p. 22.

[7] *Op. cit.*, p. 21.

[8] *Op. cit.*, p. 22.

tions' can indeed never '*contradict the outward testimony of the Scriptures*'[9] for they are just as much revelations of the Spirit as those whose deposit lies before us in Scripture. This does not mean however 'that these divine revelations are to be subjected to the test . . . of the outward testimony of the Scriptures . . . as to a more noble or certain touchstone; for *this divine revelation, and inward illumination is that which is evident and clear of itself*'.[10]

Here the Quakers forsake the solid ground of God's historical revelation in Jesus Christ and ignore the fact that God has revealed Himself fully and perfectly in Him and that therefore the only proper thing for us to do is to hear and recognise Him in the testimony of His messengers. In consequence there is no real encounter between Christ and men; everything remains within the mind of the individual. 'Inward revelations' and 'truths' are given to him; but what matters is that one truth, that only perfect revelation outside of us in Jesus Christ, which is only made present and opened to us by the Holy Spirit. The Quakers' departure from the Scripture principle is even more radical than that of the Roman Church, which still leaves Scripture as a normative authority even though it gives dogma an equal position alongside it. Nevertheless there is a clear affinity with the Quaker position. In virtue of an immediate illumination of the Holy Spirit, the Pope determines the true interpretation of Scripture and tradition. What in his case is the sole prerogative of a single individual, becomes in the Quaker view something given to every Christian by the 'inner light'. In both cases there is a departure from unconditional obedience to the Biblical testimony concerning the coming Christ and the Christ who has come.

In view both of the supreme importance attached by Quakers to the inner light and of their attitude to Holy Scripture it is only to be expected that they *have no dogma* or *confessional document*. They are the only communion growing out of the soil of the Reformation which rejects every formal confession. It takes pride in having 'thrown overboard the whole heavy cargo of theological speculations'. Their place has been taken by 'the spiritual experiences' of religious men, which are repeatedly being renewed. Yet even the Friends have certain

[9] *Op. cit.*, p. 3. [10] *Ibid.*

basic views which find expression in their various writings. Among the most important and best known of these writings is the *Apology* of Robert Barclay (*d.* 1690), already quoted several times above, and the *Book of Christian Discipline*, containing the decisions of the London Quaker Meetings.

2. Man and his Redemption

We have already mentioned the most important basic view of the Quakers, their belief in the supreme importance of the inner light. We shall appreciate this better if we turn first to their view of man. Quakers 'confess then that a *seed of sin* is transmitted to all men from Adam, . . . in which seed he gave occasion to all to sin, and it is the origin of all evil actions and thoughts in men's hearts'.[11] Human nature as such contains nothing good.[12] Reason was in fact 'the great cause of the apostasy', and conscience is 'defiled and corrupted'.[13] Therefore no 'relics of any good which Adam lost by his fall' can help man to gain salvation.[14] Yet the term *original sin* is rejected as an 'invented and unscriptural barbarism'.[15] It is not just the term which is rejected but the underlying idea that by Adam's sin original guilt has been transmitted to all men. 'We do not ascribe any whit of Adam's guilt to men, until they make it theirs by the like act of disobedience.'[16] The doctrine that original sin includes infants is an 'opinion which is cruel and contrary to the nature as well of God's mercy as justice'.[17] The latent seed of sin in man must unfold if guilt is to be incurred. Evidence that this guilt came to be known and experienced as such in all its force under God's holy judgment, is provided by the fact that Fox and his companions were 'seized' by a trembling of the whole body, and for this reason were scornfully nicknamed 'Quakers', i.e. tremblers. But, if it be right to tremble in the presence of the Divine Word, we are bound to ask how we can possibly speak of any guiltless, neutral condition of sinful man in the presence of God Himself.

Only Divine *grace* can save sinful man. Grace too is 'no less universal than the seed of sin' in man.[18] The doctrine of

[11] *Op. cit.*, p. 61. [12] *Op. cit.*, p. 54. [13] *Op. cit.*, p. 85.
[14] *Op. cit.*, p. 84. Cf. p. 57. [15] *Op.* cit., p. 61. [16] *Op. cit.*, p. 54.
[17] *Op. cit.*, p. 59. [18] *Op. cit.*, p. 62.

double predestination is rejected as 'horrible and blasphemous'.[19] Grace is not naturally present in men, but is 'a part and a great part too of the new covenant dispensation and so no consequence nor part of man's nature'.[20] It is 'in every man's and woman's heart, *in that little incorruptible seed* ready to be brought forth'.[21] It is—'in a larger sense'—Christ Himself, since 'He never is nor can be separate from that holy pure seed and light which is in all men'.[22] Of course He 'lies crucified in them by their sins and iniquities, that they may look upon him whom they have pierced, and repent, whereby he that now lies as it were slain and buried in them may come to be raised, and have dominion in their hearts over all'.[23]

Two seeds then slumber in every human heart, a sinful one and a divine one. But, whereas the sinful seed is brought to fruition by man himself, the divine one requires an intervention by God Himself. This divine act is called a 'visitation'.[24] God has 'given to every man . . . a certain day or time of visitation: during which day or time it is possible for them to be saved, and to partake of the fruit of Christ's death'.[25] This time of visitation does not embrace a man's entire life span, 'though to some it may be extended even to the very hour of death'.[26] The man who uses this opportunity and accepts God's call inwardly, will be saved even if he is among 'those who are ignorant of the death and sufferings of Christ and Adam's fall'. But a man can *resist* the light within him, whether he be a non-Christian or an unregenerate Christian, and so bring condemnation on himself.[27]

If even those who are ignorant of the sufferings and death of Christ can be saved, the question arises as to whether *the person and work of Christ* can have any significance at all for Quakers. It is plain from the *Apology* that they site the work of redemption almost exclusively in man's heart. Barclay is in fact quite unable to do justice to the biblical statements about the saving events.[28] He insists that the work of *reconciliation is not yet com-*

[19] *Op. cit.*, pp. 64ff. [20] *Op. cit.*, p. 56. [21] *Op. cit.*, p. 106.
[22] *Op. cit.*, pp. 84f. Cf. p. 117. [23] *Op. cit.*, p. 84.
[24] *Op. cit*, p 56. Cf. pp. 77ff. [25] *Op. cit.*, p. 77.
[26] *Op. cit.*, p. 80. [27] *Op. cit.*, p. 77.
[28] J. A. Möhler's comment is interesting: 'It is therefore no surprise to learn that many American Quakers regard the life of Christ purely as an allegory.

pleted, and even goes so far as to argue, unconvincingly, that this fact is expressed by the Apostle's use of the imperfect tense in 2 Cor. 5.19.[29] If Christ's own words 'It is finished' were taken to mean that redemption had been completed sixteen centuries earlier the preaching of repentance and forgiveness would be unnecessary.[30] But was not Barclay seeing something here which is true? Indeed he was, inasmuch as the work of redemption must be proclaimed to men and accepted by them today. But that is no reason for minimising the significance of Christ's work. According to Barclay God's reconciling work *cannot* be spoken of '*as if He were actually reconciled*'.[31] The 'real, true' redemption is the 'inward' one which takes place when men receive 'the light, spirit, and grace of Christ revealed to us'.[32] What, then, is the significance of Christ's work? We are 'so far reconciled to God by the death of His Son, while enemies, that we are put into a capacity of salvation',[33] 'a capacity of being reconciled to God',[34] i.e. 'a measure of that power, virtue, spirit, life and grace, that was in Christ Jesus' comes to men 'as the free gift of God'.[35] *Christ's death*, it is affirmed, is the *precondition for the giving of the divine seed*, for the inner light; *it makes possible the real, inward, redemption.* Strictly speaking, 'Christ, by His death, has removed the wrath of God, so far as to obtain remission of sins for as many as receive that grace and light that He communicates unto them and hath purchased for them by His blood'.[36] The little which Christ is said to have done for all men is reduced even further to what happens in those who experience the inner light. This conclusion is confirmed by the statement: 'But the mystery is and may be profitable *without the explicit and outward knowledge of the history*.'[37] It comes as no surprise when we read that Plato, Cicero, and other *non-Christians* '*knew Christ* and by his working in them were brought from unrighteousness to righteousness, and to love that

What Barclay had already said so often about Christ being crucified by the sin in every man, about the Inner Word suffering under the weight of that sin, and so on, clearly helped to introduce and prepare the way for the view of the historic Christ as merely a philosophical, anthropological and religious myth' (*Symbolik*, p. 527).

[29] *Apology*, p. 129.
[30] *Op. cit.*, p. 128.
[31] *Op. cit.*, p. 126.
[32] *Op. cit.*, p. 124.
[33] *Ibid.*
[34] *Op. cit.*, p. 127.
[35] *Op. cit.*, p. 124.
[36] *Op. cit.*, p. 128.
[37] *Op. cit.*, p. 83.

power by which they felt themselves redeemed'.[38] This view of Christ is still shared by present-day Quakers: 'Christ is the God who reveals Himself in eternity, who speaks directly to man: nothing in God's attitude was changed by Christ's coming.'[39] But there are other views besides this. 'In boundless love He tasted death for every man; all that inherit eternal life, of every age and of every nation under heaven, partake of the blessings of that redemption which comes through His sufferings and death.'[40]

According to Quakers, man's *justification* is his regeneration, which takes place following the divine visitation, by the growth of the seed that has been placed in every man, provided a man does not resist this visitation. Barclay's teaching was 'that the immediate, nearest, or formal cause of a man's justification in the sight of God is the revelation of God in the soul, changing, altering, and renewing the mind'.[41] Justification is '*the formation of Christ in us*, Christ born and brought forth in us'.[42] In other words, it consists in the inner light becoming a real illumination in man's soul. It sounds almost like Calvin speaking when Barclay says of the Jesus in us: 'By this also comes that communication of the goods of Christ unto us.' But the fundamental difference is at once clear when Barclay goes on: 'by which we come to be made "partakers of the divine nature",'[43] whereas Calvin interprets these words from 2 Pet. 1 in an eschatological sense. According to Barclay what we partake of in union with Christ is not the righteousness which He has won for us, but His eternity, His spirit, His power, or whatever else we care to call it. This Christ in men transforms them, makes them just, and in virtue of this transformation or sanctification they are then just. What is strange is not that Barclay should insist that justification means 'to make just'.[44] Luther, too, said that. The real danger in Barclay's doctrine is his failure to see righteousness exclusively in the Christ with whom we are united, and not in the actual holiness produced in man by the

[38] *Op. cit.*, p. 115.
[39] R. M. Jones, *An Interpretation of Quakerism.* I have been unable to trace this book (TR).
[40] *Circular Letter*, 1832, quoted by Loofs, in *R.E.*, VOL. XVI, p. 375.
[41] *Apology*, p. 136. [42] *Op. cit.*, p. 124.
[43] *Op. cit.*, p. 125. [44] *Op. cit.*, p. 131.

Spirit. So he says: 'For though properly we be not justified for them [i.e. because of works] yet we are *justified in them*: and they are necessary even as *causa sine qua non*, that is, as the cause without which none are justified.'[45] The Reformers' view 'that the best works even of the saints are defiled and polluted' in God's sight is rejected.[46] The regenerate man is *perfect*, 'free from actual sinning and transgressing of the law of God', though in such a way that a 'growth' in perfection is always possible,[47] and man's perfection is never that of God Himself.[48] 'Yet we believe that such works as naturally proceed from this spiritual birth and formation of Christ in us are pure and holy even as the root from which they come, and therefore God accepts them, justifies us in them.'[49] The departure from Christocentric thinking is unmistakably plain here. It is a case of a divine power in man transforming him. It is no wonder that Professor Möhler, a Roman Catholic, was attracted by this doctrine of justification, and could understand why 'the Quakers meet with the same objections as the Catholics, because they establish a righteousness of their own in place of the righteousness of Christ'.[50]

3. View of the Sacraments and the Church

Since Quakers regard the divine Word as an inward one, it is not surprising that they recognise no external sacramental ceremonies. The term 'sacrament' itself is rejected as being borrowed from the heathens.[51] The water baptism of John was a pointer to the coming baptism by Christ, and this is exclusively the 'Spirit baptism'.[52] According to Barclay, here too the difference between Quakers and their opponents is 'that these often times prefer the form and shadow to the power and substance'.[53] But since 'the figure gives way to the substance' 'therefore water baptism is not to continue now because it is not the baptism of Christ'.[54] In the command to baptise Christ enjoined on the apostles His own baptism, which is not water

[45] *Op. cit.*, p. 125.
[46] *Op. cit.*, p. 126.
[47] *Op. cit.*, p. 148.
[48] *Op. cit.*, p. 149.
[49] *Op. cit.*, p. 126.
[50] J. A. Möhler, *Symbolik*, p. 505.
[51] Barclay, *Apology*, p. 258.
[52] *Op. cit.*, p. 260.
[53] *Op. cit.*, p. 263.
[54] *Op. cit.*, pp. 265f.

baptism,[55] but a baptism 'into this name, virtue, and power of God', 'and not a mere formal expression of words adjoining with water baptism'.[56] Christianity therefore recognises no external badge of Christians as Judaism does by the practice of circumcision.[57]

A similar view is taken of the *Lord's Supper*. '*The breaking of bread* by Christ with His disciples *was merely a figure*' *of the* '*participation in His flesh and blood*, by which the inward man is daily nourished in the hearts of those in whom Christ dwells.'[58] The words 'This do in remembrance of me' did not mean that the meal which Jesus arranged before his death was to be an indispensable and binding feature of the New Covenant dispensation. Jesus was merely inviting the disciples 'in their eating and drinking at all times to have regard to him'.[59] Because of their weakness Paul allowed the Corinthians to celebrate an outward meal,[60] but since 'the Kingdom of God does not mean food and drink' (Rom. 14.17[61]) 'those who are dead with Christ and not only dead with Christ but buried, and also risen with him, *need not such signs*'.[62] Those who are not yet ripe for this understanding and have a tender conscience, may be allowed to celebrate a meal, provided they do not wish to burden others with it, for the day has arrived when God 'has dismissed all those ceremonies and rites, and is only to be worshipped in Spirit . . . and that to seek God in these things is . . . to seek the living among the dead'.[63]

The body of Christ which believers partake of *is the* '*heavenly seed*, that divine spiritual and celestial substance'.[64] It is one with that 'invisible principle' of which we heard at the very outset, which is implanted in the heart of every man. For this principle or seed is explicitly defined as follows: 'This we call *vehiculum Dei* or the spiritual body of Christ, the flesh and blood of Christ which came down from Heaven, by which all the saints do feed and are thereby nourished unto eternal life.'[65] When a man allows this seed to grow in his heart, when he turns towards the hidden Christ within him, or to the light, as it is

[55] *Op. cit.*, p. 271.
[56] *Op. cit.*, p. 272.
[57] *Op. cit.*, p. 269.
[58] *Op. cit.*, p. 280.
[59] *Op. cit.*, p. 294.
[60] *Op. cit.*, p 302.
[61] *Op. cit.*, p. 303.
[62] *Op. cit.*, p. 301.
[63] *Op. cit.*, p. 306.
[64] *Op. cit.*, p. 281.
[65] *Op. cit.*, p. 81.

also called, then Christ is formed in the believer.[66] His flesh and blood therefore 'is truly and really enjoyed, *as often as the soul retires into the light of the Lord*, and feels and partakes of that heavenly life by which the inward man is nourished'.[67] Eating and drinking the body and blood of Christ is the same as retiring into the inner light. The Quakers would certainly not speak of eating Christ's body at all, if this mode of speech were not suggested to them by the New Testament. Their sole concern is devout meditation, and this has nothing to do with external things such as sacramental actions.

All those 'who become obedient to the holy light and testimony of God in their hearts' constitute the '*Catholic or Universal Church*', for they are 'called and gathered truly by God'. Among them are those who have already died, and it is even possible for 'heathens, Turks, and Jews' to be members of this Catholic Church.[68] The Church is *also the congregation of believers in any one place* met together 'to wait upon God, to worship Him, and to bear a joint testimony against error, suffering for the same . . .'. They thus become like 'one family' since 'each of them watch over, teach, instruct and care for one another, according to their several measures and attainments'.[69] On the other hand it is the Devil also who prompts Churches—he is thinking of the Roman and Protestant Churches!—to assert that no one can belong to the Church without an outward profession and outward ceremonies.[70] Since all regenerate men belong together and together constitute Christ's body, neither individual Christians nor individual congregations can live unto themselves. The Friends have therefore created a *graduated organisation* of their society from the local meetings to the Yearly General Meetings. For cohesion the following measures have been taken:

God who leads men together into a congregation raises up among them 'by the inward immediate operation of his own Spirit' and 'for the preserving them in a lively fresh and powerful condition, *ministers and teachers* to instruct and teach and watch over them'.[71] Because the words of such a preacher 'proceed from the inward power and virtue' they 'reach to the

[66] *Ibid.*
[67] *Op. cit.*, p. 285.
[68] *Op. cit.*, p. 169.
[69] *Op. cit.*, p. 170.
[70] *Op. cit.*, p. 171.
[71] *Op. cit.*, p. 185.

heart of his hearers and make them approve of him and be subject unto Him'.[72] On the other hand Quakers decisively reject a regular ordained ministry, refusing, that is, to entrust these functions permanently to particular persons specially trained, externally called and paid to do them. Yet they do recognise 'that some are more particularly called to the work of the ministry' in order 'more constantly and particularly to instruct . . . and watch over their brethren'. Hence 'there is also due to them . . . such obedience and subjection as is mentioned in these testimonies of the Scripture'.[73] They have therefore developed *forms of ministry* which are performed by members provided they are illuminated by the Spirit: Recorded ministers (members of the meeting who speak often), elders, and overseers to watch over personal and corporate life. *But in principle this ministry is open to every member*, 'whether rich or poor, servant or master, young or old, yea, male or female'.[74] Only one condition is essential: the member must be filled with the Spirit.

It is significant that Quakers are not content with silent worship, but gladly accept the services given by the above-mentioned ministers. Barclay says that *preaching* constitutes '*a standing ordinance in the Church*'.[75] The only thing is that the purpose of preaching is not made clear. We have already seen that it is intended to keep the Church in a lively condition. Furthermore it is said that 'it is very appropriate and quickening when it proceeds from a true experience of the love of God in the heart'. Clearly then, the seed of the inner light carried by the individual within himself is not sufficient for him, otherwise he would not need any instruction or exhortation. This inconsistency is significant. In their depreciation of the external word of ordinary Church preaching and even of the Scriptures, are the Quakers perhaps merely reacting against a misinterpreted Scripture principle and a cold kind of preaching? Or were they precursors of Schleiermacher for whom preaching meant an expression of religious feeling? Here at least is a starting-point for our conversation with the Friends of the Inner Light.

[72] *Op. cit.*, p. 174.
[73] *Op. cit.*, p. 202.
[74] *Op. cit.*, p. 200.
[75] *Op. cit.*, p. 270.

4. A Life of Service

We cannot speak of the Quakers and their concern, without recalling how earnestly they try to live out their inner view of things. In their personal attitude to life they show clear marks of a *renunciation of the world.* Their rejection of military service and refusal to take oaths is well known. But they differ from most mystics in that they practise no self-sufficient asceticism, but, in a most exemplary way, *turn outward toward the world and its needs in ministering love.* That finds moving expression in a message of the London Yearly Meeting of 1907: 'Men today are waiting for the Gospel of Divine Love worked out in human fellowship and in the freedom of perfect service. Such freedom ... requires co-operation with each other; it means too the concentration of all our energies ... and neither of these can come without sacrifice. This sacrifice is ... the glad outpouring of our life for others, the free gift of our will to God and for our fellows ... *words cannot explain the meaning of our message* ... it needs the definition of a devoted life.'[76]

In this respect the Quakers represent a great question addressed to all Christian Churches for it is written: 'Not everyone who says to me "Lord, Lord," shall enter the Kingdom of Heaven, but he who does the will of my Father who is in Heaven' (Matt. 8.21).

It is perhaps fitting that at the end of our whole enquiry we should be confronted with this question.

[76] *Christian Discipline of the Society of Friends,* PT I, *Christian Life, Faith and Thought,* London 1927, p. 76.

APPENDIX I

THE DÜSSELDORF THESES (1933)

A Theological Declaration concerning the Form of the Church. Drawn up in Düsseldorf on 20 May 1933, by professors, pastors, elders and deacons from the Rhineland.

The providence of God has brought us to an hour when we must ask ourselves again: What is an Evangelical Church?

1. The Holy, Christian Church, whose Sole Head is Christ, is born of the Word of God, abides in the same, and hears not the voice of a stranger.

2. The Word of God speaks to us through the Holy Scriptures of the Old and New Testaments.

3. The Word of God spoken to us is our Lord Jesus Christ.

4. Jesus Christ is the Saviour of the world and the only Lord of the elect Church, which He calls out of all nations to eternal life.

5. The Church lives solely because, day by day, it is newly called and upheld, comforted and governed by its Lord.

6. The Church lives in all its members by the exercise of the ministry of preachers, teachers, elders and deacons, which was instituted and ordained by Jesus Christ.

7. The principal ministry of preachers is to proclaim God's Word to the Church and to the world, by the exposition of Scripture, and by Baptism and the Lord's Supper.

8. The ministry of teachers is to instruct the young, to train future preachers, and constantly to re-examine and test the purity and soundness of Church doctrine, and to do all this on the basis of Holy Scripture.

9. The ministry of elders consists in a special joint watchfulness over the Church's order, doctrine, and life.

10. The ministry of deacons is to care for the needy, the sick, and the helpless, no matter who they may be.

11. The authority and power of this ministry rests solely on the free grace of the Church's Lord.

12. The Church's only 'spiritual leader' is Jesus Christ, its Heavenly King; who, by His Spirit, lives on earth in everyone who serves Him in the Church, in obedience to His commission.

13. The offices of preacher, teacher, elder and deacon, together serve to edify the Church. In all the variety of ministry and gifts, each holds its promise and authority directly from the Church's Lord.

14. The earthly counterpart to the government of local congregations by the Heavenly Lord, is not the rule of one congregation over the rest, nor that of an episcopal office set over other offices, but the ministry which local congregations owe each other and seek to render each other by Synods composed of their appointed delegates.

APPENDIX II

THE BARMEN DECLARATION
(May 1934)

Theological Declaration on the Present Position of the German Evangelical Church

According to the first words of its Constitution of 11 July 1933, the German Evangelical Church is a federation of Confessional Churches of equal status, having their roots in the Reformation. The theological basis for the union of these Churches is stated in Art. 1 and Art. 2.1 of the Constitution of the German Evangelical Church, recognised by the Reich Government on 14 July 1933:

Art. 1: The inviolable foundation of the German Evangelical Church is the Gospel of Jesus Christ, as this is attested to us in Holy Scripture, and was newly brought to light in the Confessions of the Reformation. The powers which the Church needs for its mission are hereby determined and defined.

Art. 2.1: The German Evangelical Church is composed of Churches (i.e. Regional Churches).

We, as representatives of Lutheran, Reformed, and United Churches, of free Synods, Church Assemblies, and Church Societies, united in the Confessional Synod of the German Evangelical Church, declare that we stand together on the firm basis of the German Evangelical Church as a federation of German Confessional Churches. We are united by our common Confession of the One Lord of the One, Holy, Catholic and Apostolic Church.

We declare publicly to all Evangelical Churches in Germany that our common interest in this Confession, and therefore the unity of the German Evangelical Church, is in grave danger. It is threatened by the kind of doctrine and practice which is in vogue in the dominant Church party, that of the 'German Christians', and in the Church governments sponsored by them, and which has been increasingly in evidence during the first year of the existence of the German Evangelical Church. The essence of this threat is that the theological basis on which the unity of the German Evangelical Church rests is continually and systematically being evaded and made ineffective by alien principles introduced by both the leaders and spokesmen of the 'German Christians' and by the Government of the Church. If these alien principles are accepted, then, according to all the Confessions that have authority for us, the Church ceases to be the Church. If these principles are accepted therefore, the German Evangelical Church as a federation of Confessional Churches is betrayed from within.

As members of the Lutheran, Reformed and United Churches, we may and must raise our voices together in this cause today. Just because we wish to remain faithful to our various Confessions, we cannot remain silent, for we believe that, in this time of common need and trial, a common message has been given us to speak. We commit to God what this may mean for the relationships between the Confessional Churches.

In face of the errors of the 'German Christians' and the present Reich Church Government, errors which make havoc of the Church and therefore destroy the unity of the German Evangelical Church, we confess the following truths of the Gospel:

1. '*I am the way, and the truth, and the life; no one comes to the Father but by me*' (John 14.6).

'*Truly, truly, I say to you, he who does not enter the sheepfold by the door but climbs in by another way, that man is a thief and a robber. I am the door; if anyone enters by me, he will be saved*' (John 10.1,9).

Jesus Christ, as He is testified to us in Holy Scripture, is the One Word of God, which we have to hear and which we have to trust and obey in life and in death.

We reject the false doctrine that the Church can and must acknowledge as sources of its proclamation, except and beside this one Word of God, other events and powers, forms and truths, as God's revelation.

2. '*Christ Jesus, whom God made our wisdom, our righteousness and sanctification and redemption*' (1 Cor. 1.30).

As Jesus Christ is God's declaration of the forgiveness of all our sins, so, in the same way and with the same seriousness, He is God's mighty claim upon our whole life. Through Him we obtain joyful deliverance from the godless bondage of this world for the free, grateful service of His creatures.

We reject the false doctrine that there are areas of our life in which we belong not to Jesus Christ, but to other masters, realms where we do not need to be justified and sanctified by Him.

3. '*Speaking the truth in love, we are to grow up in every way into Him who is the Head, into Christ, from whom the whole body is joined and knit together*' (Eph. 4.15f).

The Christian Church is the community of brethren in which Jesus Christ acts presently as Lord in Word and Sacrament by the Holy Spirit. As the Church of pardoned sinners, in the midst of a sinful world it has to witness by its faith and obedience, its message and its order, that it is His alone, that it lives and desires to live only by His consolation and by His orders, in expectation of His coming.

We reject the false doctrine that the Church is permitted to form its message or its order according to its own desire, or according to prevailing philosophical or political convictions.

4. '*You know that the rulers of the Gentiles lord it over them and their great men exercise authority over them. It shall not be so among you: but whosoever would be great among you must be your servant*' (Matt 20.25f).

The various ministries in the Church do not provide for any lordship of some over others, but only for the exercise of that service which is entrusted to and required of the whole congregation.

We reject the false doctrine that the Church is able or at liberty apart from this ministry, to take to itself or accept special 'leaders' equipped with power to rule.

5. '*Fear God, honour the King*' (1 Pet. 2.17).

Scripture tells us that, in the as yet unredeemed world in which also the Church exists, the State has, by divine appointment, the task of maintaining law and peace, by the fullest exercise of human insight and human capacity, and by means of the threat and use of force. With gratitude and reverence towards God, the Church acknowledges the benefit of this order which He has appointed. It holds up before the world God's Kingdom, God's Commandment and righteousness, and so the responsibility of both rulers and ruled alike. It trusts and obeys the power of that Word through which God upholds all things.

We reject the false doctrine that the State should or can, beyond its own special task, become the sole and total order of human life, thus fulfilling also the Church's vocation.

We reject the false doctrine that the Church should or can, beyond its own special task, assume characteristics, functions and dignity proper only to the State, thus becoming itself an organ of the State.

6. '*Lo, I am with you always to the close of the age*' (Matt. 28.20).
'*The Word of God is not fettered*' (2 Tim. 2.9).

The Church's commission, on which its freedom rests, is in Christ's stead and so in the service of His Word and Work, to deliver to all men, by means of Preaching and Sacrament, the message of the free grace of God.

We reject the false doctrine that the Church can, in human glorification of itself, use the Word and Work of the Lord to serve any self chosen desires, purposes and plans.

The Confessional Synod of the German Evangelical Church declares that it sees in the recognition of these truths and in the rejection of these errors, the indispensable theological basis of the German Evangelical Church as a federation of Confessional Churches. It invites all who are able to accept their declaration to keep these theological principles in mind in their decisions in Church politics. It asks all whom it concerns to return to the unity of faith, love and hope.

Verbum Dei manet in aeternum.

LIST OF ABBREVIATIONS AND OF WORKS FREQUENTLY CITED

This list contains only those works frequently cited. Full details of all other works cited are given in the appropriate footnotes.

BARCLAY, ROBERT. *Apology* = *An Apology for the True Christian Divinity as the same is held forth and preached by the People, in scorn called Quakers*, 1678. 13th edn. Manchester 1869.

BARTH, KARL. *Kirchliche Dogmatik*. Zollikon—Zürich 1932-61. Eng. trans. *Church Dogmatics*. Edinburgh 1934ff.

BARTMANN, B. *Lehrbuch der Dogmatik*. 8th edn. Freiburg im Breisgau 1932.

Bekenntnisschriften (*Luth.*) = *Die Bekenntnisschriften der evangelisch-lutheranischen Kirche*. 2nd edn. Göttingen 1952, 3rd edn. 1956.

BELL, G. K. A. *Brief Sketch* = *A Brief Sketch of the Church of England*. London 1929.

CALVIN, JEAN. *Opera* = *Ioannis Calvini opera quae supersunt omnia*, edd. G. Baum *et al.* VOLS. I-LIX. Brunswick and Berlin 1863-1900. VOLS. XXIX-LXXXVII of Corpus Reformatorum.

—— *Inst.* = *Institutio Christianae Religionis. Institutes of the Christian Religion.* (1) Trans. J. Allen, London 1813; 7th edn. revised, 2 vols. London 1936. (2) Trans. H. Beveridge, 2 vols. Edinburgh 1845-6. (3) Edited J. T. McNeill and trans. Ford Lewis Battles, 2 vols. Library of Christian Classics, VOLS. XX-XXI. London 1961.

—— *Theological Treatises*, trans. and ed. J. K. S. Reid. Library of Christian Classics, VOL. XXII. London 1954.

—— *Tracts and Treatises*, ed. T. F. Torrance. 3 vols. Edinburgh 1959.

CHAMBON, J. *Maria, die Herbstreife eines Menschenkults*. Essen 1950.

C.J.C. = *Codex Juris Canonici*.

CLARKE, W. K. L. and C. HARRIS. *Liturgy and Worship*. London 1947.

COLE, H. *Calvin's Calvinism*, London 1927.

Concordia = *Concordia or Book of Concord. The Symbols of the Evangelical Lutheran Church.* Concordia Publishing House, St Louis 1957.

Corpus Confessionum, ed. C. Fabricius. Berlin 1931ff.

D. = Heinrich Denzinger, *Enchiridion symbolorum definitionum et declarationum de rebus fidei et morum.* 31st edn., ed. C. Rahner, Freiburg im Breisgau 1960. Eng. trans. *The Sources of Catholic Dogma*, trans. R. J. Deferrari, St Louis and London 1957.

Documents of the Christian Church, ed. H. Bettenson. London 1943.

Documents bearing on the problem of Christian Unity, ed. G. K. A. Bell, 1st Series. London 1924.

Ekklesia. Eine Sammlung von Selbstdarstellungen der Christlichen Kirchen, ed. F. Siegmund-Schultze. VOL. I, Gotha 1934; VOL. X, Leipzig 1939.

ELERT, W. *Morphologie des Luthertums.* 2 vols. Munich 1931-3. New edn. 1958.

The Fulness of Christ. London 1950.

Glaubensbekenntnis des Bundes evangelischer freikirchlichen Gemeinden, 29 Feb. 1944. Nordheim 1944.

GOLLWITZER, H. *Coena Domini.* Munich 1937.

HEILER, FRIEDRICH. *Urkirche und Ostkirche.* Munich 1937.

Heilslehre der Kirche. Dokumente von Pius IX bis Pius XII. Freibourg 1953.

HEPPE, HEINRICH. *Reformed Dogmatics*, trans. G. T. Thomson. London 1950. Translation of *Die Dogmatik der ev.-ref. Kirche*, 1861.

HILL. See Melanchthon, P. *Loci Communes.*

Intercommunion, edd. Donald Baillie and John Marsh. London 1952.

JULIAN, JOHN. *Dictionary of Hymnology.* London 1898, 1907.

KELLY, J. N. D. *Early Christian Creeds.* London 1950; 2nd edn. 1960.

KIDD, *Documents* = *Documents illustrative of the Continental Reformation*, ed. B. J. Kidd. Oxford 1911.

Kirche und Kosmos. Orthodoxie und Evangelisches Christentum No. 2. Witten 1949.

Lambeth Conference, 1948. *Report.*

LOOFS, F. *Symbolik* = *Symbolik oder Konfessionskunde*, VOL. I. Tübingen 1902.

LUTHER, MARTIN. E.A. = *Sämtliche Werke.* 2nd edn., ed. E. L. Enders. Erlangen 1862-84.

—— W.A. = *Werke. Kritische Gesamtausgabe*, edd. J. C. F. Knaake *et al.* Weimar 1883ff.

—— *Bondage of the Will*, trans. J. I. Packer and O. R. Johnston. Lund 1957.

—— *Commentary on Galatians*, ed. P. S. Watson. London 1953.

—— *Primary Works*, edd. and trans. H. Wace and C. A. Buchheim. London 1896.

—— *Reformation Writings*, trans. B. L. Woolf. 2 vols. London 1952, 1956.

M. = Karl Mirbt, *Quellen zur Geschichte des Papsttums und des römischen Katholizismus*. 4th edn. Tübingen 1924.

McGlothlin, W. J. *Baptist Confessions* = *Baptist Confessions of Faith*. Philadelphia 1911.

Melanchthon, Philip. *Ap. C.* = *Apologia Confessio Augustanae*. Printed in *Opera*, vols. xxvii-xxviii, also in *Concordia*, q.v.

—— *The Loci Communes of Philip Melanchthon*, trans. C. L. Hill. Boston 1944.

—— *Opera* = *Opera quae supersunt omnia*, ed. C. G. Breitschneider. Halle and Brunswick 1834-60. Corpus Reformatorum, vols. i-xxviii.

Michalescu, Jon. *Bekenntnisse und Glaubenszeugnisse* = *Die Bekenntnisse und die wichtigsten Glaubenszeugnisse der griechisch-orientalischen Kirche*. Leipzig 1904.

Möhler, J. A. *Symbolik* = *Symbolik oder Darstellung der dogmatischen Gegensatze der Katholiken und Protestanten*. Mainz 1832.

Müller, E. F. K. *Symbolik* = *Symbolik. Vergleichende Darstellung der christlichen Hauptkirchen nach ihrem Grundzüge und ihren wesentlichen Lebensäusserungen*. Erlangen 1896.

The Nature of the Church, ed. R. Newton Flew. London 1952.

New Schaff-Herzog = *New Schaff-Herzog Encyclopaedia of Religious Knowledge*, ed. S. M. Jackson. 12 vols. New York and London 1908-12.

Niemeyer, H. A. *Collectio confessionum in ecclesiis reformatis publicatarum*. Leipzig 1840.

Niesel, Wilhelm. *Bekenntnisschriften und Kirchenordnungen* = *Bekenntnisschriften und Kirchenordnungen der nach Gottes Wort reformierten Kirche*, ed. Wilhelm Niesel. 3rd edn. Zollikon 1948.

Nuelson, J. L. *Lehre des Methodismus* = *Die Lehre und die kirchengeschichtliche Bedeutung des Methodismus*. Zürich 1947.

The Orthodox Liturgy. London 1939.

Payne, E. A. *The Fellowship of Believers. Baptist Thought and Practice Yesterday and Today*. London 1944.

Peel, Albert, and Douglas Horton. *International Congregationalism*. London 1949.

Pius XII. *Mediator Dei*. Encyclical, 1947. Eng. trans. *Christian Worship*, trans. G. D. Smith. London 1957.

—— *Munificentissimus Deus*. Constitution, 1950. Eng. trans. by P. J. Hamell. London 1951.

—— *Mystici corporis Christi*. Encyclical, 1943. Eng. trans. *The Mystical Body of Jesus Christ*, trans. G. D. Smith. London 1943.

PIUS XII. *Le Pèlerinage de Lourdes*. Encyclical, 1957. Eng. trans. *Our Lady of Lourdes*, trans. V. J. Matthews. London 1957.

R.E. = J. J. Herzog, *Realencyklopädie für protestantische Theologie und Kirche*. 3rd edn., ed. A. Hauck. Leipzig 1896-1913.

ROBINSON, H. WHEELER. *Life and Faith* = *The Life and Faith of the Baptists*. London 1946.

ROUSE, RUTH, and STEPHEN NEILL. *A History of the Ecumenical Movement 1517-1948*. London 1954.

Schaff = Philip Schaff, *The Creeds of Christendom*. London 1877; 4th edn. New York 1905. VOL. I, *A History of the Creeds of Christendom*; VOL. II, *The Creeds of the Greek and Latin Churches*; VOL. III, *The Creeds of the Evangelical Protestant Churches*.

SCHMID, H. *Die Dogmatik der evangelisch-lutheranischen Kirche*. Erlangen 1843.

SEEBERG, REINHOLD. *Die Lehre Luthers*. Leipzig 1933.

SERAPHIM, METROPOLITAN. *Die Ostkirche*. Stuttgart 1950.

STRATON, H. H. *Baptists, their Message and Mission*. Philadelphia 1941.

THOMAS AQUINAS. *Summa theologica*, literally translated by the Fathers of the English Dominican Province. London 1947.

TORRANCE, T. F. *The School of Faith. The Catechisms of the Reformed Church*. London 1959.

Universal Church = World Council of Churches. Amsterdam Assembly Series, *Man's Disorder and God's Design*. London 1948. VOL. I, *The Universal Church in God's Design*.

WALKER, WILLISTON. *The Creeds and Platforms of Congregationalism*. New York 1893; Boston 1960.

WEBER, H. E. *Reformation, Orthodoxie und Rationalismus*. PT. I, *Von der Reformation zur Orthodoxie*, 2 vols., Gütersloh 1937, 1940; PT. II, *Der Geist der Orthodoxie*, Gütersloh 1951.

WESLEY, JOHN. *The Character of a Methodist*, 1739. Reprinted London 1950.

—— *Standard Sermons* = *Wesley's Standard Sermons*, ed. E. H. Sugden. 4th edn. London 1956.

—— *Works* = *The Works of the Rev. John Wesley, A.M.* 11th edn., ed. T. Jackson, London 1856.

WOYWOD, S. *The New Canon Law*. 7th edn. New York 1929.

ZANKOV, STEFAN. *The Eastern Orthodox Church*, trans. D. A. Lowrie. London 1929. Translation of *Das orthodox Christentum des Ostens, sein Wesen und seine gegenwärtige Gestalt*. Berlin 1928.

SUPPLEMENTARY BIBLIOGRAPHY

I. General

ALGERMISSEN, KONRAD. *The Christian Denominations.* St Louis 1945. (Roman Catholic.)

The Concise Encyclopaedia of Living Faiths, ed. R. C. Zaehner. London 1959.

DUMONT, C. J. *Approaches to Christian Unity.* London 1959.

LEEMING, BERNARD. *The Churches and the Church.* Westminster, Md. 1960. (Roman Catholic.)

MOLLAND, EINAR. *Christendom. A Survey of all the Christian Churches throughout the World, their Doctrines, Constitutional Forms, and Ways of Worship.* London 1959. (Contains excellent bibliography.)

ROBINSON, WILLIAM. *The Shattered Cross: The Many Churches and the One Church.* Birmingham 1957.

Union of Christendom, ed. Kenneth Mackenzie. London 1938.

ZANDER, L. A. *Vision and Action*, trans. N. Duddington. London 1952.

II. Roman Catholic Church

1. *Sources*

Acta Apostolica Sedis. Rome 1909ff.

Ancient Christian Writers. The Works of the Fathers in Translation, edd. J. Quasten, J. C. Plumpe, and W. J. Burghardt. Westminster, Md. and London 1946ff. (Translations into English of Patristic writings of the first five centuries, with introductions and substantial notes.)

BISHOP, EDMUND. *Liturgica Historica.* Oxford 1918.

BOUSCAREN, T. LINCOLN. *The Canon Law Digest.* VOL. I (1917-33), Milwaukee 1934; VOL. II (1933-42), Milwaukee 1943.

Breviarium Romanum.

Catholic Catechism (translated from German). London 1957.

Codex Iuris Canonicis. Rome 1917ff.

Corpus Iuris Canonicis, edd. A. L. Richeter and A. Friedberg. 2 vols. Leipzig 1879-81.

DENZINGER, H. *Enchiridion symbolorum, definitionum et declarationum de rebus fidei et morum.* 31st edn., ed. C. Rahner, Freiburg im

Breisgau 1960. Eng. trans. *The Sources of Catholic Dogma*, trans. R. J. Deferrari. St Louis and London 1957.

HEFELE, C. J. *A History of the Councils of the Church*, trans. W. R. Clark *et al.* 5 vols. Edinburgh 1871-96.

KING, ARCHDALE. *Liturgies of the Past*. London 1959.

—— *Liturgies of the primatial Sees*. London 1957.

—— *Liturgies of the Religious Orders*. London 1955.

—— *Liturgy of the Roman Church*. London 1957.

Library of Christian Classics, edd. John Baillie, J. T. McNeill, and H. P. Van Dusen. VOLS. I-XIII. Philadelphia and London 1953ff (Selected translations of classical Christian works from the early centuries down to the Middle Ages. Protestant.)

MANSI, J. D. *Sacrorum Conciliorum nova et amplissima collectio, in quae praeter ea quae P. Labbeus et G. Cossartus ... in lucem edidere ea omnia insuper suis in locis ... exhibentur, quae Joannes Dominicus Mansi ... evulgavit*, etc. (continued and supplemented under the editorship of Louis Petit and Jean-Baptiste Martin). 54 vols. Begun 1759; latest edn. Leipzig 1901-27.

MIRBT, KARL. *Quellen zur Geschichte des Papsttums und des römischen Katholizismus*. 4th edn. Tübingen 1924. (Protestant.)

Missale Romanum.

PARSCH, PIUS. *The Liturgy of the Mass*, trans. F. S. Eckhoff. St Louis and London 1937.

QUASTEN, J. *Patrology*. VOL. I, *The Beginnings of Patristic Literature*, London 1950; VOL. II, *Ante-Nicene Literature after S. Irenaeus*, London 1953; VOL. III, *The Golden Age of Greek Patristic Literature*, London 1960.

Rituale Romanum.

Sources of Christian Theology, ed. Paul E. Palmer. VOL. I, *Sacraments and Worship*, London 1957; VOL. II, *Sacraments and Forgiveness*, London 1959.

THOMAS AQUINAS, ST. *Philosophical Texts*, ed. and trans. T. Gilbey. Oxford 1951.

—— *Theological Texts*, ed. and trans. T. Gilbey. Oxford 1955.

WOYWOD, STANISLAUS. *The New Canon Law*. 7th edn. New York 1929.

2. *Literature*

CORBISHLEY, T. *Roman Catholicism*. London 1956.

CARRIGOU-LAGRANGE, R. *The Mother of the Saviour and our Interior Life*, trans. B. J. Kelly. Dublin 1941.

LEEMING, B. *Principles of Sacramental Theology*. London 1956.

LOEWENICH, WALTER VON. *Modern Catholicism*, trans. R. H. Fuller. London 1959.

McKENZIE, J. L. *The Two-Edged Sword.* Milwaukee 1956.

MATHEW, D. *Catholicism in England, 1535-1935.* 3rd edn. London 1955.

Mother of the Redeemer, ed. Kevin McNamara. Dublin 1959.

NEWMAN, J. H. *Essay on the Development of Christian Doctrine.* 1845; reprinted New York 1960.

PELIKAN, JAROSLAV. *The Riddle of Roman Catholicism.* Nashville 1959. (Protestant.)

The Teaching of the Catholic Church, ed. G. D. Smith. 2 vols. London 1948.

VONIER, A. *A Key to the Doctrine of the Eucharist.* In *Collected Works*, VOL. III. London 1952.

WATKIN, E. G. *Roman Catholicism in England.* Oxford 1957.

III. EASTERN ORTHODOX CHURCH

1. *Sources*

BLACKMORE, R. W. *The Doctrine of the Russian Church.* Aberdeen 1845.

BRIGHTMAN, E. F. *Liturgies Eastern and Western.* VOL. I, *Eastern Liturgies.* Oxford 1896.

BULGARIS, N. *The Holy Catechism of Nicolas Bulgaris*, trans. W. E. Daniel. London 1893.

GOGOL, N. V. *The Divine Liturgy of the Russian Orthodox Church*, trans. R. Edwards. London 1960.

Libri symbolici ecclesiae orientalis, ed. E. J. Kimmel. Jena 1843.

A Manual of Eastern Orthodox Prayers. London 1945.

The Orthodox Liturgy. London 1939.

Orthodox Spirituality. London 1945.

OVERBECK, J. J. *The Orthodox Confession of Peter Mogila.* London 1899.

SCHAFF, PHILIP. *The Creeds of Christendom.* VOL. II, *The Creeds of the Greek and Latin Churches.* London 1877; 4th edn. New York 1905.

2. *Literature*

ARSENIEV, N. *Mysticism and the Eastern Church*, trans. A. Chambers. London 1926.

BULGAKOV, S. *The Orthodox Church.* London 1935.

CONSTANTINIDES, M. *The Orthodox Church.* London 1931.

DVORNIK, F. *The Photian Schism.* Cambridge 1948.

EVERY, G. *The Byzantine Patriarchate.* London 1947.

FORTESCUE, A. *The Orthodox Eastern Church.* London 1907.

FRENCH, R. M. *The Eastern Orthodox Church.* 3rd imp. London 1961. (Contains a useful bibliography.)

HADJIANTONIOU, G. A. *Protestant Patriarch. The Life of Cyril Lucaris, Patriarch of Constantinople.* Richmond, Va. 1961.

HEADLAM, A. C. *The Teaching of the Russian Church.* London 1897.

KIDD, B. J. *The Churches of Eastern Christendom.* London 1927.

ZANKOV, S. *The Eastern Orthodox Church,* trans. D. A. Lowrie. London 1929.

ZERNOV, N. *The Christian East.* London 1956.

—— *Eastern Christendom.* London 1961.

—— *The Russians and their Church.* London 1945.

IV. LUTHERAN CHURCH

1. *Sources*

Die Bekenntnisschriften der evangelisch-lutheranischen Kirche. 3rd edn. Göttingen 1956.

Concordia or Book of Concord. The Symbols of the Evangelical Lutheran Church. Concordia Publishing House, St Louis 1957.

Concordia Triglotta, edd. F. Bente and W. H. T. Dau. St Louis 1917.

Documents illustrative of the Continental Reformation, ed. B. J. Kidd. Oxford 1911.

LUTHER, MARTIN. *Werke. Kritische Gesamtausgabe,* ed. J. C. F. Knaake. Weimar 1883ff.

—— *Sämtliche Werke.* 2nd edn. ed. E. L. Enders. Erlangen 1862-84.

—— *Luther's Works.* A new English translation, edd. J. Pelikan and H. T. Lehmann. St Louis and Richmond, Va. 1958ff. (In progress.)

—— *The Bondage of the Will,* trans. J. L. Packer and O. R. Johnston. London 1957.

—— *Early Theological Works,* ed. J. Atkinson, Philadelphia and London 1962. Library of Christian Classics, VOL. XVI.

—— *Lectures on Romans,* ed. Wilhelm Pauck. Philadelphia and London 1962. Library of Christian Classics, VOL. XV.

—— *Letters of Spiritual Counsel,* ed. T. G. Tappert. Philadelphia and London 1955. Library of Christian Classics, VOL. XVIII.

—— *Luther and Erasmus on Free Will,* edd. E. G. Rupp and P. S. Watson. Philadelphia and London 19—. Library of Christian Classics, VOL. XVII.

—— *Luther's Commentary on Galatians,* ed. P. S. Watson. London 1953.

—— *Luther's Primary Works*, edd. H. Wace and C. A. Buchheim. London 1896.

—— *Reformation Writings of Martin Luther*, trans. B. L. Woolf. 2 vols. London 1952, 1956.

MELANCHTHON, PHILIP. *Opera quae supersunt omnia*, edd. C. G. Breitschneider and H. E. Bindseil. 28 vols. Brunswick 1834-60. (VOLS. I-XXVIII of the Corpus Reformatorum.)

—— *The Loci Communes of Philip Melanchthon*, trans. C. L. Hill. Boston 1944.

—— *Melanchthon and Bucer*, ed. F. J. Taylor. Philadelphia and London 1956. Library of Christian Classics, VOL. XIX.

SCHAFF, PHILIP. *The Creeds of Christendom.* VOL. III, *The Creeds of the Evangelical Protestant Churches.* 4th edn. New York 1905.

For Lutheran liturgical texts the reader is referred to the bibliography in W. D. Maxwell, *An Outline of Christian Worship*, London 1945.

2. *Literature*

BAINTON, R. H. *Here I stand. A Life of Martin Luther.* New York 1950.

DAVIES, R. E. *The Problem of Authority in the Continental Reformers. A Study in Luther, Zwingli and Calvin.* London 1946.

DRUMMOND, A. L. *German Protestantism since Luther.* London 1951.

HILDEBRANDT, F. *Melanchthon: Alien or Ally?* London 1946.

HORTON, W. M. *Contemporary Continental Theology.* New York 1938.

KRAMM, H. H. W. *The Theology of Martin Luther.* London 1947.

PAUCK, W. *The Heritage of the Reformation.* Boston 1950.

RUPP, E. G. *The Righteousness of God.* London 1952.

—— *Studies in the Making of the English Protestant Tradition.* London 1947.

WATSON, P. S. *Let God be God.* London 1947.

ZEEDEN, F. W. *The Legacy of Luther*, trans. R. M. Bethel. London 1954.

V. REFORMED AND PRESBYTERIAN CHURCHES

1. *Sources*

CALVIN, JEAN. *Opera quae supersunt omnia*, edd. G. Baum *et al.* 59 vols. Brunswick and Berlin 1863-1900. (VOLS. XXIX-LXXXVII of the Corpus Reformatorum.)

CALVIN, JEAN. *Opera selecta*, edd. P. Barth and W. Niesel. 5 vols. Munich 1926-52.

—— *Calvin's Calvinism*, trans. H. Cole. London 1856. (*The Eternal Predestination of God*, etc.)

—— *Calvin's Tracts and Treatises*. 3 vols. Calvin Translation Society, Edinburgh 1844. Reissued, with introduction and notes by T. F. Torrance. Edinburgh 1959.

—— *Commentaries*, edd. D. W. and T. F. Torrance. Edinburgh 1960ff. (New Testament commentaries, in progress.)

—— *Commentaries*, ed. Joseph Haroutunian. Philadelphia and London 1958. Library of Christian Classics, VOL. XXIII.

—— *Concerning the Eternal Predestination of God*, trans. J. K. S. Reid. London 1961.

—— *Institutes of the Christian Religion*, trans. J. Allen. London 1813. 7th edn., revised, Philadelphia 1936.

—— *Institutes of the Christian Religion*, trans. H. Beveridge. Calvin Translation Society, Edinburgh 1845; reprinted Grand Rapids 1958.

—— *Institutes of the Christian Religion*, ed. J. T. McNeill, trans. Ford Lewis Battle. Philadelphia and London 1961. Library of Christian Classics, VOLS. XX-XXI. (Full bibliography.)

The Confession of Faith of the Assembly of Divines at Westminster, ed. S. W. Carruthers. London 1946.

Documents illustrative of the Continental Reformation, ed. B. J. Kidd. Oxford 1911.

MÜLLER, E. F. K. *Die Bekenntnisschriften der reformierten Kirche*. Leipzig 1903.

NIESEL, W. *Bekenntnisschriften und Kirchenordnungen der nach Gottes Wort reformierten Kirche*. Zürich 1938.

SCHAFF, PHILIP. *The Creeds of Christendom*. VOL. III, *The Creeds of the Evangelical Protestant Churches*. 4th edn. New York 1905.

Scots Confession, 1560, ed. G. D. Henderson. Edinburgh 1937.

TORRANCE, T. F. *The School of Faith, The Catechisms of the Reformed Church*. London 1959.

For Reformed liturgical texts and service books see the bibliography in W. D. Maxwell, *An Outline of Christian Worship*, London 1945.

2. *Literature*

AINSLIE, J. L. *The Doctrines of Ministerial Order in the Reformed Churches*. Edinburgh 1940.

BURLEIGH, J. H. S. *A Church History of Scotland.* Oxford 1960.

The Catholicity of Protestantism, edd. R. N. Flew and R. E. Davies. London 1950.

DAVIES, HORTON. *The English Free Churches.* Oxford 1952.

DONALDSON, GORDON. *The Scottish Reformation.* Cambridge 1960.

HENDERSON, G. D. *Church and Ministry.* London 1954.

—— *The Claims of the Church of Scotland.* London 1951.

—— *Presbyterianism.* Aberdeen 1954.

HENDRY, G. S. *The Westminster Confession for Today.* Richmond, Va. 1960.

HEPPE, HEINRICH. *Reformed Dogmatics*, trans. G. T. Thomson. London 1950.

HUNTER, A. M. *The Teaching of Calvin.* Glasgow 1950.

JANSEN, J. F. *Calvin's Doctrine of the Work of Christ.* London 1956.

MACGREGOR, GEDDES. *Corpus Christi: The Nature of the Church according to the Reformed Tradition.* Philadelphia 1958.

MACKAY, JOHN A. *The Presbyterian Way of Life.* New Jersey 1960.

MCNEILL, J. T. *The History and Character of Calvinism.* Oxford 1954. (Valuable bibliography.)

NIESEL, WILHELM. *The Reformed Witness and the Word of God.* Proceedings of the 17th General Council of the Alliance of Reformed Churches. Geneva 1954. (p. 127f.)

The Theology of Calvin, trans. H. Knight. London 1956.

OMAN, JOHN. *The Church and the Divine Order.* London 1911.

—— *Honest Religion.* Cambridge 1941.

PARKER, T. H. L. *The Doctrine of the Knowledge of God. A Study in the Theology of John Calvin.* London 1952.

—— *Portrait of Calvin.* London 1954.

QUISTORP, H. *Calvin's Doctrine of the Last Things*, trans. H. Knight. London 1955.

SIMPSON, P. CARNEGIE. *Church Principles.* London 1923.

—— *The Evangelical Church Catholic.* London 1934.

TORRANCE, T. F. *Calvin's Doctrine of Man.* London 1949.

—— *Conflict and Agreement in the Church.* 2 vols. London 1959-60.

VAN BUREN, P. *Christ in Our Place.* Edinburgh 1957.

WALLACE, R. S. *Calvin's Doctrine of the Christian Life.* Edinburgh 1959.

—— *Calvin's Doctrine of the Word and Sacrament.* Edinburgh 1954.

WOTHERSPOON, H. J., and J. M. KIRKPATRICK. *A Manual of Church Doctrine according to the Church of Scotland*, revised and enlarged by T. F. Torrance and R. Selby Wright. Oxford 1960.

VI. Anglican Church

1. *Sources*

Anglican Orders. The Bull of His Holiness Leo XIII and the Answer of the Archbishops of England. 1897; reprinted London 1954.

Anglo-Russian Theological Conference, 1956. *Report.* London 1958.

The Book of Common Prayer. 1662.

Catholicity. London 1947. (An Anglo-Catholic report.)

Constitutions and Canons Ecclesiastical, 1604, ed. J. V. Bullard. London 1934

Conversations between the Church of England and the Methodist Church. An Interim Statement. London 1958.

Documents bearing on the Problem of Christian Unity, ed. G. K. A. Bell. 4 vols. London 1920-57.

The Fulness of Christ. London 1950. (An evangelical Anglican report.)

Jewel, John. *The Apology of the Church of England*, 1562. Reprinted in *Works*, ed. J. Ayre. Cambridge 1845-50.

Hooker, Richard. *Of the Laws of Ecclesiastical Polity*, 1594. Reprinted in *Works*, 7th edn. 3 vols. Oxford 1888.

Lambeth Conferences, 1930, 1948, 1958. *Reports.*

Relations between Anglican and Presbyterian Churches. Joint Report. London 1957.

Rogers, T. *The Catholic Doctrine of the Church of England, An Exposition of the Thirty-Nine Articles*, 1579. Parker Society. Cambridge 1854.

Schaff, Philip. *The Creeds of Christendom.* vol. iii, *The Creeds of the Evangelical Protestant Churches.* 4th edn. New York 1905. (Latin and English texts of the Thirty-Nine Articles.)

The Thirty-Nine Articles, ed. B. J. Kidd. Oxford Church Texts, 1899.

The Two Books of Homilies Appointed to be Read in Churches. bk. i, 1547; bk. ii, 1571. Reprinted Oxford 1859.

2. *Literature*

Bell, G. K. A. *A Brief Sketch of the Church of England.* London 1929.

—— *Christian Unity. The Anglican Position.* London 1948.

Bicknell, E. J. *A Theological Introduction to the Thirty-Nine Articles*, revised by H. J. Carpenter. London 1955.

Brightman, F. E. *The English Rite.* 2 vols. London 1915.

Browne, E. H. *An Exposition of the Thirty-Nine Articles.* London 1874.

Burnet, G. *An Exposition of the Thirty-Nine Articles*, 1715; reprinted Oxford 1819.

CARDWELL, E. *A History of Conferences and other Proceedings connected with the Revision of the Book of Common Prayer.* Oxford 1849.

CHADWICK, O. *The Mind of the Oxford Movement.* London 1960.

Church Relations in England. London 1950.

CREED, J. M., and J. S. BOYS SMITH. *Religious Thought in the Eighteenth Century.* Cambridge 1934.

DAVIDSON, LORD. *The Six Lambeth Conferences, 1867-1920.* 2nd edn. London 1929.

Doctrine in the Church of England. London 1938.

EDWARDS, D. *Not Angels but Anglicans.* London 1958.

Essays Catholic and Critical, ed. E. G. Selwyn. 3rd edn. London 1934.

Essays in Anglican Self-Criticism, ed. D. M. Paton. London 1958.

GARBETT, C. *The Claims of the Church of England.* London 1947.

GIBSON, E. C. S. *The Thirty-Nine Articles.* 2nd edn. London 1898.

GORE, C. *Lux Mundi, A Series of Studies in the Religion of the Incarnation.* Oxford 1889.

GRAY, G. F. S. *The Anglican Communion.* London 1958.

HARRISON, D. E. W. *The Book of Common Prayer.* Revised edn. London 1959.

HEADLAM, A. C. *The Church of England.* 2nd edn. London 1925.

HENSON, H. HENSLEY. *Anglicanism.* London 1921.

—— *The Church of England.* Cambridge 1939.

HODGES, H. A. *Anglicanism and Orthodoxy.* London 1955.

HODGSON, L. *The Doctrine of the Church as held and taught in the Church of England.* Oxford 1946.

Liberal Evangelicalism, ed. T. G. Rogers. London 1923.

Liturgy and Worship, edd. W. K. Lowther Clarke and C. Harris. London 1947.

MASCALL, E. L. *The Recovery of Unity.* London 1958.

MASON, A. J. *The Church of England and Episcopacy.* Cambridge 1914.

MAURICE, F. D. *The Kingdom of Christ.* London 1837.

MAYFIELD, G. *The Church of England: Its members and its business.* Oxford 1958.

MORE, P. E., and F. L. CROSS. *Anglicanism.* London 1935.

NEILL, C., and J. M. WILLOUGHBY. *The Tutorial Prayer Book.* London 1959.

NEILL, S. C. *Anglicanism.* Harmondsworth 1958, revised 1960.

NICHOLLS, W. *A Comment on the Book of Common Prayer.* London 1710.

PEARSON, C. J. *An Exposition of the Creed.* 1659; reprinted London 1882.

PROCTOR, F., and W. H. FRERE. *A New History of the Book of Common Prayer.* London 1905.

RAMSAY, A. M. *From Gore to Temple. The Development of Anglican Theology 1889-1939.* London 1960.
RAWLINSON, A. E. J., and C. SMYTH. *The Genius of Anglicanism.* London 1947.
THOMAS, W. H. GRIFFITH. *The Principles of Theology.* London and New York 1930.
WAND, J. W. C. *The Church Today.* Harmondsworth 1960.
WATSON, E. W. *The Church of England.* 2nd edn. Oxford 1944.
WHEATLEY, C. *A Rational Illustration of the Book of Common Prayer.* London 1720.
WILLIAMS, A. T. P. *The Anglican Tradition in the Life of England.* London 1947.
WILLIAMS, N. P., and C. HARRIS. *Northern Catholicism.* London 1933.
WORDSWORTH, C. *Theophilus Anglicanus.* London 1843.

VII. CONGREGATIONALISM

1. *Sources*

A Book of Public Worship. Compiled by J. Huxtable, J. Marsh, R. Micklem, and J. M. Todd. London 1948; 2nd edn. 1949.
Prayers and Services for Christian Festivals. J. M. Todd. London 1951.
The Savoy Declaration of Faith and Order, 1658, ed. A. G. Matthews. London 1959. (Text also in P. Schaff. *The Creeds of Christendom*, VOL. III, *The Creeds of the Evangelical Protestant Churches.* 4th edn. New York 1905.)
WALKER, WILLISTON. *The Creeds and Platforms of Congregationalism.* New York 1893; Boston 1960.

2. *Literature*

ATKINS, G. G., and F. L. FAGLEY. *History of American Congregationalism.* Boston 1942.
Christian Worship, ed. N. Micklem. London 1936.
Congregationalism Today, ed. J. Marsh. London 1943.
DALE, R. W. *History of English Congregationalism.* London 1907.
—— *Manual of Congregational Principles.* London 1884.
DEXTER, H. M. *The Congregationalism of the last three hundred years, as seen in its Literature.* New York and London 1880.
Essays Congregational and Catholic, ed. A. Peel. London 1931.
HORTON, D. *Congregationalism: A Study in Church Polity.* London 1952.
JENKINS, D. T. *Congregationalism: A Restatement.* London 1954.
MANNING, B. L. *Essays in Orthodox Dissent.* London 1939.
MICKLEM, N. *Congregationalism and the Church Catholic.* London 1943.

NUTTALL, G. E. *Visible Saints: The Congregational Way, 1640-1660.* Oxford 1957.
PEEL, A., and D. HORTON. *International Congregationalism.* London 1952.
POWICKE, F. J. 'Brownism', in *Encyclopaedia of Religion and Ethics.* Edinburgh 1910.
WALKER, WILLISTON. 'Congregationalism', in *Encyclopaedia of Religion and Ethics.* Edinburgh 1910.

VIII. BAPTISTS

1. *Sources*

BAPTIST WORLD CONGRESS. *Reports.* 1905, 1911, 1923, 1928, 1934, 1939, 1947, 1950, 1955, 1960. Baptist World Alliance, London and Philadelphia.
MCGLOTHLIN, W. *Baptist Confessions of Faith.* London and Philadelphia 1911. Reprinted, ed. W. L. Lumpkin, Philadelphia 1960.

2. *Literature*

COOK, HENRY. *What Baptists Stand For.* Revised edn. London 1961.
JONES, PHILIP L. *A Restatement of Baptist Principles.* Philadelphia 1909.
LORD, F. T. *Baptist World Fellowship.* London 1955.
PAYNE, E. A. *The Baptist Union. A Short History.* London 1959.
—— *Fellowship of Believers.* Revised edn. London 1952.
ROBINSON, H. W. *The Life and Faith of the Baptists.* London 1946.
STRATON, H. H. *Baptists: Their Message and Mission.* Philadelphia 1941.
TORBET, R. G. *A History of the Baptists.* 2nd edn. Philadelphia 1952.
UNDERWOOD, A. C. *A History of the English Baptists.* London 1947.
WHITLEY, W. T. *A History of the British Baptists.* 2nd edn. London 1932.

IX. METHODISM

1. *Sources*

The Book of Offices. London 1936.
Minutes of the Methodist Conferences, VOL. I. London 1812.
The Sunday Service of the Methodists in North America, with other occasional services. London 1784.

WESLEY, JOHN. *The Works of the Rev. John Wesley, A.M.* 14 vols. 3rd edn. London 1829-31.

—— *Explanatory Notes upon the New Testament.* London 1755.

—— *The Journal of the Rev. John Wesley A.M.*, ed. Nehemiah Curnock. 8 vols. London 1909-16.

—— *The Letters of the Rev. John Wesley A.M.*, ed. John Telford. 8 vols. London 1931.

—— *Wesley's Standard Sermons*, ed. Edward H. Sugden. 2 vols. 4th edn. London 1956.

—— and CHARLES. *The Poetical Works of John and Charles Wesley.* Collected and arranged by George Osborn. 13 vols. London 1868-72.

2. *Literature*

BAKER, F. *A Charge to Keep.* London 1947.

BRASH, W. BARDSLEY. *Methodism.* Garden City, N.Y. 1928.

CANNON, W. R. *The Theology of John Wesley.* New York 1946.

HOLT, IVAN LEE. *The Methodists of the World.* New York 1950.

LINDSTROM, H. *Wesley and Sanctification.* London 1946.

NEELY, T. B. *Doctrinal Standards of Methodism.* New York 1918.

TOWNSEND, W. J., H. B. WORKMAN, and G. EAYRS. *A New History of Methodism.* 2 vols. London 1919.

TYERMAN, L. *The Life and Times of the Rev. John Wesley M.A.* 3 vols. London 1870-1.

WILLIAMS, C. W. *John Wesley's Theology Today.* London 1960.

YATES, A. S. *The Doctrine of Assurance, with special reference to John Wesley.* London 1952.

XI. THE SOCIETY OF FRIENDS

1. *Sources*

BARCLAY, ROBERT. *Theologiae vere Christianae apologia.* Amsterdam 1676.

—— *An Apology for the true Christian divinity as the same is held forth and preached by the people, in scorn, called Quakers.* [?Aberdeen] 1678. 13th edn. Manchester 1869.

Book of Christian Discipline of the Religious Society of Friends in Great Britain. 2nd edn. London 1911-22.

Christian Discipline of the Society of Friends. VOL. I, *Christian Life, Faith and Thought*, London 1927; VOL. II, *Christian Practice*, revised edn. London 1925; VOL. III, *Church Government*, revised edn. London 1931.

Christian Faith and Practice in the experience of the Society of Friends. London 1960. (Now forms, together with *Church Government*, the *Book of Christian Discipline.*)

FOX, GEORGE. *Journal.* 2 vols. London 1694-8. Edited by J. L. Nickalls, Cambridge 1952.

The Nature of the Church according to the Witness of the Society of Friends. London 1945. (Also printed in *Yearly Meeting Proceedings*, London 1946. For an abridgement see *The Nature of the Church*, ed. R. N. Flew, London 1952.)

PENN, WILLIAM. *A Collection of Works.* London 1726.

WOOLMAN, JOHN. *Journal and Essays*, ed. A. M. Gunmere. London 1922.

2. *Literature*

BRAITHWAITE, W. C. *The Beginnings of Quakerism.* London 1912; 2nd edn. Cambridge 1955.

—— *The Message and Mission of Quakerism.* Philadelphia 1912.

—— *The Second Period of Quakerism.* London 1919.

BRAYSHAW, A. NEAVE. *The Quakers: Their Story and Message.* Harrogate 1921; 3rd edn. London 1938.

CREASEY, MAURICE A. *Sacraments. A Quaker Approach.* London 1956.

EEG-OLOGSON, LIEF. *The Conception of the Inner Light in Robert Barclay's Theology.* Lund 1955.

GRAHAM, JOHN WILLIAM. *The Faith of a Quaker.* Cambridge 1920.

GRUBB, E. *What is Quakerism?* 3rd edn. London 1949.

HARVEY, T. EDMUND. *Workaday Saints.* London 1949.

HIBBERT, GERALD K. *Quaker Fundamentals.* 1941.

JONES, RUFUS M. *The Faith and Practice of the Quakers.* 7th edn. London 1949.

—— *An Interpretation of Quakerism.*

LOUKES, HAROLD. *The Discovery of Quakerism.* London 1960.

ROWNTREE, JOHN S. *The Society of Friends. Its Faith and Practice.* London 1901; 6th edn. London 1935.

RUSSELL, E. *The History of Quakerism.* New York 1943.

SHARPLESS, I. 'Society of Friends', in *New Schaff-Herzog Encyclopaedia of Religious Knowledge*, ed. S. M. Jackson, VOL. IV, New York and London 1909.

Studies in Quaker Thought and Practice, ed. Gerald K. Hibbert. 1936.

WOOD, H. G. *Quakerism and the Future of the Church.* London 1920.

WRAGGE, J. P. *The Faith of Robert Barclay. An Essay on his life and on the relevance of his thought for today.* London 1948.

INDEX OF SUBJECTS

INDEX OF NAMES